Basics OF Biblical Hebrew

GRAMMAR

Basics OF Biblical Hebrew

GRAMMAR

Gary D. Pratico
Miles V. Van Pelt

ZONDERVAN™

GRAND RAPIDS, MICHIGAN 49530

ZONDERVAN™

Basics of Biblical Hebrew Grammar
Copyright © 2001 by Gary Pratico and Miles Van Pelt

Requests for information should be addressed to:

Zondervan, *Grand Rapids, Michigan 49530*

Library of Congress Cataloging-in-Publication Data

Pratico, Gary Davis.
      Basics of biblical hebrew grammar / Gary D. Pratico and Miles V. Van Pelt.
        p. cm.
      Includes index.
      ISBN 0-310-23760-2
      1. Hebrew Language—Grammar.   2. Bible, O.T.—Language, style.
  I. Van Pelt, Miles, 1969– . II. Title.
  PJ4567.3.P73   2001
  492.4'82421—dc21   2001026163

This edition printed on acid-free paper.

Printed in the United States of America

---

01 02 03 04 05 06 07 08 / ❖ DC / 10 9 8 7 6 5 4 3

To Mary my Beloved

הִנָּךְ יָפָה רַעְיָתִי הִנָּךְ יָפָה

Song 4:1

To Aaron, Martha and Jon
with my love

וְאָנֹכִי וּבֵיתִי נַעֲבֹד אֶת־יְהוָה

Josh 24:15

To Laurie for her love

רְשָׁפֶיהָ רִשְׁפֵּי אֵשׁ שַׁלְהֶבֶתְיָה

Song 8:6

To Ben and Kacie

לְכוּ־בָנִים שִׁמְעוּ־לִי יִרְאַת יְהוָה אֲלַמֶּדְכֶם

Ps 34:12 [11]

גַּל־עֵינַי וְאַבִּיטָה נִפְלָאוֹת מִתּוֹרָתֶךָ

Open my eyes that I may see wonderful
things from your law.

Psalm 119:18

Table of Contents

Section 4: Introduction to the Derived Stems

Section 5: Reading and Studying Your Hebrew Bible

Appendices

Preface

As the title indicates, this grammar represents the "basics" of biblical Hebrew. From the perspective of its authorship, it represents the basics in the categories of phonology, morphology and syntax. Some will want more; others will want less. Nevertheless, this is our best judgement of what should constitute a basic, one year course in biblical Hebrew. By design, we have minimized the introduction of issues related to the historical development of the language or to the area of comparative Semitic philology. While these issues are interesting and, at times, helpful, they are often distracting and confusing to the beginning student and should be studied at the intermediate level.

We recognize that a large percentage of those who study biblical Hebrew do so in preparation for some type of pastoral or teaching ministry. For most of us, therefore, the study of Hebrew is not only an academic exercise, but also an act of obedience in the fulfillment of a calling to the ministry of God's Word. As those who have been entrusted with the preaching and teaching of God's Word and, thereby, with the oversight of his people, the study of biblical languages should constitute a fundamental and significant part of one's training. In general, the design of this grammar reflects both its scope (basic) and its primary audience (those training for biblical ministry). Some of the more notable features of its presentation are detailed below.

1. There are three parts to *Basics of Biblical Hebrew*: a grammar, a workbook and a CD-ROM that is located in the back of this volume. All practice exercises have been located in a separate workbook, *Basics of Biblical Hebrew: Workbook* (Grand Rapids: Zondervan, 2001). In the workbook, there are corresponding exercises for each chapter in the grammar. Located on the CD-ROM are a number of verb charts in color, a link to the Hebrew flashcard program FlashWorks™ and the full answer key to the workbook exercises. The charts and answer keys have been stored on the CD-ROM in PDF format so that they may be printed and used as necessary.

2. Toward the end of each chapter, vocabulary words are listed for memorization. The Hebrew words and their definitions were initially based on Larry A. Mitchell's *A Student's Vocabulary for Biblical Hebrew and Aramaic* (Grand Rapids: Zondervan, 1984). The vocabulary of this grammar includes all words occurring seventy times or more in the Hebrew Bible, excluding most proper names. Proper names have been identified for the student in

the workbook. A few words that occur less than seventy times are included because of their appearance in the grammar or workbook.

3. Throughout the grammar, frequent reference is made to statistical information in order to illustrate the relative significance or distribution of the counted item. For example, after each vocabulary word and its definition, we identify how many times that particular word occurs in the Hebrew Bible. Statistical information is also provided for certain inflected forms, grammatical constructions and other similar items. Our statistical information is derived from the Accordance module HMT-T. We acknowledge our indebtedness to this software and its developers at OakTree Software (www.OakSoft.com). We have used this invaluable resource extensively in the production of both the grammar and the workbook. We recognize, however, that this database is not without error and have corrected infrequent errors, being careful to check results whenever possible. We also recognize that discrepancies with other statistical sources do exist but have preferred the Accordance results throughout for the sake of consistency.

4. After the vocabulary section of each chapter, we have located a brief study that is intended to encourage students in their study of Hebrew. Many of these are "exegetical insights" or "biblical-theological reflections" with reference to specific Hebrew texts. A few are devoted to observations on Hebrew words or phraseology; others explore various aspects of Hebrew language that contribute to our understanding or interpretation of specific biblical passages. These studies will often emphasize a point of grammar or vocabulary studied in that particular chapter. A few are Hebrew readings that will highlight selected Hebrew verses of a biblical text with a view to grammatical, theological and exegetical commentary. All of these contributions have been written by pastors, youth leaders, graduate students and professors; and to them we express our gratitude for their contributions (see the following "Table of Insights"). This mix of contributors, with different levels of exposure to the language, should be an encouragement that any level of competence with the language can provide a better understanding of the Old Testament and enhance one's effectiveness in the communication of biblical truth.

5. We have been parsimonious with regard to the use of English punctuation so as not to clutter or confuse the appearance of the Hebrew script, especially the vowels and accent marks. This is most notable in our diminished use of commas, which would frequently obscure certain vowels. Additionally, we have chosen not to follow certain standard scholarly conventions with regard to capitalization and the use of italics and parentheses so as to present the components and concepts of the grammar with greater emphasis and clarity for the beginning student.

6. A web-site has been established to provide additional resources to complement the grammar and workbook. The address for this site is *www.basicsofbiblicalhebrew.com*. Located at this site is the Hebrew flashcard program FlashWorks^{tm} developed by William D. Mounce, the author of *Basics of Biblical Greek*. Additional teaching materials and resources for students will be posted at this site.

There are a number of people we wish to thank, especially those who helped in the production of this project: Jim Jumper, Filip Vukosavovic, Jason DeRouchie, Becky Josberger, Jun Kawashima and Mary Lewis. We are also indebted to those who were willing to test the grammar in its earlier stages: Donna Petter, Jason Bembry, Jack Klem, Alice Via, Keith Bodner and Frank Wheeler. We are grateful to Zondervan for their assistance in the production and publication of this grammar. We especially want to recognize Verlyn Verbrugge, Jack Kragt, Bob Buller, Jody DeNeef and Lee Fields. Finally, we recognize and thank Bill Mounce for his significant contributions to this project.

Gary Pratico wishes to thank the trustees and academic administration of Gordon-Conwell Theological Seminary for their many levels of support and encouragement, including the sabbatical year which was devoted exclusively to this publication.

Miles Van Pelt would like to thank Professor John Hartley of Azusa Pacific University for his profound investments in an unlikely student. I would also like to thank Larry and Martha Armitstead for all of their support and help. But most of all, I especially thank my wife Laurie, who, in many ways, has contributed more to this project than I myself have contributed.

Gary D. Pratico
Miles V. Van Pelt
May 2001

Table of Insights

Chapter 1

The Hebrew Alphabet

1.1 The Hebrew alphabet consists of twenty-three consonants or letters. It is written from right to left. The first step in learning Hebrew requires that you memorize the alphabet in order. You will also want to learn the names of the Hebrew letters, how each letter is pronounced and the transliterated value of each.

Hebrew Letter	Name	Pronunciation	Transliteration
א	Aleph	silent	ʾ
ב	Bet	*b* as in *boy*	*b*
ג	Gimel	*g* as in *God*	*g*
ד	Dalet	*d* as in *day*	*d*
ה	He	*h* as in *hay*	*h*
ו	Waw	*w* as in *way*	*w*
ז	Zayin	*z* as in *Zion*	*z*
ח	Ḥet	*ch* as in *Bach*	ḥ
ט	Tet	*t* as in *toy*	ṭ
י	Yod	*y* as in *yes*	*y*
כ	Kaf	*k* as in *king*	*k*
ל	Lamed	*l* as in *lion*	*l*
מ	Mem	*m* as in *mother*	*m*
נ	Nun	*n* as in *now*	*n*
ס	Samek	*s* as in *sin*	*s*
ע	Ayin	silent	ʿ
פ	Pe	*p* as in *pastor*	*p*
צ	Tsade	*ts* as in *boots*	ṣ
ק	Qof	*k* as in *king*	*q*
ר	Resh	*r* as in *run*	*r*
שׂ	Sin	*s* as in *sin*	ś
שׁ	Shin	*sh* as in *ship*	š
ת	Taw	*t* as in *toy*	*t*

1.2   **Pronouncing א and ע.** You have just learned that א and ע are silent, lacking any phonetic value. While א is indeed silent, the consonant ע does have some phonetic value. For English speakers, however, the pronunciation of ע is so subtly nuanced that, for all practical purposes, we are considering it too as silent. When these two consonants are encountered in a word, they will take on the sound, or phonetic value, of their assigned vowel. This means that if an א or ע is assigned an "a" vowel, they will sound like an "a." If assigned an "o" vowel, they will sound like an "o." You will not study Hebrew vowels until chapter 2. At this point, therefore, it is only important to know that א and ע are silent and will take on the sound of their assigned vowels.

1.3   As mentioned above, Hebrew is written from right to left, *not* left to right as in English. In the following order, beginning on the right, carefully study and memorize the twenty-three consonants of the Hebrew alphabet.

א ב ג ד ה ו ז ח ט י כ ל מ נ ס ע פ צ ק ר שׁ שׂ ת

1.4   **Final Forms.** Five of the Hebrew letters have final forms. That is to say, when one of these letters occurs at the end of a word, it is written differently than when it appears at the beginning or in the middle of a word. *The changing of a letter's form, however, does not change its pronunciation or transliteration.* The five final forms are listed below. These final forms must also be memorized. Remember that the Hebrew examples are written from right to left, whereas the transliteration of the Hebrew examples is written from left to right.

Regular Form	Final Form	Example	Transliteration	Translation
כ	ך	דרך	*drk*	(road, way)
מ	ם	עם	*ʿm*	(nation, people)
נ	ן	זקן	*zqn*	(old man, elder)
פ	ף	כסף	*ksp*	(money, silver)
צ	ץ	ארץ	*ʾrṣ*	(earth, land)

1.5   *Begadkephat* **Letters.** Six of the Hebrew consonants have two possible, but closely related, pronunciations. Collectively, these are known as the *begadkephat* consonants. This term is simply a mnemonic device allowing for the easy memorization of these six letters (בגדכפת). To distinguish between the two pronunciations, a dot called a Daghesh Lene was inserted into the consonantal character (בּגּדּכּפּתּ). The presence of the Daghesh Lene indicates a hard pronunciation and its absence denotes a soft pronunciation. *A Daghesh Lene will only appear in the begadkephat letters.* The student should learn the different pronunciations indicated below. You will also notice that each letter without the Daghesh Lene is transliterated with a small horizontal line either below or above the English character. Memorize both the pronunciation and the transliteration.

Begadkephat Letter	*Pronunciation*	*Transliteration*
בּ	*b* as in *boy*	*b*
ב	*v* as in *vine*	*b̲*
גּ	*g* as in *God*	*g*
ג	*gh* as in *aghast*	*ḡ*
דּ	*d* as in *day*	*d*
ד	*dh* as in *the*	*d̲*
כּ	*k* as in *king*	*k*
כ	*ch* as in *Bach*	*k̲*
פּ	*p* as in *pastor*	*p*
פ	*ph* as in *alphabet*	*p̄*
תּ	*t* as in *toy*	*t*
ת	*th* as in *thin*	*t̲*

1.6   **Gutturals.** Four of the Hebrew letters are called *gutturals*. They are called gutturals because they are pronounced in the back of the throat. The guttural consonants are א, ע, ה and ח. Sometimes ר will also behave like a guttural. For now, you only need to memorize which of the consonants are gutturals. Later you will learn certain rules that govern the use of these consonants.

1.7 **Easily Confused Letters**. For the beginning student, certain pairs or groups of consonants can sometimes look alike and become confused (just as in English with the capital I and lowercase l in the word "Idol"). You have probably observed also that different Hebrew letters can sound alike (just as in English with the *c* in *cat* and the *k* in *kite*). In order to avoid any confusion, it is sometimes helpful to compare the following characters and carefully note the distinguishing features. There is no need to memorize these consonant groups. It is only important that you are able to distinguish between the different letters and sounds.

Hebrew consonants that look alike:

1. בּ (Bet) and כ (Kaf)
2. ג (Gimel) and נ (Nun)
3. ה (He) and ח (Ḥet) and ת (Taw)
4. שׂ (Sin) and שׁ (Shin)
5. ם (final Mem) and ס (Samek)
6. ד (Dalet) and ר (Resh)
7. צ (Tsade) and ע (Ayin)
8. ו (Waw) and ז (Zayin)
9. ו (Waw) and ן (final Nun)
10. ך (final Kaf) and ן (final Nun)

Hebrew consonants that sound alike:

1. ט (Tet) and תּ (Taw with Daghesh Lene)
2. כּ (Kaf with Daghesh Lene) and ק (Qof)
3. ס (Samek) and שׂ (Sin)

1.8 **Transliteration**. It is important to learn the system of transliteration presented above, not for the purpose of pronouncing or reading biblical Hebrew, but for studying other books that refer to Hebrew words without using Hebrew characters. Many commentaries, word study books, theological dictionaries and other language tools do not use Hebrew font characters but a transliteration system whereby Hebrew letters are assigned equivalent letters from the English alphabet. In most instances, these books will list their system of transliteration somewhere at the beginning, usually between the table of contents and the first chapter or section. Some transliteration values are easily confused, so study the following transliterations carefully and observe the distinctions.

1. ᵓ (א) and ᶜ (ע). These are the most unusual transliteration symbols.
2. h (ה) and ḥ (ח)
3. ṭ (ט) and t (ת) and ṯ (ת)
4. s (ס) and ṣ (צ) and ś (שׂ) and š (שׁ)
5. You will also want to review the different transliteration symbols for the *begadkephat* letters listed in 1.5. Remember that the consonants *without the Daghesh Lene*, with the soft pronunciation, have a horizontal line above or below the letter.

1.9 **Numerical Values.** Hebrew does not have a separate set of characters to represent numbers (like the English 1, 2, 3, etc.). Rather, each letter of the Hebrew alphabet represents a numerical value. The consonants א through ט represent numbers 1-9. Consonants י through צ represent numbers 10-90 in multiples of 10 (10, 20, 30, etc.). And ק through ת represent numbers 100, 200, 300 and 400 (שׁ and שׂ both represent 300). For a full presentation of the Hebrew numerical system, see chapter 11 (Hebrew Numbers).

1.10 **Summary.** Before you move on to the exercises for this chapter, be sure that you are comfortable with the following summary. When possible, treat the exercises like a quiz, not using your book to answer the questions. Then go back and make corrections with your book. This will give you an idea of what material you have mastered and the material you need to study further.

1. Memorize the twenty-three consonants of the Hebrew alphabet in order. Be able to write out the alphabet completely from right to left. You should also know the name, pronunciation and transliteration value of each letter.
2. Five letters of the Hebrew alphabet (כ, מ, נ, פ and צ) have final forms (ך, ם, ן, ף and ץ). These must be memorized. Note that a final ך (Kaf) will frequently appear with two dots (ךּ).

3. Six Hebrew consonants are known as *begadkephat* letters (בְּגַדְכְּפַת). They are capable of two different pronunciations, hard and soft. These pronunciations are distinguished by the presence or absence of a Daghesh Lene. The distinction in pronunciation and transliteration must be memorized.

4. Four Hebrew consonants are called gutturals: א, ע, ה and ח. Remember that ר may also behave like a guttural.

1.11   **The Hebrew Acrostic.** Knowledge of the Hebrew alphabet opens the door of understanding to the Hebrew acrostic or alphabetical psalms. These are biblical poems in which consecutive units (either lines, verses or groups of verses) begin with sequential letters of the Hebrew alphabet. No doubt such a linguistic device provides a simple memory aid to the listener while still communicating the intensity and passion of the poet. For instance, the individual verses of Ps 9-10, 25, 34, and 145 begin with words whose first letters are, consecutively, the letters of the Hebrew alphabet. In Ps 37, the opening letters of alternate verses are arranged according to the sequence of the alphabet. Another variation occurs in Ps 111 and 112, where each line (rather than each verse) begins with successive letters of the Hebrew alphabet. The most elaborate acrostic biblical poem is Ps 119. This artistically shaped poem consists of twenty-two sections, each comprised of eight verses. These units feature twenty-two letters of the Hebrew alphabet, with all eight verses of a given unit beginning with the same letter of the alphabet.

As an artistic device, the acrostic uses both structure and content to express totality and completeness. Thus, everything from A to Z (or א to ת) is praised regarding the qualities of God (Ps 111 and 145), the just man (Ps 112), the virtuous woman (Prov 31:10-31) or the beauty of the law (Ps 119). Conversely, the writer of the book of Lamentations uses the acrostic to communicate the complete sense of grief over Jerusalem's fall. What is notable about the acrostic is that such an artificial scheme did not stand in the way of producing literature of a high order full of passion and thoughtfulness.

Roger Valci
Pastor, Christian Life Center
Santa Cruz, California

1.12 **Advanced Information: Traditional and Modern Pronunciation.**[1] The pronunciation of modern or Israeli Hebrew differs in a number of ways from what is considered to be the traditional or ancient pronunciation. The most notable differences involve the pronunciation of ג, ד, ת and ו. With the three *begadkephat* consonants, the forms without Daghesh Lene are pronounced just like the forms with Daghesh Lene in modern Hebrew.

Consonant	Traditional Pronunciation	Modern Pronunciation
ג	*gh* as in *aghast*	*g* as in *God*
ד	*dh* as in *the*	*d* as in *day*
ת	*th* as in *thin*	*t* as in *toy*
ו	*w* as in *way*	*v* as in *vine*

---

[1] Periodically, throughout the chapters of this grammar, you will come across a section like this one entitled "Advanced Information." This material is not required but often helpful and interesting.

Chapter 2

The Hebrew Vowels

2.1   **Hebrew Vowels.** You might be surprised to learn that originally the Hebrew language had no *written* system of vowels. This does not mean, however, that Hebrew vowels did not exist. While they did not exist in written form, they had always been present in the *spoken* form of the language. If we were to take the vowels out of the English writing system, these vowels would still be present in the spoken form. Let us use the English translation of Deut 6:5 as an example: "Love the Lord your God with all your heart." Without the vowels, we are left with a series of consonants, much like the ancient written form of Hebrew: Lv th Lrd yr Gd wth ll yr hrt. In order to read this sentence out loud, you would need to rely on your knowledge of English and supply the necessary vowels. In the same way, when Joshua read the entire law of Moses to the Israelites (Josh 8), he had before him a consonantal text with no vowels. This required Joshua to supply from memory the necessary vowels when reading. Fortunately for us, this is not the case today. In the second half of the first millennium A.D., a group of dedicated scribes called *Masoretes* became concerned with preserving the oral tradition or spoken form of Hebrew. They developed an elaborate system of vowel notation called *pointing*. This pointing system was designed to preserve the spoken system of vowels in the written text. Because the masoretic scribes considered the biblical text to be sacred, their vowel symbols were designed in such a way as never to alter the original consonantal text. To do this, the Masoretes developed vowel symbols that were placed under, inside (to the left) or above the consonantal characters. Let us look once again at Deut 6:5 but this time in Hebrew. You will notice that the consonants are exactly the same in both examples. In the second example, however, the masoretic vowel pointing system has been added. Notice that the majority of symbols exist below the consonants with occasional symbols inside (to the left) or over the consonants.

ואהבת את יהוה אלהיך בכל לבבך (without vowels)

וְאָהַבְתָּ אֵת יְהוָה אֱלֹהֶיךָ בְּכָל לְבָבְךָ (with vowels)

2.2 **Hebrew Vowel Charts.** In the following charts, the Hebrew vowels are presented in four major vowel classes: short, changeable long, unchangeable long and reduced. Within these vowel classes, there are five vowel types (a, e, i, o, u), though not all are attested in each of the vowel classes. Each vowel will appear with the consonant בֿ in order to show the position of the vowel with respect to its consonant. It is important to note that the vowel is pronounced after the consonant with which it is associated. For example, בַ is pronounced *ba* and not *ab* and בֹ is pronounced *bo* and not *ob*. Remember that while Hebrew is written from right to left, English transliteration is written from left to right.

Study each of the following vowel charts with care. For each vowel, you should be able to identify its vowel class, vowel name and transliteration. The transliteration system is fairly simple for vowels. All a-type vowels are transliterated with some form of the letter a. This is the same for each subsequent class of vowels. In transliteration, changeable long vowels have a horizontal line (macron) over the letter: *ā, ē, ō*. Unchangeable long vowels have a small upside down "v" (circumflex) over the letter: *â, ê, î, ô, û*. Short vowels are unaltered: *a, e, i, o, u*. Reduced vowels exhibit what looks like a small "u" placed above the letter: *ă, ě, ŏ*. For now, do not be concerned about the physical similarity between the Qamets (בָ, changeable long *ā*) and the Qamets Hatuf (בָ, short *o*). You will learn how to distinguish between them in the next chapter.

Finally, you should begin the process of becoming familiar with the pronunciation value of each vowel. Learning the sound for each vowel will take some time. Be patient.

2.3   Hebrew Vowel Chart 1: Short Vowels.

	Symbol	Vowel Name	Pronunciation	Transliteration
a-type	בַ	Pathach	*a* as in *bat*	*a*
e-type	בֶ	Seghol	*e* as in *better*	*e*
i-type	בִ	Hireq	*i* as in *bitter*	*i*
o-type	בָ	Qamets Hatuf	*o* as in *bottle*	*o*
u-type	בֻ	Qibbuts	*u* as in *ruler*	*u*

2.4   Hebrew Vowel Chart 2: Changeable Long Vowels. In our system of vowel classification (2.15), i-type and u-type vowels are not attested in the changeable long category.

	Symbol	Vowel Name	Pronunciation	Transliteration
a-type	בָ	Qamets	*a* as in *father*	ā
e-type	בֵ	Tsere	*e* as in *they*	ē
o-type	בֹ	Holem	*o* as in *role*	ō

2.5   Hebrew Vowel Chart 3: Unchangeable Long Vowels.

	Symbol	Vowel Name	Pronunciation	Transliteration
a-type	בָי	Qamets Yod	*ou* as in *bought*	â
e-type	בֵי	Tsere Yod	*e* as in *they*	ê
	בֶי	Seghol Yod	*e* as in *better*	ê
i-type	בִי	Hireq Yod	*i* as in *machine*	î
o-type	בוֹ	Holem Waw	*o* as in *role*	ô
u-type	בוּ	Shureq	*u* as in *ruler*	û

2.6 **Hebrew Vowel Chart 4: Reduced Vowels**. In this class, i-type and u-type vowels are not attested.

	Symbol	Vowel Name	Pronunciation	Transliteration
a-type	בֲ	Hateph Pathach	*a* as in *amuse*	$\breve{a}$
e-type	בֱ	Hateph Seghol	*a* as in *amuse*	$\breve{e}$
o-type	בֳ	Hateph Qamets	*a* as in *amuse*	$\breve{o}$

2.7 **Shewa**. You will notice in vowel chart 4 that each reduced vowel (בֲ, בֱ, בֳ) exhibits a pair of vertical dots on the right side of the vowel symbol. These vertical dots also occur without an accompanying vowel (בְ). This vowel sign is called *Shewa*. The Shewa is not listed in the above vowel charts because it is not like any other vowel. It does not belong to any phonetic class: a, e, i, o, u. There are two types of Shewa in Hebrew: *Silent Shewa* and *Vocal Shewa*. The Silent Shewa has a zero value and is never pronounced and never transliterated. The Vocal Shewa maintains a *hurried* pronunciation and sounds like the *a* in *amuse*. It is transliterated either as an upside-down *e* (בְ, bə) or as a superscript *e* (בְ, b^e). In the next chapter, you will learn how to distinguish between Silent and Vocal Shewa.

2.8 **Holem over the שׂ and שׁ**. In some instances, when the vowel symbol Holem (בֹ) is used with שׂ (Sin) or שׁ (Shin), the two dots combine into one dot over the consonant. For example, we would expect to see something like יֹשְׂבִים (yōš^ebîm) with two distinct dots. But the two dots will sometimes combine into a single dot (יֹשְׁבִים) which will serve two purposes. It distinguishes between שׁ (š) and שׂ (ś) and it also serves as the changeable long *ō* vowel (Holem). You will learn in the next chapter that *all initial consonants must be followed by a vowel*. Given this rule, the dot over the שׂ, in the above example, must also function as the Holem vowel.

2.9 **Daghesh Forte**. There is another pointing symbol to be discussed at this point, the *Daghesh Forte*. You know his brother, the Daghesh Lene. In chapter 1, you learned that six Hebrew consonants have two different pronunciations - the *begadkephat* letters. In order to distinguish between the two pronunciations, a small dot (Daghesh Lene) was inserted into the consonant (בּ for the hard *b* and ב for the soft *v*). The Daghesh Forte looks exactly like the Daghesh Lene. The effect of the Daghesh Forte, however, is to *double the consonant in which it occurs*. For example, the Hebrew word הַשָּׁמַיִם (the heavens) has a Daghesh Forte located in the Shin (שׁ). When pronouncing or transliterating this word, therefore, it should be rendered with two Shins (שׁשׁ), *haššāmayim*. The Daghesh Forte can occur in any consonant except the gutturals (א, ע, ה, ח) and ר. The gutturals and ר, therefore, will never take a Daghesh Lene or Forte. Also like the Daghesh Lene, a Daghesh Forte can occur in a *begadkephat* consonant. It is important to note that when a Daghesh Forte occurs in a *begadkephat* consonant, it doubles the hard pronunciation and not the soft. In the next chapter, you will learn how to tell the difference between the Daghesh Lene and the Daghesh Forte when they appear in *begadkephat* letters.

2.10   **Vowel Letters**. We must conclude our study of the Hebrew vowels by discussing what are called *vowel letters*. The ancient Hebrew scribe was well aware of the difficulties associated with reading texts without vowels. To this end, as early as the tenth century B.C., the innovative scribes would use, on occasion, certain Hebrew consonants to indicate different vowel sounds. The consonants א and ה were generally used to indicate the *a* vowels. The י was used to indicate the *i* and *e* vowels and the ו was used to indicate *u* and *o* vowels. A good example of this phenomenon is the variable spelling of David's name. Originally it was spelled דוד (*dwd*). But later, it was spelled דויד (*dwyd*). In the second example, you will notice the insertion of י to indicate the *i* vowel in the second half of the name. The י is not functioning as a consonant but as a vowel. In other words, certain Hebrew letters can be either consonantal or vocalic. By far, the י and ו are the most frequently used vowel letters. The unchangeable long vowels can also be called vowel letters. For example, the most common vowel letters are Hireq Yod (יִ), Holem Waw (וֹ) and Shureq (וּ).

2.11   **Defective Writing**. You have just learned that certain vowels (unchangeable long vowels) use a consonant in the formation of their symbol and that these are called vowel letters. Sometimes, a vowel letter is written without the consonant י or ו. This phenomenon, known as *defective writing*, occurs with measured frequency. It should also be noted that when these vowels are written with the consonants it is called *full writing*. The full or defective spelling of a word makes no difference in the meaning of a word. Study the following chart and memorize how each of these vowel letters will appear when written defectively.

	Full Writing		*Defective Writing*	
	בוֹ	➤	בֹ	Holem Waw to Holem
Example	שׁוֹפָר	➤	שֹׁפָר	ram's horn
	בוּ	➤	בֻ	Shureq to Qibbuts
Example	מַדּוּעַ	➤	מַדֻּעַ	why?
	בִּי	➤	בִ	Hireq Yod to Hireq
Example	דָּוִיד	➤	דָּוִד	David

There is no certain way to always predict when a vowel will be written defectively. Familiarity with vocabulary and frequent exposure to this phenomenon will help you in the identification of defectively spelled words. Study a few more examples.

תּוֹרוֹת	➤	תּוֹרֹת	laws
מוֹעֵד	➤	מֹעֵד	meeting place
עַמּוּד	➤	עַמֻּד	pillar
שְׁבוּעָה	➤	שְׁבֻעָה	oath

2.12 **Summary**. After working through this chapter, you should be able to identify the Hebrew vowel symbols by name. You should also be able to write, pronounce and transliterate the vowels (including the Shewa, בְּ). In other words, make sure that you master the information in the summary below before moving on to the exercises.

1. **Summary Hebrew Vowel Chart**

	a	*e*	*i*	*o*	*u*
Short	בַ Pathach	בֶ Seghol	בִ Hireq	בָ Qamets Hatuf	בֻ Qibbuts
Changeable Long	בָ Qamets	בֵ Tsere		בֹ Holem	
Unchangeable Long	בִי Qamets Yod	בֵי / בֶי Tsere Yod / Seghol Yod	בִי Hireq Yod	בוֹ Holem Waw	בוּ Shureq
Reduced	בֲ Hateph Pathach	בֱ Hateph Seghol		בֳ Hateph Qamets	

2. The Daghesh Forte (בּ) doubles the consonant in which it appears. It can occur in any consonant except the gutturals and ר.

3. The unchangeable long vowels (2.5) may also be called vowel letters because of the presence of י or ו in the formation of the vowel symbol.

4. Defective writing is that phenomenon in which a vowel letter is written without the consonant י or ו. There are three patterns of defective writing to be learned.

בוֹ	➤	בֹ	Holem Waw to Holem
בוּ	➤	בֻ	Shureq to Qibbuts
בִי	➤	בִ	Hireq Yod to Hireq

2.13 **Jots and Tittles.** "Think not that I am come to destroy the law, or the prophets: I am not come to destroy, but to fulfill. For verily I say unto you, Till heaven and earth pass, one jot or one tittle shall in no wise pass from the law, till all be fulfilled" (Matt 5:17-18 AV).

A "jot" refers to the Yod (י) in Hebrew, which is the smallest letter in the alphabet. The "tittle," literally "horn," probably refers to those smallest of marks that distinguish similar letters from each other, such as Dalet (ד) which has a tittle, and Resh (ר) which does not.

Gordon P. Hugenberger
Senior Pastor, Park Street Church
Boston, Massachusetts

2.14 **The Spelling of David's Name.** Given that David lived before the invention of internal vowel letters (*matres lectionis*) in Hebrew, it is certain that he and his contemporaries would have spelled his name as דוד rather than דויד. Consistent with this assumption, the spelling דוד appears in a recently discovered ninth century B.C. Aramaic inscription from Tel Dan. While there are difficulties in the interpretation of the inscription, this word offers the earliest extra-biblical reference to David.

Reflecting this same early spelling convention, the "shorter" (defective) spelling דָּוִד appears 669 out of 672 times in Samuel and Kings. On the other hand, the "full" (*plene*) spelling, דָּוִיד, appears in every one of the 272 occurrences of this name in the post-Exilic books of Chronicles and Ezra-Nehemiah. Ezekiel occupies a mid-point in this transition: "David" appears twice as דָּוִד (37:24-25) and twice as דָּוִיד (34:23-24).

In view of this development, it is remarkable that the book of Isaiah consistently spells "David" using the earlier "defective" spelling דָּוִד (Isa 7:2, 13; 16:5; 22:9, 22; 29:1; 37:35; 38:5; 55:3). This practice is expected for Isaiah 1-39, chapters which are generally attributed to the eighth century B.C. prophet Isaiah. The example in chapter 55, however, is tantalizing, even if it is not decisive, because many modern scholars date Isaiah 40-55 to the late Exilic or post-Exilic period.

Gordon P. Hugenberger
Senior Pastor, Park Street Church
Boston, Massachusetts

2.15   **Advanced Information: Alternative Vowel Classification**. Originally, there were only three vowel classes in Hebrew: a-class, i-class and u-class. The other vowel classes (e-class and o-class) developed later. The e-class developed from the original i-class and the o-class developed from the original u-class. For this reason, most grammarians prefer to divide Hebrew vowels into three (a, i, u) rather than five (a, e, i, o, u) classes. By doing this, e-class vowels are considered to be a subset of the i-class and o-class vowels are considered to be a subset of the u-class. Other grammarians, however, divide Hebrew vowels into the five classes with which most students are familiar from their study of English. In this grammar, we have adopted the five-class system. For your reference, the following chart shows both categorization systems together. Note that this information is not presented for memorization but so that you might be familiar with other grammar presentations.

	a-class	*i-class*		*u-class*	
	a	*e*	*i*	*o*	*u*
Short	בַּ	בֶּ	בִּ	בָּ	בֻּ
Changeable Long	בָּ	בֵּ		בֹּ	
Unchangeable Long	בָּי	בֵּי / בֶּי	בִּי	בֹּו בּוֹ	בּוּ
Reduced	בֲּ	בֱּ		בֳּ	

Chapter 3

Syllabification and Pronunciation

3.1   Now that we have covered the Hebrew system of consonants and vowels, it becomes important to refine our ability to pronounce Hebrew words correctly. To do so, it is necessary to work on the issue of syllabification.[1] Syllabification is simply the process of dividing words into syllables, the basic sounds of each word. In most English dictionaries, entries are commonly syllabified to aid with pronunciation. Examples include bib-li-cal, gram-mar and in-tro-duc-tion. Some words have only one syllable (monosyllabic) and, therefore, they have no syllable divider: dog, cat, friend. In English, we do this instinctively. But since we are not native speakers of Hebrew, we will not have the instincts needed to correctly syllabify Hebrew words. For this reason, we will have to rely on certain rules and principles to aid us in this process.

3.2   **Two Rules of Syllabification.** In order to divide Hebrew words into syllables, you must begin with two simple rules.

1. *Every syllable must begin with one consonant and have only one vowel.* In Hebrew, therefore, a syllable does not begin with a vowel (with one exception to be discussed in 5.7.2). The Hebrew word for "word" is דָּבָר and is syllabified as דָּ|בָר (dā-ḇār). This example has two syllables, each beginning with a consonant and each having only one vowel.

2. *There are only two types of syllables: open and closed.* Open syllables end with a vowel and closed syllables end with a consonant. These two types of syllables are present in the above example, דָּ|בָר (dā-ḇār). The first syllable, דָּ (dā), is open because it ends in a vowel. The second syllable, בָר (ḇār), is closed because it ends in a consonant. It is that simple!

---

[1] Your pronunciation of Hebrew will improve with an understanding of syllabification. These issues are important because proper pronunciation will enhance your ability to memorize and retain elements of the language.

17

These two rules are the essence of this chapter. The remainder of the chapter will discuss more specific issues and potential difficulties with the application of these rules to Hebrew words.

3.3   **Hebrew Accents**. *Hebrew words are usually accented (stressed) on the last syllable.* What this means is that the force of pronunciation is usually given to the last syllable. Using דָּבָר as an example, the stress or force of pronunciation falls on the last syllable, בָר (*bār*). Cultivating the ability to stress the last syllable in Hebrew words will be difficult for most of us since we typically stress the first syllable in English. You should also note that there are some Hebrew words that are not stressed on the last syllable. The stress in these words will be indicated by an accent mark over the stressed syllable. For example, the Hebrew word for "book" is סֵפֶר (סֵ|פֶר, *sē-p̄er*). This word happens to be stressed on the first syllable. This is indicated by the accent mark over the Samek (סֵ). If a Hebrew word is stressed on the last syllable, however, no accent mark is used. If the stress falls to any other syllable, it is indicated with an accent mark.

3.4   **Syllable Classification**. In Hebrew, syllables are classified by their proximity to the accent.[2]

1. *Tonic*. The accented syllable is called the tonic (or tone) syllable. Once again, using the example דָּבָר, the syllable בָר (*bār*) is the tonic syllable because it is the accented syllable. In the example סֵפֶר, the syllable סֵ (*sē*) is the tonic syllable because it is the accented syllable.

2. *Pretonic*. Syllables in the pretonic position occur *before the tonic syllable*. In the example דָּבָר, the syllable דָּ (*dā*) is pretonic because it occurs *before* the tonic syllable.

3. *Propretonic*. The syllable occurring *before the pretonic syllable* is called the propretonic syllable. In the examples דְּבָרִים (דְּ|בָ|רִים, transliterated *dᵉ-bā-rîm*) and סְפָרִים (סְ|פָ|רִים, transliterated *sᵉ-pā-rîm*), the syllables דְּ (*dᵉ*) and סְ (*sᵉ*) are propretonic syllables because they occur before the pretonic syllable.

---

[2] An alternative system of syllable classification also exists for which the location of the accent is not determinative. In this system, the *ultima* is the last syllable of a word. The *penultima* is the next-to-last syllable and the *antepenultima* is the syllable before the penultima.

3.5   **The Daghesh and Syllabification**. You will remember from chapter 2 that the *begadkephat* consonants can take a Daghesh Lene (hardening the sound of the consonant) and all consonants, except the gutturals and ר, can take a Daghesh Forte (doubling the consonant). The *Daghesh Lene* does not affect syllabification. The *Daghesh Forte*, however, does affect syllabification because it doubles the value of the consonant. For example, the Hebrew word for "you" is אַתָּה. Inside the second letter of this word is a *Daghesh Forte* (תּ). Because the *Daghesh Forte* doubles the value of a consonant, it must be rendered twice in transliteration, *ʾattāh* (note the double "t"). Since the Taw (תּ) is doubled, it functions *both* as the final consonant of the first syllable and the first consonant of the second syllable, *ʾat-tāh*. In order to syllabify the Hebrew word, you would need to draw a vertical line through the Daghesh Forte in the Taw (תּ). In this grammar, however, syllabification of words with a *Daghesh Forte* is rendered in the following manner, אַתָּ|תָה. Note that the gray character (ת) does not really exist except to demonstrate the doubling power of the *Daghesh Forte*. The following examples are intended to illustrate further the syllabification of the Daghesh Forte.

חֻקָּה	⟩	חֻקָּ|קָה
יַבָּשָׁה	⟩	יַבָּ|בָּ|שָׁה
אוּרִיָּה	⟩	אוּ|רִיָּ|יָה
תְּפִלָּה	⟩	תְּ|פִלָּ|לָה

So far, things are relatively simple. There is, however, one potentially confusing issue. The *begadkephat* letters can take either a *Daghesh Forte* or a *Daghesh Lene*. How can you tell which *Daghesh* is being used in a *begadkephat* letter? Here are a few simple rules.

1. *The Daghesh in a begadkephat is a Forte if preceded by a vowel* (אַתָּה, תּ preceded by the Pathach vowel).

2. *The Daghesh in a begadkephat is a Lene if preceded by a consonant* (מַלְכָּה, כּ preceded by ל with Silent Shewa). You will learn how to distinguish between Vocal and Silent Shewa in the next section.

3. *A begadkephat letter at the beginning of a word takes a Daghesh Lene unless the previous word ends in a vowel* (דָּבָר, ד with Daghesh Lene begins the word).

3.6   **The Shewa and Syllabification**. In section 2.7, you learned that there are two types of Shewas in Hebrew: *Silent Shewa* and *Vocal Shewa*. The Silent Shewa has a zero value and is never pronounced or transliterated. The Vocal Shewa maintains a hurried pronunciation and sounds like the *a* in *amuse*. It is transliterated either as an upside-down *e* (בְּ, *bə*) or as a superscript *e* (בְּ, *b^e*). *The Vocal Shewa will always occur in an open syllable*. A Silent Shewa will always come at the end of a closed syllable, that is, after a short vowel.

We now need to learn how to distinguish between a Vocal and a Silent Shewa. There are two simple rules.

1. *The Shewa is silent if it is immediately preceded by a short vowel.* This is just a different way of saying, as above, that a Silent Shewa will always come at the end of a closed syllable. Consider the Shewa in the word מַלְכָּה (*malkāh*), meaning "queen." It is immediately preceded by a short vowel (Pathach under the מ) and it comes at the end of a closed syllable. Consider the following applications of this first rule.

   a. A Shewa is silent when immediately preceded by a short vowel. For example, in פַּרְעֹה (*par-ʿōh*), the Shewa under the ר is preceded by the short *a* vowel and, therefore, is silent.

   b. The first of two contiguous (side-by-side) Shewas within a word is silent. For example, the Shewa under the שׁ of מִשְׁפְּטֵי is silent and the Shewa under the פ is vocal. The word is syllabified מִשׁ|פְּ|טֵי (*miš-p^e-ṭê*).

   c. A Shewa at the end of a word is silent as in כָּתַבְתְּ. Both Shewas in this form are silent. The word is syllabified as כָּ|תַבְתְּ (*kā-ṭaḇt*). This is the only exception to the above principle.

2. *The Shewa is vocal if not immediately preceded by a short vowel.* That is to say, in all other circumstances, the Shewa is vocal. Consider the following applications of this second rule:

   a. Initial Shewa is always vocal as in בְּרָכָה (*b^e-rā-ḵāh*).

   b. The second of two contiguous (side-by-side) Shewas within a word is vocal as in מִשְׁפְּטֵי (*miš-p^e-ṭê*). The Shewa under the **פ** is vocal because it is preceded by the consonant **שׁ** and not a short vowel. The Shewa under the **שׁ** is silent.

c. A Shewa under any consonant with Daghesh Forte is vocal as in **הַמְּלָכִים** (*ham-mᵉ-lā-ḵîm*). The Daghesh in the **מּ** must be Forte because it is not a *begadkephat* letter.

d. A Shewa after a long vowel is vocal as in **כֹּתְבִים** (*kō-ṯᵉ-ḇîm*). The Shewa is preceded by the changeable long *ō* vowel and, therefore, is vocal.

It is important at this point to note that the gutturals cannot take a Vocal Shewa but they can take a Silent Shewa as in **שָׁמַעְתָּ** (*šā-maᶜ-tā*). The Shewa under the **ע** comes at the end of a closed syllable and it is immediately preceded by a short vowel. It is, therefore, silent.

When dealing with the Shewa in Hebrew, remember to keep it simple. *A Shewa is silent if it is immediately preceded by a short vowel. In all other circumstances, it is vocal.*

3.7 **Qamets and Qamets Hatuf.** You already know from section 2.2 that two vowels look exactly alike, the Qamets (**בָ**, changeable long *ā*) and the Qamets Hatuf (**בָ**, short *o*). How do you tell the difference? In general, the Qamets occurs much more frequently than the Qamets Hatuf. So when in doubt, defer to the Qamets. Since, however, this method is not error free, the following rules are given.

1. The Qamets Hatuf (**בָ**, short *o*) occurs only in a *closed and unaccented syllable*. In **חָכְמָה** (*ḥoḵ-māh*), the vowel under the **ח** is a Qamets Hatuf since it occurs in a closed syllable that is unaccented. The vowel under the **מ** is a Qamets since it occurs in an accented syllable. The word occurring most frequently with the Qamets Hatuf is **כָּל** (*kol*) which means "all," "each" or "every."

2. The Qamets (**בָ**, changeable long *ā*) prefers an open, pretonic syllable or a closed, accented syllable. In the example **דָּבָר**, both vowels are Qamets. The first is in an open, pretonic syllable. The second is in a closed, accented syllable (see 3.14 for further discussion of syllable preferences).

3. A small symbol called *Metheg* may also be used to distinguish between Qamets and Qamets Hatuf.[3] The Metheg is a small vertical line that is placed beneath a consonant and to the left of a vowel as in בָּתִּים (*bāt-tîm*). In this word, the Metheg is the vertical line to the left of the Qamets under the בּ. In terms of vowel identification, the Metheg occurs with the Qamets and not with the Qamets Hatuf. For example, in the word בָּתִּים (houses), the vowel symbol under the בּ could be taken either as Qamets or Qamets Hatuf. The appearance of the Metheg to the left of the vowel (בָּתִּים) identifies it as Qamets and not Qamets Hatuf. In the word חָכְמָה (wisdom), however, the vowel under the ח is Qamets Hatuf (short *o*) and, therefore, is not marked with Metheg. The Shewa under the כ is silent because it comes at the end of a closed syllable that contains a short vowel.

3.8 **Furtive Pathach**. You have learned that Hebrew vowels are pronounced after the consonant with which they are associated (בַּ is rendered *ba* and not *ab*). There is, however, one minor exception to this rule. *When a word ends in ח or ע, a Pathach may appear beneath this consonant and must be pronounced and transliterated before the guttural.* This special use of the Pathach is called the *Furtive Pathach*. In terms of syllabification, the Furtive Pathach is not considered to be a full vowel nor is it counted in syllabification. Note the following examples.

בֹּרֵחַ	*bōrēaḥ*	➤	בֹּ‖רֵחַ	*bō-rēaḥ*
נֹטֵעַ	*nōṭēaʿ*	➤	נֹ‖טֵעַ	*nō-ṭēaʿ*
רָקִיעַ	*rāqîaʿ*	➤	רָ‖קִיעַ	*rā-qîaʿ*
רוּחַ	*rûaḥ*	➤	רוּחַ	*rûaḥ* (monosyllabic)

3.9 **Quiescent א**. When א occurs without a vowel, it is *quiescent* as in חַטָּאת (sin). When the א is quiescent, it is not considered to be a consonant with reference to the rules of syllabification. This word should be divided as חַ‖טָּאת.

---

[3] Though there are other uses of the Metheg, in this grammar the Metheg will be used only to distinguish between Qamets and Qamets Hatuf in ambiguous circumstances.

3.10 **Hebrew Diphthong**. In Hebrew, there is a cluster of consonants and vowels that always act together as a unit. Technically, this phenomenon is called a *diphthong*. *Diphthong* is a grammatical term used to identify sounds normally distinct but now functioning as a single unit. The most common Hebrew diphthong is ֫יַ (*ayi*). Syllables that contain this diphthong are considered to be closed. Note the following examples for syllabification.

שָׁמַיִם *šāmayim* ➤ שָׁ|מַיִם *šā-mayim*

בַּיִת *bayit* ➤ בַּיִת *bayit* (monosyllabic)

3.11 **Summary**. In the following summary, all major rules for syllabification are listed. These rules are not to be rigorously memorized but rather understood and applied to the syllabification and pronunciation of Hebrew words.

1. Every syllable must begin with a consonant and have only one vowel (with very few exceptions).

2. There are only two types of syllables: open and closed. Open syllables end with a vowel and closed syllables end with a consonant.

3. A *Daghesh Forte* doubles the consonant in which it occurs and must be divided in syllabification.

4. A *Daghesh* in a *begadkephat* consonant is a *Lene* if preceded by a consonant and a *Forte* if preceded by a vowel.

5. A *Daghesh Forte* in a *begadkephat* consonant doubles the hard sound and never the soft sound.

6. The gutturals and ר cannot take *Daghesh Lene* or *Daghesh Forte*.

7. A Shewa is *vocal* in the following circumstances: if it occurs under the first consonant of a word; if it is the second of two contiguous Shewas within a word; if it is under any consonant with a Daghesh Forte; if it is after any long vowel.

8. A Shewa is *silent* in the following circumstances: if it is preceded immediately by a short vowel; if it is the first of two contiguous Shewas within a word; if it is at the end of a word.

9. A guttural cannot take a Vocal Shewa but it can take a Silent Shewa as in שָׁמָעְתָּ (שָׁ|מָֽעְ|תָּ).

10. Unlike the gutturals, the consonant ר can take Vocal Shewa.

11. The reduced vowels (בֲ, בֱ, בֳ) always occur in open syllables. They are never silent.

12. The Metheg may be used to distinguish between Qamets and Qamets Hatuf. The Metheg occurs with Qamets and not with Qamets Hatuf (בָּתִּים).

13. Furtive Pathach is not considered to be a full vowel nor is it counted in syllabification. It must, however, be pronounced and transliterated before the guttural.

14. When א occurs without a vowel, it is *quiescent* as in חַטָּאת (sin).

15. Syllables that contain the *diphthong* (יַ) are considered to be closed.

3.12   **Vocabulary.** The numbers in parentheses indicate how many times that word occurs in the Hebrew Bible.

אָדָם	man, Adam (562)
אֶרֶץ	earth, land (2,505); feminine
אֱלֹהִים	God, gods (2,602)
אָב	father (1,211)
אֵל	God, god, the high god El (317)
בֵּן	son (4,941)
בַּיִת	house (2,047)
דָּבָר	word, matter, thing (1,454)
יוֹם	day (2,301)
יִשְׂרָאֵל	Israel (2,507)
יְרוּשָׁלַם	Jerusalem (643); יְרוּשָׁלַיִם (alternate form)
יְהוָה	Yahweh, Lord (6,828)
מִצְרַיִם	Egypt (682)
מֹשֶׁה	Moses (766)

מֶ֫לֶךְ   king (2,530)

סוּס   horse (138)

עֶ֫בֶד   servant (803)

פַּרְעֹה   Pharaoh (274)

שָׁנָה   year (878)

שֵׁם   name (864)

3.13 **The Imperative Summons to Praise**. Of the many names and descriptive titles by which God is called in the Old Testament, only one is his personal name. He is called יהוה (commonly translated as "Lord" or rendered as "Yahweh"). The name is composed of four consonants and thus known as the *tetragrammaton* (Greek: "having four letters"). The divine name may also appear as a shortened independent form as in Ex 15:2: עָזִּי וְזִמְרָת יָהּ (the Lord is my strength and my song). The form יָהּ is the shortened form of the *tetragrammaton*. The name is also attested in shortened forms that are commonly used in the formation of personal names such as יְהוֹנָתָן (Jonathan, "Yahweh has given"), יְהוֹשָׁפָט (Jehoshaphat, "Yahweh has judged"), יוֹאֵל (Joel, "Yahweh is God") or יְהוֹרָם (Jehoram, "Yahweh is exalted").

The shortened independent form occurs primarily in poetry and is perhaps most common in the spelling of "hallelujah" as in Ps 135:3, הַלְלוּ־יָהּ כִּי־טוֹב יְהוָה (Praise the Lord for he is good!). The verse begins with a verbal form that will not be studied until chapter 27. It is a Piel Imperative 2mp verb from the root הָלַל which means "to praise." As an Imperative form, it translates "you praise" or simply "praise." You recognize the shortened form of the divine name (יָהּ) which is attached to the Imperative with the raised horizontal line that is known as Maqqef. You now understand the etymology of "hallelujah" (the imperative summons to praise). The call to praise may also appear without a Maqqef as in the first verse of Ps 106: הַלְלוּיָהּ (Praise the Lord!). This grammatical form is the same as that in Ps 135:3.[4]

As you might expect, the most frequent use of the verbal root הָלַל in expression of praise to God is in the book of Psalms, especially in the

---

[4] Note also that the call to praise may be phrased with the full spelling of the tetragrammaton and the accusative marker: הַלְלוּ אֶת־יְהוָה (Praise the Lord!) as in Ps 117:1.

so-called Hallelujah Psalms that are found in several groups (Ps 104-106; 111-113; 115-117; 135; 146-150). Here, the imperative summons to praise may appear as an integral part of the psalm (135:3) or it may serve as a liturgical introduction[5] and/or conclusion[6] with either of the spellings detailed above. It is significant to note that most of these occurrences are plural, emphasizing (though not uniquely) the congregational and communal dimension of praise. Praise can manifest itself in speaking (Jer 31:7), singing (Ps 69:30) and with dancing and musical instruments (Ps 149:3). However offered, corporately or individually, praise is a vital response to God. The book of Psalms concludes:

> Let everything that breathes praise the Lord.
> Praise the Lord!
> (Ps 150:6)

Gary D. Pratico
Professor of Old Testament
Gordon-Conwell Theological Seminary
South Hamilton, Massachusetts

3.14   **Advanced Information: Vowels and Their Syllable Preferences**. As you know from chapter 2, Hebrew vowels are grouped into four categories: short, changeable long, unchangeable long and reduced. The vowels of each category prefer to be in certain types of syllables. A vowel's preference for a particular type of syllable is determined by two primary factors: the type of syllable (open or closed) and the proximity of the syllable to the accent. Awareness of a vowel's syllable preference will help with syllabification and pronunciation, and will enable you to identify and explain changes in a word's spelling.

1.   *Short Vowels*. Short vowels prefer either *closed, unaccented* syllables or *open, accented* syllables.

> עָ|בְד   short vowel in a closed, unaccented syllable (בֶד)
>
> עָ|בְד   short vowel in an open, accented syllable (עָ)

---

[5]   Ps 106:1; 111:1; 112:1; 113:1; 117:1; 135:1; 146:1; 147:1; 148:1; 149:1; 150:1.

[6]   Ps 104:35; 105:45; 106:48; 113:9; 115:18; 116:19; 135:21; 146:10; 147:20; 148:14; 149:9; 150:6.

2. *Long Vowels*. Long vowels (changeable or unchangeable) prefer either *closed, accented* syllables or *open, pretonic* syllables.

    דָּ|בָר   long vowel in a closed, accented syllable (בָר)

    דָּ|בָר   long vowel in an open, pretonic syllable (דָּ)

3. *Vocal Shewa and Reduced Vowels*. Vocal Shewa and reduced (Hateph) vowels prefer *open, propretonic* syllables. The reduced vowels appear with guttural consonants in the open, propretonic position.[7]

    דְּ|בָ|רִים   Vocal Shewa in an open, propretonic syllable (דְּ)

    אֱ|לֹ|הִים   reduced vowel in an open, propretonic syllable (אֱ)

---

[7] Of course, there are exceptions to this general rule, for example, with the stem vowel of certain forms of the Imperfect verb (see 15.4.7).

Chapter 4

Hebrew Nouns

4.1   **Introduction**. Hebrew nouns function just like English nouns. They are used to indicate a person, place, thing or idea. Like English, Hebrew nouns can be either *singular* or *plural* in number. But, unlike English, they can also be *dual* in number, indicating a plurality of two (i.e., two eyes, two hands, etc.). Hebrew nouns also have gender. They are either *masculine* or *feminine*.

In English, most nouns are pluralized with the addition of an "s" or "es." For example, when the noun *prophet* is pluralized it becomes *prophets*. The letter "s" was added to make the singular into a plural. Hebrew nouns pluralize in much the same way. Different endings are added to singular nouns in order to indicate the plural and dual forms. In Hebrew, however, the plural ending for a masculine noun is different from the plural ending for a feminine noun. The following noun chart illustrates how masculine and feminine nouns are pluralized.

4.2   **Plural and Dual Endings on Masculine and Feminine Nouns**

	Masculine Noun	*Feminine Noun*
Singular	סוּס horse	תּוֹרָה law
Plural	סוּסִים horses	תּוֹרוֹת laws
Dual	סוּסַיִם two horses	

4.3   **Gender and Number**. Hebrew nouns are either *masculine* or *feminine*, though a few nouns are both masculine and feminine. With regard to a noun's number, it may be either *singular*, indicating one; *plural*, indicating more than one; or *dual*, indicating two.

Masculine singular nouns are *endingless* nouns, that is, they have *no distinctive endings*. The plural and dual masculine endings are very distinct and, for this reason, easy to identify. Masculine plural nouns usually end in ים as in סוּסִים (horses) or דְּבָרִים (words). Masculine dual nouns end in ַיִם as in סוּסַיִם (two horses) or עֵינַיִם (two eyes).

28

In contrast to endingless masculine singular nouns, feminine singular nouns are *usually* marked with distinctive endings. The most common ending is הָ as in תּוֹרָה (law). Additionally, the endings תְ and תֶ are distinctly feminine as in בַּת (daughter) and תִּפְאֶרֶת (glory, beauty). Feminine plural nouns end in וֹת as in מְלָכוֹת (queens) or תּוֹרוֹת (laws). Feminine dual nouns end in יִם as in יָדַיִם (two hands). You will notice that *the dual ending is the same for both masculine and feminine nouns*. Usually words for paired body parts (hands, feet, eyes, ears) utilize the dual ending.

It is important to understand that feminine nouns (grammatical gender) do not refer only to feminine things (natural gender) or masculine nouns only to masculine things. For example, the Hebrew word for "law" is תּוֹרָה and it is feminine. This does not mean, however, that laws apply only to women. What the gender of a Hebrew noun indicates is the *pattern of inflection* it will usually follow. In other words, masculine nouns take one set of endings for pluralization and feminine nouns take another. But, of course, grammatical gender and natural gender do correspond in most Hebrew nouns. For example, the word for "daughter" (בַּת) in Hebrew is feminine and, therefore, grammatical and natural gender correspond. Likewise, the Hebrew word for "son" (בֵּן) is masculine, so natural and grammatical gender once again correspond. The following chart summarizes all possible endings for the pluralization of masculine and feminine nouns.

4.4   Summary of Noun Endings.

	Masculine Noun	*Feminine Noun*
Singular	endingless	הָ /תְ /תֶ
Plural	יִם	וֹת
Dual	יִם	יִם

4.5   The following word lists contain examples of singular, plural and dual nouns. You will quickly realize how simple it is to identify the gender and number of most nouns by learning the few endings in the above chart.

Masculine Singular (ms)	*Masculine Plural* (mp)	*Feminine Singular* (fs)	*Feminine Plural* (fp)	*Mas/Fem Dual*
סוּס	סוּסִים	מַלְכָּה	מְלָכוֹת	יוֹמַיִם
מֶלֶךְ	מְלָכִים	תּוֹרָה	תּוֹרוֹת	פַּעֲמַיִם
דָּבָר	דְּבָרִים	חוֹמָה	חוֹמוֹת	רַגְלַיִם
יֶלֶד	יְלָדִים	בַּת	בָּנוֹת	יָדַיִם
יוֹם	יָמִים	קֶשֶׁת	קְשָׁתוֹת	עֵינַיִם

4.6 **Lexical Form**. When in doubt with regard to a word's meaning or form, you will have to look it up in what is called a Hebrew lexicon (Hebrew dictionary). When looking up a noun in the lexicon, you must search for its lexical form. *The lexical form for any noun is the singular form.* For example, if you were to search for the definition of סוּסִים or סוּסָיִם, you would have to look under סוּס, the masculine singular form. Likewise, if you were to search for the feminine plural תּוֹרוֹת, you would find it listed in its singular or lexical form, תּוֹרָה. In almost every instance, the lexical form of a noun will be the form you have memorized as vocabulary.

4.7 **Exceptions to the Rules**. As with every set of rules or patterns, there are always exceptions. Some of the most common exceptions are listed below.

1. *Endingless Feminine Nouns.* You have learned that all masculine singular nouns are endless but not all endless nouns are masculine singular. In a few instances, feminine singular nouns are also endless. For example, the nouns אֶרֶץ (land), עִיר (city) and אֶבֶן (stone) are endless but also feminine. The only way to be certain of any noun's gender is to look it up in the lexicon (dictionary). But do not be confused by this irregularity. The gender of a noun does not change its meaning, only its pattern of pluralization. Whether a noun like יָד (hand) is masculine or feminine, pluralized with יִם (masculine) or וֹת (feminine), makes absolutely no difference with regard to its meaning.

2. *Exception to Normal Pluralization.* In a very few instances, singular nouns of one gender take the plural endings of the other gender.

For example, the Hebrew word for "father" is אָב and it is masculine. We would expect, therefore, that this masculine singular noun would take the masculine plural ending. This is not the case, however, as the plural of אָב is אָבוֹת. But again, such irregularity is no cause for confusion. If you know that the Hebrew word for "father" is אָב and that וֹת is a plural ending, then אָבוֹת must mean "fathers." Similarly, even though שָׁנָה (year) is a feminine noun, it is commonly pluralized as שָׁנִים (years) with the masculine plural ending. All such irregularities will be noted in the vocabulary sections throughout the grammar.

3. *Special Dual Nouns.* You know that Hebrew nouns can be *dual* in number and as such indicate a plurality of two as in יָדַיִם meaning "*two* hands." There are three special Hebrew words, however, that are *always dual in form.* They are שָׁמַיִם (heaven, heavens), מִצְרַיִם (Egypt) and מַיִם (water). These three nouns occur frequently and should be memorized.

4. *Irregular Stem Change.* Some Hebrew nouns will alter their actual (consonantal) stem when they add their plural endings. The *stem* of a noun refers to the *original combination of consonants* that make up a particular word. This type of irregularity is the most difficult to identify. For example, the plural of יוֹם (day) is יָמִים (days), the plural of אִישׁ (man) is אֲנָשִׁים (men) and the plural of אִשָּׁה (woman) is נָשִׁים (women).[1] In some instances, letters are lost; in others they are added when forming the plural. There are not many Hebrew words that undergo this type of change and all such irregularities will be identified in the vocabulary sections throughout the grammar.

5. *Defective Spelling of וֹת.* Occasionally, the feminine plural ending וֹת will be spelled ֹת, with a Holem rather than a Holem Waw. For example, the Hebrew word for "congregation" is עֵדָה. The ending clearly indicates that this is a feminine noun. Normally we would expect to see עֵדוֹת in the plural. Sometimes, however, the feminine plural form appears as עֵדֹת. This shorter spelling is called "defective spelling" or "defective writing." The longer or full form is called the *plene* (Latin for "full") spelling. Defective

---

[1] The noun אִשָּׁה (woman) pluralizes with the masculine plural ending (נָשִׁים).

spelling is that spelling which does not use the vowel letters (see 2.12.4). Once again, the change is minor. Both spellings have the same type of vowel and are pronounced exactly the same.

4.8   **Basic Patterns of Noun Pluralization**. You have probably noticed that most nouns undergo significant vowel changes with the addition of plural endings. For example, observe the vowel changes from the singular מֶלֶךְ (king) to the plural מְלָכִים (kings). In fact, relatively few nouns pluralize without altering the vowels of the noun stem in some way. These changes are occasioned by a shift in both accent and syllable structure when plural endings are added. Carefully study the following basic patterns of noun pluralization.

1. *Pluralization with No Change*. There are a number of nouns that are pluralized simply with the addition of the masculine or feminine plural ending. In other words, there are no changes in the vocalization (vowel pattern) of the noun itself. Nouns of this type may be monosyllabic with an unchangeable long vowel.

שִׁיר song	➤	שִׁירִים songs
אוֹת sign	➤	אוֹתוֹת signs

   Nouns of this type may also be composed of two syllables with Shewa or Hateph Pathach in the first syllable and an unchangeable long vowel in the second syllable.

חֲלוֹם dream	➤	חֲלוֹמוֹת dreams
רְחוֹב street	➤	רְחוֹבוֹת streets

2. *Pluralization with Propretonic Reduction*. Two-syllable nouns that are accented on the final syllable and have either Qamets or Tsere in the first or pretonic syllable will experience what is called "propretonic reduction" with the addition of plural endings. With the addition of the plural endings, the Qamets or Tsere is placed in an open, propretonic syllable. In an open, propretonic syllable, the Qamets or the Tsere will *reduce to Shewa*. This is called *propretonic reduction* (3.14.3)

דָּבָר word	➤	דְּבָרִים words
לֵבָב heart	➤	לְבָבוֹת hearts

Nouns with an initial guttural consonant cannot take a Vocal Shewa but prefer Hateph Pathach.

עָנָן	cloud	➤	עֲנָנִים	clouds
חָצֵר	courtyard	➤	חֲצֵרוֹת	courtyards

Note that nouns with an unchangeable long vowel in the first syllable will *not* experience propretonic reduction.

כּוֹכָב	star	➤	כּוֹכָבִים	stars

3. *Pluralization of Segholate Nouns.* All two-syllable nouns that are *accented on the first syllable* are classified as Segholate nouns. Both masculine and feminine nouns appear in this class. They are called Segholate nouns because they typically have two Seghol vowels as in the following examples: מֶלֶךְ (king), אֶרֶץ (earth, land), דֶּרֶךְ (road, way), פֶּסֶל (idol) and חֶרֶב (sword). Other vowel patterns also appear in this class, usually with at least one Seghol vowel as in the following examples: סֵפֶר (book), בֹּקֶר (morning) and זֶרַע (seed). The nouns בַּעַל (lord) and נַעַר (young man) are also Segholate nouns because they are accented on the first syllable even though they exhibit a vowel pattern without a Seghol vowel. While the vowel pattern of Segholate nouns will vary in the singular, they will *always have the same vowel pattern in the plural.* Carefully study the following plural forms of Segholate nouns and note that each plural form has the same vowel pattern with Vocal Shewa or a Hateph vowel under the first consonant and Qamets under the second consonant.

מֶלֶךְ	king	➤	מְלָכִים	kings
נֶפֶשׁ	life	➤	נְפָשׁוֹת	lives
חֶרֶב	sword	➤	חֲרָבוֹת[2]	swords
סֵפֶר	book	➤	סְפָרִים	books
בֹּקֶר	morning	➤	בְּקָרִים	mornings
זֶרַע	seed	➤	זְרָעִים	seeds

---

[2] Gutturals cannot take a Vocal Shewa (3.6.2). In such instances, they will take a reduced vowel, usually Hateph Pathach.

בַּעַל lord   ➤   בְּעָלִים lords

נַעַר boy   ➤   נְעָרִים boys

4. *Pluralization of Geminate Nouns.* Geminate nouns appear to have only two consonants (Biconsonantal) as in עַם (people). Actually, Geminate nouns originally had three consonants. For example, the Hebrew word for "people" (עַם) was originally spelled עמם. There are still a few Geminate nouns in biblical Hebrew that occasionally preserve both Geminate consonants such as לֵבָב (heart). What makes this noun class unique is that the last two consonants of the original stem are identical. The term "Geminate" comes from the Latin *gemini*, meaning "twins." Over the years, however, the two identical consonants became one. When Geminate nouns are pluralized, *the consonant that originally appeared twice will now be written once with Daghesh Forte.* The Daghesh Forte represents the lost Geminate consonant. The "twin" has reappeared, not as a consonant, but as a Daghesh Forte.[3] Observe the following examples.

עַם people   ➤   עַמִּים peoples (original root עמם)

חֵץ arrow   ➤   חִצִּים arrows (original root חצץ)

חֹק statute   ➤   חֻקִּים statutes (original root חקק)

5. *Irregular Pluralization.* Finally, there are numerous nouns that are irregular and unpredictable in their pluralization. Below are some of the most common examples.

אִישׁ man   ➤   אֲנָשִׁים men

אִשָּׁה woman   ➤   נָשִׁים women

עִיר city   ➤   עָרִים cities

אָב father   ➤   אָבוֹת fathers

---

[3] Note, however, that not all Biconsonantal nouns were originally Geminate nouns. For example, the nouns אָב (father), בֵּן (son) and שֵׁם (name) are Biconsonantal but not Geminate. When these nouns pluralize, there is no Daghesh Forte: אָבוֹת (fathers), בָּנִים (sons) and שֵׁמוֹת (names).

בַּ֫יִת	house	➤	בָּתִּים	houses
בַּת	daughter	➤	בָּנוֹת	daughters
בֵּן	son	➤	בָּנִים	sons
יוֹם	day	➤	יָמִים	days

4.9   Summary.

1. Hebrew nouns have both *gender* and *number*. With regard to gender, a noun will be either *masculine* or *feminine*, rarely both. With regard to number, a noun will be *singular*, *plural* or *dual*.

2. Masculine singular nouns are endingless. Masculine plural nouns have the םי ָ ending. Masculine dual nouns have the םִי ַ֫ ending.

3. The most common feminine singular ending is ה ָ but ת ֶ and ת ַ are well-attested. Feminine singular nouns may also be endingless. Feminine plural nouns have the וֹת ending. Feminine dual nouns have the םִי ַ֫ ending which is the same as the masculine dual. Feminine singular nouns that end in ה ָ will not be identified as feminine in the vocabulary sections or in the grammar's lexicon.

4. Exceptions to these standard rules or patterns include:

   a. *Endingless Feminine Nouns.* All masculine singular nouns are endingless but a few feminine singular nouns are also endingless. Examples include עִיר (city) and אֶ֫בֶן (stone).

   b. *Exception to Normal Pluralization.* A few singular nouns of one gender take the plural endings of the other gender. For example, אָב (father) is a masculine singular noun but takes a feminine plural ending, אָבוֹת (fathers).

   c. *Special Dual Nouns.* A few nouns are always dual in form but usually singular in meaning (מַ֫יִם, dual in form but translated as singular, "water").

   d. *Irregular Stem Change.* A few nouns change their (consonantal) stem when forming the plural. For example, אִישׁ (man) becomes אֲנָשִׁים (men) in the plural.

   e. *Defective Spelling of* וֹת. Sometimes, the feminine plural ending וֹת will be spelled ת, with a Holem rather than a Holem Waw. For example, עֵדָה (congregation) is usually spelled עֵדֹת in the plural, with Holem rather than Holem Waw.

5. Most nouns undergo a change in vowel pattern with the addition of plural endings. Be certain that you understand the patterns of noun pluralization that are discussed in section 4.8.

6. A Hebrew dictionary is called a *lexicon*. When looking up words you must search for them by their *lexical form*. The lexical form of a Hebrew noun is the *singular form*.

4.10 Vocabulary. Endingless feminine nouns will be identified in the vocabulary sections throughout the grammar.

אֲדֹנָי	Lord; אָדוֹן lord, master (774)
אָח	brother (629); אַחִים (irregular plural)
אִישׁ	man, husband (2,198); אֲנָשִׁים (irregular plural)
אִשָּׁה	woman, wife (779); נָשִׁים (irregular plural)
בַּת	daughter (603); בָּנוֹת (irregular plural); feminine
גּוֹי	people, nation (560)
דֶּרֶךְ	way, road (712); masculine/feminine
הַר	mountain, mountain range (558); הָרִים (plural)
כֹּהֵן	priest (750)
לֵב	heart (854); לֵבָב (alternate form)
מַיִם	water (586)
נֶפֶשׁ	life, soul (757); feminine
נָבִיא	prophet (317)
סֵפֶר	book, scroll (191)
עַיִן	eye, spring (900); עֵינַיִם (dual); feminine
עִיר	city (1095); עָרִים (irregular plural); feminine
צָבָא	army, host (486); צְבָאוֹת (plural)
קוֹל	voice, sound (505)
רֹאשׁ	head, chief, top (600)
תּוֹרָה	law, teaching, Torah (223)

4.11 **Kinship Terms and God's Relationship with His People.** Some of the first vocabulary words a student learns in Hebrew are some of the richest theological terms in the Old Testament. Several of these words are kinship terms that provide the conceptual framework for understanding Israel's relationship with Yahweh and with each other. אָב is the common word for "father" but one that also means, by extension, "ancestor." The "children of Israel" (בְּנֵי־יִשְׂרָאֵל) were literally the *sons* of Jacob, also named Israel. Jacob was the grandson of Abraham whose name was changed from "Father is lofty" (Abram) to "Father of multitudes" (Abraham). Metaphorically, אָב may refer to the originator or leader of a group. The head of a tribal unit (Deut 26:5), a musical guild (Gen 4:21), or a religious group (2 Kgs 6:21) may be a "father." Abraham becomes, in the New Testament, the father of the faithful (Gal 3:7, 29; Rom 4:11-16). Most significantly, God is seen as the spiritual father of his people.

Israel is sometimes described as Yahweh's firstborn "son" (בֵּן). "When Israel was a child," writes Hosea (11:1), "I loved him. And out of Egypt I called my son" (בְּנִי). In Ezek 16, Israel is allegorically pictured as God's adopted daughter (born originally to Amorite and Hittite parents) who eventually becomes his wife. The most common way that God refers to corporate Israel is as "my people." In almost 250 cases (concentrated in Exodus and in the prophets), God uses the term עַמִּי. Implicit in this term is a covenant relationship. Yahweh bought Israel out of bondage and at Mt. Sinai presented her with the terms for this relationship. Exodus records the inauguration of the covenant; the prophets describe its breakdown and hope for renewal.

The fatherhood of God for Israel is, from a theological perspective, inseparably bound to the fraternal relationship between the members of the community. אַחִים (brothers) are not simply those with whom there are blood ties; they are all those who share in the covenant God made with the "extended family" called Israel. The community of Israel was to be understood, fundamentally, as the family of God. Misunderstanding and abusing the rights and privileges of another member of the community was a capital crime. In Deut 24:7 we read, "If a man is caught kidnapping one of his fellow Israelites [אָחָיו] and treats him as a slave or sells him, the kidnapper must die" (cf. Lev 25:46).

Interestingly, Israel's neighbors were viewed as אַחִים as well. Tyre was condemned for ignoring a "treaty of *brotherhood*" and Edom was to be judged for mistreating *brother* Israel (Amos 1:9,11). These statements are likely the result of real treaties made between the parties. But they also hint at a perspective on God's universal relationship with all nations as vassals. Amos, quoting the Lord, asks, "Are not you Israelites the same to me as the Cushites? ... Did I not bring Israel up from Egypt, the Philistines from Caphtor, and the Arameans from Kir?" (Amos 9:7). In similarly explicit covenant language, Isaiah predicts a time when "The Lord Almighty will bless them, saying, 'Blessed be Egypt my people, Assyria my handiwork, and Israel my inheritance'" (Isa 19:25).

Tim Laniak
Assistant Professor of Old Testament
Gordon-Conwell Theological Seminary
Charlotte, North Carolina

4.12   Advanced Information: Rules of Shewa. In various sections of this grammar, we will refer to the Rules of Shewa. Here, the two basic Rules of Shewa and two exceptions are presented.

1. *The First Rule of Shewa*. Hebrew will not allow two contiguous (side-by-side) Vocal Shewas. When two side-by-side Shewas occur within a word, you have learned that the first is silent and the second is vocal. What happens, however, when two side-by-side Shewas would occur at the beginning of a word? In such a circumstance, the two Vocal Shewas become Hireq in a closed syllable. In other words, two Vocal Shewas become a single syllable in which there are no Vocal Shewas. For example, the prefixing of the preposition לְ (to, for) to נְבִיאִים (prophets) would produce לְנְבִיאִים but two Vocal Shewas are not allowed at the beginning of a word. The application of the first Rule of Shewa produces לִנְבִיאִים (for prophets).

2. *Exception to the First Rule of Shewa*. The application of the first Rule of Shewa produces a different spelling if the word begins with the syllable יְ as in יְהוּדָה (Judah). Again, the prefixing of the preposition לְ (to) to יְהוּדָה (Judah) would produce לְיְהוּדָה but two Vocal Shewas at the beginning of a word are not allowed.

In the case of a word that begins with the יְ syllable, the application of the Rule of Shewa produces לִיהוּדָה (to Judah) with Hireq Yod. Remember that this spelling is only with a word that begins with the יְ syllable.

3. *The Second Rule of Shewa.* A second Rule of Shewa applies to syllables that have a guttural consonant followed by a reduced or Hateph vowel. For example, the prefixing of the preposition בְּ (in) to חֲלוֹם (dream) would produce בְּחֲלוֹם but this combination of syllables is not allowed. A Vocal Shewa cannot precede a guttural with a reduced vowel. Application of this second Rule of Shewa produces בַּחֲלוֹם (in a dream). With this spelling, the preposition takes the corresponding short vowel (Pathach) of the reduced vowel (Hateph Pathach).

4. *Exception to the Second Rule of Shewa.* There is one very important exception to the second Rule of Shewa. When a preposition like לְ is prefixed to אֱלֹהִים (God), the result is לֵאלֹהִים (to God). The appearance of the Tsere under the לֹ is occasioned by the quiescing (silencing) of the א. This exception occurs only with אֱלֹהִים. After a few encounters, this spelling will be recognized immediately.

Chapter 5

Definite Article and Conjunction Waw

5.1 **Introduction.** In English, a noun will be either *definite* or *indefinite*. Nouns are definite when they appear with the definite article "the" as in *the* student, *the* book and *the* teacher. Nouns are indefinite when they appear either without the definite article or with the indefinite article "a" or "an" as in *a* student, *a* book or *an* instructor. In Hebrew, there is no indefinite article (see 5.12 below). Therefore, מֶ֫לֶךְ may be translated as either "king" or "a king." For this reason, words occurring without the definite article should be considered indefinite unless otherwise indicated. There are three types of definite nouns in Hebrew. The most common definite nouns are those occurring with the Hebrew definite article. Proper nouns (Egypt) and nouns with possessive pronouns (your book) are also considered to be definite. In this chapter, we will concentrate on nouns with the Hebrew definite article. In general, the Hebrew definite article functions much like the English definite article.

5.2 **Form of the Hebrew Definite Article.** The Hebrew word for "king" or "a king" is מֶ֫לֶךְ. As it appears, the noun is indefinite. In Hebrew, a noun is made definite by *prefixing the definite article which consists of* הַ *plus a Daghesh Forte in the first consonant of the noun.*

Definite Article

הַמֶּ֫לֶךְ

Thus מֶ֫לֶךְ (a king) becomes הַמֶּ֫לֶךְ (*the* king). You can see how easy it is to identify the definite article in the following examples.

Indefinite Noun		Definite Noun	
נָבִיא	a prophet	הַנָּבִיא	the prophet
זָקֵן	an elder	הַזָּקֵן	the elder

סוּס	a horse	הַסּוּס	the horse
שֹׁפֵט	a judge	הַשֹּׁפֵט	the judge

5.3 **The Article and Initial *Begadkephat* Consonants.** You know that words with an initial *begadkephat* consonant will appear with a Daghesh Lene as in בַּיִת (house), דֶּרֶךְ (road, way) and גִּבּוֹר (warrior). When adding the definite article to these words, the Daghesh Lene is replaced by a Daghesh Forte. The following examples show that nothing really changes in the spelling, though the original Daghesh Lene is now a Daghesh Forte with the addition of the article.

Indefinite Noun		*Definite Noun*	
בַּיִת	a house	הַבַּיִת	the house
דֶּרֶךְ	a road	הַדֶּרֶךְ	the road
גִּבּוֹר	a warrior	הַגִּבּוֹר	the warrior

5.4 **The Article and Initial Guttural Consonants.** An important part of the definite article is the Daghesh Forte that is inserted into the first consonant of the noun. But you know that the gutturals and ר cannot take a Daghesh Forte. They reject it. What happens, then, when the initial consonant of a noun is a guttural or ר?

1. *Compensatory Lengthening.* With the initial gutturals א, ר and ע, the rejection of the Daghesh Forte results in what is called *compensatory lengthening*. This means that the Pathach (short *a*) vowel of the definite article הַ lengthens to a Qamets (changeable long *ā*) as in הָ.[1] In this way, the definite article *compensates* for the loss of the Daghesh Forte by the *lengthening* of its vowel (short a to long *ā*), thus *compensatory lengthening*. The definite article is still easy to identify as the following examples illustrate.

Indefinite Noun		*Definite Noun*	
אִישׁ	a man	הָאִישׁ	the man
אִשָּׁה	a woman	הָאִשָּׁה	the woman

---

[1] There are three patterns of compensatory lengthening with which you need to become familiar. Each pattern involves the lengthening of a short vowel to a changeable long vowel: Pathach lengthens to Qamets (בַּ ≻ בָּ), Hireq lengthens to Tsere (בִּ ≻ בֵּ) and Qibbuts lengthens to Holem (בֻּ ≻ בֹּ).

רֹאשׁ a head   הָרֹאשׁ the head

עִיר a city   הָעִיר the city

2. *Virtual Doubling.* When ה or ח is the first consonant of a noun, the rejection of the Daghesh Forte results in what is called virtual doubling. Virtual doubling is the *rejection of the Daghesh Forte without the lengthening of the Pathach* (short *a*) *vowel*. For example, the Hebrew word for "palace" is הֵיכָל. With the addition of the definite article, it is rendered הַהֵיכָל, "*the* palace." Another example is חוֹמָה (wall) and it is rendered as הַחוֹמָה (*the* wall). Notice how the ה and the ח reject the Daghesh Forte but the Pathach vowel *does not lengthen* in either example. This is virtual doubling.

3. *Irregular Seghol Vowel.* Before nouns that begin with an unaccented עָ, הָ or חָ (חָ may also be accented), the definite article appears with the Seghol (short *e*) vowel and without the Daghesh Forte (הֶ). Observe, for example, how the Hebrew word חָכָם (wise man) becomes הֶחָכָם (*the* wise man).

5.5 **The Article with Initial יְ and מְ.** With few exceptions, words that begin with יְ or מְ give up the Daghesh Forte that is associated with the definite article. For example, יְלָדִים (boys) becomes הַיְלָדִים (the boys) or מְרַגְּלִים (spies) becomes הַמְרַגְּלִים (the spies). In both instances, the Daghesh Forte is given up but the Pathach vowel (short *a*) is not lengthened. This is similar to the issue of virtual doubling with gutturals mentioned above. Notice that with the loss of the Daghesh Forte, each word loses a syllable.

5.6 **Vowel Changes.** You now know that a Hebrew noun is rendered definite by the prefixing of the definite article (ה plus a Daghesh Forte in the first consonant of the noun). You also know that there are some minor variations to this standard construction, especially with initial guttural consonants. There are a few nouns that deviate from these rules. But none of these changes should concern you too much. It is good to be aware of exceptions and variations to the standard pattern. But it is more important for you to *concentrate on what does not change*. The presence of the prefixed ה never changes. That is, no matter what the vowels or the Daghesh Forte do or do not do, the ה is unaltered.

Secondly, the stem of the noun will rarely change with the addition of the definite article. Therefore, if you know your vocabulary and understand that a prefixed ה indicates the definite article, you will rarely have any trouble identifying nouns with the definite article in Hebrew.

In a small group of words, the prefixing of the definite article occasions slight changes in the vocalization of the noun. In the following examples, note that *the vowel under the first consonant of each noun has changed to Qamets* with the prefixing of the definite article.

אֶ֫רֶץ	earth	⟩	הָאָ֫רֶץ	the earth
עַם	people	⟩	הָעָם	the people
גַּן	garden	⟩	הַגַּן	the garden
הַר	mountain	⟩	הָהָר	the mountain
אֲרוֹן	ark	⟩	הָאָרוֹן	the ark

5.7 **The Conjunction וְ.** In the vocabulary for this lesson, you are given the basic form of the conjunction וְ (and, but, also, even). This word occurs more frequently than any other word in the Hebrew Bible with over 50,000 occurrences. On average, therefore, the conjunction וְ occurs about 2.5 times per verse. When it appears, it is always prefixed to another word and so never occurs independently. In other words, "and a man" is written in Hebrew as וְאִישׁ with the conjunction וְ prefixed to אִישׁ (man). This conjunction has four basic spelling possibilities, depending on the vocalization of the word to which it is prefixed.

1. Before most consonants, the conjunction will appear as וְ (the way it is spelled in the lexicon). It occurs this way about fifty percent of the time. Note the following examples.

וְעֶ֫בֶד	and a servant
וְאִשָּׁה	and a woman
וְהָאִשָּׁה	and the woman
וְאִישׁ	and a man
וְהָאִישׁ	and the man

2. There are two circumstances in which the conjunction will appear as וּ (Shureq).

   a. It is spelled with Shureq (וּ) before the consonants בּ, מ or פּ (the so-called labial consonants). This is sometimes referred to as the "bump" rule because the word "bump" contains the transliterated values of בּ, מ and פּ. Note the following examples and observe that initial *begadkephat* consonants (for example, בַּיִת) will lose the Daghesh Lene when the conjunction is prefixed (וּבַיִת).

וְ + בֵּין	➤	וּבֵין	and between
וְ + בַּיִת	➤	וּבַיִת	and a house
וְ + מֶלֶךְ	➤	וּמֶלֶךְ	and a king
וְ + פַּרְעֹה	➤	וּפַרְעֹה	and Pharaoh

   b. The conjunction וְ is also spelled with Shureq (וּ) before most consonants having a Vocal Shewa. Note the following examples.

וְ + נְעָרִים	➤	וּנְעָרִים	and young men
וְ + זְרָעִים	➤	וּזְרָעִים	and seeds
וְ + סְפָרִים	➤	וּסְפָרִים	and books
וְ + שְׁמוּאֵל	➤	וּשְׁמוּאֵל	and Samuel

   There is an exception to this rule. If the conjunction וְ is prefixed to a word that begins with the syllable יְ then these two syllables contract to וִי as illustrated by the following example.

   | וְ + יְהוּדָה | ➤ | וִיהוּדָה | and Judah |

3. Before a reduced or Hateph vowel, the conjunction is spelled with the corresponding short vowel of the Hateph vowel. For example, the Hebrew word for "dream" is חֲלוֹם and with the conjunction it is וַחֲלוֹם (and a dream). The conjunction is spelled with *Pathach* (וַ) because it is prefixed to a word beginning with the reduced vowel *Hateph Pathach* (חֲ). Note the following additional examples.

אֲנָשִׁים + וְ   ⤙   וַאֲנָשִׁים   and men

אֱמֶת + וְ   ⤙   וֶאֱמֶת   and truth

חֳלִי + וְ   ⤙   וָחֳלִי   and sickness

There is one important exception to this rule. When אֱלֹהִים (God) occurs with the conjunction וְ it is spelled וֵאלֹהִים (and God).

4. The conjunction וְ may also be spelled with a Qamets (וָ) before monosyllabic words and certain words with an initial accent.

צֹאן + וְ   ⤙   וָצֹאן   and sheep

לֶחֶם + וְ   ⤙   וָלֶחֶם   and bread

Let us end our discussion of the conjunction וְ with a final point of encouragement. In addition to this conjunction, there are only six other words in the Hebrew Bible that begin with the consonant ו (three proper nouns, two common nouns and one adjective). These six words occur only eighteen total times in the Hebrew Bible. Therefore, when you see the consonant ו at the beginning of a Hebrew word, you should expect the conjunction over ninety-nine percent of the time. In other words, regardless of the vowel occurring under an initial ו, you know that it is the Hebrew conjunction.

5.8   Summary.

1. In general, the Hebrew definite article *functions* much like the English definite article. There is no indefinite article in Hebrew.

2. A noun is made definite by prefixing the definite article which consists of הַ plus the Daghesh Forte in the first consonant of the noun.

Definite Article

הַמֶּלֶךְ

3. The Daghesh Lene of an initial *begadkephat* consonant is replaced by a Daghesh Forte with the prefixing of the definite article.

4. Gutturals and ר reject the Daghesh Forte of the definite article.

   a. *Compensatory Lengthening.* With initial א, ר and ע, the rejection of the Daghesh Forte results in the lengthening of the Pathach (short *a*) to a Qamets (long *ā*); הַ changes to הָ.

   b. *Virtual Doubling.* With initial ה and ח, the Daghesh Forte is rejected but the Pathach vowel *does not lengthen*.

   c. *Irregular Seghol Vowel.* When nouns begin with unaccented עָ, הָ or חָ (חָ may also be accented), the definite article appears with a Seghol vowel and without the Daghesh Forte, הֶ.

5. Despite the variation of vowels beneath the ה of the definite article, *concentrate on what does not change*. The ה of the article will never change and the spelling of the noun will rarely change.

6. The Hebrew conjunction וְ (and, but, also, even) is the most frequently occurring word in the Hebrew Bible. This conjunction has four basic spelling possibilities.

   a. Before most consonants, the conjunction will appear as וְ.

   b. Before ב, מ or פ ("bump" rule) and syllables beginning with Vocal Shewa, the conjunction will appear as וּ (Shureq).

   c. Before a Hateph vowel, the conjunction is spelled with the corresponding short vowel of the Hateph vowel.

   d. Before monosyllabic words and certain words with initial accent, the conjunction is spelled with Qamets (וָ).

5.9   Vocabulary.

אֵשׁ	fire (376); feminine
הֵיכָל	palace, temple (80)
וְ	and, but, also, even (51, 524)
זָהָב	gold (392)
חֶרֶב	sword (413); feminine
חַי	(noun) life, lifetime; (adjective) living (255)
יֶלֶד	male child, boy (89)

יָם	sea, west (396)
כֶּסֶף	silver (403)
כֹּה	thus, so (577)
מָקוֹם	place (401)
מִשְׁפָּט	judgement, custom, justice (425)
מִזְבֵּחַ	altar (403)
נְאֻם	utterance, declaration (376)
עוֹלָם	forever, eternity (439)
עָנָן	clouds (87)
רוּחַ	wind, spirit (378); usually feminine
שַׁעַר	gate (375)
שָׁמַיִם	heaven(s), sky (421)
שַׂר	official, leader, prince (425)

5.10 **The Long Nose of God.** Of the many wonders to be found in the Word of God, few surpass the revelation of the character of God. For example, we know that God is the creator of all things (Gen 1:1-2:3; Isa 45:6) and the redeemer of his people (Ex 14; Isa 43:1) and that by these actions he has demonstrated his immeasurable and unparalleled power. Another way we learn about the character of God is by certain divinely inspired descriptions of God, such as "majestic in holiness" or "awesome in glory" (Ex 15:11). Yet, perhaps the most remarkable way in which we learn about the character of God is when God describes himself. For example, in Scripture God has described himself as compassionate (רַחוּם in Ex 34:6), gracious (חַנּוּן in Ex 34:6) and holy (קָדוֹשׁ in Lev 11:45; 19:2). These are some of the most well-known attributes of God's character. However, you might be surprised to discover that God has also described himself as having a "long nose."

This unique description of God's character is first found in Exodus 34:6, when God came and stood with Moses to proclaim his name. We read in the text, "And he passed in front of Moses, proclaiming, 'The Lord, the Lord, the compassionate and gracious God, slow to anger, abounding in love and faithfulness'" (NIV). What is translated as "slow to anger" in English is the Hebrew expression אֶרֶךְ אַפַּיִם, literally "long of nose." This expression may also be translated as "patient" or "longsuffering"

(KJV). In Hebrew, the idiom "long of nose" was used to describe someone who was patient or slow to anger (Prov 14:29). Conversely, a person "short of nose" (קְצַר־אַפַּיִם as in Prov 14:17) was considered to be impatient or quick-tempered, much like the modern English idioms "hothead" or "short fuse."

The theological significance of God's long nose is not to be underestimated. Because God is patient, his people do not perish. Because God's nose is long, he has not treated us as we deserve. In the New Testament we are encouraged to "bear in mind that God's patience means salvation" (2 Peter 3:15; cf. 3:9). Reflecting on these realities, the psalmist has put it this way:

> The Lord is compassionate and gracious,
> slow to anger [long of nose], abounding in love.
> He will not always accuse,
> nor will he harbor his anger forever;
> he does not treat us as our sins deserve
> or repay us according to our iniquities.
> (Ps 103:8-10, NIV).

Miles V. Van Pelt
Ph.D. candidate
The Southern Baptist Theological Seminary
Louisville, Kentucky

5.11   **Advanced Information: Special Uses of the Definite Article**. There are a few special uses of the Hebrew article that do not correspond to English usage. Below are a few of the most common special uses.

    1. *Demonstrative Adjective*. The definite article may, at times, be used like a demonstrative adjective (this, that).

        אָנֹכִי מְצַוְּךָ הַיּוֹם   I am commanding you *the* day (literally).
                           I am commanding you *this* day (today).

    2. *Vocative Use*. *Vocative* is a term used to indicate *direct address*. This means that a definite article can be used on names or titles when a speaker is referring to the person with whom he or she is talking (usually translated "O king," "O man," "O Lord," etc.).

וַיִּקְרָא לֵאמֹר הַמֶּלֶךְ   And he called saying, "*the* king" (literally).
And he called saying, "*O* king."

3. *Superlative Use.* The definite article may be used to indicate the superlative use of adjectives (good/best or high/highest).

הַטּוֹב וְהַיָּשָׁר   the good and the upright (literally)
the *best* and the *most* upright

4. *Possessive Pronoun.* The definite article may, at times, be used like a possessive pronoun (my, his, her, your, etc.).

וְלָקַח דָּוִד הַכִּנּוֹר   And David took *the* harp (literally).
And David took *his* harp.

5.12   **Advanced Information: Indefinite Article.** Hebrew has no indefinite article. Sometimes, however, the Hebrew word for "one," אֶחָד (ms) or אַחַת (fs), is used like the English indefinite article *to mark indefinite nouns.*

אִישׁ אֶחָד   *one* man (literally)
a man or *a certain* man

אִשָּׁה אַחַת   *one* woman (literally)
a woman or *a certain* woman

Chapter 6

Hebrew Prepositions

6.1   **Introduction.** The study of prepositions in Hebrew is straightforward and uncomplicated. Hebrew prepositions function like English prepositions. They are used to describe relationships between words. For example, these relationships can be spatial as in *under* the book, *on* the book, *over* the book. These relationships can also be temporal as in *before* class, *during* class, *after* class. Many other relationships also exist. The word following the preposition is called the *object* of the preposition. In Hebrew, there are three types of prepositions to be studied: independent prepositions, Maqqef prepositions and inseparable prepositions. This classification is based on a preposition's form and relationship to its object, not meaning.

6.2   **Independent Prepositions.** The majority of Hebrew prepositions *stand alone* and, for this reason, are called *independent*. This is just like the English preposition. The following examples illustrate how simple it is to work with this type of preposition.

לִפְנֵי הַמֶּ֫לֶךְ	before the king
תַּ֫חַת הָעֵץ	under the tree
אַחַר הַמַּבּוּל	after the flood
בֵּין הַמַּ֫יִם	between the water(s)

6.3   **Maqqef Prepositions.** Prepositions of this type are always joined to their objects by a raised horizontal stroke called a *Maqqef*. Among the most common prepositions of this type are עַל־ (on, upon, concerning), אֶל־ (to, toward), עַד־ (until, as far as) and מִן־ (from). In the following examples, you will see the Maqqef used to join these prepositions to their objects.

עַל־הָאֶ֫בֶן	upon the stone
אֶל־הַהֵיכָל	to the temple
עַד־הַנָּהָר	as far as the river
מִן־הָאָ֫רֶץ	from the land

50

6.4   **Inseparable Prepositions.** These prepositions are prefixed directly to their objects and never occur independently. In other words, they are *inseparable* from their objects. There are only three inseparable prepositions to be learned.[1]

בְּ   in, by, with

לְ   to, for

כְּ   like, as, according to

1. Before most consonants, the inseparable prepositions will appear with Vocal Shewa as בְּ, לְ or כְּ (the way each is spelled in the lexicon). The following examples illustrate how these prepositions are prefixed to their objects.

    בְּשָׂדֶה   in a field

    לְנַעַר   for a young man

    כְּמֶלֶךְ   like a king

2. Before a reduced or Hateph vowel, the inseparable prepositions take the corresponding short vowel of the Hateph vowel. This is the same type of rule that you have already learned for the conjunction וְ (5.7.3).[2]

    כַּאֲנָשִׁים   like men

    בֶּאֱמֶת   in truth

    לֶחֳלִי   for sickness

3. Before consonants with Vocal Shewa, the inseparable prepositions are spelled with Hireq. This is due to the fact that two contiguous (side-by-side) Vocal Shewas cannot stand at the beginning of a word (4.12.1).[3]

---

[1] Though there are only three inseparable prepositions, together they occur 38,932 times in the Hebrew Bible: בְּ occurs 15,559 times; כְּ occurs 3,053 times; and לְ occurs 20,320 times. Due to their frequency, it is important that students become familiar with these prepositions.

[2] When an inseparable preposition is prefixed to אֱלֹהִים (God), it is spelled לֵאלֹהִים (to God). This spelling follows the exception to the second Rule of Shewa (4.12).

[3] If an inseparable preposition (בְּ, for example) is prefixed to a word beginning with יְ then it will contract to בִי as in בִּיהוּדָה (in Judah). In other words, בְּ plus יְהוּדָה becomes בִּיהוּדָה. This is similar to what you learned for Rule of Shewa (4.12.2)

לִנְבִיאִים   for prophets

לִבְרִית   for a covenant

4. In nouns *with the definite article*, the prefixing of the preposition is somewhat unusual. The vowel and Daghesh Forte of the definite article are retained but the consonant of the preposition replaces the ה of the definite article. The following examples illustrate this process.

שָׂדֶה	a field	➤	הַשָּׂדֶה	the field
		➤	בַּשָּׂדֶה	in the field
אֵשׁ	a fire	➤	הָאֵשׁ	the fire
		➤	בָּאֵשׁ	in the fire
נַעַר	a boy	➤	הַנַּעַר	the boy
		➤	לַנַּעַר	to *or* for the boy
מֶלֶךְ	a king	➤	הַמֶּלֶךְ	the king
		➤	כַּמֶּלֶךְ	like the king

6.5   **The Form of the Preposition מִן.** This preposition deserves special consideration because it occurs both as a Maqqef preposition and as an inseparable preposition.

1. Frequently, the preposition מִן is simply joined to its object by the Maqqef as in מִן־הַבַּיִת (from the house) or מִן־הַמַּלְכָּה (from the queen).

2. The preposition מִן can also occur as an inseparable preposition. When this happens, the נ of the preposition assimilates into the first consonant of the noun to which it is prefixed. The assimilated נ is subsequently represented by a Daghesh Forte. For example:

מִן־מֶלֶךְ from a king ➤ מִמֶּלֶךְ from a king

The Daghesh Forte in the second מ of מִמֶּלֶךְ represents the assimilated נ of the original preposition. The Daghesh Forte that results from the assimilated נ behaves in the same way as the Daghesh Forte of the definite article construction. The following explanations show how the Daghesh Forte interacts with *begadkephat* and guttural consonants.

---

and the conjunction וְ (5.7.2).

a. When מִן is inseparably prefixed to a word beginning with a *begadkephat* consonant, the Daghesh Lene of the *begadkephat* consonant becomes a Daghesh Forte as in בַּיִת (a house) ≻ מִבַּיִת (from a house). The Daghesh Forte in the בּ of מִבַּיִת represents the assimilated נ of the preposition.

b. When מִן is inseparably prefixed to a word beginning with a guttural consonant, the guttural rejects the Daghesh Forte of the assimilating נ with the result that the Hireq (short *i*) under the מ of the preposition lengthens to Tsere (changeable long *ē*) as in מֵאִישׁ (from a man) or מֵעִיר (from a city). The lengthening of Hireq to Tsere is another example of *compensatory lengthening*.[4] When מִן is prefixed to words with the definite article, the ה of the article is retained as in מֵהָאָרֶץ (from the land).

c. When מִן is inseparably prefixed to a word beginning with ח, the Daghesh Forte is rejected but without compensatory lengthening as in מִחוּץ (from outside). This is called *virtual doubling* (see 5.4.2). In other instances, however, compensatory lengthening will occur, as in מֵחֶרֶב (from a sword).

6.6   **The Use of the Preposition מִן.** Because of the frequency with which the preposition מִן occurs (7,592 times), it is worth studying a few of its special uses.

1. *Comparative Use.* In English, adjectives are used to express the comparative and superlative ideas: *big* becomes *bigger* (comparative) or *biggest* (superlative) and *good* becomes *better* or *best*. In Hebrew, the preposition מִן is often used to indicate the comparative or "better than" idea. The following examples illustrate this usage.

---

[4] This is your second encounter with compensatory lengthening. The first occurrence appeared with the definite article: Pathach to Qamets (5.4 .1). A second pattern of compensatory lengthening now occurs with the prefixing of the מִן preposition: Hireq to Tsere.

טוֹבָה חָכְמָה מִזָּהָב

> *Literally*:   Wisdom is *good from* gold.
>
> *Comparatively*:   Wisdom is *better than* gold .

טוֹב הַסֵּפֶר הַזֶּה מִסֵּפֶר הַהוּא

> *Literally*:   This book is *good from* that book.
>
> *Comparatively*:   This book is *better than* that book.

The comparative use of מִן can also communicate the nuance of "too... for" as in the following example.

קָשָׁה הָעֲבוֹדָה מֵהָאֲנָשִׁים

> *Literally*:   The work is difficult *from* the men.
>
> *Comparatively*:   The work is *too* difficult *for* the men.

2. *Superlative Use*. In Hebrew, the preposition מִן may be used with כֹּל (all, each, every) in the formation of a superlative מִכֹּל, literally "from every." The following example illustrates this usage.

עָרוּם מִכֹּל חַיַּת הַשָּׂדֶה

> *Literally*:   *clever from every* living thing of the field
>
> *Superlatively*:   *the most clever* living thing of the field

3. *Partitive Use*. The partitive use of מִן is the way that Hebrew expresses a part or portion of something. The following examples illustrate this usage.

מִפְּרִי

> *Literally*:   *from* a fruit
>
> *Partitively*:   *some of* the fruit

מֵהָאֲנָשִׁים

> *Literally*:   *from* the men
>
> *Partitively*:   *some of* the men

6.7   The Definite Direct Object Marker. In Hebrew prose, definite direct objects are usually marked with אֶת/אֶת־. The direct object is the word that receives the action of the verb. For example, in the sentence "God created the earth," the word "earth" is the direct object of the verb "created." The direct object "earth" is also a *definite* direct object because it has the *definite* article, "the earth." In Hebrew, the definite direct object marker, also called the accusative marker, is spelled exactly the same as the preposition אֶת/אֶת־ which translates "with." In most instances, context will enable you to distinguish between these two forms. Consider the following sentence.

כָּתַב אֶת־הַדְּבָרִים בַּסֵּפֶר   He wrote the words in the book.

The masculine plural noun דְּבָרִים (words) is the direct object of the verb כָּתַב (he wrote). This direct object is definite, that is, it has the definite article (הַדְּבָרִים). As the definite direct object of the verb, it is marked with אֶת־. Note that the definite direct object marker is not translated. It is a word that has a grammatical function but no translation value. A few more examples will help to illustrate the use of the object marker.

בָּרָא אֱלֹהִים אֵת הַשָּׁמַיִם   God created the heavens.

נָתַן הַנָּבִיא אֶת־הַסֵּפֶר לַמֶּלֶךְ   The prophet gave the book to the king.

בָּנָה הַמֶּלֶךְ אֶת־הַהֵיכָל הַגָּדוֹל   The king built the great temple.

In each of the examples above, the direct objects are considered to be definite because each has the definite article. Proper nouns (שְׁמוּאֵל, Samuel) and nouns with pronominal suffixes (סוּסִי, my horse) are also considered to be definite. Therefore, direct objects that are proper nouns or nouns with pronominal suffixes will also be marked with אֶת/אֶת־. Study the following sentences and be certain that you understand why the object marker is present.

שָׁמַר הַמֶּלֶךְ אֶת־הַמִּצְוָה וְאֶת־הַתּוֹרוֹת   The king observed the commandment and the laws.

שָׁלַח הַנָּבִיא אֶת־הַמַּלְאָךְ אֶל־הָעִיר   The prophet sent the messenger to the city.

אָהַב דָּוִד אֶת־יְהוֹנָתָן   David loved Jonathan.

נָתַן הַמֶּלֶךְ אֶת־תּוֹרוֹתָיו לְעָם   The king gave his laws to the people.

If the direct object of a verb is not definite, then the definite direct object marker is not used. In the following examples, the direct objects are indefinite and, therefore, the definite direct object marker is not present.

בָּנָה הַמֶּלֶךְ הֵיכָל גָּדוֹל   The king built a great temple.

בָּנָה הַנַּעַר בַּיִת קָטֹן בָּעִיר   The young man built a small house in the city.

6.8   Summary.

1. Hebrew prepositions function like English prepositions. The word following the preposition is called the *object* of the preposition. There are three types of Hebrew prepositions: independent, Maqqef and inseparable.

2. Independent prepositions stand alone. Maqqef prepositions are joined to their objects by a raised horizontal stroke called a *Maqqef*. Inseparable prepositions are prefixed directly to their objects.

3. The inseparable prepositions בְּ (in, by, with), לְ (to, for) and כְּ (like, as, according to) are prefixed directly to their objects and never occur independently.

   a. Before most consonants, the inseparable prepositions will appear with Vocal Shewa as בְּ, לְ or כְּ.

   b. Before a reduced or Hateph vowel, the inseparable prepositions are spelled with the corresponding short vowel of the Hateph vowel.

   c. Before consonants with Vocal Shewa, the inseparable prepositions are spelled with Hireq because of the application of Rule of Shewa (4.12.1).

   d. In nouns with the definite article, the vowel and Daghesh Forte of the definite article are retained but the consonant of the preposition replaces the הַ of the definite article.

4. The preposition מִן occurs both as a Maqqef preposition and as an inseparable preposition. When occurring as an inseparable preposition, the נ assimilates into the following consonant and

appears as a Daghesh Forte. This Daghesh Forte is rejected by gutturals, resulting in either compensatory lengthening or virtual doubling.

5. The preposition מִן can be used *comparatively* (as in "better than"); *superlatively* with כֹּל (מִכֹּל, as in "the most"); and partitively (as in "some of").

6. In Hebrew prose, definite direct objects are usually marked with אֵת/־אֶת (the accusative marker). The definite direct object marker is never translated. It is a word that has a grammatical function but no translation value.

6.9 Vocabulary.

אַחַר	behind, after (718); also as אַחֲרֵי
אֵת	with (890); also as ־אֶת
אֵת	definite direct object marker, not translated (10,978); also as ־אֶת
אֶל	to, unto, toward (5,518); also as ־אֶל
בֵּין	between (409); וּבֵין with the conjunction וְ
בְּ	in, against, by, with (15,559)
בְּתוֹךְ	in the midst, middle (420)
חָכְמָה	wisdom, experience, shrewdness (153); note that the vowel under ח is Qamets Hatuf
כְּ	like, as, according to (3,053)
כֹּל	all, each, every, whole (5,415); also as ־כָּל
לְפְנֵי	before, in the presence of (1,102)
לְ	to, toward, for (20,320)
לְמַֽעַן	for the sake of, on account of, in order that (272)
מִן	from (7,592); also as ־מִן
מַֽעַל	above (140); often with מִן (מִמַּֽעַל)
מִצְוָה	command, commandment (184); מִצְוֹת (plural)
עַד	(spatial) to, unto, as far as; (temporal) until, while (1,263)

עַל	on, upon, against (5,777); also as עַל־
עַל־דְּבַר	because of, on account of (46)
עִם	with (1,048)
פֶּה	mouth (498)
שָׂדֶה	field (329)
תַּחַת	beneath, under, instead of (510)

6.10   **Who Is Like You?** Of the so-called Minor Prophets, Micah is one of the better known to modern readers. He was a contemporary of Isaiah in the latter half of the eighth century B.C. and he prophesied to both Judah and Israel. He delivers a direct and powerful message of judgement upon each nation and its political and religious leadership. The language of judgement is graphic and startling (3:1-12), mediated with conviction and moral outrage (3:8). God's judgement is just (1:3-5; 2:1-2; 3:9-12). The sins of the people demand it. Micah is a purveyor of judgement to be sure, but amidst the prediction of certain doom, the prophet mediates the divine promise of restoration and the coming of God's kingdom through the appearance of a Saviour (4:1-4; 5:2). With reference to this unique blend of divine justice (we get what we deserve) and divine mercy (we don't get what we deserve), the prophet declares מִי־אֵל כָּמוֹךָ toward the end of the book (7:18). A simple grammatical construction, the question is composed of the interrogative pronoun מִי, the divine title אֵל and the preposition כְּ with a 2ms pronominal suffix (Who is a God like you?). Despite the use of the interrogative pronoun, the question neither demands nor expects a response. It is rhetorical. Micah expects no raised hand in the gallery of his readership. Though deities abound in the pantheons of ancient Israel's neighbors, no candidates will be identified as God's equal because the God of Israel and the attributes of his character are unique, especially his mercy: justice tempered with mercy, a portrait consistent with the divine self-revelation in Ex 34:5-7.

The consummate expression of divine mercy with which the book of Micah ends (7:18-20) finds its expression at the beginning of the composition (1:1) with the identification of the prophet's name. In Hebrew, the name Micah is spelled מִיכָה (Micah 1:1) or מִיכָיְהוּ (Judg 17:1, 4). The name is composed of the interrogative pronoun מִי, the preposition כְּ and a shortened form of the divine name (Who is like Yahweh?). In Hebrew, the link between the prophet's name (1:1) and his message of divine mercy in 7:18 (מִי־אֵל כָּמוֹךָ) is unmistakable. The question without an answer, which stands as a declaration and affirmation of the unique and merciful character of God, echoes throughout the Old Testament.

> Who is like you, O Lord, among the gods?
> Who is like you, majestic in holiness,
> terrible in glorious deeds, doing wonders?
> (Ex 15:11)

> All my bones say, "O Lord, who is like you?"
> (Ps 35:10)

Gary D. Pratico
Professor of Old Testament
Gordon-Conwell Theological Seminary
South Hamilton, Massachusetts

6.11 **Advanced Information: Compound Prepositions.** Some Hebrew prepositions are formed by combining two different prepositions (or a preposition and a noun) in order to make a new preposition.

1. Several high frequency prepositions are formed from the noun פָּנֶה (face) which is attested only in the plural (פָּנִים). The following are among the most important forms.

   לִפְנֵי before, in the presence of (פָּנִים + לְ)

   מִפְּנֵי away from, out from, from the presence of, from before, on account of, because of (פָּנִים + מִן)

   מִלִּפְנֵי away from, from before, from the presence of, on account of (פָּנִים + לְ + מִן)

   עַל־פְּנֵי in the face of, in the sight of, in front of, before, up against, opposite to (פָּנִים + עַל־)

2. The following are some common prepositions that are created by the compounding of two different prepositions.

מֵעַל	from upon	➤	מִן is prefixed to עַל
מִתַּחַת	from under	➤	מִן is prefixed to תַּחַת
מֵאֵת	from with	➤	מִן is prefixed to אֵת

3. The following prepositions are created by the compounding of a noun with a preposition.

עַל־דְּבַר	on account of	➤	עַל is prefixed to דְּבָר
בְּתוֹךְ	in the midst of	➤	בְּ is prefixed to תָּוֶךְ
מִתּוֹךְ	from the midst of	➤	מִן is prefixed to תָּוֶךְ

Chapter 7

Hebrew Adjectives

7.1 **Introduction.** Hebrew adjectives function just like English adjectives. They are used to modify, describe, characterize or classify nouns. In other words, adjectives modify nouns with a certain amount of increased specificity. For example, the noun "king" can be modified by any number of different adjectives such as "*righteous* king" or "*wicked* king." Whatever you want to say about a king, you can say it with adjectives.

7.2 **The Inflection of Adjectives.** Hebrew adjectives inflect (change their form) in order to indicate gender and number. They are inflected in four forms: masculine singular and masculine plural, feminine singular and feminine plural. The good news is that the inflectional endings for adjectives are the same endings that you have already learned for nouns. Observe how the Hebrew adjective טוֹב (good) is inflected.

	Inflected Adjective		*Inflectional Endings*	
	Masculine	*Feminine*	*Masculine*	*Feminine*
Singular	טוֹב	טוֹבָה		הָ
Plural	טוֹבִים	טוֹבוֹת	יִם	וֹת

7.3 **Notes on the Inflection of Adjectives.** There are a few additional things that you should know about Hebrew adjectives.

1. *Hebrew adjectives agree in gender and number with the nouns they modify.* This means that an adjective modifying a feminine noun will take a feminine ending. Likewise, an adjective modifying a masculine noun will take a masculine ending. For example, סוּס טוֹב is translated as "good horse" or "a good horse." The noun סוּס is masculine and so the adjective טוֹב must also be masculine *in form*. Likewise, מַלְכָּה טוֹבָה is translated as "good queen" or "a good queen." The noun מַלְכָּה is feminine and so the adjective טוֹבָה must also be feminine *in form* because adjectives

61

modifying feminine nouns take feminine endings. *The gender of an adjective does not change the meaning of an adjective.*

2. *Adjectives that are plural in form are singular in translation value.* In other words, they do not translate with any kind of plural meaning. For example, מְלָכוֹת טוֹבוֹת is translated "*good* queens." The reason the adjective טוֹבוֹת is plural *in form* is due to the fact that the noun it is modifying is plural. In Hebrew, the number of an adjective does not change the meaning of an adjective, unless the adjective is used substantively (7.4.3).

3. Unlike טוֹב, *most adjectives undergo vowel changes when the inflectional endings are added.* These patterns of change are similar to those that occur in nouns (see 7.10 for various patterns of adjectival inflection).

7.4   The Use of Adjectives. We now turn our attention to adjectival usage. In other words, how do adjectives modify or relate to nouns? Adjectival usage falls into three categories: attributive, predicative and substantive.

1. *Attributive Use.* When an adjective directly modifies a noun, it is being used attributively. In the examples "*good* student" and "*big* book," the adjectives directly modify the nouns. In Hebrew, attributive adjectives follow, or come after, the noun they are modifying. The modifying adjective must also agree with the noun in gender, number and definiteness. The term "definiteness" refers to the presence (definite) or absence (indefinite) of the definite article. The following examples illustrate the attributive use of the adjective.

אִישׁ טוֹב	good man *or* a good man
הָאִישׁ הַטּוֹב	the good man
אִשָּׁה טוֹבָה	good woman *or* a good woman
הָאִשָּׁה הַטּוֹבָה	the good woman
אֲנָשִׁים טוֹבִים	good men
הָאֲנָשִׁים הַטּוֹבִים	the good men

נָשִׁים טוֹבוֹת[1]   good women

הַנָּשִׁים הַטּוֹבוֹת   the good women

In each of the above examples, be certain that you understand the agreement between noun and adjective in the categories of gender, number and definiteness (or indefiniteness).

2. *Predicative Use.* This use of the adjective does not directly modify a noun but rather asserts something about it. In the examples "the student is *good*" or "the book is *big*," the adjectives assert something about the nouns so as to create a predication. In English, a form of the verb "to be" is used to indicate the predicative relationship. In Hebrew, the predicative relationship is indicated when an adjective matches the noun in gender and number *but not definiteness*. The predicate adjective never takes the definite article. With regard to word order, the adjective may either precede or follow the noun. The following examples illustrate the predicative use of the adjective.

הָאִישׁ טוֹב / טוֹב הָאִישׁ   The man is good.

הָאִשָּׁה טוֹבָה / טוֹבָה הָאִשָּׁה   The woman is good.

הָאֲנָשִׁים טוֹבִים / טוֹבִים הָאֲנָשִׁים   The men are good.

הַנָּשִׁים טוֹבוֹת / טוֹבוֹת הַנָּשִׁים   The women are good.

In the examples above that illustrate the predicate usage, there is no form of the Hebrew verb "to be." The "is" or "are" translations are supplied because of the predicative relationship between the noun and the adjective. In this usage, a predication is created with a noun and with an adjective without the definite article. The noun can also be a proper name as in יָשָׁר שְׁמוּאֵל (Samuel is upright) or יָפָה רוּת (Ruth is beautiful). Verbless clauses with predicate adjectives should be translated only with the English present tense of the verb "to be" as in צַדִּיק הַנָּבִיא (the prophet *is* righteous) or צַדִּיקִים הַנְּבִיאִים (the prophets *are* righteous). Apart from context, you should not supply the English

---

[1] The plural of אִשָּׁה is נָשִׁים. This is an example of irregular pluralization (4.7.4). Even though נָשִׁים takes the masculine plural ending, it is still feminine. The adjective will agree with natural gender and not grammatical gender.

past tense of the verb "to be." A verbless clause can be translated with the past tense ("was" or "were") but only if a past tense verbal form is present or if warranted by context.

Given that the predicate adjective never takes the definite article, certain constructions may pose ambiguity. For example, אִישׁ טוֹב can be translated either as "a good man" or as "a man is good." In such instances, only context will suggest whether the usage is attributive or predicative.

3. *Substantive Use*. Adjectives may be used independently as nouns. In such cases, there will be no noun for the adjective to modify. The Hebrew adjective meaning "wise" is חָכָם. Used substantively, by itself, it means "a wise one" or "a wise man." Likewise, with the definite article, הֶחָכָם is translated "the wise one" or "the wise man."

7.5 **Lexical Form**. The lexical form of a Hebrew adjective is always the *masculine singular* form. This is different than a noun for which the lexical form is masculine *or* feminine singular, depending on the gender of the noun.

7.6 **The Directional Ending**. In Hebrew, a special ending may be added to a word in order to express the idea of *motion toward someone or something*. This special ending is the *directional ending* הָ (it is always unaccented). In terms of meaning, the use of the directional ending הָ is the same as a prepositional phrase with אֶל־ (to, toward). Compare the following examples.

אֶל־הָאָרֶץ	to (toward) the land
אַרְצָה	to (toward) the land

In the second example above, the noun אֶרֶץ (land) appears with the directional ending and is translated just like the first example with the preposition אֶל־ (to, toward). This directional ending occurs 1,091 times in the Hebrew Bible. In the examples below, the directional ending has been added to words that occur frequently with this ending. You will also note in the following examples that vowel changes are clearly observable in most words. It is better, however, to master recognition through frequency of encounter rather than attempting to memorize all the spelling changes.

בַּיִת	house	⟩	הַבַּיְתָה	to (toward) the house
עִיר	city	⟩	הָעִירָה	to (toward) the city
שָׁמַיִם	heaven	⟩	הַשָּׁמַיְמָה	to heaven, heavenward
מִצְרַיִם	Egypt	⟩	מִצְרַיְמָה	to (toward) Egypt
הַר	mountain	⟩	הָהָרָה	to (toward) the mountain
שָׁם	there	⟩	שָׁמָּה	to there, to that place
יָם	sea, west	⟩	יָמָּה	toward the sea, toward the west, westward

Now that you have studied the Hebrew directional ending (הָ), it might be helpful to review the other הָ endings that you have encountered.

1. Feminine singular *nouns* may end in הָ as in תּוֹרָה (law). The ending is accented.

2. Feminine singular *adjectives* may end in הָ as in גְּדוֹלָה (great). The ending is accented.

3. In later chapters, you will learn that prepositions, nouns and the definite direct object marker may take a 3fs pronominal suffix that consists of הָ as in לָהּ (to her) or סוּסָהּ (her horse). Note, however, that the הּ of the 3fs pronominal suffix has a dot within it that is called *Mappiq*.

7.7 Summary.

1. Hebrew adjectives inflect in order to indicate gender and number. They are inflected in four forms: masculine singular and masculine plural, feminine singular and feminine plural. The inflectional endings for adjectives are the same endings that you have already learned for nouns.

2. Hebrew adjectives agree in gender and number with the nouns they modify. The gender of an adjective does not change the meaning of an adjective.

3. Adjectives that are plural in form are singular in translation value. The number of an adjective does not change the translation value of an adjective.

4. Adjectival usage falls into three categories: attributive, predicative and substantive.

a. *Attributive* adjectives follow the noun they modify and agree in gender, number and definiteness (or indefiniteness).

b. *Predicative* adjectives either precede or follow the noun they modify and agree in gender and number only. Predicative adjectives never take the definite article.

c. *Substantive* adjectives are used independently as nouns. In such cases, there will be no noun for the adjective to modify.

5. In Hebrew, the directional ending הָ may be added to the end of a word in order to express the idea of motion toward someone or something. The directional ending is always unaccented and is translated "to" or "toward."

7.8   Vocabulary.

אֶחָד	one (976)
גָּדוֹל	great (527)
דַּל	poor (48)
זָקֵן	(adjective) old; (noun) old man, elder (180)
חָכָם	wise (138)
טוֹב	good (535)
יָפֶה	beautiful (43)
יָשָׁר	straight, right, upright, just (119)
כֵּן	thus, so (741)
מְאֹד	very, exceedingly (300)
מְעַט	a few, little (101)
עַתָּה	now (435)
צַדִּיק	righteous, just (206)
קֹדֶשׁ	(noun) holy, holy thing (470)
קָדוֹשׁ	(adjective) holy (117)
קָטֹן	small, insignificant (86)
קָרוֹב	near, imminent (75)
קָשֶׁה	difficult (36)
רָחוֹק	(adjective) far, distant; (noun) distance (84)

רַב	much, many (439)
עַר	evil, wicked (331)
רָשָׁע	wicked, guilty (264)
שִׁיר	song (78)

7.9 **Was David Just a Boy When He Fought Goliath?** To make David's defeat of Goliath in 1 Samuel 17 seem more relevant to Sunday School classes, it is sometimes stressed that David was just a "boy" (perhaps ten or eleven years old?) at the time he killed the giant. In support, it is emphasized that he was the youngest of the eight sons of Jesse. Moreover, many English translations of the Bible report that Saul objected to David's plan to fight, saying that "you are only a boy" (1 Sam 17:33), using the word נַעַר, and that Goliath despised David because "he was only a boy" (1 Sam 17:42), using the same word (נַעַר).

While the term נַעַר stresses David's inexperience, it does not require or suggest that he was a pre-teen. Had this been the case, it would be hard to explain the relevance of Saul's promise to the victor of his daughter's hand in marriage in 1 Sam 17:25; 18:17-19. Moreover, 1 Sam 17:38-39 explains that David's difficulty with Saul's helmet and armor was not that they did not fit him but that "he was not used to them."

The term נַעַר (young man) frequently appears as a contrastive term for זָקֵן (old man), as in Gen 19:4 and Ex 10:9. It can even refer to an infant (Ex 2:6; 1 Sam 1:22). It is also, however, regularly used to refer to young men, whether married or not, perhaps with the restriction that these individuals be childless or at least have some kind of dependent status. For example, the soon-to-be married Shechem is called a נַעַר (young man) in Gen 34:19; the sexually immoral and perhaps married, but as yet childless sons of Eli are so termed in 1 Sam 2:17; and the married, but as yet childless Absalom is so termed in 2 Sam 14:21; 18:5, 12, 29, 32.

Gordon P. Hugenberger
Senior Pastor, Park Street Church
Boston, Massachusetts

7.10   **Advanced Information: Basic Patterns of Adjectival Inflection.** For
the most part, those changes that occur with adjectives are the same as
those that occur with nouns (4.8). Below are some of the most common
patterns of adjectival inflection. These patterns demonstrate how an
adjective's vowels will change when inflected for gender and number.

1. *Adjectival Inflection with No Change.* Certain adjectives, like the
    monosyllabic adjective טוֹב, do not change with the addition of
    inflectional endings.

	Masculine	Feminine
Singular	טוֹב	טוֹבָה
Plural	טוֹבִים	טוֹבוֹת

2. *Adjectival Inflection with Propretonic Reduction.* Review 4.8.2 for
    discussion of propretonic reduction. In adjectives, with the
    addition of inflectional endings, a changeable long vowel (Qamets
    or Tsere) in an open, propretonic syllable will reduce to Vocal
    Shewa. This type of change occurs when the open, pretonic
    syllable of the masculine singular adjective becomes propretonic
    with the addition of inflectional endings. Study the following
    examples with propretonic reduction.

    a. Adjectives with the vowel pattern of גָּדוֹל (great)

	Masculine	Feminine
Singular	גָּדוֹל	גְּדוֹלָה
Plural	גְּדוֹלִים	גְּדוֹלוֹת

    b. Adjectives with the vowel pattern of זָקֵן (old)

	Masculine	Feminine
Singular	זָקֵן	זְקֵנָה
Plural	זְקֵנִים	זְקֵנוֹת

    c. Adjectives with the vowel pattern of יָשָׁר (upright, right)

	Masculine	Feminine
Singular	יָשָׁר	יְשָׁרה
Plural	יְשָׁרִים	יְשָׁרוֹת

Adjectives with an initial guttural consonant cannot take a Vocal Shewa but prefer Hateph Pathach.

	Masculine	*Feminine*
Singular	חָכָם	חֲכָמָה
Plural	חֲכָמִים	חֲכָמוֹת

3. *Inflection of Adjectives Ending in* הֶ ָ. Adjectives like קָשֶׁה (difficult) can be difficult to recognize because the הֶ ָ ending is dropped when the inflectional endings are added. It must be recognized, for example, that קָשִׁים derives from קָשֶׁה before a form like this can be located in the lexicon.

	Masculine	*Feminine*
Singular	קָשֶׁה	קָשָׁה
Plural	קָשִׁים	קָשׁוֹת

4. *Inflection of Geminate Adjectives*. Like Geminate nouns (4.8.4), Geminate adjectives such as רַב (great, many) will take a Daghesh Forte in the second consonant with the addition of inflectional endings.

	Masculine	*Feminine*
Singular	רַב	רַבָּה
Plural	רַבִּים	רַבּוֹת

Note that Geminate adjectives like רַע (evil), with a guttural for the second consonant, cannot take the Daghesh Forte. Because the guttural rejects the Daghesh Forte, the Pathach under the ר undergoes compensatory lengthening.

	Masculine	*Feminine*
Singular	רַע	רָעָה
Plural	רָעִים	רָעוֹת

Chapter 8

Hebrew Pronouns

8.1 **Introduction**. A pronoun is a word that replaces a noun. The noun that a pronoun refers back to is called the *antecedent*. Stated differently, the antecedent of a pronoun is the word or words for which the pronoun stands. In the example, "Moses was one hundred and twenty years old when he died," the word "he" is a pronoun that refers back to "Moses," the antecedent. In Hebrew, there are personal, demonstrative, relative and interrogative pronouns. Hebrew pronouns function much like their English counterparts.

8.2 **Independent Personal Pronouns**. In Hebrew, the independent personal pronoun is labelled "independent" because it stands alone and is not prefixed or suffixed to another word. Personal pronouns can be first, second or third person and either singular or plural. First person pronouns refer to the person speaking (I, we). Second person pronouns refer to the person being spoken to (you). Third person pronouns refer to the person or thing spoken of (he, she, it, they). The second and third person pronouns have both masculine and feminine forms. First person pronouns, however, are *common*, meaning that they may refer to either masculine or feminine nouns (they are not inflected for gender). In Hebrew, independent personal pronouns are *subjective*, meaning they are used as the subject of a verb, never as the object of the verb. Personal pronouns may also appear as the subject of a verbless clause. For this reason, they are sometimes called *subject pronouns*. The Hebrew independent personal pronouns are listed below. Note that some pronouns have more than one form or spelling.

8.3 Independent Personal Pronoun Paradigm.

	Singular		*Plural*	
1 Common	אֲנִי, אָנֹכִי	I	אֲנַ֫חְנוּ[1]	we
2 Masculine	אַתָּה	you	אַתֶּם	you
2 Feminine	אַתְּ	you	אַתֵּ֫נָה[2]	you
3 Masculine	הוּא	he/it	הֵם, הֵ֫מָּה	they
3 Feminine	הִיא, הוּא[3]	she/it	הֵן, הֵ֫נָּה	they

8.4 The Use of the Independent Personal Pronoun. The independent personal pronouns and their translations should be memorized as vocabulary. Hebrew personal pronouns often occur in conjunction with verbs. They may also be used, however, in a predicative relationship with nouns or adjectives in verbless clauses. The following examples illustrate how the independent personal pronouns are used with other nouns or adjectives in a predicative relationship.

אֲנִי יְהוָה	I am Yahweh (the Lord).
הוּא נָבִיא צַדִּיק	He is a righteous prophet.
אַתָּה מֶ֫לֶךְ טוֹב	You (2ms) are a good king.
אַחִים אֲנַ֫חְנוּ	We are brothers
הִיא אִשָּׁה חֲכָמָה	She is a wise woman.
אַתֶּם בָּעִיר הַגְּדוֹלָה	You (2mp) are in the great city.

In terms of normal word order in a verbless clause, the independent personal pronoun may precede or follow the noun or adjective. As with the predicative use of the adjective (7.4.2), a form of the verb "to be" in the present tense must be supplied.

8.5 Demonstrative Pronouns and Adjectives. The English demonstratives are "this," "these," "that" and "those." They may be used either as adjectives (*this* man, *those* women) or as pronouns (*this* is the man,

---

[1] The alternate forms אֲנוּ and נַ֫חְנוּ occur only seven total times.

[2] The alternate form אַתֵּן occurs only one time.

[3] The alternate 3fs form הִוא is found only in the first five books of the Old Testament.

those are the women). Demonstratives increase the level of a word's specificity beyond that of the definite article. The level of specific reference increases from "*a* man," to "*the* man," to "*this* man." Hebrew demonstratives function like English demonstratives.

8.6   Demonstrative Paradigm.

	Singular		*Plural*	
Masculine	זֶה	this	אֵלֶּה	these
Feminine	זֹאת	this	אֵלֶּה	these
Masculine	הוּא	that	הֵם, הֵמָּה	those
Feminine	הִיא	that	הֵן, הֵנָּה	those

1. The masculine and feminine singular forms, הוּא and הִיא, are identical to the third person masculine and feminine independent personal pronouns. In most instances where ambiguity exists, the larger context of the sentence will enable you to make the appropriate choice. Note the ambiguity in the following examples.

    הוּא הָאִישׁ   He is the man.   (personal pronoun)
                    That is the man.   (demonstrative pronoun)

    הִיא הָאִשָּׁה   She is the woman.   (personal pronoun)
                    That is the woman.   (demonstrative pronoun)

2. The demonstrative אֵלֶּה (these) is both masculine and feminine plural. Remember that the designation for this phenomenon is "common," meaning *not inflected for gender*. In other words, this common form can modify either masculine or feminine nouns.

3. There are a few variant or alternative forms for some of the demonstratives. These forms should not be memorized because of their infrequency.

    זֶה   ➤   הַלָּזֶה and הַלָּז
    זֹאת   ➤   הַלֵּזוּ, זֹו and זוֹ
    אֵלֶּה   ➤   אֵל

8.7   The Use of the Hebrew Demonstratives. Hebrew demonstratives may be used either as adjectives (*this* man, *those* women) or as pronouns (*this* is the man, *those* are the women).

1. *Demonstrative Adjectives.* When a Hebrew demonstrative is functioning as an adjective, it will *follow* the noun it modifies and agree in gender, number *and definiteness*. This is just like the attributive use of adjectives as explained in 7.4.1 The following examples illustrate the use of demonstrative adjectives.

הָאִישׁ הַזֶּה	this man
הָאִשָּׁה הַזֹּאת	this woman
הָאִישׁ הַהוּא	that man
הָאִשָּׁה הַהִיא	that woman
הָאֲנָשִׁים הָאֵלֶּה	these men
הַנָּשִׁים הָאֵלֶּה	these women
הָאֲנָשִׁים הָהֵם	those men
הַנָּשִׁים הָהֵנָּה	those women

In each of these examples, be certain that you understand the agreement between the noun and demonstrative adjective in the categories of gender, number and definiteness. Note that the demonstrative follows the noun in every instance. You should also note that when a modifying adjective is introduced, it is placed between the noun and demonstrative adjective. It must also agree in gender, number and definiteness.

הָאִישׁ הַטּוֹב הַזֶּה	this good man
הָאִשָּׁה הַטּוֹבָה הַזֹּאת	this good woman
הָאִישׁ הַטּוֹב הַהוּא	that good man
הָאִשָּׁה הַטּוֹבָה הַהִיא	that good woman
הָאֲנָשִׁים הַטּוֹבִים הָאֵלֶּה	these good men
הַנָּשִׁים הַטּוֹבוֹת הָאֵלֶּה	these good women
הָאֲנָשִׁים הַטּוֹבִים הָהֵם	those good men
הַנָּשִׁים הַטּוֹבוֹת הָהֵנָּה	those good women

2. *Demonstrative Pronouns.* When a Hebrew demonstrative is functioning as a pronoun, it will *precede* the noun and agree in

gender and number *but not definiteness*. This is just like the predicative use of adjectives (7.4.2). The following examples illustrate the use of demonstrative pronouns.

זֶה הָאִישׁ	This is the man.
זֹאת הָאִשָּׁה	This is the woman.
הוּא הָאִישׁ	That is the man.
הִיא הָאִשָּׁה	That is the woman.
אֵלֶּה הָאֲנָשִׁים	These are the men.
אֵלֶּה הַנָּשִׁים	These are the women.
הֵם הָאֲנָשִׁים	Those are the men.
הֵנָּה הַנָּשִׁים	Those are the women.

When a modifying adjective is introduced, it is placed after the noun it modifies. It will agree in gender, number and definiteness with the noun it is modifying.

זֶה הָאִישׁ הַטּוֹב	This is the good man.
אֵלֶּה הָאֲנָשִׁים הַטּוֹבִים	These are the good men.
הִיא הָאִשָּׁה הַטּוֹבָה	That is the good woman.
הֵנָּה הַנָּשִׁים הַטּוֹבוֹת	Those are the good women.

8.8   **Relative Pronoun.** The relative pronouns in English are "who," "that" and "which." A relative pronoun introduces a relative clause that modifies a noun. A relative clause is composed of the relative pronoun and the clause that it introduces. In the sentence "happy is the person *who studies Hebrew*," the clause "who studies Hebrew" is a relative clause modifying the noun "person." In Hebrew, the word אֲשֶׁר functions as the relative pronoun.[4] The form of this word never changes. In other words, it does not inflect to indicate the gender and number of its antecedent (the noun it is modifying). The relative pronoun אֲשֶׁר may appear either with or without the Maqqef. In the following

---

[4] In addition to אֲשֶׁר, the particle שֶׁ also functions as a relative pronoun, occurring 142 times in the Hebrew Bible (mostly in poetry). Like the definite article, it is prefixed to a word with a Daghesh Forte in the first consonant (where possible) as in שֶׁטּוֹב (who is good).

examples, you will notice that when אֲשֶׁר functions as a relative pronoun introducing a relative clause, it immediately follows the noun it is modifying.

הָעֵץ אֲשֶׁר בְּתוֹד־הַגָּן	the tree *that* (is) in the middle of the garden
הֶהָרִים אֲשֶׁר־תַּחַת הַשָּׁמָיִם	the mountains *that* (are) under the heavens
הַמֶּלֶךְ אֲשֶׁר בְּחַרְתֶּם	the king *whom* you chose
דָּוִד אֲשֶׁר בְּבֵית יְהוָה	David, *who* (is) in the house of the Lord

8.9 **Interrogative Pronouns**. Interrogative pronouns are used to ask a question. In Hebrew, the main interrogative pronouns are מִי (who? whom?) and מָה (what?). These pronouns do not inflect and can appear with or without the Maqqef. The vocalization of מִי does not change. The vocalization of מָה, however, may change slightly. In addition to מָה, this interrogative is also spelled מַה and מֶה. When spelled as מַה, a Daghesh Forte will usually appear in the first consonant of the following word (unless that consonant is a guttural). It is not essential to know what causes these vocalization changes. It is easier simply to be aware of the three spelling options. The following examples illustrate how these interrogative pronouns are used.

מַה־שְּׁמוֹ	What (is) his name?
מֶה־עָשִׂיתָ	What have you done?
מָה הַחֲלוֹם הַזֶּה	What (is) this dream?
מִי־אַתָּה	Who (are) you?
מִי־הָאִישׁ הַזֶּה	Who (is) this man?
מִי הָאֲנָשִׁים הָאֵלֶּה	Who (are) these men?

8.10 **The Interrogative Particle הֲ**. In addition to the interrogative pronouns above, Hebrew also has an interrogative particle.[5] In Hebrew, questions are not created with punctuation as in English (?). Rather, interrogative clauses (sentences asking a question) are created with the use of certain

---

[5] The interrogative particle הֲ occurs 513 times in the Hebrew Bible.

interrogative pronouns or with a form of the particle הַ prefixed to the first word of the sentence. Consider the following examples.

שָׁלַח הַמֶּלֶךְ אֶת־הַנָּבִיא   The king sent the prophet.

הֲשָׁלַח הַמֶּלֶךְ אֶת־הַנָּבִיא   Did the king send the prophet?

The first example is a statement; the second is a question. In the second example, the sentence begins with a verb to which the interrogative particle הַ has been prefixed. The question has been created by the prefixing of the interrogative particle. The spelling of the particle will change, depending on the spelling of the form to which it is prefixed. The rules are quite simple.

1. Prefixed to most consonants, it is הֲ as in the example above.

2. Prefixed to a guttural consonant or any consonant with Shewa, it is normally הַ.

3. Prefixed to a guttural consonant followed by Qamets, the spelling of the particle is הֶ.

There is the possibility of confusing the interrogative particle with the definite article. To avoid confusion, it will be helpful to remember the following clues.

1. The interrogative particle does not normally have an associated Daghesh Forte as does the definite article.[6]

2. With some frequency, the interrogative particle will be prefixed to a verbal form or another particle. Verbs and particles, of course, will not take the definite article.

3. The Hateph Pathach (הֲ) of the interrogative particle (as it appears with most consonants) is not the spelling of the definite article.

8.11 Summary.

1. A pronoun is a word that replaces a noun. The noun that the pronoun refers back to is called the *antecedent*.

2. A *personal pronoun* is a pronoun that replaces a noun referring to a person or thing. It can be first, second or third person and

---

[6] Infrequently, the prefixing of the interrogative particle may occasion the doubling of the following consonant but this is anomolous.

either singular or plural. First person pronouns are labelled "common," meaning that they may refer to either masculine or feminine nouns (not inflected for gender). Second and third person pronouns have both masculine and feminine forms.

	Singular		*Plural*	
1 Common	אֲנִי ,אָנֹכִי	I	אֲנַ֫חְנוּ	we
2 Masculine	אַתָּה	you	אַתֶּם	you
2 Feminine	אַתְּ	you	אַתֵּ֫נָה	you
3 Masculine	הוּא	he/it	הֵם ,הֵ֫מָּה	they
3 Feminine	הִיא ,הוּא	she/it	הֵן ,הֵ֫נָּה	they

3. The Hebrew demonstratives may be used either as adjectives (*this* man, *those* women) or as pronouns (*this* is the man, *those* are the women).

	Singular		*Plural*	
Masculine	זֶה	this	אֵ֫לֶּה	these
Feminine	זֹאת	this	אֵ֫לֶּה	these
Masculine	הוּא	that	הֵם ,הֵ֫מָּה	those
Feminine	הִיא	that	הֵן ,הֵ֫נָּה	those

a. When a Hebrew demonstrative is functioning as an adjective, it will *follow* the noun it modifies and agree in gender, number *and definiteness* (הָאִישׁ הַזֶּה, this man).

b. When a Hebrew demonstrative is functioning as a pronoun, it will *precede* the noun it modifies and agree in gender and number *but not definiteness* (זֶה הָאִישׁ, this is the man).

4. The word אֲשֶׁר (who, which, that) functions as the Hebrew relative pronoun. The form of this word never changes.

5. In Hebrew, the most common interrogative pronouns are מִי (who? whom?) and מָה (what?). These words do not inflect and can appear with or without the Maqqef.

6. Another way Hebrew asks a question is with the interrogative particle הֲ. This particle is prefixed to the first word of the interrogative clause (sentence asking a question). Usually, it is spelled הֲ. However, it also occurs as הַ (before most guttural consonants and consonants with Shewa) and הֶ (before guttural consonants with Qamets).

8.12 Vocabulary.

אֹהֶל	tent (348)
אַחֵר	another (166)
אֵיךְ	how? (61); also as אֵיכָה (17)
אֶלֶף	thousand, tribe, clan (497)
אֲשֶׁר	who, which, that (5,503)
בְּהֵמָה	cattle, animal(s) (190)
גַּם	also, indeed (762)
דָּם	blood (361)
הֲ	interrogative particle (513)
טָהוֹר	clean, pure (96)
כַּאֲשֶׁר	as, when (511)
כִּי	because, for, that (4,487)
כְּסִיל	stupid, dull (75)
לָמָּה	why? (178); also as לָמָה
מָה	what? how? (571)
מַדּוּעַ	wherefore? why? (72)
מִי	who? (424)
עָנִי	poor, afflicted (80)
שֶׁמֶן	oil (193)
שֹׁפֵט	judge (68)

8.13 I Myself Have Given. In English, the subject of the verb and the verb itself are two separate words, e.g., "I (subject) wrote (verb)" or "he (subject) spoke (verb)." In Hebrew, however, the subject and the verb are one word as in כָּתַבְתִּי (I wrote) or אָמַר (he said). Thus Hebrew uses one word where English uses two words. But when a biblical writer wanted to emphasize the subject, he would place an independent personal pronoun just before the verb, as in אֲנִי כָּתַבְתִּי (I *myself* wrote). The first word, אֲנִי, is not necessary but serves to emphasize the subject's involvement in the action of the verb.

An example of the emphatic use of the independent personal pronoun is found in Lev 17:11, one of the clearest verses in the Old Testament on the theology of sacrifice. Here the Lord says, "For the life of the flesh is in the blood, and I *myself* have given it [וַאֲנִי נְתַתִּיו] to you upon the altar to make atonement for your lives, for it is the blood, by means of the life, that makes atonement." On the one hand, God says that sacrificial blood is for the purpose of making atonement. On the other hand, however, he emphasizes that *he himself* is the one who provides the means for atonement in the first place. This is an important reversal of how we normally think about sacrifice, namely, as something *we* give to God. This verse turns that idea completely on its head. It is God who has given to us! As in the New Testament, then, God shows his grace not only by granting forgiveness, but by providing sinners with the means of forgiveness to begin with. This is the same idea expressed in Rom 5:8, "But God demonstrates his own love for us in this way: while we were still sinners, Christ died for us."

Jay Sklar
Ph.D. candidate
Cheltenham and Gloucester College of Higher Education
Cheltenham, England

8.14   Advanced Information: More Interrogative Pronouns. In addition to
מָה (what?), מִי (who?) and the interrogative particle הֲ, Hebrew possesses
a number of other interrogative words as well. Some of the more
common interrogatives are listed below for your reference.

1. לָמֶה or לָמָה (why?)

אֵלִי אֵלִי לָמָה עֲזַבְתָּנִי
My God, my God, *why* have you forsaken me?
(Ps 22:2 [English 22:1])

לָמָּה תַעֲשֶׂה כֹה לַעֲבָדֶיךָ
Why have you done thus to your servants?
(Ex 5:15)

2. אֵיךְ or אֵיכָה (how?)

וְאֵיךְ אֶעֱשֶׂה הָרָעָה הַגְּדֹלָה הַזֹּאת וְחָטָאתִי לֵאלֹהִים
How could I do this great evil
and sin against God?
(Gen 39:9)

אֵיכָה נֵדַע אֶת־הַדָּבָר
How may we know the word?
(Deut 18:21)

3. אֵי or אַיֵּה (where?)

וַיֹּאמֶר יְהוָה אֶל־קַיִן אֵי הֶבֶל אָחִיךָ
And the Lord said to Cain,
"Where is Abel your brother?"
(Gen 4:9)

אַיֵּה שָׂרָה אִשְׁתֶּךָ
Where is Sarah your wife?
(Gen 18:9)

Chapter 9

Hebrew Pronominal Suffixes

9.1   **Introduction.** In the last chapter, we studied the *subjective* (he, she, we) independent personal pronouns. In this chapter, we will study pronouns that can be either *possessive* (his, her, our) or *objective* (him, her, us). In Hebrew, these possessive and objective pronouns appear as *suffixes* on nouns, prepositions and the definite direct object marker. For this reason, they are called *pronominal suffixes*. When appearing on nouns, they are possessive as in "his book" or "her wisdom." When appearing on prepositions or the definite direct object marker, they are objective as in "to them," "for them," or "them."

9.2   **The Pronominal Suffixes.** In Hebrew, there are two sets of pronominal suffixes to be learned, Type 1 and Type 2. Both types have the same possessive and objective translation values. As suffixes, these pronouns are appended to the end of a word.

	Type 1 Suffixes	Type 2 Suffixes	Translation Possessive/Objective
1cs	יִ	יִ	my / me
2ms	ךָ	יךָ	your / you
2fs	ךְ	יִךְ	your / you
3ms	וֹ	יו	his / him
3fs	הָ	יהָ	her / her
1cp	נוּ	ינוּ	our / us
2mp	כֶם	יכֶם	your / you
2fp	כֶן	יכֶן	your / you
3mp	הֶם	יהֶם	their / them
3fp	הֶן	יהֶן	their / them

9.3   **Notes on the Pronominal Suffixes**. The chart with Type 1 and Type 2 suffixes constitutes the essence of this chapter. The remainder of the chapter simply illustrates *how* these pronominal suffixes appear on different words.

1. With few exceptions, Type 1 suffixes occur with singular nouns and Type 2 suffixes occur with plural nouns.

2. All pronominal suffixes have person, gender and number. Gender is distinguished in all second and third person forms, both singular and plural. The first person singular and plural forms are common, meaning not inflected for gender.

3. In general, there are many similarities in form between Type 1 and Type 2 suffixes, especially in the plural. All Type 2 suffixes have י as part of their spelling. It is the presence of this י that will enable you to distinguish between the two types.

4. Note the dot in the ה of the Type 1 3fs suffix (הּ). This is not a Daghesh Lene or a Daghesh Forte. The Daghesh Lene occurs only in a *begadkephat* consonant and the Daghesh Forte cannot occur in the gutturals or ר. This dot in a final ה is called *Mappiq* and frequently marks the 3fs suffix.

5. A few alternate forms exist for the Type 1 pronominal suffixes. They should not give you too much trouble but are important forms to memorize. You will encounter these alternate forms on selected nouns below.

	Type 1 Suffix		*Alternate Form*
1cs	יָ	➤	נִי
3ms	וֹ	➤	הוּ
3fs	הָ	➤	הָ
3mp	הֶם	➤	מָ
3fp	הֶן	➤	ןָ

9.4 **Masculine Nouns with Pronominal Suffixes.**[1] It has already been explained that pronominal suffixes on nouns express possession (9.1). Singular nouns use Type 1 suffixes and plural nouns use Type 2 suffixes. The following paradigms use the masculine noun סוּס (horse) to illustrate how masculine nouns receive their pronominal suffixes.

	Type 1 Suffixes		Type 2 Suffixes	
	Noun ms	*Translation*	*Noun mp*	*Translation*
1cs	סוּסִי	my horse	סוּסַי	my horses
2ms	סוּסְךָ	your horse	סוּסֶיךָ	your horses
2fs	סוּסֵךְ	your horse	סוּסַיִךְ	your horses
3ms	סוּסוֹ	his horse	סוּסָיו	his horses
3fs	סוּסָהּ	her horse	סוּסֶיהָ	her horses
1cp	סוּסֵנוּ	our horse	סוּסֵינוּ	our horses
2mp	סוּסְכֶם	your horse	סוּסֵיכֶם	your horses
2fp	סוּסְכֶן	your horse	סוּסֵיכֶן	your horses
3mp	סוּסָם	their horse	סוּסֵיהֶם	their horses
3fp	סוּסָן	their horse	סוּסֵיהֶן	their horses

9.5 **Notes on Masculine Nouns with Pronominal Suffixes.**

1. It is important to understand that singular nouns can take both singular and plural pronominal suffixes. In the same way, plural nouns can take both singular and plural pronominal suffixes. For example, the singular noun סוּס can take both a singular suffix as in סוּסִי (*my* horse) or a plural suffix as in סוּסֵנוּ (*our* horse). In these two examples, the noun is singular in both instances but the pronominal suffix is singular in the first example and plural in the second example.

2. When pronominal suffixes are added to masculine plural nouns, the masculine plural ending (יִם) is dropped. With the absence of this ending, a masculine noun is recognizable as plural only by the use of Type 2 pronominal suffixes.

---

[1] Endingless feminine singular nouns are also included in this category.

3. If a feminine noun takes a masculine plural ending (4.7), then it will also follow the masculine plural pattern above. For example, the feminine noun עִיר (city) takes the masculine plural ending, עָרִים (cities). When a pronominal suffix is added, this feminine noun continues to act like a masculine noun, עָרֶיכֶם (your cities).

4. Be careful to note the important distinction between the 1cs suffixes on singular and plural nouns: סוּסִי (my horse) and סוּסַי (my horses). With the singular noun, the suffix is Hireq Yod. With the plural noun, the suffix is Pathach Yod.

5. In the masculine singular noun paradigm above, the alternate endings appear in the forms סוּסָם (with 3mp suffix) and סוּסָן (with 3fp suffix). Once again, it is important to memorize the Type 1 alternate suffixes.

6. Nouns ending in הָ will frequently drop this ending before adding pronominal suffixes. For example, שָׂדֶה (field) becomes שָׂדְךָ (your field) or שָׂדִי (my field). In order to locate these nouns in a lexicon, you must be able to recognize that the הָ ending has been dropped.

9.6 Feminine Nouns with Pronominal Suffixes.[2] Feminine nouns also take Type 1 suffixes in the singular and Type 2 suffixes in the plural. The following chart uses the feminine noun תּוֹרָה (law) to illustrate how feminine nouns ending in הָ receive their pronominal suffixes.

---

[2] This category covers feminine singular nouns that end in הָ.

	Type 1 Suffixes		Type 2 Suffixes	
	Noun fs	*Translation*	*Noun fp*	*Translation*
1cs	תּוֹרָתִי	my law	תּוֹרוֹתַי	my laws
2ms	תּוֹרָתְךָ	your law	תּוֹרוֹתֶיךָ	your laws
2fs	תּוֹרָתֵךְ	your law	תּוֹרוֹתַיִךְ	your laws
3ms	תּוֹרָתוֹ	his law	תּוֹרוֹתָיו	his laws
3fs	תּוֹרָתָהּ	her law	תּוֹרוֹתֶיהָ	her laws
1cp	תּוֹרָתֵנוּ	our law	תּוֹרוֹתֵינוּ	our laws
2mp	תּוֹרַתְכֶם	your law	תּוֹרוֹתֵיכֶם	your laws
2fp	תּוֹרַתְכֶן	your law	תּוֹרוֹתֵיכֶן	your laws
3mp	תּוֹרָתָם	their law	תּוֹרוֹתֵיהֶם	their laws
3fp	תּוֹרָתָן	their law	תּוֹרוֹתֵיהֶן	their laws

9.7   Notes on Feminine Nouns with Pronominal Suffixes.

1. When a feminine singular noun ending in הָ (as in תּוֹרָה) receives a pronominal suffix, the ה is replaced by ת. In other words, the feminine singular noun תּוֹרָה becomes תּוֹרַת before receiving a pronominal suffix.[3] Note the presence of this ת in every form of the feminine singular paradigm above. The inability to recognize this ת as indicative of feminine singular nouns ending in הָ will prevent the identification of its lexical form.

2. Unlike masculine plural nouns, feminine plural nouns retain their plural ending (וֹת). In this case, both the feminine plural ending and the use of Type 2 pronominal suffixes identify these nouns as plural.

9.8   Vowel Changes in Nouns with Pronominal Suffixes. In the above discussion, the nouns סוּס and תּוֹרָה were selected because their vowels do not change with the addition of pronominal suffixes. The majority of nouns, however, will experience vowel changes with the addition of suffixes. Note the following examples.

---

[3] It must be understood that this is a descriptive analysis of how this feminine singular noun receives pronominal suffixes.

Lexical Form		*Suffix Form*	*Translation*
דָּבָר	➣	דְּבָרִי	my word
דָּבָר	➣	דִּבְרֵיהֶן	their (fp) words
בַּיִת	➣	בֵּיתְךָ	your (ms) house
מָוֶת	➣	מוֹתוֹ	his death

Some of these vowel changes are predictable and follow prescribed rules, but many will deviate from expected patterns. Rather than focus on the changing vowels, however, it is preferable to concentrate on what does not change. Notice that in each of the above forms, the basic consonants do not change. The pronominal suffixes will also remain unchanged. You should be able to identify most nouns with pronominal suffixes in the Hebrew Bible with three capabilities: (1) the memorization of all Type 1 and Type 2 pronominal suffixes, (2) reasonable recall of vocabulary and (3) the use of a standard lexicon.

9.9   **Monosyllabic Nouns with Pronominal Suffixes**. There are a number of high frequency monosyllabic nouns that will add י to their stem before a pronominal suffix. This occurs only when the noun is singular. As you will observe from the following paradigms, the addition of this י to singular nouns with Type 1 suffixes may cause them to be confused with plural nouns having Type 2 suffixes. With regard to consonants, both paradigms are identical. The singular noun paradigm, however, has Hireq Yod throughout (אָחִיךָ, your brother). The plural noun paradigm varies its vowel but never has Hireq Yod (אַחֶיךָ, your brothers). Recognizing this distinction now will prevent confusion later. The singular noun אָח (brother) and its plural אַחִים (brothers) are presented below with Type 1 and Type 2 suffixes.

	Type 1 Suffixes		Type 2 Suffixes	
	Noun ms	*Translation*	*Noun mp*	*Translation*
1cs	אָחִי	my brother	אַחַי	my brothers
2ms	אָחִיךָ	your brother	אַחֶיךָ	your brothers
2fs	אָחִיךְ	your brother	אַחַיִךְ	your brothers
3ms	אָחִיו[4]	his brother	אֶחָיו	his brothers
3fs	אָחִיהָ	her brother	אַחֶיהָ	her brothers
1cp	אָחִינוּ	our brother	אַחֵינוּ	our brothers
2mp	אֲחִיכֶם	your brother	אֲחֵיכֶם	your brothers
2fp	אֲחִיכֶן	your brother	אֲחֵיכֶן	your brothers
3mp	אֲחִיהֶם	their brother	אֲחֵיהֶם	their brothers
3fp	אֲחִיהֶן	their brother	אֲחֵיהֶן	their brothers

9.10 **Prepositions with Pronominal Suffixes**. In Hebrew, prepositions also take pronominal suffixes. When doing so, the pronominal suffixes are objective rather than possessive. In other words, they usually function as the object of the preposition as in "to *him*," "for *her*," "with *me*," etc. Some prepositions take Type 1 suffixes and others take Type 2. You need not concern yourself with a preposition's suffix preference. On prepositions, the translation value is the same for both types. The following charts illustrate how certain prepositions receive their pronominal suffixes. The inseparable preposition לְ (to, for) takes Type 1 suffixes. The preposition עַל (on, upon) takes Type 2 suffixes.

---

[4] This form also occurs with the alternate 3ms ending הוּ, אָחִיהוּ (his brother).

	Type 1	Translation	Type 2	Translation
1cs	לִי	to me	עָלַי	on me
2ms	לְךָ	to you	עָלֶיךָ	on you
2fs	לָךְ	to you	עָלַיִךְ	on you
3ms	לוֹ	to him	עָלָיו	on him
3fs	לָהּ	to her	עָלֶיהָ	on her
1cp	לָנוּ	to us	עָלֵינוּ	on us
2mp	לָכֶם	to you	עֲלֵיכֶם	on you
2fp	לָכֶן	to you	עֲלֵיכֶן	on you
3mp	לָהֶם	to them	עֲלֵיהֶם	on them
3fp	לָהֶן	to them	עֲלֵיהֶן	on them

9.11   Notes on Prepositions with Pronominal Suffixes.

1. The presentation of prepositions with pronominal suffixes is straightforward. Some variation in the spelling of the pronominal suffixes will be observed with certain prepositions. With relatively few exceptions, however, these variations should not occasion much difficulty in terms of recognizing the person, gender and number of the suffix. The emphasis must be on recognition and not on the ability to produce these forms in Hebrew.

2. Once again, some prepositions take Type 1 suffixes. The prepositions לְ (to, for), בְּ (in, on), עִם (with) and אֵת (with) all take Type 1 suffixes. Prepositions that take Type 2 suffixes include: עַל (on, upon), אֶל (to, for), תַּחַת (under) and אַחֲרֵי (after). With regard to translation, a preposition's suffix preference is of little importance. You should be comfortable identifying prepositions with either type of pronominal suffix.

9.12 **The Prepositions כְּ and מִן with Pronominal Suffixes** These two prepositions are spelled differently when pronominal suffixes are added.

	כְּ	*Translation*	מִן	*Translation*
1cs	כָּמוֹנִי	like me	מִמֶּנִּי	from me
2ms	כָּמוֹךָ	like you	מִמְּךָ	from you
2fs	כָּמוֹךְ	like you	מִמֵּךְ	from you
3ms	כָּמוֹהוּ	like him	מִמֶּנּוּ	from him
3fs	כָּמוֹהָ	like her	מִמֶּנָּה	from her
1cp	כָּמוֹנוּ	like us	מִמֶּנּוּ	from us
2mp	כָּכֶם	like you	מִכֶּם	from you
2fp	כָּכֶן	like you	מִכֶּן	from you
3mp	כָּהֶם	like them	מֵהֶם	from them
3fp	כָּהֵן	like them	מֵהֵן[5]	from them

9.13 **Notes on כְּ and מִן with Pronominal Suffixes.**

1. With the preposition כְּ, the forms with singular and 1cp suffixes exhibit a longer, alternate spelling of the preposition, כְּמוֹ. In the forms with second and third person plural suffixes, the spelling of the preposition exhibits the shorter form. Note the presence of the alternate endings in the forms with 1cs (כָּמוֹנִי), 3ms (כָּמוֹהוּ) and 3fs (כָּמוֹהָ) suffixes.

2. With the preposition מִן, the forms with singular and 1cp suffixes also exhibit a longer, alternate spelling of the preposition. In the forms with second and third person plural suffixes, the spelling of the preposition has the shorter form. Note the presence of alternate endings throughout the paradigm. Special attention should be given to forms with 3ms (מִמֶּנּוּ) and 1cp (מִמֶּנּוּ) suffixes since they are identical. When confronted by this form, context should enable you to make the correct choice.

---

[5] The 3fp suffix on מִן may also be written as מֵהֵנָּה (3 times). It occurs only two times in the form written above in the paradigm.

9.14 **The Definite Direct Object Marker and the Preposition אֶת/אֵת־ with Pronominal Suffixes**. The object marker אֶת/אֵת־ takes Type 1 pronominal suffixes. It is translated as a personal pronoun in the objective or accusative case. Be careful not to confuse the object marker with the preposition אֶת/אֵת־ meaning "with." While sharing the same lexical form, these two words can be distinguished by their vowels after pronominal suffixes have been added. The object marker is distinguished by a Holem vowel over the initial consonant (אֹתִי). It is Seghol in the 2mp and 2fp forms (אֶתְכֶם). The preposition is distinguished by the presence of a Hireq vowel under the initial consonant (אִתִּי). The preposition also has a Daghesh Forte in the ת. These are important distinctions to remember. Both paradigms are listed below for comparison.

	Object Marker	*Translation*	*Preposition*	*Translation*
1cs	אֹתִי	me	אִתִּי	with me
2ms	אֹתְךָ	you	אִתְּךָ	with you
2fs	אֹתָךְ	you	אִתָּךְ	with you
3ms	אֹתוֹ	him	אִתּוֹ	with him
3fs	אֹתָהּ	her	אִתָּהּ	with her
1cp	אֹתָנוּ	us	אִתָּנוּ	with us
2mp	אֶתְכֶם	you	אִתְּכֶם	with you
2fp	אֶתְכֶן	you	אִתְּכֶן	with you
3mp	אֹתָם	them	אִתָּם	with them
3fp	אֹתָן	them	אִתָּן	with them

9.15 **עַם and עִם with Pronominal Suffixes**. The preposition עִם (with)[6] and the noun עַם (people) with pronominal suffixes can be easily confused. Both are listed below for comparison. The most significant difference between the two words is the vowel that appears under the first consonant. The preposition has Hireq (עִמִּי, with me) and the noun has Pathach (עַמִּי, my people). Both words take a Daghesh Forte in the מ when pronominal suffixes are added.

---

[6] The Hebrew prepositions עַם and אֵת־ are both translated "with."

	Preposition	Translation	Noun	Translation
1cs	עִמִּי	with me	עַמִּי	my people
2ms	עִמְּךָ	with you	עַמְּךָ	your people
2fs	עִמָּךְ	with you	עַמֵּךְ	your people
3ms	עִמּוֹ	with him	עַמּוֹ	his people
3fs	עִמָּהּ	with her	עַמָּהּ	her people
1cp	עִמָּ֫נוּ	with us	עַמֵּ֫נוּ	our people
2mp	עִמָּכֶם	with you	עַמְּכֶם	your people
2fp	עִמָּכֶן	with you	עַמְּכֶן	your people
3mp	עִמָּם	with them	עַמָּם	their people
3fp	עִמָּן	with them	עַמָּן	their people

9.16 Summary.

1. Pronominal suffixes are *possessive* (my, his, her) when appearing on nouns and *objective* (me, him, her) when appearing on prepositions.

2. All pronominal suffixes have person, gender and number.

3. There are two sets of pronominal suffixes to be learned, Type 1 (for singular nouns and selected prepositions) and Type 2 (for plural nouns and selected prepositions). Both types have the same possessive and objective translation values. As a general observation, Type 2 suffixes are distinguished by the presence of י throughout their spelling.

4. The dot in the Type 1 3fs suffix is called *Mappiq* (הּ). It is neither the Daghesh Forte nor the Daghesh Lene.

5. Singular nouns can take both singular and plural pronominal suffixes. Plural nouns can also take both singular and plural pronominal suffixes.

6. Singular nouns take Type 1 pronominal suffixes; plural nouns take Type 2.

7. With masculine plural nouns, the plural ending (ים ָ) is lost when pronominal suffixes are added (סוּסַי, my horses). Feminine nouns retain their plural inflectional ending (תּוֹרוֹתַי, my laws).

8. When a feminine singular noun ending in ה ָ (תּוֹרָה) receives a pronominal suffix, the ה is replaced by ת (תּוֹרָתִי, my law).

9. When a noun ending in ה ֶ (שָׂדֶה) receives a pronominal suffix, the final ה simply drops off and is *not* replaced by ת (שָׂדִי, my field).

10. Certain singular monosyllabic nouns will add י (appears as Hireq Yod with Type 1 suffixes) to their stem before a pronominal suffix (אָח, "brother" becomes אָחִיךָ, "your brother").

11. Prepositions may take either Type 1 or Type 2 pronominal suffixes. Which type of suffix a preposition prefers is of little significance because the translation value is the same for both types.

12. With the addition of pronominal suffixes, the prepositions כְּ (like, as, according to) and מִן (from) exhibit longer, alternate spellings in all forms with singular and 1cp suffixes (כָּמוֹךָ and מִמְּךָ).

13. The object marker אֶת־ takes Type 1 pronominal suffixes. It is translated as a personal pronoun in the objective or accusative case. Be careful not to confuse the object marker with the preposition אֶת־ meaning "with."

14. The Type 1 and Type 2 pronominal suffix paradigms are presented below. The alternate Type 1 suffixes are also included and must be memorized.

	Type 1 Suffixes	Type 1 Alternate	Type 2 Suffixes	Translation
1cs	יָ	נִי	יָ	my/me
2ms	ךָ		יךָ	your/you
2fs	ךְ		יךְ	your/you
3ms	וֹ	הוּ	יו	his/him
3fs	הָ	הָ	יהָ	her/her
1cp	נוּ		ינוּ	our/us
2mp	כֶם		יכֶם	your/you
2fp	כֶן		יכֶן	your/you
3mp	הֶם	ם	יהֶם	their/them
3fp	הֶן	ן	יהֶן	their/them

9.17 Vocabulary.

אוֹ	or (321)
אַיִן	there is not, there are not (791); also as אֵין
אַף	nostril, nose, anger (277); אַפַּיִם (dual)
בֹּקֶר	morning (213)
בָּקָר	cows, herd(s), cattle (183)
בְּרָכָה	blessing (71)
הֵן	behold! (107)
הִנֵּה	behold! lo! (1,061)
חַטָּאת	sin (297); feminine
יֵשׁ	there is, there are (138)
כָּבוֹד	glory, honor (200)
כְּלִי	vessel, utensil (325)
לֶחֶם	bread, food (340)

לְבַד   (adverb) alone; (preposition) besides (161)

מִשְׁפָּחָה   family, clan (304)

מִלְחָמָה   war, battle (319)

סָבִיב   all around, surrounding, neighborhood (338)

עַם   people (1,869)

עֵץ   tree, (329); עֵצִים (plural)

9.18   **A Cherished Name of God.** God has been called by many names, titles and epithets throughout the Old Testament. He is called אֵל (God), a designation that is frequent in poetical literature (especially Psalms and Job). This name is commonly compounded with other descriptive titles (Gen 14:18-21; 16:13; 17:1; 21:33; 31:13; Ps 29:3; Isa 12:2). Each is expressive of some aspect of God's person and character, though none can encompass the fullness of his being. A common designation for God in the Hebrew Bible is אֱלֹהִים (God), a plural form with singular meaning that implies the fullness of deity.[7]

As revealed in Ex 3:13-15 and 6:2-8, there is only one personal name for God in the Old Testament. That name is יהוה ("Yahweh" or "Lord"), a form composed of four consonants and called the *tetragrammaton*. The name יהוה is also the covenant name for God in the faith of ancient Israel.[8] This name is also attested in shortened forms that are commonly used in the formation of personal names such as Elijah (אֵלִיָּהוּ or אֵלִיָּה) which translates "(My) God is Yahweh."

But one of the most cherished names of God in the Old Testament is עִמָּנוּ אֵל ("Immanuel" or "Emmanuel"). Most readers will be familiar with the name and its meaning but now you can understand its etymology in Hebrew. It is composed of two words in its three occurrences in Isaiah (7:14; 8:8, 10). The name is composed of the preposition עִם (with) to which has been affixed the 1cp pronominal suffix (us).[9] The divine name אֵל comes at the end of the form. The

---

[7] The designation אֱלֹהִים occurs 2,602 times in the Hebrew Bible.

[8] The name יהוה occurs 6,828 times in the Hebrew Bible. Given that this is God's covenant name, it is instructive that it occurs with the greatest frequency in Jeremiah (726 times), Psalms (695 times) and Deuteronomy (550 times).

[9] You learned this form (עִמָּנוּ) in section 9.15 of the grammar.

name עִמָּנוּ אֵל means "God (is) with us." The etymology is easy; the theology of the name is profound. The name is cherished because it bespeaks the depth of God's grace and mercy that he gives his presence, and even himself (Matt 1:23), to his human creation. Beyond its specific context in Isa 7:14, the name עִמָּנוּ אֵל has come to symbolize and summarize the story of biblical revelation. It is a narrative through time that documents the promise of divine presence and the relentless movement of redemption, by divine initiative, from heaven to earth. This is sometimes called the "Immanuel theme" in covenant theology. The theme begins in Eden with the intimate and unhindered fellowship between God and his human creation and it concludes with the restoration of that fellowship in the events of Rev 21:1-4.

> Behold, the dwelling of God is with men.
> He will dwell with them,
> and they shall be his people,
> and God himself will be with them.
> (Rev 21:3)

Gary D. Pratico
Professor of Old Testament
Gordon-Conwell Theological Seminary
South Hamilton, Massachusetts

9.19 **Advanced Information.** The following prepositions occur frequently with pronominal suffixes. You should not have any trouble identifying these forms but they are listed for your reference.

	בְּ	Translation	אֶל	Translation
1cs	בִּי	in me	אֵלַי	to me
2ms	בְּךָ	in you	אֵלֶ֫יךָ	to you
2fs	בָּךְ	in you	אֵלַ֫יִךְ	to you
3ms	בּוֹ	in him	אֵלָיו	to him
3fs	בָּהּ	in her	אֵלֶ֫יהָ	to her
1cp	בָּ֫נוּ	in us	אֵלֵ֫ינוּ	to us
2mp	בָּכֶם	in you	אֲלֵיכֶם	to you
2fp	בָּכֶן	in you	אֲלֵיכֶן	to you
3mp	בָּהֶם	in them	אֲלֵיהֶם	to them
3fp	בָּהֶן	in them	אֲלֵיהֶן	to them

	תַּ֫חַת	Translation	אַחֲרֵי	Translation
1cs	תַּחְתַּי	under me	אַחֲרַי	after me
2ms	תַּחְתֶּ֫יךָ	under you	אַחֲרֶ֫יךָ	after you
2fs	תַּחְתֶּ֫יִךְ	under you	אַחֲרַ֫יִךְ	after you
3ms	תַּחְתָּיו	under him	אַחֲרָיו	after him
3fs	תַּחְתֶּ֫יהָ	under her	אַחֲרֶ֫יהָ	after her
1cp	תַּחְתֵּ֫ינוּ	under us	אַחֲרֵ֫ינוּ	after us
2mp	תַּחְתֵּיכֶם	under you	אַחֲרֵיכֶם	after you
2fp	תַּחְתֵּיכֶן	under you	אַחֲרֵיכֶן	after you
3mp	תַּחְתֵּיהֶם	under them	אַחֲרֵיהֶם	after them
3fp	תַּחְתֵּיהֶן	under them	אַחֲרֵיהֶן	after them

Chapter 10

Hebrew Construct Chain

10.1 **Introduction.** There is no word for "of" in biblical Hebrew. Rather, Hebrew expresses the "of" (possessive) relationship between two nouns by what is called the *construct chain*. For those who have studied Greek, the construct chain is Hebrew's rough equivalent to the genitive case. This grammatical relationship is created by placing two or more nouns side by side. Observe the following examples.

קוֹל הָאִישׁ   the voice *of* the man

מֶלֶךְ הָאָרֶץ   the king *of* the land

עֶבֶד הַמֶּלֶךְ   the servant *of* the king

In the above examples, there is no explicit Hebrew word for "of." Rather, it is implied by the fact that each set of nouns is side by side, that is, in a construct chain. In most instances, two different translations are possible. For example, קוֹל הָאִישׁ may be translated as either "the voice of the man" or "the man's voice." Similarly, עֶבֶד הַמֶּלֶךְ may be translated as either "the servant of the king" or "the king's servant." While studying the construct chain in this chapter, the "of" translation is used throughout.

10.2 **Basic Grammar of the Hebrew Construct Chain.**

1. *Construct and Absolute States.* Utilizing the imagery of a chain, there are two links in the Hebrew construct chain, the *construct* link and the *absolute* link. The first of the two nouns in the construct chain is called the *construct noun* and is said to be in the *construct state*. The second of the two nouns is called the *absolute noun* and is said to be in the *absolute state*. The absolute form of a noun is also its lexical form.

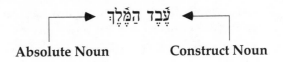

Absolute Noun   **Construct Noun**

In a construct chain, there is only one absolute noun and the absolute noun is always the last noun in the chain. However, multiple construct nouns may appear in a construct chain. You should also note that when two nouns are "in construct," no other words or particles may separate them. In other words, the "chain" cannot be broken.

2. *Definiteness and Indefiniteness.* Construct chains are either entirely definite (*the ... of the ...*) or entirely indefinite (*a ... of a ...*) but the construct noun will not take the definite article. The definiteness or indefiniteness of a construct chain is determined by the definiteness or indefiniteness of the absolute noun. Therefore, a construct chain is definite if the absolute noun is definite and indefinite if the absolute noun is indefinite. If the absolute noun is definite, so are all the construct nouns linked to it. If the absolute noun is indefinite, so are all the construct nouns linked to it. In the following examples, the construct chains are indefinite because the absolute nouns are indefinite.

קוֹל אִישׁ	*a* voice of *a* man
מֶלֶךְ אֶרֶץ	*a* king of *a* land
עֶבֶד מֶלֶךְ	*a* servant of *a* king

Using the same nouns, notice how the following construct chains are entirely definite because the absolute nouns are definite.

קוֹל הָאִישׁ	*the* voice of *the* man
מֶלֶךְ הָאָרֶץ	*the* king of *the* land
עֶבֶד הַמֶּלֶךְ	*the* servant of *the* king

Even though the construct nouns lack the definite article, they are considered to be definite because the absolute nouns are definite. Remember that a noun is considered to be definite under three circumstances: (1) if it has the definite article as in הַמַּלְכָּה (the queen); (2) if it has a pronominal suffix as in סוּסוֹ (his horse); or (3) if it is a proper noun as in שְׁמוּאֵל (Samuel). Note how the following construct chains are definite. In the first two examples, the construct chain is definite because the absolute noun is a proper noun. In the last two examples, the construct chain is definite because the absolute noun has a pronominal suffix.

אֲבִי אַבְרָהָם	*the* father of *Abraham*
עֶבֶד שְׁמוּאֵל	*the* servant of *Samuel*
בֵּית מַלְכִּי	*the* house of *my* king
סֵפֶר אָבִיהוּ	*the* book of *his* father

3. *Multiple Construct Nouns.* It has already been explained that *multiple construct nouns may appear in a given construct chain* but there is only one absolute noun for each construct chain. In instances where multiple construct nouns appear, each construct noun is translated with the key word "of" and they all depend upon the absolute noun for definiteness. In the following examples, the construct chains contain more than one noun in the construct state.

עֶבֶד אֲחִי הַמֶּלֶךְ	the servant of the brother of the king
עֶבֶד בֵּית הַמֶּלֶךְ	the servant of the house of the king
דִּבְרֵי מֶלֶךְ הָאָרֶץ	the words of the king of the land
כָּל־מִשְׁפַּחַת בֵּית־אֲבִי[1] אִמּוֹ	all of the family of the house of the father of his mother (Judg 9:1)

4. *Construct Chains Linked with Maqqef.* The nouns of a construct chain are sometimes joined by Maqqef.[2]

בֶּן־דָּוִד	the son of David
כָּל־הָעָם	all of the people
בֵּית־אָבִי	the house of my father

---

[1] The form כָּל־ (with Qamets Hatuf) is the construct of כֹּל (all, each, every).

[2] The use of the Maqqef indicates that the two joined words form a single accented unit. In other words, the first word gives up its primary accent to the second word and the entire chain is pronounced as if it were a single word. This process is known technically as "proclisis," whereby the first word becomes "proclitic" to the second word.

10.3   Construct Chains with Adjectives.

1. *Attributive Adjectives.* It has already been explained that the nouns of a construct chain cannot be separated by other words. For this reason, when an adjective modifies either the construct or absolute noun, it must follow the entire chain. Like any attributive adjective, it must agree with the noun it modifies in gender, number and definiteness. In the following examples, דְּבַר is the construct form of דָּבָר and מֶלֶךְ is both the construct and absolute (lexical) form of this noun.

דְּבַר הַמַּלְכָּה הַטּוֹב	the *good word* of the queen The adjective is masculine singular, modifying the construct noun.
דְּבַר הַמַּלְכָּה הַטּוֹבָה	the word of the *good queen* The adjective is feminine singular, modifying the absolute noun.
מֶלֶךְ הָאָרֶץ הַטּוֹב	the *good king* of the land The adjective is masculine singular, modifying the construct noun. The noun אֶרֶץ is feminine singular.
מֶלֶךְ הָאָרֶץ הַטּוֹבָה	the king of the *good land* The adjective is feminine singular, modifying the absolute noun.

In the following construct chains, the adjective may modify either the construct or the absolute noun. In ambiguous constructions like these, context must be your guide. Note that דִּבְרֵי is the construct form of דְּבָרִים and עֶבֶד is both the construct and absolute (lexical) form of this noun.

דְּבַר הַמֶּלֶךְ הַטּוֹב	the *good word* of the king *or* the word of the *good king*
דִּבְרֵי הַמְּלָכִים הַטּוֹבִים	the *good words* of the kings *or* the words of the *good kings*
עֶבֶד הַנָּבִיא הָרַע	the *evil servant* of the prophet *or* the servant of the *evil prophet*

2. *Demonstrative Adjectives.* Just like attributive adjectives, demonstrative adjectives must also follow the construct chain. The following examples illustrate this point. Note that אֵשֶׁת is the construct form of אִשָּׁה (woman, wife).

אֵשֶׁת הָאִישׁ הַזֶּה	the wife of *this man*
אֵשֶׁת הָאִישׁ הַטּוֹב הַזֶּה	the wife of *this good man*
דִּבְרֵי הַנָּבִיא הָאֵלֶּה	*these words* of the prophet
דִּבְרֵי הַנָּבִיא הַזֶּה	the words of *this prophet*
דִּבְרֵי הַנָּבִיא הַטּוֹב הַזֶּה	the words of *this good prophet*
דְּבַר הַנָּבִיא הַזֶּה	the word of *this* prophet *or* *this* word of the prophet
דִּבְרֵי הַנְּבִיאִים הָאֵלֶּה	*these words* of the prophets *or* the words of *these prophets*

3. *Adjectives in the Construct State.* You have already learned that an adjective may be used substantively, like a noun. As such, a substantival adjective can appear, just like a noun, in the construct state. The following examples illustrate this point.

יְפַת מַרְאֶה	beautiful of form (יְפַת is the fs construct of יָפֶה)
חֲכַם־לֵב	wise of heart (חֲכַם is the ms construct of חָכָם)
קְדוֹשׁ יִשְׂרָאֵל	the Holy One of Israel (קְדוֹשׁ is the ms construct of קָדוֹשׁ)

10.4 **Construct Nouns with Inseparable Prepositions.** Although a construct noun does not take a definite article, it may appear with one of the inseparable prepositions (בְּ, לְ, כְּ) as in בְּבֵית דָּוִד, meaning "*in the* house of David." In this example, the construct noun בַּיִת has the prefixed preposition בְּ. The entire chain is definite because the absolute noun is a proper noun. Note the loss of the Daghesh Lene in the second ב of בְּבֵית because this *begadkephat* consonant is now preceded by a vowel (Vocal Shewa).

10.5 **The Spelling of Nouns in the Construct State.** In many instances, the singular construct noun and its lexical form are identical in spelling. Examples include סוּס (horse or horse of), קוֹל (voice or voice of) and מֶלֶךְ (king or king of). Most construct nouns, however, are spelled differently than their lexical form. *These changes are occasioned by the fact that a construct noun surrenders its primary accent. As such, only the absolute noun has the primary accent and the entire construct chain is pronounced as though it were a single word.* The changes in spelling that occur with nouns in the construct state are similar to those changes that a noun undergoes when taking a pronominal suffix. Although a standard lexicon will provide the construct form for most nouns, a few rules will enable you to identify most of the changes on your own.

1. *Vowel Reduction.* Because the construct noun loses its primary accent, the vowels of the construct noun will often reduce or change their length. The following rules apply to endingless nouns, either masculine or feminine (excluding Segholate nouns).

    a. In the construct state, *Qamets (and sometimes Tsere) changes to Pathach in a final closed syllable.*

Absolute			Construct	
מִשְׁפָּט	judgement	➤	מִשְׁפַּט	judgement of
מִדְבָּר	wilderness	➤	מִדְבַּר	wilderness of
מַלְאָךְ	angel	➤	מַלְאַךְ	angel of

    In certain words, Tsere may also change to Pathach in a final closed syllable. For example, מִזְבֵּחַ (altar) becomes מִזְבַּח (altar of) in the construct state.

    b. In the construct state, *Qamets or Tsere change to Vocal Shewa in an open, unaccented syllable.*

Absolute			Construct	
נָבִיא	prophet	➤	נְבִיא	prophet of
שָׁלוֹם	peace	➤	שְׁלוֹם	peace of
מָקוֹם	place	➤	מְקוֹם	place of

c. Frequently, both of the rules in 1a-b will apply to the formation of a noun in the construct state. In other words, the vowels in both syllables will reduce.

Absolute			Construct	
דָּבָר	word	＞	דְּבַר	word of
לֵבָב	heart	＞	לְבַב	heart of
קָהָל	assembly	＞	קְהַל	assembly of
זָקֵן	elder	＞	זְקַן	elder of
חָצֵר	court	＞	חֲצַר	court of

d. The monosyllabic nouns כֹּל (all) and בֵּן (son) occur more frequently in the construct state than any other nouns in the Hebrew Bible.[3] In the construct state, these nouns (and others like them) will experience reduction of the changeable long vowel to its corresponding short vowel.

Absolute			Construct	
בֵּן	son	＞	בֶּן	son of
כֹּל	all	＞	כָּל	all of
יָד	hand	＞	יַד	hand of

2. The masculine plural ים ָ and dual יִם ַ endings change to ֵי in the construct state and then the above rules (1a-b) are applied to produce the construct form. This too is an important type of change to memorize.

Absolute			Construct	
אֱלֹהִים	God	＞	אֱלֹהֵי	God of
בָּנִים	sons	＞	בְּנֵי	sons of
עֵינַיִם	two eyes	＞	עֵינֵי	(two) eyes of
דְּבָרִים	words	＞	דִּבְרֵי[4]	words of

---

[3] In the construct state, בֶּן occurs 4,649 times and כָּל occurs 4,556 times. Together, these two words constitute almost 20% of all construct nouns in the Hebrew Bible.

[4] This example involves both propretonic reduction and the application of Rule of Shewa (3.15).

3. Feminine singular nouns with the הָ ending change this ending to תְ and then the above rules (1a-b) are applied to produce the construct form.[5] This is an important type of change to memorize.

Absolute			*Construct*	
תּוֹרָה	law	➤	תּוֹרַת	law of
מַלְכָּה	queen	➤	מַלְכַּת	queen of
שָׁנָה	year	➤	שְׁנַת	year of

4. Feminine plural nouns ending in וֹת retain this diagnostic ending and then the above rules (1a-b) are applied to produce the construct form.

Absolute			*Construct*	
מַמְלָכוֹת	kingdoms	➤	מַמְלְכוֹת	kingdoms of
שֵׁמוֹת	names	➤	שְׁמוֹת	names of
שָׂדוֹת	fields	➤	שְׂדוֹת	fields of
בְּרָכוֹת	blessings	➤	בִּרְכוֹת[6]	blessings of

5. Certain singular monosyllabic nouns add Hireq Yod to their stem in the construct state. You will recall that this also occurs when these same nouns take pronominal suffixes. You must be careful not to confuse this Hireq Yod with the 1cs pronominal suffix.

Absolute			*Construct*	
אָב	father	➤	אֲבִי	father of
אָח	brother	➤	אֲחִי	brother of

Compare the above construct forms with אָבִי (my father) and אָחִי (my brother).

6. A small group of nouns that occur with some frequency in the construct state are characterized by the diphthong יַ֫ (3.10). Two

---

[5] As in section 9.7, it must be understood that this is a descriptive analysis of how certain feminine singular absolute nouns become constructs.

[6] This last example involves application of the Rule of Shewa (3.15). The Qamets under the ר in בְּרָכוֹת changes to Shewa according to 1b above (בְּרְכוֹת) in the construct state. Two initial, side-by-side Vocal Shewas are not permitted and so Rule of Shewa is applied, producing בִּרְכוֹת (blessings of).

such nouns are בַּיִת (house) and עַיִן (eye, spring). In the construct state this diphthong changes to Tsere Yod (יַ֫ changes to יֵ). The construct forms of these nouns are much more common than their absolute or lexical forms.[7] For this reason, it is important to memorize both the absolute and construct forms as vocabulary. All such irregular construct forms will be listed in the vocabulary sections throughout the grammar.

Absolute			*Construct*	
בַּיִת	house	>	בֵּית	house of
עַיִן	spring	>	עֵין	spring of

7. *Segholate Nouns.* The singular absolute or lexical form of a Segholate noun is identical to its singular construct form. In other words, מֶ֫לֶךְ may be translated as either "king" in the absolute state or "king of" in the construct state. The plural construct form follows the pattern of מַלְכֵי (kings of).[8]

Absolute			*Construct*	
מֶ֫לֶךְ	king	>	מֶ֫לֶךְ	king of
עֶ֫בֶד	servant	>	עֶ֫בֶד	servant of
מְלָכִים	kings	>	מַלְכֵי	kings of
עֲבָדִים	servants	>	עַבְדֵי	servants of

8. Nouns ending in הָ have a singular construct form with an הֵ ending.

Absolute			*Construct*	
שָׂדֶה	field	>	שְׂדֵה	field of
מַחֲנֶה	camp	>	מַחֲנֵה	camp of

---

[7] The noun בַּיִת occurs a total of 2,047 times in the Hebrew Bible. In 477 instances (23%), it appears in the absolute state or lexical form. It appears 1,570 times (77%) in the construct state (בֵּית). Likewise, עַיִן occurs 83 times (9%) in the absolute state but 817 times (91%) in the construct state (עֵין).

[8] Frequently, in the construct plural of Segholate nouns (such as מַלְכֵי and עַבְדֵי in this section), the Daghesh Lene that is expected in the *begadkephat* consonant after the Silent Shewa is given up. This loss of Daghesh Lene (in a *begadkephat* consonant) after a closed syllable will be encountered in other circumstances (18.7).

10.6 Summary.

1. Hebrew expresses the "of" (possessive) relationship between two nouns by placing them side by side, in a *construct chain*.

2. A construct chain may have one or more nouns in the construct state but only one noun in the absolute state. The absolute noun is always last in the construct chain.

3. Construct chains are either definite (*the ... of the ...*) or indefinite (*a ... of a ...*). The definiteness or indefiniteness of a construct chain is determined by the definiteness or indefiniteness of the absolute noun. The construct noun will not take the definite article. Therefore, a construct chain is definite if the absolute noun is definite and indefinite if the absolute noun is indefinite.

4. Nouns in a construct chain may be linked by Maqqef as in בֶּן־דָּוִד (the son of David).

5. When two or more nouns are "in construct," no other words or particles may separate them. For this reason, modifying adjectives must follow the construct chain as in מֶלֶךְ הָאָרֶץ הַטּוֹב (the good king of the land).

6. Although a construct noun does not take a definite article, it may appear with one of the inseparable prepositions as in בְּבֵית דָוִד (*in* the house of David).

7. Most construct nouns change their spelling in comparison to their absolute or lexical forms. This is the result of the construct noun surrendering its primary accent or stress to the absolute noun in the construct chain. The most significant changes are listed below.

   a. In the construct form of endingless nouns (except for Segholate nouns), Qamets (and sometimes Tsere) changes to Pathach in a final closed syllable. Qamets and Tsere change to Vocal Shewa in an open, unaccented syllable (or a reduced vowel with gutturals).

   b. The masculine plural (◌ִים) and dual (◌ַיִם) endings are replaced by ◌ֵי in the construct state and the rules of vowel reduction are applied.

c. The הָ ending of a feminine singular noun changes to תְ in the construct state and the rules of vowel reduction are applied.

d. Feminine plural nouns ending in וֹת retain this diagnostic ending in the construct and the rules of vowel reduction are applied.

e. Certain singular monosyllabic nouns add Hireq Yod to their stem as in אֲבִי (father of).

f. The singular absolute or lexical form of a Segholate noun is identical to its singular construct form. The plural construct form follows the pattern of מַלְכֵי (kings of).

g. Nouns ending in הֶ have a singular construct ending in הֵ as in שְׂדֵה (field of).

10.7 Vocabulary.

אֶבֶן	stone (276); feminine
אֲדָמָה	ground (222)
אֹיֵב	enemy (285)
בָּשָׂר	flesh (270)
בְּרִית	covenant (287); feminine
גְּבוּל	boundary, territory (241)
חַיִל	strength, wealth, army (246)
חֶסֶד	loyalty, kindness, devotion, steadfast love (249)
חֹדֶשׁ	new moon, month (283)
יָד	hand (1,627); יָדוֹת (plural); feminine
מָוֶת	death (153); מוֹת (irregular construct form)
מַטֶּה	rod, staff, tribe (252)
מִדְבָּר	pasturage, wilderness (270)
עוֹד	yet, still, again (491)
עֵת	time (297); feminine

עֹלָה   burnt offering (286)

פָּנִים   face (2,126); פְּנֵי (construct)

צֹאן   flock, small herd of sheep or goats (274)

רֶגֶל   foot (251); feminine

10.8   Marry a Prostitute?

לֵךְ קַח־לְךָ אֵשֶׁת זְנוּנִים וְיַלְדֵי זְנוּנִים כִּי־זָנֹה תִזְנֶה הָאָרֶץ
מֵאַחֲרֵי יְהוָה

Go marry a woman of prostitution and have children of prostitution
because the land is completely committing prostitution
away from Yahweh (Hos 1:2).

In Hos 1, we are confronted with an interpretational question: Did God
actually command Hosea to marry a prostitute? Some commentators
have answered in the affirmative, even suggesting that Hosea's wife
probably turned to prostitution sometime after their marriage, and
Hosea, looking back at his past at a later point when he was seeking an
analogy for Israel's unfaithfulness to Yahweh, re-cast the story of his
marriage as if he had been commanded to marry a prostitute in the
first place. However, these interpreters do not necessarily have Hebrew
grammar on their side.

There are three words for "prostitute" in Hebrew: קְדֵשָׁה (cult prostitute),
זֹנָה (common prostitute) and כֶּלֶב (male prostitute). None of the three
is used here. Instead, a special *construct* term appears: the word אִשָּׁה
(construct אֵשֶׁת) for a woman or wife is used in combination with a
governing noun in the masculine plural, זְנוּנִים. In Hebrew, the masculine
plural is the standard way to convey abstraction - in this case, not
"prostitute" but the concept of "prostitution," i.e., in theological contexts,
the opposite of "faithfulness." Moreover, a noun in the construct is
often related logically to its governing noun in the manner of "something
characterized by" so that אֵשֶׁת זְנוּנִים would tend to mean "a woman
characterized by [the abstract concept of] prostitution" rather than
literally "a prostitute." Further, Hosea's children are called יַלְדֵי זְנוּנִים,
"children of prostitution" in a precisely parallel Hebrew construct, i.e.,
"children characterized by [the abstract concept of] prostitution" rather

than "children of a prostitute." Additionally, the verse goes on to say that the land (of Israel) זָנֹה תִזְנֶה, "is completely committing prostitution."

Thus the same thing is being said about Hosea's wife, about his future children and about the land of Israel in general - and in no case is the literal meaning apparently related to actually selling sex. All of this fits in well with the way that the Hebrew root in question, זנה, is used elsewhere in Hosea (and other prophetical contexts, especially Ezekiel), to convey the sense of "ultimate [religious] unfaithfulness" to Yahweh. In other words, Hosea 1:2 is conceptually parallel to Isa 64:4 or Ps 14:2-3 (cf. Rom 3:10-12). It makes the point, not that Hosea actually married a prostitute, but that in his day, all Israel has abandoned Yahweh's covenant, so that even Hosea's wife and children - no matter whom he married - would be tainted by the same unfaithfulness that "the land" in general displayed.

Douglas Stuart
Professor of Old Testament
Gordon-Conwell Theological Seminary
South Hamilton, Massachusetts

10.9 **Advanced Information: The Superlative**. In section 6.6.2, you learned that the preposition מִן may be used with כֹּל (all, each, every) in the formation of a superlative construction (מִכֹּל). This is only one of several ways that Hebrew can express the superlative idea. Two additional superlative constructions in Hebrew are detailed below.

1. Perhaps the most common superlative construction is created by the use of an adjective that has been made definite by the definite article, a pronominal suffix or the construct state. Of course, not all "definite" adjectives will translate as superlatives but context will suggest the possibility.

    מִן־הַקָּטֹן וְעַד־הַגָּדוֹל (literally) "from the small one to the great one" or (superlatively) "from the *smallest* one to the *greatest* one" (1 Sam 30:19)

מִגְּדוֹלָם וְעַד־קְטַנָּם   (literally) "from the great one of them to the small one of them" or (superlatively) "from the *greatest* of them to the *least* of them" (Jonah 3:5)

הַקָּטֹן אֶת־אָבִינוּ הַיּוֹם   (literally) "the young one is with our father today" or (superlatively) "the *youngest* one is with our father today" (Gen 42:13)

הַיָּפָה בַּנָּשִׁים   (literally) "the beautiful one among (the) women" or (superlatively) "the *most beautiful* one among (the) women" (Song 1:8)

בְּנוֹ הַקָּטָן   (literally) "his young son" or (superlatively) "his *youngest* son" (Gen 9:24)

קְטֹן בָּנָיו   (literally) "the young one of his sons" or (superlatively) "the *youngest* one of his sons" (2 Chr 21:17)

2. Another superlative construction consists of two nouns in the construct state where the construct noun is singular and the absolute noun is plural and definite. In this construction, the two nouns must be the same.

קֹדֶשׁ הַקֳּדָשִׁים   "the holy of holies," meaning the *most* holy place (Ex 26:33)

אֲדֹנֵי הָאֲדֹנִים   "the Lord of lords," meaning the *greatest* Lord (Deut 10:17)

שִׁיר הַשִּׁירִים   "the song of songs," meaning the *greatest* song (Song 1:1)

Chapter 11

Hebrew Numbers

11.1 **Introduction**. Biblical Hebrew does not have a separate set of numerical symbols (1, 2, 3, etc.) like we do in English. Rather, Hebrew numbers are written out (see chart below). In Hebrew, there are both cardinal and ordinal numbers. Cardinal numbers are used for counting (one, two, three, etc.) and ordinal numbers are used to indicate position in a series (first, second, third, etc.).

11.2 **Cardinal Numbers: One through Ten**. In Hebrew, cardinal numbers have masculine and feminine forms. They also occur in both the absolute and construct states. It is not necessary to memorize all of the following forms. Instead, memorize only the masculine absolute forms and then note the types of changes that occur in the remaining forms. Those changes indicating gender and state should be familiar to you from your study of previous chapters. You will need to give special attention to the spelling of numbers *one* and *two*.

	Masculine		**Feminine**	
	Absolute	*Construct*	*Absolute*	*Construct*
One	אֶחָד	אַחַד	אַחַת	אַחַת
Two	שְׁנַ֫יִם	שְׁנֵי	שְׁתַּ֫יִם	שְׁתֵּי
Three	שָׁלֹשׁ	שְׁלֹשׁ	שְׁלֹשָׁה	שְׁלֹ֫שֶׁת
Four	אַרְבַּע	אַרְבַּע	אַרְבָּעָה	אַרְבַּ֫עַת
Five	חָמֵשׁ	חֲמֵשׁ	חֲמִשָּׁה	חֲמֵ֫שֶׁת
Six	שֵׁשׁ	שֵׁשׁ	שִׁשָּׁה	שֵׁ֫שֶׁת
Seven	שֶׁ֫בַע	שְׁבַע	שִׁבְעָה	שִׁבְעַת
Eight	שְׁמֹנֶה	שְׁמֹנֶה	שְׁמֹנָה	שְׁמֹנַת
Nine	תֵּ֫שַׁע	תְּשַׁע	תִּשְׁעָה	תִּשְׁעַת
Ten	עֶ֫שֶׂר	עֶ֫שֶׂר	עֲשָׂרָה	עֲשֶׂ֫רֶת

1. With number *one*, the masculine form is spelled with דּ (אֶחָד) and the feminine form with ת (אַחַת). The number *one* is used like an *adjective*. As such, it follows the noun it modifies and agrees in gender and definiteness. When used in the construct state, it will precede an absolute noun that is usually plural.

בֵּן אֶחָד	one son	בַּת אַחַת	one daughter
הַבֵּן הָאֶחָד	the one son	הַבַּת הָאַחַת	*the one daughter*
אַחַד הַבָּנִים	one of the sons	אַחַת הַבָּנוֹת	one of the daughters

2. With number *two*, the masculine form is spelled with נ (שְׁנַיִם) and the feminine with ת (שְׁתַּיִם). Note that both forms are dual in number. The number *two* is classified as a *noun* and agrees in gender with the other noun to which it is related. The absolute and construct forms are used interchangeably without any apparent change in meaning.

בָּנִים שְׁנַיִם	two sons	בָּנוֹת שְׁתַּיִם	two daughters
שְׁנַיִם בָּנִים	two sons	שְׁתַּיִם בָּנוֹת	two daughters
שְׁנֵי בָּנִים	two sons	שְׁתֵּי בָּנוֹת	two daughters

3. With numbers *three* through *ten*, there is no change in spelling, except to indicate gender and state. Like number *two*, these numbers are classified as nouns but they *do not agree in gender* with the other nouns to which they are related. In other words, masculine numbers are used with feminine nouns and feminine numbers are used with masculine nouns. Note also that while the numbers are singular in form, the nouns are plural.

שְׁלֹשָׁה בָּנִים	three sons	שָׁלוֹשׁ בָּנוֹת	three daughters
בָּנִים שְׁלֹשָׁה	three sons	בָּנוֹת שָׁלוֹשׁ	three daughters
שְׁלֹשֶׁת בָּנִים	three sons	שְׁלֹשׁ בָּנוֹת	three daughters

4. Numbers *two* through *ten* may also occur with pronominal suffixes. These suffixes are added to the construct forms of the number.

שְׁנֵיהֶם	two of them	שְׁתֵּיהֶן	two of them
שְׁנֵיכֶם	two of you	שְׁתֵּיכֶן	two of you
שְׁנֵינוּ	two of us	שְׁתֵּינוּ	two of us

11.3 **Cardinal Numbers: Eleven through Nineteen.** Numbers *eleven* through *nineteen* are formed with a combination of the number *ten* and *one* through *nine*. For example, the Hebrew number *eleven* is אַחַד עָשָׂר, a combination of *one* (אֶחָד) and *ten* (עֶשֶׂר).

	With Masculine Nouns	With Feminine Nouns
Eleven	אַחַד עָשָׂר	אַחַת עֶשְׂרֵה
	עַשְׁתֵּי עָשָׂר	עַשְׁתֵּי עֶשְׂרֵה
Twelve	שְׁנֵי עָשָׂר	שְׁתֵּי עֶשְׂרֵה
	שְׁנֵים עָשָׂר	שְׁתֵּים עֶשְׂרֵה
Thirteen	שְׁלֹשָׁה עָשָׂר	שְׁלֹשׁ עֶשְׂרֵה
Fourteen	אַרְבָּעָה עָשָׂר	אַרְבַּע עֶשְׂרֵה
Fifteen	חֲמִשָּׁה עָשָׂר	חֲמֵשׁ עֶשְׂרֵה
Sixteen	שִׁשָּׁה עָשָׂר	שֵׁשׁ עֶשְׂרֵה
Seventeen	שִׁבְעָה עָשָׂר	שְׁבַע עֶשְׂרֵה
Eighteen	שְׁמֹנָה עָשָׂר	שְׁמֹנֶה עֶשְׂרֵה
Nineteen	תִּשְׁעָה עָשָׂר	תְּשַׁע עֶשְׂרֵה

1. Note that *eleven* and *twelve* have alternate forms. The alternate forms for *eleven* (with עַשְׁתֵּי) occur only nineteen times in the Hebrew Bible.

2. Most of the time, these numbers occur with plural nouns. A few nouns, however, appear regularly in the singular. When singular nouns of this type occur with these numbers, they are translated as plural nouns.

שְׁנֵי עָשָׂר אִישׁ	twelve men (Josh 3:12)
שְׁלֹשׁ עֶשְׂרֵה שָׁנָה	thirteen years (1 Kgs 7:1)
אַרְבָּעָה עָשָׂר יוֹם	fourteen days (Ex 12:6)
חֲמִשָּׁה עָשָׂר שֶׁקֶל	fifteen shekels (Lev 27:7)

11.4   Cardinal Numbers: Twenty through Ninety Nine.

Twenty	עֶשְׂרִים
Thirty	שְׁלֹשִׁים
Forty	אַרְבָּעִים
Fifty	חֲמִשִּׁים
Sixty	שִׁשִּׁים
Seventy	שִׁבְעִים
Eighty	שְׁמֹנִים
Ninety	תִּשְׁעִים

1. עֶשְׂרִים (twenty) is the masculine plural form of עֶשֶׂר (ten). Numbers *thirty* through *ninety* (by ten) are the masculine plural forms of *three* through *nine*. For example, שִׁשִּׁים (sixty) is the plural form of שֵׁשׁ (six).

2. In Hebrew, *twenty-one* and other such numbers occur either as "twenty and one" or, less frequently, as "one and twenty."

עֶשְׂרִים וְאַחַת	twenty-one (2 Kgs 24:18)
שִׁבְעִים וְשִׁבְעָה	seventy-seven (Gen 4:24)
תִּשְׁעִים וָתֵשַׁע	ninety-nine (Gen 17:24)
שְׁנַיִם וּשְׁלֹשִׁים	thirty-two (Num 31:40)

11.5   Cardinal Numbers: One Hundred and Higher.

One Hundred	מֵאָה	(construct מְאַת; plural מֵאוֹת)
Two Hundred	מָאתַיִם	(dual form of מֵאָה)
Three Hundred	שְׁלֹשׁ מֵאוֹת	
One Thousand	אֶלֶף	(plural אֲלָפִים)
Two Thousand	אַלְפַּיִם	(dual form of אֶלֶף)
Three Thousand	שְׁלֹשֶׁת אֲלָפִים	
Ten Thousand	רְבָבָה	(also רִבּוֹ and רִבּוֹא)
Twenty Thousand	רִבּוֹתַיִם	(dual form of רְבָבָה)
Thirty Thousand	שְׁלֹשׁ רִבּוֹת	

1. The numbers *one hundred* (מֵאָה), *one thousand* (אֶלֶף), and *ten thousand* (רְבָבָה) should be memorized.

2. Note that *two hundred* (מָאתַיִם) is the dual form of *one hundred* (מֵאָה), *two thousand* (אַלְפַּיִם) is the dual form of *one thousand* (אֶלֶף) and *twenty thousand* (רִבּוֹתַיִם) is the dual form of *ten thousand* (רְבָבָה).

3. The remaining numerical sequences (*three hundred, four hundred, five hundred, six hundred,* etc.) follow the pattern exhibited by *three hundred* (שְׁלֹשׁ מֵאוֹת), *three thousand* (שְׁלֹשֶׁת אֲלָפִים) and *thirty thousand* (שְׁלֹשׁ רִבּוֹת).

11.6 **Ordinal Numbers**. The ordinal numbers are used to express position in a series (first, second, third, etc.). In Hebrew, ordinal numbers have both masculine and feminine forms.

	Masculine	*Feminine*
First	רִאשׁוֹן	רִאשׁוֹנָה
Second	שֵׁנִי	שֵׁנִית
Third	שְׁלִישִׁי	שְׁלִישִׁית
Fourth	רְבִיעִי	רְבִיעִית
Fifth	חֲמִישִׁי	חֲמִישִׁית
Sixth	שִׁשִּׁי	שִׁשִּׁית
Seventh	שְׁבִיעִי	שְׁבִיעִית
Eighth	שְׁמִינִי	שְׁמִינִית
Ninth	תְּשִׁיעִי	תְּשִׁיעִית
Tenth	עֲשִׂירִי	עֲשִׂירִית

1. The ordinal רִאשׁוֹן (first) is derived from the noun רֹאשׁ (head, chief, beginning). The remaining ordinals share a common root with their corresponding cardinal number. For example, שֵׁשׁ (six) and שִׁשִּׁי (sixth) share a common root.

2. With ordinals *second* through *tenth*, the masculine form is distinguished from the feminine form by a final ת in the feminine. In other words, masculine ordinals end with יִ as in שְׁלִישִׁי and feminine ordinals end with יִת as in שְׁלִישִׁית.

3. Ordinal numbers are classified as *adjectives*. When attributive, they follow the noun they modify and usually agree in gender and definiteness.

בַּיּוֹם הָרִאשׁוֹן   on the first day (Lev 23:7)

בַּיּוֹם הַשְּׁבִיעִי   on the seventh day (Gen 2:2)

יוֹם הַשִּׁשִּׁי   the sixth day (Gen 1:31)

4. For ordinals greater than *tenth*, cardinal numbers are used.

וּשְׁלֹשׁ־עֶשְׂרֵה שָׁנָה   and the thirteenth year (Gen 14:4)

בִּשְׁלֹשִׁים וָשֶׁבַע שָׁנָה   in the thirty-seventh year (Jer 52:31)

בִּשְׁנַת הָאַרְבָּעִים   in the fortieth year (1 Chr 26:31)

11.7 Summary.

1. Cardinal numbers are used for counting (one, two, three, etc.) and ordinal numbers are used to indicate position in a series (first, second, third, etc.).

2. In Hebrew, cardinal numbers have both masculine and feminine forms. They also occur in the absolute and construct states. In most instances, you need only to memorize the masculine absolute forms.

3. While cardinal number *one* functions like an adjective, numbers *two* and higher function like nouns. Note that numbers *three* through *ten* do not agree in gender with the noun to which they are related.

4. Cardinal numbers *eleven* through *nineteen* are formed with a combination of the number *ten* and *one* through *nine*. For example, the Hebrew number *eleven* is עָשָׂר אַחַד, a combination of *one* (אַחַד) and *ten* (עָשָׂר).

5. In Hebrew, the number *twenty-one* and other such numbers occur as either "twenty and one" or, less frequently, as "one and twenty."

6. Ordinal numbers are classified as adjectives and have both masculine and feminine forms. Masculine ordinals end in ֹי. as with שְׁלִישִׁי (third) and feminine ordinals end in ֹית. as with שְׁלִישִׁית (third).

11.8 Vocabulary.

אַמָּה	forearm, cubit (249)
אֵם	mother (220); feminine
בֶּגֶד	garment (216)
זֶרַע	seed, offspring, descendant, child (229)
חָצֵר	permanent settlement, court, enclosure (192)
לַיְלָה	night (234)
לָכֵן	therefore (200)
מוֹעֵד	appointed place or time, season (224)
מַחֲנֶה	camp, army (215)
מַלְאָךְ	messenger, angel (213)
מַעֲשֶׂה	work (235)
נַעַר	lad, youth (240)
נַחֲלָה	inheritance (222)
עָוֹן	transgression, iniquity (231)
קֶרֶב	inward part, midst (227)
רַק	only (109)
שָׁלוֹם	peace, health (242)
שָׁם	there (835)
תָּמִיד	continually, regularly (104)

11.9   Martin Luther (1483-1546): On the Importance of the Biblical Languages. Martin Luther was the German leader of the Protestant Reformation, who, by the study of the Scriptures in their original languages, found the grace of God and the freedom from sin that only comes by that grace. On this ground, he became convinced that reading Greek and Hebrew was one of the greatest privileges and responsibilities of the Reformation preacher, so as to preserve a pure gospel. Few arguments for the importance of biblical languages are clearer than Luther's 1524 treatise, "To the Councilmen of All Cities in Germany That They Establish and Maintain Christian Schools." The following is an excerpt from this work.

> And let us be sure of this we will not long preserve the gospel without the languages. The languages are the sheath in which this sword of the Spirit is contained; they are the casket in which this jewel is enshrined; they are the vessel in which this wine is held; they are the larder in which this food is stored; and, as the gospel itself points out, they are the baskets in which are kept these loaves and fishes and fragments. If through our neglect we let the languages go (which God forbid!), we shall ... lose the gospel ...

> Experience too has proved this and still gives evidence of it. For as soon as the languages declined to the vanishing point, after the apostolic age, the gospel and faith and Christianity itself declined more and more ... On the other hand, now that the languages have been revived, they are bringing with them so bright a light and accomplishing such great things that the whole world stands amazed and has to acknowledge that we have the gospel just as pure and undefiled as the apostles had it, that it has been wholly restored to its original purity, far beyond what it was in the days of St. Jerome and St. Augustine ...

> Yes, you say, but many of the fathers were saved and even became teachers without the languages. That is true. But how do you account for the fact that they so often erred in the Scriptures?... Even St. Augustine himself is obliged to confess... that a Christian teacher who is to expound the Scriptures must know Greek and Hebrew in addition to Latin. Otherwise, it is

impossible to avoid constant stumbling; indeed, there are plenty of problems to work out even when one is well versed in the languages.

There is a vast difference therefore between a simple preacher of the faith and a person who expounds Scripture, or, as St. Paul puts it, a prophet. A simple preacher (it is true) has so many clear passages and texts available through translations that he can know and teach Christ, lead a holy life, and preach to others. But when it comes to interpreting Scripture, and working with it on your own, and disputing with those who cite it incorrectly, he is unequal to the task; that cannot be done without languages. Now there must always be such prophets in the Christian church who can dig into Scripture, expound it, and carry on disputations. A saintly life and right doctrine are not enough. Hence languages are absolutely and altogether necessary in the Christian church, as are the prophets or interpreters; although it is not necessary that every Christian or every preacher be such a prophet, as St. Paul points out in I Corinthians 12 and Ephesians 4 …

Since it becomes Christians then to make good use of the Holy Scriptures as their one and only book and it is a sin and a shame not to know our own book or to understand the speech and words of our God, it is a still greater sin and loss that we do not study languages, especially in these days when God is offering and giving us men and books and every facility and inducement to this study, and desires his Bible to be an open book. O how happy the dear fathers would have been if they had had our opportunity to study the languages and come thus prepared to the Holy Scriptures! What great toil and effort it cost them to gather up a few crumbs, while we with half the labor—yes, almost without any labor at all—can acquire the whole loaf! O how their effort puts our indolence to shame! Yes, how sternly God will judge our lethargy and ingratitude!

Here belongs also what St. Paul calls for in I Corinthians 14, namely, that in the Christian church all teachings must be judged. For this a knowledge of the language is needful above all else. The preacher or teacher can expound the Bible from beginning to end as he pleases, accurately or inaccurately, if there is no one there to judge whether he is doing it right or wrong. But in order to judge, one must have a knowledge of the languages; it cannot be done in any other way. Therefore, although faith and the gospel may indeed be proclaimed by simple preachers without a knowledge of languages, such preaching is flat and tame; people finally become weary and bored with it, and it falls to the ground. But where the preacher is versed in the languages, there is a freshness and vigor in his preaching, Scripture is treated in its entirety, and faith finds itself constantly renewed by a continual variety of words and illustrations. Hence, Psalm 129 likens such scriptural studies to a hunt, saying to the deer God opens the dense forests; and Psalm 1 likens them to a tree with a plentiful supply of water, whose leaves are always green.[1]

---

[1] Martin Luther, "To the Councilmen of All Cities in Germany That They Establish and Maintain Christian Schools," in *Luther's Works*, ed. W. Brandt and H. Lehman (Philadelphia: Muhlenberg Press, 1962) 357-366.

Chapter 12

Introduction to Hebrew Verbs

12.1   **Introduction.** At this point in your study of Hebrew, you have hopefully mastered the essential elements of Hebrew nouns and nominals. It is now time to study the Hebrew verbal system. Verbs are those words used to describe an action (he *studied*) or state of being (she *is wise*). In the Hebrew Bible, there are just over 23,000 verses. In the midst of these verses are found almost 72,000 verbs. This means that, on average, there are approximately three verbs in each verse. These statistics demonstrate that you must understand the Hebrew verbal system in form, function and meaning to succeed in the language. In this chapter, you will learn about the basic grammatical issues relating to verbs. *However, there is no need to memorize the Hebrew verbal forms in this chapter.* They are simply examples that illustrate the topics under discussion.

12.2   **Roots and Stems.** You are about to discover that many of the nouns you have memorized as vocabulary have verbal counterparts. The following nouns, for example, are listed with their verbal counterparts.

מֶלֶךְ	king	➤	מָלַךְ to reign
דָּבָר	word	➤	דִּבֶּר to speak
מִשְׁפָּט	judgement	➤	שָׁפַט to judge

Notice how each pair shares a common set of consonants and related definitions. The reason for this relationship is due to the fact that they share a common root. It is very important to understand the distinction between a root and those words derived from that root. It is a distinction between root and stem. Hebrew roots are typically composed of three consonants (triconsonantal), occasionally two (biconsonantal). *A root represents the origin or simplest form from which any number of Hebrew words are derived.* From a root, therefore, any number of nouns or verbs may be derived. *A stem is the most basic form of any word derived from a root.* For example, from the triconsonantal root מלך comes the noun stems מֶלֶךְ (king), מַלְכָּה (queen), מַלְכוּת (kingdom) and the verb stem מָלַךְ (to reign, be king). Once again, notice how each different word shares a common set of consonants and related definitions. This relationship is based upon the sharing of a common root. The system of deriving different words or stems from a common root should be a point of encouragement for students since it can take some of the pain out of vocabulary memorization. You should also understand, however, that roots never exist as real words, only those words that derive from a common, abstracted root. Technically, the whole concept of a word's root is a grammatical abstraction, that is, roots do not really exist as real words in the language. This "abstraction" is based upon the existence of related words sharing a common set of consonants and definitions.

12.3   **Person, Gender and Number.** In English, a verb by itself does not have person, gender or number (study). It must be supplied by the addition of a personal pronoun (she studied). In Hebrew, however, most verbs have person, gender and number. These verbal characteristics are indicated in Hebrew verbs by certain patterns of inflection. For example, the verb כָּתַב means "he wrote" and the verb כָּתְבָה means "she wrote." The different endings indicate person, gender and number. In Hebrew, therefore, a verb's person, gender and number are indicated in the verbal form itself. These endings will be discussed in the following chapters. Even though most Hebrew verbs are capable of indicating person, gender and number by themselves, they may also occur with independent personal pronouns. For example, both כָּתַבְתִּי and אֲנִי כָּתַבְתִּי are translated "I wrote." Because Hebrew verbs by themselves indicate person, gender and number, the addition of an independent personal pronoun typically expresses emphasis. With regard to person, Hebrew verbs can be first person (I, we), second person (you) or third person (he, she, it, they). With regard to number, Hebrew verbs will be either singular (I, you, he, she, it) or plural (we, you, they). And with regard to gender, Hebrew verbs will be either masculine (he), feminine (she), or common, meaning either masculine or feminine (I, we).

12.4   Chart: Summary of Person, Gender and Number.

Person		
	First	I, we
	Second	you
	Third	he, she, it, they
Gender	*Masculine*	referring to *masculine* subjects
	Feminine	referring to *feminine* subjects
	Common	referring to *masculine or feminine* subjects
Number	*Singular*	referring to *one* person or thing
	Plural	referring to *more than one* person or thing

12.5   Introduction to Verbal Stems. In the Hebrew verbal system, there are seven major stems: the Qal stem, Niphal stem, Piel stem, Pual stem, Hiphil stem, Hophal stem and Hithpael stem. The Qal stem is the basic or simple verbal stem. From the Qal stem all other verbal stems are formed. For this reason, *the Niphal through Hithpael stems are called "derived stems" because their forms are derived or based on the Qal stem.* Verbal stems tell us two things about the action or meaning of a verb: the *type of verbal action* and the *voice of verbal action.*

In Hebrew, there are three basic categories of verbal action: simple action (to break), intensive action (to smash into pieces) and causative action (to cause to break). There are also three basic categories of verbal voice: active, passive and reflexive. *The voice of a verb indicates the relationship between the subject of a verb and the action of the verb.* Stated differently, voice indicates whether the subject acts or is acted upon. With the active voice, the subject of the verb is performing the action of the verb. In the example "David defeated the enemy," *David* is the subject of the verb "defeated" and he is performing the action. With the passive voice, the subject of the verb is receiving the action of the verb. In the example "David *was* defeated by the enemy," David is no longer performing the action of the verb but receiving the verbal action. With the reflexive voice, the subject of the verb is both doing and receiving the action of the verb. In the example "David dressed *himself*," David is both performing and receiving the verbal action. Notice that the sentence was rendered reflexive by using an English "reflexive" pronoun (himself).

12.6 **English and Hebrew Spelling of the Verbal Stems with Diagnostics.**
The names of the Hebrew verbal stems might seem strange at first.
They sound strange to us because they are the traditional Hebrew
names. The Qal (קַל) is the basic verbal stem. The term "Qal" means
"simple" with reference to the fact that the root is unaugmented, nothing
has been added to it. The six derived conjugations have names that are
constructed on the verbal root פעל, inflecting each in its Perfect, third
masculine singular (3ms) form. You should carefully study how the
names are constructed because their spelling preserves certain diagnostic
points of vocalization. Note that in the following chart, you will see
references to what is called a "stem vowel." In Hebrew, *the stem vowel
is that vowel which is associated with the second consonant of the verbal root.*

English Spelling		*Hebrew Spelling*	*Spelling Diagnostics*
Qal	➤	קַל	unaugmented
Niphal	➤	נִפְעַל	נ prefix; Pathach stem vowel
Piel	➤	פִּעֵל	Hireq-Tsere vowel pattern
Pual	➤	פֻּעַל	Qibbuts-Pathach vowel pattern
Hiphil	➤	הִפְעִיל	ה prefix; Hireq Yod stem vowel
Hophal	➤	הָפְעַל	הָ prefix;[1] Pathach stem vowel
Hithpael	➤	הִתְפַּעֵל	הִת prefix; Tsere stem vowel

12.7 **The Hebrew Verbal Stems.** In this section, we will briefly discuss the
significance of the Qal and derived stems in terms of their verbal action
and voice. Please note that what follows is a simple preview of basic
information. These issues will receive further attention in subsequent
chapters.

Simple Active

1. **Qal.** The Qal is the simple or basic verbal stem. Qal verbs are
active in voice, though a few passive forms do exist. The Qal
stem also exhibits the *simple* or unnuanced type of action. An
example of a verb in the Qal stem is שָׁמַע meaning "he heard."

---

[1] The vowel under the ה prefix of the Hophal stem is Qamets Hatuf.

Simple
Passive/
Reflexive

2. **Niphal**. The Niphal stem is used to express *simple* action with either a *passive* or *reflexive* voice. In other words, whatever a verb means in the Qal stem, it becomes passive or reflexive in the Niphal stem. An example of a verb in the Niphal stem is נִשְׁמַע meaning "he *was* heard" (passive) or "he heard *himself*" (reflexive). Notice the change in spelling from שָׁמַע (Qal) to נִשְׁמַע (Niphal). The most notable difference between the two forms is the prefixing of נ to the Niphal stem. The name "Niphal" *will remind you* that every verb in the Niphal stem takes a נ prefix. This prefix is unique to the Niphal stem and so distinguishes it from the other verbal stems.

Intensive
Active

3. **Piel**. The Piel stem is sometimes used to express an *intensive* type of action with an *active* voice.[2] In other words, the simple action of the Qal stem will take on some type of intensive nuance in the Piel stem. For example, the verb שָׁבַר means "he broke" in the Qal stem. The Piel form, however, is שִׁבֵּר and means "he smashed into pieces." Notice the change in spelling from שָׁבַר (Qal) to שִׁבֵּר (Piel). The distinguishing characteristics of the Piel stem are a unique vowel pattern and the presence of a Daghesh Forte in the second root consonant.

Intensive
Passive

4. **Pual**. The Pual is the passive form of the Piel. The Pual stem, therefore, is used to express an *intensive* type of action with a *passive* voice. For example, the Piel verb שִׁבֵּר means "he smashed into pieces." The Pual form, however, would be שֻׁבַּר and is translated "he (it) *was* smashed into pieces." Notice how a form of the English verb "to be" (was) is used to make the translation passive. Like the Piel, the Pual stem is also distinguished by the presence of a Daghesh Forte in the second consonant of the verbal root. Notice also the Qibbuts-Pathach vowel pattern in the Pual form of the verb. This vowel pattern will distinguish the Pual stem from the corresponding Piel stem form.

---

[2] We recognize the difficulty of characterizing the varieties of action denoted by the Piel stem (also Pual and Hithpael) with a single designation like "intensive." Such a designation is, however, a helpful starting point for the beginning student. Additionally, it is legitimate to think of the factitive and iterative as "types" of intensive action.

Causative Active

5. **Hiphil**. The Hiphil stem is used to express *causative* action with an *active* voice. For example, the verb מָלַךְ means "he was king" or "he reigned" in the Qal stem. The Hiphil form, however, is הִמְלִיךְ and means "he *caused* to reign" or "he *made* (someone) king." Notice the change in spelling from מָלַךְ (Qal) to הִמְלִיךְ (Hiphil). The most notable differences between the two forms are the prefixing of הַ to the first root consonant and the Hireq Yod stem vowel. The presence of הַ and the Hireq Yod stem vowel make identifying the Hiphil stem very easy.

Causative Passive

6. **Hophal**. The Hophal is the passive form of the Hiphil. The Hophal stem, therefore, is used to express *causative* action with a *passive* voice. For example, the Hiphil verb הִמְלִיךְ means "he made (someone) king." The Hophal form is הָמְלַךְ and it is translated "he *was* made king." Notice how הַ is prefixed to both the Hiphil and Hophal, clearly distinguishing them from the previous stems. The Hiphil and Hophal are distinguished from one another by their prefix and stem vowels.

Intensive Reflexive

7. **Hithpael**. The Hithpael stem is used to express an *intensive* type of action with a *reflexive* (or sometimes passive) voice. For example, the verb חָבָא means "he hid" in the Qal stem. The Hithpael form is הִתְחַבֵּא and it means "he hid *himself*." Notice the drastic change in spelling from חָבָא (Qal) to הִתְחַבֵּא (Hithpael). The most notable differences between the two forms are the prefixing of הִתְ to the first root consonant and the Daghesh Forte in the second root consonant. At this point, it is helpful to note that all verbs exhibiting an intensive type of action (Piel, Pual and Hithpael) insert a Daghesh Forte into the second consonant of the verbal root. This is a "diagnostic" feature of the intensive stems. The term "diagnostic" means that the presence of the Daghesh Forte in the second root consonant is a feature that identifies or diagnoses the intensive verbal stems. When you examine a Hebrew verb and see this diagnostic feature, you will be able to successfully identify or diagnose the verbal stem being used.

12.8   Chart: Summary of Basic Verbal Stem Meaning.

	Simple Action	*Intensive Action*	*Causative Action*
Active Voice	**Qal**	**Piel**	**Hiphil**
Passive Voice	**Niphal**	**Pual**	**Hophal**
Reflexive Voice	**Niphal**	**Hithpael**	

12.9   Summary of Verbal Translation Values. Once again, there is no need to memorize the Hebrew forms. They appear only for the sake of illustration. Review the spelling patterns and the translation values for each of the verbal stems.

Verbal Stem	*Verbal Form*	*Translation Value*
Qal	שָׁמַע	he heard
Niphal	נִשְׁמַע	he was heard
Piel	שִׁבֵּר	he smashed into pieces
Pual	שֻׁבַּר	he (it) was smashed into pieces
Hiphil	הִמְלִיךְ	he made king
Hophal	הָמְלַךְ	he was made king
Hithpael	הִתְחַבֵּא	he hid himself

It is important to note that most Hebrew verbs are not attested in each of the basic verbal stems. Some verbs are not even attested in the Qal stem. For example, the Hebrew verb meaning "to love" is אָהַב and it does not occur in the Hophal stem. Similarly, the Piel verb דִּבֶּר (to speak) does not occur in the Qal stem.

12.10   Verbal Stems and Verbal Meaning. The meaning of a verb in the Qal may be different when that same verb appears in another stem. This is one of the major reasons why it is important to understand the verbal stems as presented above. For example, the Hebrew verb שָׁבַר in the Qal means "to break." This same verb in the Piel stem (שִׁבֵּר) means "to smash into pieces." In this and many other instances, the relationship between the two meanings is apparent in light of the discussion above. In other instances, however, understanding the change in verbal meaning between the different stems is not as apparent. For example, the verb בָּרַךְ means "to kneel" in the Qal. This same verbal root in the Piel stem means "to bless." Always consult a lexicon to be certain of a verb's meaning in a given stem.

Having studied verbal stems and how they affect verbal meaning, we now turn to verbal conjugations and how they denote verbal function. In other words, *verbal stems are used to indicate verbal meaning* and *verbal conjugations are used to denote verbal function.*

12.11 **Introduction to the Verbal Conjugations.** In English, verbs are conjugated in order to express different verbal functions. The term "conjugation" is used to describe the inflected verbal forms that express particular verbal functions. Some verbal conjugations are also used to express what is called "tense." The term "tense" is used to indicate the relationship between the time of the verbal action and the time of speaking. For example, an English verb may be conjugated in the present tense in order to express action taking place but not yet complete, that is, incomplete or *imperfective* action.

> *Singular:* I study, you study, he/she/it studies
> *Plural:*   we study, you study, they study

This same verb may also be conjugated in the past tense in order to express action that has been completed, that is, *perfective* action.

> *Singular:* I studied, you studied, he/she/it studied
> *Plural:*   we studied, you studied, they studied

This verb may also be conjugated in the future tense in order to express action not yet begun but expected in the future.

> *Singular:* I will study, you will study, he/she/it will study
> *Plural:*   we will study, you will study, they will study

English verbs may also be conjugated as Participles (studying), Infinitives (to study) or Imperatives (study!). Each English verb takes on a different form (study, studies, studied, studying, to study) in order to express a different verbal function. In Hebrew, there are eight basic verbal conjugations: Perfect, Imperfect, Imperative, Cohortative, Jussive, Infinitive Construct, Infinitive Absolute and Participle. This means that a verb in the Qal may be conjugated any one of eight different ways, depending on what verbal function the author intends. In most cases, the change in verbal function will be identifiable by a change in verbal form. Each of the derived stems (Niphal, Piel, Pual, etc.) may also be conjugated in any one of these eight different conjugations. In Hebrew, therefore, there are seven verbal stems (Qal and the derived stems) and eight verbal conjugations (Perfect, Imperfect, etc.). For example, the Qal verb שָׁמַע may be conjugated in any one of eight different ways depending on the intended function of the verb (Qal Participle, Qal Infinitive, Qal Imperative, etc.). This same verb in the Niphal stem may also be conjugated in any one of the eight different Hebrew conjugations (Niphal Participle, Niphal Infinitive, Niphal Imperative, etc.). The following chapters will take you step by step through each verbal stem and each verbal conjugation. At this point, however, it will be helpful to briefly define the function of each Hebrew verbal conjugation.

1. **Perfect**. The Perfect conjugation is used to express a *completed action* or a *state of being*. When used to describe a completed action (either in reality or in the mind of the speaker), the Hebrew Perfect may be translated by the English past tense (he studied), present perfect (he has studied), past perfect (he had studied) or future perfect (he will have studied). When used to describe a state of being, it will be translated with the English present tense

Completed Action (he is wise). The Hebrew Perfect may also be translated by the English present tense with verbs of perception or attitude (he knows, he loves). It must be emphasized that the Hebrew Perfect does not have tense (time of action) apart from context and issues of syntax. Rather, it signifies aspect (type of action). The Perfect aspect designates a verbal action with its conclusion envisioned in the mind of the speaker or writer. To state it differently, *the Perfect aspect denotes completed action, whether in the past, present or future*.

2. **Imperfect**. The Imperfect conjugation is used to express *incomplete action* and is usually translated by the English present tense (I
Incomplete Action study) or future tense (I will study). The action of the verb occurs either at the time of speaking or after the time of speaking. The Hebrew Imperfect is also used to denote habitual or customary action, whether in the past, present or future (he

prays regularly, he used to pray). The Imperfect may also be rendered by one of several modal values (would, could, should, may, might, can, etc.). These modal translation values are suggested by various contextual considerations. It must also be emphasized that, like the Perfect, the Hebrew Imperfect does not have tense (time of action) apart from context and issues of syntax. It too signifies aspect (type of action). The Imperfect aspect designates a verbal action for which, in the mind of the speaker or writer, the conclusion is not in view. To state it differently, *the Imperfect aspect denotes incomplete action, whether in the past, present or future.*

3. **Imperative.** The next three conjugations (Imperative, Cohortative and Jussive) are *volitional* conjugations, meaning they are used *to express some type of command, wish or desire.* The Imperative

2nd Person Command conjugation is used primarily to express direct commands, demanding immediate action from the one being addressed. It can also be used to request permission or communicate a request. The Hebrew Imperative occurs only in the second person. For example, "(You) *defend* the cause of the weak!"

4. **Cohortative.** This second volitional conjugation is used much like the Imperative, to express a wish, request or command. It

1st Person Volitional may also be used, however, to express purpose (in order to) or result (resulting in). The Cohortative conjugation occurs in the first person, for example, "*Let* me (first person singular) *honor* the Lord!" or "*Let* us (first person plural) *honor* the Lord!"

5. **Jussive.** The Jussive conjugation is also used to express either some type of mild command or strong wish. Strictly speaking, it occurs only in the third person, singular and plural. For example, "*May* the Lord (third person) *give* to me another son." To sum

3rd Person Volitional up the volitional conjugations, all three are used to express some type of command, request or desire. Context will help determine which volitional nuance is intended by the author. The Cohortative occurs in the first person (I, we), the Imperative in the second person (you) and the Jussive in the third person (he, she, it, they).

6. **Infinitive Construct**. An Infinitive is a verbal noun. In Hebrew, there are two Infinitive forms: the Infinitive Construct and the Infinitive Absolute. The Infinitive Construct may function much like an English Infinitive, usually translated with the preposition "to" plus a verb as in "to study" or "to learn." Like a noun, it can be used as the subject (*to study* is hard work) or object of a verb (I want *to study*). It may also be used in a number of other ways that will be detailed in chapter 20.

Verbal Noun

7. **Infinitive Absolute**. The Hebrew Infinitive Absolute has no real English counterpart. It may be used in conjunction with other verbs to emphasize or intensify the verbal action. It may also be used in the place of an Imperative to express a command. In special instances, it can be used with other verbs to express two verbal actions occurring at the same time, that is, contemporaneous action.

Verbal Noun

8. **Participle**. A Participle is a verbal adjective. As such, it has both verbal and adjectival characteristics. Verbally, it expresses some type of verbal action such as "studying" or "learning." Adjectivally, it is used much like a Hebrew adjective: attributively, predicatively or substantively.

Verbal Adjective

12.12 Strong and Weak Verbs. Hebrew verbs are classified as either strong or weak. Strong verbs have no weak consonants. Weak verbs, however, have at least one weak root consonant. The weak consonants are the gutturals and ר. For example, the verbs קָטַל, כָּתַב and קָבַץ are strong verbs and שָׁמַע, מָצָא and עָלָה are weak verbs. The consonants י and נ are also considered weak *but only when they appear as the first consonant of the verbal root* as in יָשַׁב and נָפַל and only in certain conjugations. Biconsonantal and Geminate verbal roots are also considered to be weak. Biconsonantal roots have two rather than three root consonants as in קָם (he arose). Geminate roots are those in which the second and third root consonants are identical as in סָבַב (he surrounded). When studying the various Hebrew conjugations, you will first learn the strong verb forms and then the weak verb forms. The following chart provides you with examples of weak verbal roots and their system of classification. The roman numerals that are used in their classification indicate which root letter is weak: "I" indicates the first root position; "II" the second root position; and "III" the third root position.

12.13 The Classification of Weak Verbal Roots.

	Verb	Description
I-Guttural	עָמַד	guttural in first root position
II-Guttural	גָּאַל	guttural in second root position
III-ח/ע	בָּרַח	ח or ע in third root position
III-א	מָצָא	א in third root position
III-ה	בָּנָה	ה in third root position
I-י	יָשַׁב	י in first root position
I-נ	נָפַל	נ in first root position
Doubly Weak	עָלָה	I-Guttural *and* III-ה
Biconsonantal	קָם	only two root consonants[3]
Geminate	סָבַב	identical second and third consonants

12.14 **Word Order in the Hebrew Verbal Sentence.** In English, the ordering of words in a sentence helps to identify the function of those words. For example, in the sentence "Jacob loved Rachel," *Jacob* is the subject of the verb because his name precedes the verb. Additionally, *Rachel* is the object of the verb because her name follows the verb. If the sentence was "Rachel loved Jacob," then *Rachel* would be the subject and *Jacob* the object because of their positions in the sentence. In English, normal word order is subject-verb-object. In Hebrew, however, normal word order for a verbal sentence is *verb-subject-object* as the following example illustrates.

בָּרָא אֱלֹהִים אֵת הַשָּׁמַיִם וְאֵת הָאָרֶץ

God created the heavens and the earth (Gen 1:1).

In this example, the verb is in first position (בָּרָא), the subject in second position (אֱלֹהִים) and the two objects follow the subject (הַשָּׁמַיִם and הָאָרֶץ). It must be acknowledged, however, that there are frequent variations and exceptions to this "normal" ordering of words in a Hebrew sentence. For example, it is not uncommon for the direct object to stand at the beginning of a Hebrew sentence for the purpose of emphasis as the following example illustrates.

---

[3] Biconsonantal verbs are also called "Hollow" or II-י/ו verbs (see 14.12).

אֶת־יְהוָה אֱלֹהֶיךָ תִּירָא

Yahweh your God you shall fear (Deut 10:20).

In this example, observe how the direct object (אֶת־יְהוָה אֱלֹהֶיךָ) precedes the verb (תִּירָא) for the purpose of emphasis. A discussion of issues related to sentence syntax is presented in chapter 23.

12.15 **Parsing Hebrew Verbs.** In the following chapters, you will learn how to "parse" Hebrew verbs. Parsing is the process whereby you will identify a verb's stem, conjugation, person, gender, number and lexical form. For example, the verb נִשְׁמַע is parsed as a Niphal Perfect third masculine singular (3ms) from שָׁמַע. You will get plenty of practice parsing verbs in the following chapters.

12.16 **Lexical Form for Hebrew Verbs.** The lexical form of any triconsonantal verb is the *Qal Perfect 3ms*. This is also the form of the verb that you will be memorizing as vocabulary. With Biconsonantal verbs, however, you will memorize a different lexical form (14.12).

12.17 **Summary.**

1. Verbs are those words used to describe an action or state of being.

2. A *root* represents the origin or simplest form from which any number of Hebrew words are derived. Most Hebrew verbs are triconsonantal.

3. Hebrew verbs can indicate person, gender and number by certain patterns of *inflection*.

4. Hebrew verbs may appear in seven different *stems*: the Qal and six derived stems (Niphal, Piel, Pual, Hiphal, Hophal, Hithpael). These stems indicate verbal action (simple, intensive, causative) and verbal voice (active, passive, reflexive).

5. Hebrew verbs may be inflected in eight different conjugations: Perfect, Imperfect, Imperative, Cohortative, Jussive, Infinitive Construct, Infinitive Absolute and Participle. The term "conjugation" is used to describe the inflected verbal forms that express particular verbal functions.

6. At the end of this chapter, we have included an illustration that attempts to graphically represent the relationship between Hebrew roots, stems and conjugations.

7. Hebrew verbs are classified as either *strong* or *weak* verbs. Weak verbs are those verbs having at least one weak root consonant. Strong verbs have no weak consonants.

8. Though frequent exceptions and variations do exist, the normal word order for a Hebrew verbal sentence is *verb-subject-object*.

9. The process of "parsing" a verb involves the identification of the verbal stem, conjugation, person, gender, number and lexical form.

10. The *lexical form* of any triconsonantal verb is the Qal Perfect 3ms.

12.18 Vocabulary.

Verbs

אָכַל	to eat (820)
אָמַר	to say (5,316)
הָלַךְ	to go, walk (1,554)
הָיָה	to be, happen, become (3,576)
יָצָא	to go (come) out, go (come) forth (1,076)
יָשַׁב	to sit, dwell, inhabit (1,088)
נָתַן	to give (2,016)
עָשָׂה	to do, make (2,632)
רָאָה	to see (1,311)
שָׁבַת	to cease, rest (71)
שָׁמַע	to hear, give ear to, obey (1,165)

Nouns

אֲרוֹן	ark, chest (202)
מִנְחָה	gift, offering (211)
שַׁבָּת	Sabbath, rest (111)

Other

אַךְ	only, surely (161)
אַל	no, not (729)
אִם	if, then (1,070)
לֹא	no, not (5,193)

12.19 Ulrich Zwingli (1484-1531): Languages are Gifts of the Holy Ghost. The beginning of the Reformation in Switzerland dates from the New Testament lectures of Ulrich Zwingli in 1519, just three years after his own study of the Scriptures led him to question and finally renounce the teaching of the Roman Church. Foundational to all of Zwingli's ministry was his conviction that the Scriptures bear sole authority in the life of the Christian.

Zwingli wrote a treatise on the proper godly education of youth, within which he emphasizes the necessity for the biblical languages. The following is an excerpt from this treatise.

> Once a young man is instructed in the solid virtue which is formed by faith, it follows that he will regulate himself and richly adorn himself from within: for only he whose whole life is ordered finds it easy to give help and counsel to others.

> But a man cannot rightly order his own soul unless he exercises himself day and night in the Word of God. He can do that most readily if he is well versed in such languages as Hebrew and Greek, for a right understanding of the Old Testament is difficult without the one, and a right understanding of the New is equally difficult without the other.

> But we are instructing those who have already learned the rudiments, and everywhere Latin has the priority. In these circumstances I do not think that Latin should be altogether neglected. For an understanding of Holy Scripture it is of less value than Hebrew and Greek, but for other purposes it is just as useful. And it often happens that we have to do the business of Christ amongst those who speak Latin. No Christian should use these languages simply for his own profit or pleasure: for languages are gifts of the Holy Ghost.

After Latin we should apply ourselves to Greek. We should do this for the sake of the New Testament, as I have said already. And if I may say so, to the best of my knowledge the Greeks have always handled the doctrine of Christ better than the Latins. For that reason we should always direct our young men to this source. But in respect of Greek as well as Latin we should take care to garrison our souls with innocence and faith, for in these tongues there are many things which we learn only to our hurt: wantonness, ambition, violence, cunning, vain philosophy and the like. But the soul … can steer safely past all these if it is only forewarned, that is, if at the first sound of the voices it pays heed to the warning: Hear this in order to shun and not to receive.

I put Hebrew last because Latin is in general use and Greek follows conveniently. Otherwise I would willingly have given Hebrew precedence, for in many places even amongst the Greeks those who are ignorant of Hebrew forms of speech have great difficulty in attempting to draw out the true sense of Scripture. But it is not my purpose to speak exhaustively of these languages.

If a man would penetrate to the heavenly wisdom, with which no earthly wisdom ought rightly to be considered, let alone compared, it is with such arms that he must be equipped. And even then he must still approach with a humble and thirsting spirit.[4]

---

[4] Ulrich Zwingli, "On the Education of Youth," in *Zwingli and Bullinger*, The Library of Christian Classics: Ichthus Edition, ed. G. W. Bromiley (Philadelphia: The Westminster Press, 1953) 108-09.

Verbal Root, Stems & Conjugations

Root
קטל

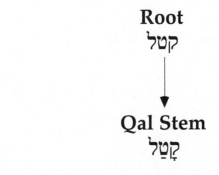

Qal Stem
קָטַל

Derived Stems

Niphal	Piel	Pual	Hiphil	Hophal	Hithpael
נִקְטַל	קִטֵּל	קֻטַּל	הִקְטִיל	הָקְטַל	הִתְקַטֵּל

Verbal Conjugations

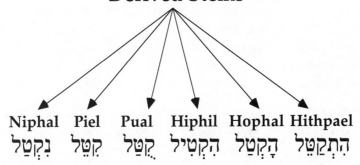

Perfect
Imperfect
Imperative
Cohortative
Jussive
Inf Construct
Inf Absolute
Participle

Chapter 13

Qal Perfect - Strong Verbs

13.1 **Introduction.** Of the almost 72,000 verbs in the Hebrew Bible, over two-thirds (50,699 verbs) occur in the Qal stem. For this reason, significant attention will be given to the various forms of the Qal stem in the following chapters. Only after the Qal stem has been mastered will the derived stems be studied. In this grammar, memorization of paradigms will be kept to a minimum. Only in your study of the Qal stem will paradigm memorization be required. Once we move into the derived stems, no further paradigm memorization is required. Instead, you will learn a system of *diagnostic* indicators whereby identification of the derived stems and their conjugations are made possible without the burden of memorizing paradigms. The use of *diagnostic* indicators is an important and unique feature of this grammar. It should make learning the Hebrew verbal system much easier than the traditional method of paradigm memorization for the conjugations of the derived stems.

13.2 **The Qal Stem.** The Qal is the simple or basic verbal stem. Qal verbs are *active* in voice, though a few passive forms do exist. The Qal stem also exhibits the *simple* or unnuanced type of action. An example of a verb in the Qal stem is קָטַל meaning "he killed." The simple action of the Qal stem is further divided into transitive, intransitive and stative.

1. *Transitive.* Transitive verbs may take a direct object. In the example "the prophet wrote the book," the word "book" is the direct object of the verb "wrote" because it receives the verbal action.

2. *Intransitive.* Intransitive verbs cannot take a direct object. In the example "the king perished in the battle," the verb "perished" cannot take a direct object. Other examples of intransitive verbs include "to live," "to die" and "to fast."

3. *Stative.* Stative verbs are used to describe a state of being. In the example, "the priest is old," the verbal construction "is old" describes the state or condition of the subject (the priest). In English, a stative (or state-of-being) idea is expressed with a form of the verb "to be" (is) and an adjective (old). In Hebrew,

a stative idea is expressed through various verbs themselves, such as כָּבֵד (to be heavy) and קָטֹן (to be small). Most stative verbs are considered to be intransitive because they cannot take a direct object.

13.3 **The Perfect Conjugation**. The Perfect conjugation is used to express a *completed action* or *state of being*. When used to describe a completed action (either in reality or in the mind of the speaker), the Hebrew Perfect may be translated by the English past tense (he studied), present perfect (he has studied), past perfect (he had studied) or future perfect (he will have studied). When used to describe a state of being, it will be translated with the English present tense (he is wise). The Hebrew Perfect may also be translated by the English present tense with verbs of perception or attitude (he knows, he loves). It must be emphasized that the Hebrew Perfect does not have tense (time of action) apart from context and issues of syntax. Rather, it signifies aspect (type of action). The Perfect aspect designates a verbal action with its conclusion envisioned in the mind of the speaker or writer. To state it differently, *the Perfect aspect denotes completed action, whether in the past, present or future*.

13.4 **Introduction to Qal Perfect Strong Verbs**. The Perfect conjugation is sometimes called the "suffix" conjugation. It has been called the suffix conjugation because different inflectional endings or *sufformatives* are added to the Qal stem in order to indicate person, gender and number. *The following Qal Perfect paradigm must be memorized with a view to both writing and oral recitation*. When writing out the paradigm, exact spelling of all consonants, vowels and accent marks is required. When practicing oral recitation, be as clear and precise as possible. Be sure to make a distinction in pronunciation, for example, between the Qamets and Pathach. This type of precision will aid in the subsequent spelling of verbal forms. In the following paradigm, both the complete verbal paradigm and the Perfect sufformatives are listed together. This should help you to identify the distinctive endings used to indicate person, gender and number. In every Perfect conjugation of the derived stems, whether Qal, Niphal, Piel, etc., the sufformatives are the same. For this reason, it is important to memorize these endings now.

13.5   The Qal Perfect Paradigm of the Strong Verb.

	Sufformative	*Perfect*	*Translation*
3ms		קָטַל	he killed
3fs	הָ֖	קָטְלָה	she killed
2ms	תָּ	קָטַ֫לְתָּ	you killed
2fs	תְּ	קָטַלְתְּ	you killed
1cs	תִּי	קָטַ֫לְתִּי	I killed
3cp	וּ	קָטְלוּ	they killed
2mp	תֶּם	קְטַלְתֶּם	you killed
2fp	תֶּן	קְטַלְתֶּן	you killed
1cp	נוּ	קָטַ֫לְנוּ	we killed

13.6   Notes on the Qal Perfect Paradigm of the Strong Verb.

1. The ordering of this paradigm might seem a bit unusual. The presentation of forms moves from third person to the second and first person, singular then plural. Notice how the paradigm begins with the third masculine singular (3ms) form, קָטַל. This is the *lexical form*. Because the third masculine singular form is also the lexical form, its definition may be listed as "to kill" in the lexicon. It is, however, never translated this way when used in a sentence. In a sentence, קָטַל translates "he killed." This is also the only Perfect form that does not have a sufformative. Most strong triconsonantal verbal roots follow this same vowel pattern in the third masculine singular form. The following graphic illustrates the common vowel pattern of the Qal Perfect 3ms strong verb.

Qal Perfect 3ms
Strong Verb

קָטַל

2. With regard to gender, three forms of the Perfect conjugation are listed as *common, meaning not inflected for gender*. The common

forms are first person singular (קָטַ֫לְתִּי) and plural (קָטַ֫לְנוּ) and third person plural (קָטְלוּ). As common forms, these verbs may be used with either masculine or feminine subjects.

3. Once you have mastered the spelling and pronunciation of the Qal Perfect paradigm listed above, you are encouraged to practice the Perfect inflection with other strong verbs. The following verbs are given as examples for practice: יָשַׁב (to sit, dwell, inhabit), זָכַר (to remember), כָּתַב (to write), שָׁמַר (to keep, observe) and קָבַץ (to gather). Remember, both the vocalization (vowel pattern) and sufformatives (inflectional endings) will remain the same for these verbs. Only the root consonants will change as you work with different verbs. In order to show the uniformity of these verbal forms, their full paradigms are presented in the next section.

4. Note the presence of the Metheg in the 3fs (קָֽטְלָה) and 3cp (קָֽטְלוּ) forms which serves to identify the vowel as Qamets and *not* Qamets Hatuf.

13.7 The Qal Perfect Paradigm of Other Strong Verbs. Based on your memorization of the קָטַל paradigm above, you should be able to generate the full Qal Perfect paradigm for each of the following strong verbs. Only the verbal root consonants will change.

	יָשַׁב to dwell	זָכַר to remember	כָּתַב to write	שָׁמַר to keep	קָבַץ to gather
3ms	יָשַׁב	זָכַר	כָּתַב	שָׁמַר	קָבַץ
3fs	יָֽשְׁבָה	זָכְרָה	כָּתְבָה	שָׁמְרָה	קָֽבְצָה
2ms	יָשַׁ֫בְתָּ	זָכַ֫רְתָּ	כָּתַ֫בְתָּ	שָׁמַ֫רְתָּ	קָבַ֫צְתָּ
2fs	יָשַׁבְתְּ	זָכַרְתְּ	כָּתַבְתְּ	שָׁמַרְתְּ	קָבַצְתְּ
1cs	יָשַׁ֫בְתִּי	זָכַ֫רְתִּי	כָּתַ֫בְתִּי	שָׁמַ֫רְתִּי	קָבַ֫צְתִּי
3cp	יָֽשְׁבוּ	זָכְרוּ	כָּתְבוּ	שָׁמְרוּ	קָֽבְצוּ
2mp	יְשַׁבְתֶּם	זְכַרְתֶּם	כְּתַבְתֶּם	שְׁמַרְתֶּם	קְבַצְתֶּם
2fp	יְשַׁבְתֶּן	זְכַרְתֶּן	כְּתַבְתֶּן	שְׁמַרְתֶּן	קְבַצְתֶּן
1cp	יָשַׁ֫בְנוּ	זָכַ֫רְנוּ	כָּתַ֫בְנוּ	שָׁמַ֫רְנוּ	קָבַ֫צְנוּ

13.8   **Verbal Roots Ending in ת.** When a verbal root ending in ת receives a suffformative beginning with ת, the two identical consonants become one consonant with a Daghesh Forte. In other words, תת is written as תּ. As you have observed from the above paradigms, five of the Perfect suffformatives begin with ת. These five Perfect forms of the Hebrew verb כָּרַת (to cut) illustrate this point.

כָּרַ֫תָּ	2ms	you cut
כָּרַתְּ	2fs	you cut
כָּרַ֫תִּי	1cs	I cut
כְּרַתֶּם	2mp	you cut
כְּרַתֶּן	2fp	you cut

As you can see, the two identical consonants have become one consonant. The final ת of the verbal root has assimilated into the initial ת of the Perfect suffformative. The presence of the first (assimilated) ת is indicated by the placement of the Daghesh Forte in the ת of the suffformative; תת is written as תּ.

13.9   **Verbal Roots Ending in נ.** Similar to the discussion in the preceding section, when a verbal root ending in נ receives a Perfect suffformative beginning with נ, the two identical consonants become one consonant with Daghesh Forte. The only suffformative that begins with נ is the 1cp (נוּ). Observe, therefore, that the 1cp form of שָׁכַן (to dwell) is written as שָׁכַ֫נּוּ. You would expect to see two Nuns in this form, the last letter of the verbal root and the first letter of the 1cp suffformative. The two identical consonants, however, become one consonant; ננ is written as נּ. This process of assimilation of נ in the 1cp form is also observable in those Perfect forms that have suffformatives beginning with ת. In other words, נת can also become תּ. For example, the 1cs form of the verb נָתַן (to give) is נָתַ֫תִּי. The final נ of the verbal root has assimilated into the ת of the suffformative and its presence is represented by the Daghesh Forte (see 14.18 for the Qal Perfect paradigm of נָתַן).

13.10 **Stative Verbs: Perfect.** You learned above that stative verbs are used to describe a state of being. More specifically, they describe the state or condition of the subject (he is old, she is wise) rather than describing a verbal action (he wrote, she observed).[1] Stative verbs are classified by

---

[1] Most stative verbs are intransitive, that is, they do not take a direct object.

their stem vowel. *The stem vowel is the vowel that is associated with the second root consonant.* For example, in the strong verb paradigms above, the stem vowel is Pathach as in שָׁמַר ,קָטַל and זָכַר. With stative verbs, however, the stem vowel is variable as the following examples illustrate.

Pathach-Stative	גָּדַל	to be(come) great
	חָכַם	to be wise
Tsere-Stative	כָּבֵד	to be heavy
	זָקֵן	to be old
Holem-Stative	קָטֹן	to be small
	יָכֹל	to be able

Presented above are three different types of stative verb. Each type is distinguished by its stem vowel. The Pathach-Stative is spelled just like the other strong verbs you have studied in this chapter. The Tsere-Stative and Holem-Stative, however, are spelled with a different stem vowel in some forms. Their full paradigms are presented below.

| | גָּדַל | כָּבֵד | קָטֹן |
	Pathach-Stative	Tsere-Stative	Holem-Stative
3ms	גָּדַל	כָּבֵד	קָטֹן
3fs	גָּדְלָה	כָּבְדָה	קָטְנָה
2ms	גָּדַלְתָּ	כָּבַדְתָּ	קָטֹנְתָּ
2fs	גָּדַלְתְּ	כָּבַדְתְּ	קָטֹנְתְּ
1cs	גָּדַלְתִּי	כָּבַדְתִּי	קָטֹנְתִּי
3cp	גָּדְלוּ	כָּבְדוּ	קָטְנוּ
2mp	גְּדַלְתֶּם	כְּבַדְתֶּם	קְטָנְתֶּם
2fp	גְּדַלְתֶּן	כְּבַדְתֶּן	קְטָנְתֶּן
1cp	גָּדַלְנוּ	כָּבַדְנוּ	קָטֹנּוּ

Though rare, certain verbs that are spelled like a stative may be transitive as illustrated by שָׂנֵה (to hate). This verb can take a direct object.

Notes:

1. The Pathach-Stative (גָּדַל) is spelled just like the regular strong verb. There are no spelling changes in this paradigm.

2. With the Tsere-Stative, the Tsere stem vowel appears only in the 3ms form (כָּבֵד). All other forms are spelled just like the regular strong verb.

3. With the Holem-Stative, an o-class stem vowel appears throughout the paradigm (except in the 3fs and 3cp). The only change in this paradigm, therefore, is the o-class stem vowel. In every other way, it is vocalized just like the regular strong verb. Note the o-class vowel Qamets Hatuf in the 2mp (קְטָנְתֶּם) and 2fp (קְטָנְתֶּן) forms. You should also note that in the 1cp form (קָטֹנּוּ), the נ of the verbal root has assimilated into the נ of the Perfect sufformative and is represented by the Daghesh Forte.

4. Stative verbs are closely related to their corresponding adjectives. For example, the form זָקֵן is either the Qal Perfect 3ms stative verb (he is old) or the masculine singular adjective (old). Note the following additional examples.

Stative Verb Qal Perfect 3ms		Adjective Masculine Singular	
כָּבֵד	to be heavy	כָּבֵד	heavy
מָלֵא	to be full	מָלֵא	full
טָמֵא	to be unclean	טָמֵא	unclean
רָעֵב	to be hungry	רָעֵב	hungry

The difference, however, between a stative verb and its corresponding adjective is that one is inflected as a verb (above) and the other as an adjective: כָּבֵד (ms), כְּבֵדִים (mp), כְּבֵדָה (fs), כְּבֵדוֹת (fp). Note that identical forms exist only in the Qal Perfect 3ms and masculine singular adjective (כָּבֵד). In this case, you will need to rely on context in order to correctly identify the form. The Qal Perfect 3fs (כָּבְדָה) and feminine singular adjective (כְּבֵדָה) are similar but should not be confused.

13.11 **Parsing.** The parsing of Perfect verbs involves the identification of the verbal stem, conjugation, person, gender, number and verbal root. When parsing, give the appropriate information in the proper order as the following examples illustrate. Though it is given below, translation is not a required part of parsing information.

זָכַ֫רְתִּי	Qal Perfect 1cs	זָכַר	I remembered
שָׁמַ֫רְתְּ	Qal Perfect 2fs	שָׁמַר	you observed

13.12 **The Negative Particle לֹא.** Perfect (and Imperfect) verbs are negated with the particle לֹא, usually translated "not." It may also be spelled לוֹא.[2] The negative particle is always placed immediately before the verb. The following examples illustrate how this particle is used.

לֹא שְׁמַרְתֶּם אֶת־הַתּוֹרוֹת	You did *not* observe the laws.
לֹא זָכַרְתָּ אֶת־הַבְּרִית	You did *not* remember the covenant.

13.13 **The Particle הִנֵּה.** The word הִנֵּה (also as הֵן and הֶן־) is commonly translated "behold" in many, often older, translations. In vocabulary, this is the translation value that is to be memorized and it is the basic meaning given in most standard lexicons. Translated in this way, it could be called a demonstrative interjection but this is only one of its many uses and nuances. This particle has no exact equivalent in English.

הִנֵּה appears over 1,000 times in the Hebrew Bible. It can stand alone or take Type 1 pronominal suffixes (those attached to singular nouns). The attested forms with pronominal suffixes are presented in the following chart.

1cs	הִנֵּ֫נִי/הִנְנִי	1cp	הִנֶּ֫נּוּ/הִנְנוּ
2ms	הִנְּךָ	2mp	הִנְּכֶם
2fs	הִנֵּךְ	2fp	
3ms	הִנּוֹ	3mp	הִנָּם

While the particle הִנֵּה is used in a number of different ways, three common uses are detailed below.

---

[2] The negative particle לֹא occurs 5,193 times in the Hebrew Bible. It appears with the full spelling לוֹא 188 times.

1. The particle הִנֵּה may be used to add emphasis or to stress the importance of something (demonstrative interjection).

וַיַּרְא אֱלֹהִים אֶת־כָּל־אֲשֶׁר עָשָׂה וְהִנֵּה־טוֹב מְאֹד

And God saw all that he had made, and
behold, (it was) very good (Gen 1:31).

הִנֵּה עֵין יְהוָה אֶל־יְרֵאָיו

Behold, the eye of the Lord is upon
the ones who fear him (Ps 33:18).

2. The particle הִנֵּה may be used to indicate the immediate presence of someone or something with an emphasis on immediacy and urgency (predicator of existence).

וְהִנֵּה אָנֹכִי עִמָּךְ

And *behold*, I am with you (Gen 28:15).

וַיֹּאמֶר הִנֵּנִי

And he said, "*I am here*" (Gen 22:1). The form הִנֵּנִי (literally, "behold me") is the particle הִנֵּה with 1cs pronominal suffix.

3. The particle הִנֵּה may be used to introduce a fact or situation upon which a subsequent statement is based.

וַיֹּאמֶר שְׁמוּאֵל אֶל־כָּל־יִשְׂרָאֵל הִנֵּה שָׁמַעְתִּי בְקֹלְכֶם
לְכֹל אֲשֶׁר־אֲמַרְתֶּם לִי וָאַמְלִיךְ עֲלֵיכֶם מֶלֶךְ

And Samuel said to all of Israel, "*Behold*, I have listened to all
that you have said to me and (therefore) I will
cause a king to reign over you" (1 Sam 12:1).

הִנֵּה־נָא יָדַעְתִּי כִּי אִשָּׁה יְפַת־מַרְאֶה אָתְּ וְהָיָה כִּי־יִרְאוּ
אֹתָךְ הַמִּצְרִים . . . וְהָרְגוּ אֹתִי וְאֹתָךְ יְחַיּוּ

Behold, I know that you are a woman with a beautiful
appearance and (so) when the Egyptians see you . . .
they will kill me but let you live (Gen 12:11-12).

13.14 Summary.

1. The Qal stem is the simple or basic verbal stem. It is used to express *simple action* with an *active voice*.

2. The simple action of the Qal stem may be either *transitive* (taking a direct object), *intransitive* (not taking a direct object) or *stative* (describing a state of being).

3. The Perfect conjugation is used to express a *completed action* and is translated with the English past tense (also with the English present perfect, past perfect and future perfect tenses). It may also be used to describe a *state of being* and, as such, will be translated with the English present tense.

4. The Perfect conjugation is also called the "suffix" conjugation because different inflectional endings or *sufformatives* are added to the verbal root in order to indicate person, gender and number.

5. You must memorize the Qal Perfect paradigm of the strong verb. You must also memorize the Perfect sufformatives.

6. When a verbal root ending in ת receives a sufformative beginning with ת, the two identical consonants become one consonant with a Daghesh Forte; תת is written as תּ (כָּרַ֫תָּ).

7. When a verbal root ending in נ receives a Perfect sufformative beginning with נ, the two identical consonants become one consonant with Daghesh Forte; ננ is written as נּ (שָׁכַ֫נּוּ). This final נ of the verbal root may also assimilate into the initial ת of those sufformatives that begin with ת, that is, נת is written as תּ (נָתַ֫תִּי).

8. Stative verbs are classified by their stem vowel. *The stem vowel is the vowel that is associated with the second root consonant.* The Pathach-Stative (גָּדַל) is spelled just like the regular strong verb. The Tsere-Stative has a Tsere stem vowel only in the Qal Perfect 3ms (כָּבֵד). The Holem-Stative has an o-class stem vowel in all forms (קָטֹן), except the 3fs and 3cp.

9. Perfect (and Imperfect) verbs are negated with the particle לֹא. This particle is always placed immediately before the verb.

10. The particle הִנֵּה is commonly translated as "behold." It may be used to add emphasis (demonstrative interjection), to indicate the immediate presence of someone or something (predicator of existence), or to introduce a fact or situation upon which a subsequent statement is based.

13.15 Vocabulary.

Verbs

בָּרַךְ	to bless (327)
זָכַר	to remember (235)
זָקֵן	to be(come) old (26)
חָזַק	to be(come) strong (290)
יָדַע	to know (957)
כָּבֵד	to be heavy (114)
כָּתַב	to write (225)
מָלֵא	to be full, fill, fulfill (252)
מָלַךְ	to reign, be king (350)
מָצָא	to find (457)
פָּקַד	to visit, number, appoint (304)
שָׁכַב	to lie down, have sexual intercourse (213)
שָׁלַח	to stretch out, let go, send (847)
שָׁמַר	to keep, watch, guard, observe (469)

13.16 At Your Service. הִנֵּה is a particle that may mark temporal and spatial immediacy. Typically found in direct discourse, this particle often appears with a pronominal suffix to emphasize the subject who is available *here and now*. The traditional translation "behold" is not only outdated in modern English but it fails to convey the full freight of meaning this common particle carries. For example, הִנֵּנִי may be translated "Here I am" or "I'm ready now" or, more colloquially, "At your service." This simple response is a motif in the story of the binding of Isaac. When God prepares to test Abraham, he calls his covenant partner by name. The respectful response is הִנֵּנִי (Gen 22:1). When Isaac wants an explanation for their journey, he calls his father and gets the same response: הִנֵּנִי (22:7). At the point in the story when the angel calls to Abraham, his answer again is הִנֵּנִי (22:11). Abraham is rewarded for his unqualified availability and unhesitating readiness to obey, qualities implicit in the simple response הִנֵּנִי. This is the response Samuel gives first to Eli and then to the Lord when he is called in the night (1 Sam 3). It is also the response Isaiah gives to the question "Whom shall I send?" in Isa 6:8: "*Here I am.* Send me!"

For a sense of immediacy, an author will often use the construction הִנֵּה (often with a suffix) plus a Participle. For example, Yahweh says to Noah in Gen 6:17, "*I am about to* bring the flood" (וַאֲנִי הִנְנִי מֵבִיא אֶת־הַמַּבּוּל). No prophet uses this form more than Jeremiah (some 150 times) who is intent on emphasizing the *imminence* of God's judgement. For example, Jer 11:11 reads, "*Surely I am about to* bring upon them evil" (הִנְנִי מֵבִיא אֲלֵיהֶם רָעָה). The most common use of this construction in Jeremiah (and throughout the Old Testament) is with the verb בּוֹא. Jeremiah says twenty-one times, "The days are approaching when ..." (הִנֵּה יָמִים בָּאִים). Although this phrase typically introduces the threat of judgement, the good news in Jeremiah is that *God's grace is also imminent.* In 23:5 God promises the coming of a Righteous Branch; in 30:3, the restoration of their fortunes; and in 31:31, a new covenant.

Tim Laniak
Assistant Professor of Old Testament
Gordon-Conwell Theological Seminary
Charlotte, North Carolina

Chapter 14

Qal Perfect - Weak Verbs

14.1 **Introduction.** Now that you have studied the Qal Perfect forms of the strong verb, we turn to the Qal Perfect inflection of various weak verb types. In chapter 12, you learned that weak verbs are those verbs having one or more weak root consonants. The presence of a weak consonant in a verbal root can cause changes in the vocalization or spelling of the verb. In order to successfully identify or parse weak verbal forms, these changes must be studied and, in many cases, memorized. All such weak variations are identifiable only in comparison with the strong verb form. You should not work through this chapter of the grammar, therefore, until you have mastered the Qal Perfect strong verb paradigm in the previous chapter.

14.2 **I-Guttural, II-Guttural and III-ה/ע Weak Verbs.** I-Guttural weak verbs have a guttural for the first root consonant as in עָמַד meaning "to stand." II-Guttural weak verbs have a guttural for the second root consonant as in בָּחַר meaning "to choose." III-ה/ע weak verbs have either ה or ע for the third root consonant as in לָקַח, meaning "to take" or שָׁמַע meaning "to hear." These weak verbs are studied together because they exhibit a similar type of change compared to the strong verb paradigm. The changes in the I-Guttural and II-Guttural paradigms are minor and you have already learned the rule that governs them. It has to do with the relationship between gutturals and the Vocal Shewa. You will recall from section 3.6 that *a guttural cannot take a Vocal Shewa but prefers the reduced a-vowel, Hateph Pathach.* For this reason, the few Vocal Shewas that occur in the strong verb paradigm will change to a Hateph Pathach when the strong consonant is replaced by a guttural consonant. In the three weak paradigms listed below, there are only five total changes. The strong verb paradigm is also included for comparison. *Please note that, despite any changes in vocalization due to the presence of a guttural consonant, the Perfect sufformatives do not change.*

	I-Guttural	II-Guttural	III-ח/ע	Strong
3ms	עָמַד	בָּחַר	שָׁמַע	קָטַל
3fs	עָמְדָה	בָּחֲרָה	שָׁמְעָה	קָטְלָה
2ms	עָמַׁדְתָּ	בָּחַׁרְתָּ	שָׁמַׁעְתָּ	קָטַׁלְתָּ
2fs	עָמַדְתְּ	בָּחַרְתְּ	שָׁמַ֫עַתְּ	קָטַלְתְּ
1cs	עָמַׁדְתִּי	בָּחַׁרְתִּי	שָׁמַׁעְתִּי	קָטַׁלְתִּי
3cp	עָמְדוּ	בָּחֲרוּ	שָׁמְעוּ	קָטְלוּ
2mp	עֲמַדְתֶּם	בְּחַרְתֶּם	שְׁמַעְתֶּם	קְטַלְתֶּם
2fp	עֲמַדְתֶּן	בְּחַרְתֶּן	שְׁמַעְתֶּן	קְטַלְתֶּן
1cp	עָמַׁדְנוּ	בָּחַׁרְנוּ	שָׁמַׁעְנוּ	קָטַׁלְנוּ

14.3 **I-Guttural, II-Guttural and III-ח/ע Weak Notes**. The following notes and observations will help as you work through these paradigms.

1. In the I-Guttural and II-Guttural paradigms, the Vocal Shewas have changed to the reduced a-vowel, Hateph Pathach due to the presence of the guttural consonants (בְּחַרְתֶּם ,עֲמַדְתֶּן ,עֲמַדְתֶּם, בָּחֲרוּ). Because the changes in vocalization are minor and follow a standard rule, there is no need to memorize the I-Guttural and II-Guttural paradigms listed above. You should memorize, however, the rule governing these changes. Once again, it is important to have first memorized the Qal Perfect strong verb paradigm. If you know the strong verb paradigm and the rule governing the gutturals and Vocal Shewa, then you will not have to memorize these weak verb paradigms.

2. In the III-ח/ע paradigm, the Silent Shewa under the guttural of the 2fs form שָׁמַ֫עַתְּ has changed to Pathach. This is the only change to be noted in this weak verb class. There is no need to memorize the full paradigm on account of this minor change. You should simply be aware of the anomaly.

14.4 **III-א Weak Verbs**. These weak verbs have א for the third root consonant as in מָצָא meaning "to find." The changes in this type of weak verb are considerable compared to the last three weak verb classes. You will recall from section 3.9 that an א is silent when there is no vowel under it as in the noun חַטָּאת (sin). With III-א weak verbs, the א is silent in almost every inflected form. For this reason, the changes in vocalization are significant when compared to the strong verb paradigm. Because these changes are so pronounced, *memorization of the III-א paradigm is required.*

	III-א	*Strong*
3ms	מָצָא	קָטַל
3fs	מָצְאָה	קָטְלָה
2ms	מָצָאתָ	קָטַלְתָּ
2fs	מָצָאת	קָטַלְתְּ
1cs	מָצָאתִי	קָטַלְתִּי
3cp	מָצְאוּ	קָטְלוּ
2mp	מְצָאתֶם	קְטַלְתֶּם
2fp	מְצָאתֶן	קְטַלְתֶּן
1cp	מָצָאנוּ	קָטַלְנוּ

14.5   **III-א Weak Notes.** The following notes and observations will help as you work through the III-א weak verb paradigm.

1. The differences begin with the first form in the paradigm. The 3ms form (מָצָא) does not have the standard vowel pattern previously illustrated for all strong triconsonantal verbal forms. All III-א and III-ה weak verbs exhibit the following pattern in their 3ms or lexical form.

Qal Perfect 3ms
III-א / III-ה
בנה / מצא

2. The stem vowel (the vowel under the second root consonant) has changed from Pathach to Qamets in all but two forms in the above paradigm (3fs and 3cp).

3. Because of the quiescent **א**, the expected Shewa under the third root consonant of many of the inflected forms is no longer necessary.

4. You will notice that the Daghesh Lene, normally in the initial consonant of the five sufformatives beginning with a **ת**, is absent. For example, the 1cs sufformative **תִּי** has become **תִי**, losing the Daghesh Lene. This loss is occasioned by the quiescing of the **א** in pronunciation. When this happens, the **ת** is preceded by a vowel sound and, therefore, loses the Daghesh Lene. Remember, however, that though the **א** is not pronounced, it is essential to the spelling of the word.

5. The changes in this paradigm are significant enough to warrant memorization of the entire paradigm. Be certain that you can recite and write the full Qal Perfect paradigm of **מָצָא** (to find).

14.6   **III-ה Weak Verbs**. These weak verbs have **ה** for the third root consonant as in **בָּנָה**, meaning "to build." As with III-**א** weak verbs, the changes in this weak class are considerable compared to the strong verb paradigm. The most significant change in this paradigm is the loss of the final **ה** root consonant in every form of the Perfect. For this reason, and because of the frequency of III-**ה** verbs, *memorization of the following paradigm is required.*

	III-ה	*Strong*
3ms	בָּנָה	קָטַל
3fs	בָּנְתָה	קָטְלָה
2ms	בָּנִֽיתָ	קָטַ֫לְתָּ
2fs	בָּנִית	קָטַלְתְּ
1cs	בָּנִֽיתִי	קָטַ֫לְתִּי
3cp	בָּנוּ	קָטְלוּ
2mp	בְּנִיתֶם	קְטַלְתֶּם
2fp	בְּנִיתֶן	קְטַלְתֶּן
1cp	בָּנִֽינוּ	קָטַ֫לְנוּ

14.7   III-ה Weak Notes.

1. The vowel pattern learned for III-א weak verbs is the same for III-ה weak verbs in the 3ms.

2. It has already been mentioned that the irregularities of this weak verb are occasioned by the loss of the final ה *in every form of the paradigm*. The ה in the 3ms form (בָּנָה) is not a root consonant but rather a vowel letter (also called a *mater lectionis*) used for the final vowel of this form (2.10).

3. Another unusual feature of this paradigm is the ת in the 3fs form (בָּנְתָה). The ת will distinguish the 3fs form from the 3ms form.

4. It is important to observe that all second and first person forms, both singular and plural, have a distinctive or diagnostic stem vowel. In each of these forms, the stem vowel is Hireq Yod (for example, בָּנִיתָ). It is helpful to understand that III-ה verbs were originally III-י and the stem vowel of a form like בָּנִיתָ is reminiscent of the original consonant in third root position (see also 22.8.4). In the Qal conjugation, the diagnostic Hireq Yod stem vowel will help you to identify the III-ה class of verbs.

5. Lastly, as in the III-א paradigm, the Daghesh Lene in the sufformatives beginning with ת is absent. This loss of the Daghesh Lene is due to the fact that the *begadkephat* consonant (ת) is now preceded by a vowel, the distinctive Hireq Yod stem vowel.

14.8   Doubly Weak Verbs. Verbs of this type have more than one weak consonant as part of their verbal root. Most of the verbs in this weak class are both III-ה and I-Guttural or II-Guttural.[1] The Perfect paradigm

---

[1] Examples include רָעָה (to feed, graze, tend flocks), עָשָׂה (to do, make), חָרָה (to become angry) and הָרָה (to conceive, become pregnant). However, not all doubly

of a doubly weak verb will combine the spelling variations of its two weak consonants. However, once you have mastered the types of changes that occur in the weak verbs presented in 14.2-7, you should have little difficulty identifying the Qal Perfect forms of doubly weak verbs. Because of their frequency, two doubly weak III-ה verbs will be studied here: רָאָה (to see) and עָלָה (to go up). The first is III-ה/II-Guttural and the second is III-ה/I-Guttural

	III-ה/ II-Gutt	III-ה/ I-Gutt	*Strong Verb*
3ms	רָאָה	עָלָה	קָטַל
3fs	רָאֲתָה	עָלְתָה	קָטְלָה
2ms	רָאִֽיתָ	עָלִֽיתָ	קָטַֽלְתָּ
2fs	רָאִית	עָלִית	קָטַלְתְּ
1cs	רָאִֽיתִי	עָלִֽיתִי	קָטַֽלְתִּי
3cp	רָאוּ	עָלוּ	קָטְלוּ
2mp	רְאִיתֶם	עֲלִיתֶם	קְטַלְתֶּם
2fp	רְאִיתֶן	עֲלִיתֶן	קְטַלְתֶּן
1cp	רָאִֽינוּ	עָלִֽינוּ	קָטַֽלְנוּ

14.9   Doubly Weak Notes.

1. In both doubly weak paradigms, the changes learned for III-ה verbs are fully present: (1) the loss of final ה in every form; (2) the insertion of ת in the 3fs form; (3) the presence of the diagnostic Hireq Yod stem vowel; and (4) the loss of the Daghesh Lene in the suffformatives beginning with ת.

2. In these doubly weak verbal roots, the changes occasioned by the III-ה weak verb class are combined with the changes caused by the presence of additional guttural consonants. These types of changes should be familiar to you by now. In the 3fs form (רָאֲתָה), the expected Vocal Shewa under the guttural א has changed to the Hateph Pathach because a guttural cannot take a

---

weak verbs are III-ה. For example, the verbs אָהַב (to love), אָחַז (to seize) and חָטָא (to sin) are doubly weak but not III-ה.

Vocal Shewa but rather prefers the Hateph Pathach vowel. For the same reason, the 2mp (עֲלִיתֶם) and 2fp (עֲלִיתֶן) forms have the Hateph Pathach under the initial guttural consonant. Although the full memorization of these paradigms might be helpful, it is not considered essential if you have already memorized the paradigm of the III-ה weak verb and remember that gutturals reject the Vocal Shewa.

14.10 Geminate Verbs. Verbs of this class have identical second and third root consonants as in סָבַב meaning "to go around." Other examples include אָרַר (to curse) and תָּמַם (to be finished). Verbs of this type exhibit two major changes. In most forms, the first Geminate consonant assimilates into the second Geminate consonant and is represented as a Daghesh Forte. Secondly, there is the insertion of a "connecting" vowel, the Holem Waw (וֹ), between the verbal root and the sufformative. The presence of the Holem Waw "connecting" vowel is a helpful way to identify the Qal Perfect of Geminate verbs. In the following paradigms, three Geminate verbs are presented for study. Only the first paradigm, using סָבַב, needs to be memorized.

	Geminate Strong	*Geminate Weak 1*	*Geminate Weak 2*	*Strong Verb*
3ms	סָבַב	אָרַר	תַּם	קָטַל
3fs	סָבְבָה	אָרְרָה	תַּמָּה	קָטְלָה
2ms	סַבּוֹתָ	אָרֹותָ	תַּמֹּותָ	קָטַלְתָּ
2fs	סַבּוֹת	אָרֹות	תַּמֹּות	קָטַלְתְּ
1cs	סַבּוֹתִי	אָרֹותִי	תַּמֹּותִי	קָטַלְתִּי
3cp	סָבְבוּ	אָרְרוּ	תַּמּוּ	קָטְלוּ
2mp	סַבּוֹתֶם	אֲרֹותֶם	תַּמֹּותֶם	קְטַלְתֶּם
2fp	סַבּוֹתֶן	אֲרֹותֶן	תַּמֹּותֶן	קְטַלְתֶּן
1cp	סַבּוֹנוּ	אָרֹונוּ	תַּמֹּונוּ	קָטַלְנוּ

14.11 Geminate Notes. All initial observations are directed primarily toward the forms of the Geminate verb סָבַב.

1. Note that all first and second person forms, both singular and plural, assimilate the first Geminate consonant into the second Geminate consonant with a resulting Daghesh Forte. In other words, בַב is written as בּ in the first and second person forms, singular and plural. This Daghesh Forte is a diagnostic feature of the Qal Perfect Geminate verb.

2. Additionally, all first and second person forms, both singular and plural, exhibit the Holem Waw (וֹ) connecting vowel. The presence of Holem Waw between the verbal root and the Perfect sufformative is a diagnostic feature of the Qal Perfect Geminate verb.

3. By now, you should expect the loss of Daghesh Lene in the initial ת of the sufformative when preceded by a vowel.

4. The verb אָרַר differs from סָבַב in one way. In the second and first person forms, singular and plural, the Geminate consonant rejects the Daghesh Forte and the Pathach under the א becomes Qamets due to compensatory lengthening.

5. Finally, with regard to the paradigm of תָּמַם, the Geminate consonants have assimilated in all forms and remain as a Daghesh Forte (except in the 3ms). Unlike the 3fs and 3cp forms of many Geminate verbs, note the presence of the Daghesh Forte in the Geminate consonant of these two forms (תַּמָּה and תַּמּוּ).

14.12 Biconsonantal Verbs. The study of verb forms to this point has been concerned with triconsonantal verbal roots, that is, roots composed of three consonants. The verbs have been either strong or weak but all of them have been composed of three consonants. We now begin the study of the so-called "Biconsonantal" class of weak verbs. As the name indicates, these verbs are composed of two consonants. Examples include קָם (to rise), שָׂם (to set, put) and בָּא (to enter).

Biconsonantal verbs are also called "Hollow" or II-י/ו verbs. These designations reflect the fact that Biconsonantal verbs, in some conjugations, exhibit a medial vowel letter. In the Perfect conjugation, however, these vowel letters are not present. Only in the Imperfect and related conjugations do they appear. It is important to note, at this point, that the lexical or dictionary form of a Biconsonantal verb is *not* the Qal Perfect 3ms form as in most verbs. These verbs are listed in the lexicon under their Infinitive Construct forms and, as such, appear with their vowel letters. In other words, קָם is listed under קוּם, שָׂם under שִׂים and בָּא under בּוֹא.

Carefully study the Qal Perfect paradigms of these three Biconsonantal verbs. The Perfect of קוּם should be memorized.

	Biconsonantal Paradigms			Strong
	Strong[2]	*Strong*	*Weak*	*Verb*
3ms	קָם	שָׂם	בָּא	קָטַל
3fs	קָ֫מָה	שָׂ֫מָה	בָּ֫אָה	קָטְלָה
2ms	קַ֫מְתָּ	שַׂ֫מְתָּ	בָּ֫אתָ	קָטַ֫לְתָּ
2fs	קַמְתְּ	שַׂמְתְּ	בָּאת	קָטַלְתְּ
1cs	קַ֫מְתִּי	שַׂ֫מְתִּי	בָּ֫אתִי	קָטַ֫לְתִּי
3cp	קָ֫מוּ	שָׂ֫מוּ	בָּ֫אוּ	קָטְלוּ
2mp	קַמְתֶּם	שַׂמְתֶּם	בָּאתֶם	קְטַלְתֶּם
2fp	קַמְתֶּן	שַׂמְתֶּן	בָּאתֶן	קְטַלְתֶּן
1cp	קַ֫מְנוּ	שַׂ֫מְנוּ	בָּ֫אנוּ	קָטַ֫לְנוּ

14.13 Biconsonantal Notes.

1. With the strong Biconsonantal paradigms (קוּם and שִׂים), *all third person forms* have Qamets under the first root consonant, while all other forms (first and second person) have Pathach.

2. In the weak paradigm (בּוֹא), *all forms* have Qamets under the first root consonant.

3. In the weak Biconsonantal paradigm, the א is quiescent as in III-א triconsonantal verbs. For this reason, the expected Daghesh Lene in the initial ת of selected Perfect sufformatives is absent.

---

[2] Though Biconsonantal verbs are considered weak, a "strong" Biconsonantal verb is one without a guttural consonant (קוּם). The verb בּוֹא, however, is considered to be a "weak" Biconsonantal verb because of the presence of the guttural (א).

14.14 **Summary**. At this point, you might feel a bit overwhelmed. All of the changes and variations presented in these weak verb paradigms can be intimidating at first. With time and continued exposure to weak verb forms, you will become more and more familiar with these changes. Actually, the variations observed in weak verbs are based upon only a few standard rules or patterns.

1. Of first importance is the need to memorize the strong verb paradigm and the Perfect sufformatives (chapter 13). The Perfect sufformatives will not change, despite any weakness in the verbal root.

2. Guttural consonants cannot take a Vocal Shewa and will prefer some type of a-vowel, usually Hateph Pathach. This accounts for changes in I-Guttural, II-Guttural and doubly weak verbs.

3. With III-א weak verbs, the א is quiescent. This causes the loss of the Daghesh Lene in the ת of the Perfect sufformatives because the ת is now preceded by a vowel.

4. With III-ה weak verbs, the final ה of the verbal root is lost in all forms of the Qal Perfect paradigm. All second and first person forms of this paradigm, both singular and plural, have the diagnostic Hireq Yod stem vowel (בָּנִיתָ). Additionally, the Daghesh Lene that is expected in the ת of the Perfect sufformatives is lost because this *begadkephat* consonant is preceded by a vowel (the Hireq Yod stem vowel).

5. With Geminate verbs like סָבַב (to go around), expect the assimilation of the first Geminate consonant into the second Geminate consonant with a resulting Daghesh Forte in all first and second person forms (סַבּוֹתָ). The Holem Waw (וֹ) connecting vowel is also a diagnostic feature of this weak verb class. As with III-א and III-ה verbs, the Daghesh Lene that is expected in the ת of the Perfect sufformative is lost because it is preceded by a vowel.

14.15 **Qal Perfect Paradigms: Strong and Weak Verbs**. The III-א, III-ה, Geminate and Biconsonantal paradigms must be memorized. You should be able to identify the forms of other weak verbs, given your knowledge of certain rules or patterns of inflection learned in this chapter.

Strong	*I-Gutt*	*II-Gutt*	*III-ח/ע*	*III-א*	*III-ה*	*Doubly Weak*	*Gem Verbs*	*Bicon Verbs*
קָטַל	עָמַד	בָּחַר	שָׁמַע	מָצָא	בָּנָה	עָלָה	סָבַב	קָם
קָטְלָה	עָמְדָה	בָּחֲרָה	שָׁמְעָה	מָצְאָה	בָּנְתָה	עָלְתָה	סָבְבָה	קָמָה
קָטַלְתָּ	עָמַדְתָּ	בָּחַרְתָּ	שָׁמַעְתָּ	מָצָאתָ	בָּנִיתָ	עָלִיתָ	סַבּוֹתָ	קַמְתָּ
קָטַלְתְּ	עָמַדְתְּ	בָּחַרְתְּ	שָׁמַעַתְּ	מָצָאת	בָּנִית	עָלִית	סַבּוֹת	קַמְתְּ
קָטַלְתִּי	עָמַדְתִּי	בָּחַרְתִּי	שָׁמַעְתִּי	מָצָאתִי	בָּנִיתִי	עָלִיתִי	סַבּוֹתִי	קַמְתִּי
קָטְלוּ	עָמְדוּ	בָּחֲרוּ	שָׁמְעוּ	מָצְאוּ	בָּנוּ	עָלוּ	סָבְבוּ	קָמוּ
קְטַלְתֶּם	עֲמַדְתֶּם	בְּחַרְתֶּם	שְׁמַעְתֶּם	מְצָאתֶם	בְּנִיתֶם	עֲלִיתֶם	סַבּוֹתֶם	קַמְתֶּם
קְטַלְתֶּן	עֲמַדְתֶּן	בְּחַרְתֶּן	שְׁמַעְתֶּן	מְצָאתֶן	בְּנִיתֶן	עֲלִיתֶן	סַבּוֹתֶן	קַמְתֶּן
קָטַלְנוּ	עָמַדְנוּ	בָּחַרְנוּ	שָׁמַעְנוּ	מָצָאנוּ	בָּנִינוּ	עָלִינוּ	סַבּוֹנוּ	קַמְנוּ

14.16 Vocabulary.

Verbs

בּוֹא	to go in, enter, come (2,591)
בָּנָה	to build (377)
יָלַד	to bring forth, bear (499)
יָרֵא	to fear, be afraid (317)
יָרַד	to go down (382)
לָקַח	to take (967)
מוּת	to die (854)
נָפַל	to fall (435)
נָשָׂא	to lift up, bear, carry (659)
עָלָה	to go up (894)
עָבַר	to pass over, transgress (553)

עָמַד   to stand (524)

קוּם   to rise, arise, stand (627)

קָרָא   to call, meet, read aloud (740)

שׁוּב   to turn, return (1,076)

שִׂים   to set, put, place (588)

Other

פֹּה   here (82)

14.17 We Have Not Come To an End.

חַסְדֵי יְהוָה כִּי לֹא־תָמְנוּ כִּי לֹא־כָלוּ רַחֲמָיו

The steadfast love of the Lord never ceases,
his mercies never come to an end.
Lam 3:22 (RSV)

Most of us are familiar with this English translation of Lam 3:22. Frequently, commentators and scholars have suggested that this text, as it presently stands, has suffered corruption in the history of its transmission. The first half of the verse does not seem straightforward, and the form תָמְנוּ (Qal Perfect 1cp of תָּמַם) is difficult because the root is both Geminate *and* stative. Many emend תָמְנוּ (Qal Perfect 1cp) to תַּמּוּ (Qal Perfect 3cp) on the basis of parallelism with כָלוּ (Qal Perfect 3cp) in the second half of the verse.[3] The second half of the verse is clear and may be translated "for his mercies have not come to an end." The emended line of text is translated "the steadfast love of Yahweh does not cease" (so RSV, NRSV, NJPS). Thus חַסְדֵי יְהוָה is considered the subject of the verb and כִּי is either considered emphatic or ignored. It is possible to consider that if חַסְדֵי יְהוָה is the subject, then it has been removed from the כִּי clause and placed at the front of the verse for emphasis. The dislocation of clause elements, or fronting, is not normal, however, in a כִּי clause (i.e., embedded sentence).

---

[3] Whether we read תָמְנוּ or תַּמּוּ, it must be noted that either form is pausal (see 36.3) and so the expected Pathach has been lengthened to Qamets. The non-pausal form תַּמְנוּ is attested elsewhere twice (Num 17:28 and Ps 64:7) and is clearly Qal Perfect 1cp.

Is it possible to make sense of the text by reading the verb as it currently stands? A function of כִּי that is standard is to nominalize its clause, i.e. reduce the entire clause to the level of a nominal (functioning as a noun). We would then have a verbless clause in which the construct phrase חַסְדֵי יְהוָה is the subject and the nominalized clause כִּי לֹא־תָמְנוּ is the predicate. Taken this way, it would be translated "The steadfast love of Yahweh is that we have not come to an end." This makes better sense of כִּי and the order of the words in the text. The argument to emend the text on the basis of parallelism is not strong; even when parallelism is synonymous, the parallel lines may say something slightly different from each other.

The text is saying something more powerful than that the steadfast love of the Lord never ceases. It is saying that it is due to the steadfast love of the Lord that we, the people of God, do not come to an end and, in this way, his mercies never fail. It is always better to patiently study the text as it stands than to rashly assume a corrupt text and emend it.

Peter J. Gentry
Associate Professor of Old Testament
The Southern Baptist Theological Seminary
Louisville, Kentucky

14.18 Advanced Information: נָתַן and הָיָה. Both נָתַן meaning "to give" and הָיָה meaning "to be" occur frequently throughout the Hebrew Bible. The multiple weaknesses of these verbal roots can, in certain forms, make their identification difficult. Their Qal Perfect forms are listed below.

	נָתַן *to give*	הָיָה *to be*	*Strong Verb*
3ms	נָתַן	הָיָה	קָטַל
3fs	נָתְנָה	הָיְתָה	קָטְלָה
2ms	נָתַתָּ	הָיִיתָ	קָטַלְתָּ
2fs	נָתַתְּ	הָיִית	קָטַלְתְּ
1cs	נָתַתִּי	הָיִיתִי	קָטַלְתִּי
3cp	נָתְנוּ	הָיוּ	קָטְלוּ
2mp	נְתַתֶּם	הֱיִיתֶם	קְטַלְתֶּם
2fp	נְתַתֶּן	הֱיִיתֶן	קְטַלְתֶּן
1cp	נָתַנּוּ	הָיִינוּ	קָטַלְנוּ

Notes: נָתַן and הָיָה.

1. In the Perfect conjugation of נָתַן, the final נ of the verbal root has assimilated into the first consonant of the Perfect sufformative in all first and second person forms.

2. With one minor deviation, the verb הָיָה inflects just like other III-ה verbs in the Qal Perfect. Note the presence of the Hateph Seghol in the 2mp (הֱיִיתֶם) and 2fp (הֱיִיתֶן) forms. The guttural ה cannot take a Vocal Shewa and, therefore, takes a reduced vowel (Hateph Seghol with הָיָה).

14.19 **Advanced Information:** יָרֵא **and** מוּת. The following verbs are both weak *and* stative. The verb יָרֵא (to be afraid) is III-א and מוּת (to die) is Biconsonantal.

	יָרֵא to be afraid	מוּת to die	Strong Verb
3ms	יָרֵא	מֵת	קָטַל
3fs	יָרְאָה	מֵתָה	קָטְלָה
2ms	יָרֵאתָ	מַתָּה [4]	קָטַלְתָּ
2fs	יָרֵאת	מַתְּ	קָטַלְתְּ
1cs	יָרֵאתִי	מַתִּי	קָטַלְתִּי
3cp	יָרְאוּ	מֵתוּ	קָטְלוּ
2mp	יְרֵאתֶם	מַתֶּם	קְטַלְתֶּם
2fp	יְרֵאתֶן	מַתֶּן	קְטַלְתֶּן
1cp	יָרֵאנוּ	מַתְנוּ	קָטַלְנוּ

---

[4] Note the assimilation of the final root consonant into the sufformative. This occurs in the 2ms, 2fs, 1cs, 2mp and 2fp forms.

Chapter 15

Qal Imperfect - Strong Verbs

15.1 **Introduction.** The Imperfect is the second major Hebrew verbal conjugation to be studied. Of the over 50,000 occurrences of the Qal stem in the Hebrew Bible, the Imperfect conjugation occurs 21,951 times, approximately forty-three percent of Qal stem occurrences.[1] Like the Perfect conjugation, the Imperfect inflects, or changes its form, in order to indicate person, gender and number.

15.2 **The Meaning of the Qal Imperfect.** The Imperfect conjugation is used to express *incomplete action* and is usually translated by the English present tense (I study) or future tense (I will study). The action of the verb occurs either at the time of speaking or after the time of speaking. The Hebrew Imperfect is also used to denote habitual or customary action, whether in the past, present or future (he prays regularly, he used to pray). The Imperfect may also be rendered by one of several modal values (would, could, should, may, might, can, etc.). These modal translation values are suggested by context and various issues of syntax. It must also be emphasized that, like the Perfect, the Hebrew Imperfect does not have tense (time of action) apart from context and issues of syntax. It too signifies aspect (type of action). The Imperfect aspect designates a verbal action for which, in the mind of the speaker or writer, the conclusion is not in view. To state it differently, *the Imperfect aspect denotes incomplete action, whether in the past, present or future.*

15.3 **The Form of the Qal Imperfect.** Recall that the Perfect conjugation is called the *suffix* conjugation because inflectional suffixes called *sufformatives* are attached to the verbal stem in order to indicate person, gender and number. The Imperfect conjugation is called the *prefix* conjugation because inflectional prefixes called *preformatives* are added to all Imperfect verbal forms. This preformative distinguishes the Imperfect conjugation from all other conjugations. It should also be

---

[1] The Imperfect conjugation in the remaining derived stems totals 9,303 occurrences. These statistics count both the regular Imperfect and the Imperfect with Waw Conversive.

noted, however, that half of the Imperfect verbal forms also take their own Imperfect sufformatives. The Imperfect paradigm must be memorized with a view to both writing and oral recitation. When writing out the paradigm, exact spelling of all consonants, vowels and accent marks is required. The preformatives and sufformatives of the Qal Imperfect are the same for all Imperfect forms in the derived stems, strong and weak verbs.

	Suffor-mative	Imperfect Paradigm	Prefor-mative	Translation
3ms		יִקְטֹל	יִ	he will kill
3fs		תִּקְטֹל	תִּ	she will kill
2ms		תִּקְטֹל	תִּ	you (ms) will kill
2fs	יִ	תִּקְטְלִי	תִּ	you (fs) will kill
1cs		אֶקְטֹל	אֶ	I will kill
3mp	וּ	יִקְטְלוּ	יִ	they (mp) will kill
3fp	נָה	תִּקְטֹלְנָה	תִּ	they (fp) will kill
2mp	וּ	תִּקְטְלוּ	תִּ	you (mp) will kill
2fp	נָה	תִּקְטֹלְנָה	תִּ	you (fp) will kill
1cp		נִקְטֹל	נִ	we will kill

15.4 Notes on the Qal Imperfect Strong Verb Paradigm.

1. Once again, precise memorization of this paradigm is essential. The careful memorization of this Qal Imperfect paradigm will prevent the need to memorize other Imperfect paradigms in subsequent chapters. All Imperfect verbs in the derived stems use these same preformatives and sufformatives.

2. As in the Perfect, the Imperfect paradigm moves from third person to first person, singular then plural.

3. In the Qal stem, only the Imperfect conjugation has a verbal preformative. Knowing this fact will make identification of Imperfect forms much easier. In the Qal, all preformative consonants have the Hireq vowel, except the 1cs form which has Seghol (אֶקְטֹל).

4. You have probably already noticed that two sets of forms are identical in the Imperfect paradigm. In each instance, context must provide the proper identification. Having duplicate forms, however, does make paradigm memorization easier!

תִּקְטֹל   both 3fs and 2ms (she will kill *or* you will kill)

תִּקְטֹלְנָה   both 3fp and 2fp (they will kill *or* you will kill)

5. In the Perfect, the third person plural form קָטְלוּ (they killed) is common. In the Imperfect, the third person plural is inflected for gender and so there are two third person forms: יִקְטְלוּ (3mp) and תִּקְטֹלְנָה (3fp).

6. The Imperfect prefix תֹ is a *begadkephat* letter. An initial *begadkephat* letter will normally have a Daghesh Lene as is seen in the above paradigm.

7. The stem vowel is Holem, except in those forms that have suf-formatives that consist of a vowel (2fs, 3mp and 2mp), wherein the Holem stem vowel is reduced to Vocal Shewa.

8. With some frequency in the Hebrew Bible (252 times), the 3mp and the 2mp forms will be written with a final ן as in יִקְטְלוּן or תִּקְטְלוּן. This final ן is called *Nun Paragogicum*. Verbs with this final Nun may also be spelled defectively (meaning that the vowel letter Shureq is written as Qibbuts) as in יִקְטְלֻן or תִּקְטְלֻן.

9. The following graphic identifies the prefix and stem vowels that are diagnostic of the Qal Imperfect. These diagnostics must be memorized. Note that the Silent Shewa under ק is not considered to be diagnostic.

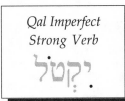

Qal Imperfect
Strong Verb

יִקְטֹל

15.5 **The Qal Imperfect Paradigm of Other Strong Verbs.** The paradigms below are not to be memorized. You should be able to reproduce them once you have memorized the forms of קָטַל listed above. Note the Daghesh Lene in the second root consonant of the Imperfect forms of זָכַר, כָּתַב and קָבַץ. The presence of the Daghesh Lene is due to the fact that these *begadkephat* letters are preceded by a consonant and not a vowel (see 3.5).

	זָכַר to remember	כָּתַב to write	שָׁמַר to keep	קָבַץ to gather
3ms	יִזְכֹּר	יִכְתֹּב	יִשְׁמֹר	יִקְבֹּץ
3fs	תִּזְכֹּר	תִּכְתֹּב	תִּשְׁמֹר	תִּקְבֹּץ
2ms	תִּזְכֹּר	תִּכְתֹּב	תִּשְׁמֹר	תִּקְבֹּץ
2fs	תִּזְכְּרִי	תִּכְתְּבִי	תִּשְׁמְרִי	תִּקְבְּצִי
1cs	אֶזְכֹּר	אֶכְתֹּב	אֶשְׁמֹר	אֶקְבֹּץ
3mp	יִזְכְּרוּ	יִכְתְּבוּ	יִשְׁמְרוּ	יִקְבְּצוּ
3fp	תִּזְכֹּרְנָה	תִּכְתֹּבְנָה	תִּשְׁמֹרְנָה	תִּקְבֹּצְנָה
2mp	תִּזְכְּרוּ	תִּכְתְּבוּ	תִּשְׁמְרוּ	תִּקְבְּצוּ
2fp	תִּזְכֹּרְנָה	תִּכְתֹּבְנָה	תִּשְׁמֹרְנָה	תִּקְבֹּצְנָה
1cp	נִזְכֹּר	נִכְתֹּב	נִשְׁמֹר	נִקְבֹּץ

15.6　Stative Verbs: Imperfect. In chapter 13, you studied the inflection of stative verbs in the Qal Perfect. You will recall that stative verbs are classified by their stem vowel: Pathach (גָּדַל), Tsere (כָּבֵד) or Holem (קָטֹן). This variation in stem vowel caused differences in the spelling of certain Perfect forms. For example, the Tsere-Stative has a Tsere stem vowel in the Qal Perfect 3ms (כָּבֵד). Additionally, the Holem-Stative has an o-class stem vowel throughout (קָטֹנְתָּ). With the Imperfect inflection of stative verbs, however, the stem vowel is Pathach regardless of the stem vowel in the Perfect.

	Perfect		Imperfect
Pathach-Stative	גָּדַל	➤	יִגְדַּל
Tsere-Stative	כָּבֵד	➤	יִכְבַּד
Holem-Stative	קָטֹן	➤	יִקְטַן

As you can see, the stem vowel is Pathach in each of the above Imperfect forms. Note that the Pathach stem vowel of the Imperfect stative is distinct from the Holem stem vowel of the regular Imperfect strong verb form (יִקְטֹל). Apart from this change in stem vowel, however, the Imperfect conjugation of the stative verb follows the regular strong verb pattern. Note, however, the assimilation of the third consonant of the verbal root (ן) into the נ of the Imperfect sufformative in the 3fp and 2fp forms of קָטֹן (תִּקְטֹ֫נָּה)

	גָּדֵל Pathach- Stative	כָּבֵד Tsere- Stative	קָטֹן Holem- Stative
3ms	יִגְדַּל	יִכְבַּד	יִקְטֹן
3fs	תִּגְדַּל	תִּכְבַּד	תִּקְטֹן
2ms	תִּגְדַּל	תִּכְבַּד	תִּקְטֹן
2fs	תִּגְדְּלִי	תִּכְבְּדִי	תִּקְטְנִי
1cs	אֶגְדַּל	אֶכְבַּד	אֶקְטֹן
3mp	יִגְדְּלוּ	יִכְבְּדוּ	יִקְטְנוּ
3fp	תִּגְדַּ֫לְנָה	תִּכְבַּ֫דְנָה	תִּקְטֹ֫נָּה
2mp	תִּגְדְּלוּ	תִּכְבְּדוּ	תִּקְטְנוּ
2fp	תִּגְדַּ֫לְנָה	תִּכְבַּ֫דְנָה	תִּקְטֹ֫נָּה
1cp	נִגְדַּל	נִכְבַּד	נִקְטֹן

15.7 **Lexical Form.** The lexical form for most Imperfect verbs is the Qal Perfect 3ms. The Qal Perfect 3ms is the standard lexical form for most verbs regardless of stem or conjugation.

15.8 **Parsing.** When asked to parse Qal Imperfect verbs, you will be required to identify the verbal stem, conjugation, person, gender, number and verbal root. When parsing, give the required information in the proper order as the following examples illustrate. Though given below, translation is not a required part of the parsing information.

יִשְׁמְעוּ	Qal Imperfect 3mp	שָׁמַע	they will hear
יִמְלֹךְ	Qal Imperfect 3ms	מָלַךְ	he will reign (be king)

15.9   Negation of the Imperfect: The Particles לֹא and אַל.

1. Like the Perfect, the Imperfect is also negated with לֹא.[2] This
    negative particle is always placed immediately before the verb.
    In addition to the use of the negative particle to simply negate
    the verb, there is a special use of לֹא before an Imperfect. In the
    Ten Commandments (Decalogue), the combination of לֹא plus
    the Imperfect is used for an absolute or permanent prohibition.

לֹא תַעֲשֶׂה	you shall not make (Ex 20:4)
לֹא תִשָּׂא	you shall not take (Ex 20:7)
לֹא תִּרְצָח	you shall not kill (Ex 20:13)
לֹא תִּנְאָף	you shall not commit adultery (Ex 20:14)
לֹא תִּגְנֹב	you shall not steal (Ex 20:15)
לֹא תַעֲנֶה	you shall not answer (Ex 20:16)
לֹא תַחְמֹד	you shall not covet (Ex 20:17)

2. The negative particle אַל is also used with an Imperfect verb[3] to
    express an immediate, specific and non-durative prohibition.[4] In
    other words, prohibitions with לֹא are permanent and absolute;
    prohibitions with אַל are immediate and specific. This particle is
    often prefixed to the verb with Maqqef (אַל־).

אַל־תִּכְתֹּב בַּסֵּפֶר	Do not write in the book!
אַל־תִּירָא	Do not fear! (Gen 15:1)
אַל־תִּשְׁמְעוּ אֶל־דִּבְרֵי נְבִיאֵיכֶם	Do not listen to the words of your prophets! (Jer 27:14)

15.10   Summary.

1. The Qal stem is used to express *simple action* with an *active voice*.
    The Imperfect conjugation is used to express an *incomplete action*
    which may be translated with either the English present or future
    tense.

---

[2] The combination of לֹא plus the Imperfect occurs 2,654 times in the Hebrew
     Bible.

[3] See also the discussion of the Jussive in 18.15.

[4] The combination of אַל plus the Imperfect occurs 678 times in the Hebrew
     Bible.

2. The Imperfect conjugation is also called the *prefix* conjugation because every form takes a verbal prefix called a *preformative*. The prefixes are unique to the Imperfect conjugation in the Qal and derived stems.

3. The following graphic identifies the preformative and stem vowels that are diagnostic of the Qal Imperfect. These diagnostics must be memorized.

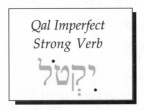

Qal Imperfect
Strong Verb
יִקְטֹל

4. With the Imperfect inflection of stative verbs, the stem vowel is Pathach (יִכְבַּד) and not Holem (יִקְטֹל).

5. The Qal Perfect 3ms is the standard lexical form for most verbs, regardless of stem or conjugation.

6. Imperfect verbs are usually negated with the negative particle לֹא. In addition to this use, the negative particle לֹא may be used before an Imperfect verb to express an absolute or permanent prohibition. The negative particle אַל before an Imperfect is used to express an immediate and specific prohibition (see 18.5, 15).

15.11 Vocabulary.

Verbs

חָיָה	to live (282)
יָכֹל	to be able (193)
כָּרַת	to cut off, make a covenant (289)
סוּר	to turn (297)
עָנָה	to answer (316)
עָבַד	to serve (289)

Nouns

אֹזֶן	ear (188); feminine
אַיִל	ram (171)

גִּבּוֹר   warrior, mighty man (160)

זֶבַח   sacrifice (162)

צְדָקָה   righteousness (159)

צָפוֹן   north (153); feminine

Other

אָז   then, since (141)

אַף   also, even (133)

פֶּן־   lest (133)

15.12 Cursed Is Anyone Who Hangs on a Tree. Reflecting the numerous references in the New Testament to Jesus' death on a "tree" (Acts 5:30; 10:39; 13:29; 16:24; Gal 3:13; 1 Pet 2:24), Jehovah's Witnesses sometimes object to the claim of orthodox Christianity that Jesus died on a cross.

In Deut 21:22-23, Israel is told that if an individual is executed and if, in addition, his body is hung "on a tree" (עַל־עֵץ), the corpse should not be allowed to remain all night, but it should be buried that same day because "he who is hanged is accursed of God."

While עֵץ can refer to a natural tree, there is nothing in the context of Deut 21 that requires that the term be so restricted. The Hebrew term עֵץ has a broad range of meaning. It can refer to a single tree, stand of trees, wood (as a substance), or any object made from wood. Although crucifixion did not exist in the Old Testament period, the fact that עֵץ is used, for example, to refer to the wooden gallows on which the accursed Haman and his ten sons were hung (Esther 7:10; 9:25) amply justifies the New Testament's application of Deut 21:22-22 to a Roman cross.

It is true that outside the New Testament the Greek term for "tree" (ξύλον) is not ordinarily used to refer to a cross. Nevertheless, it has a range of meaning that parallels that of the Hebrew term עֵץ. Although this Greek word typically refers to a "tree" (Luke 23:31) or to "wood" (1 Cor 3:12), it can also refer to a variety of objects made from wood, such as clubs (Matt 26:47; Luke 22:52) and stocks (Acts 16:24).

The early believers, as recorded by Luke, seemed to go out of their way to describe the cross in a manner that could hardly be more offensive to Jewish ears: it was a "tree" (ξύλον). Indeed, as Gal 3:13

implies, the remarkable tendency to use "tree" with reference to our Lord's crucifixion finds its probable source in Deut 21:22-23 where the Septuagint employs ξύλον to translate עֵץ. Consistent with the curse pronounced in that text, the Old Testament abounds with examples where the accursed enemies of God and his people were made to hang on trees (the king of Ai in Josh 8:29; the five Amorite kings in Josh 10:26; Absalom in 2 Sam 18:9 and following; perhaps the seven sons of Saul for their attempted genocide against the Gibeonites in 2 Sam 21; and certainly Haman and his ten sons in Esther 7:10; 9:25 for their attempted genocide against the Jews). Likewise, the use of trees as the expected place for exposure to divine judgement and wrath (Judg 4:5) may illumine that infamous tree in Eden, which the Lord surely intended to serve for the damnation of Satan himself. Tragically, it became instead the place where judgement was pronounced against the first Adam, who, ironically, "hid from the Lord God among the *trees.*"

As observed by G. B. Caird, hanging on a tree "is not a description of the Crucifixion which would naturally occur to a bystander. It is a quotation from Deuteronomy xxi. 22f. … Surely no Christian preacher would have chosen to describe the death of Jesus in terms which drew attention to the curse of God resting upon the executed criminal, unless he had first faced the scandal of the Cross and had come to believe that Jesus had borne the curse on behalf of others."[5] In light of the Old Testament associations of an עֵץ as the locus for divine wrath, "the message of the cross is foolishness to those who are perishing, but to us who are being saved it is the power of God" (1 Cor 1:18).

Gordon P. Hugenberger
Senior Pastor, Park Street Church
Boston, Massachusetts

---

[5] G. B. Caird, *The Apostolic Age* (London: Duckworth, 1955) 40.

Chapter 16

Qal Imperfect - Weak Verbs

16.1 **Introduction.** Compared to the Perfect, the Imperfect conjugation of weak verbs exhibits significantly more variation. The addition of both preformatives *and* sufformatives to weak verbal roots increases the likelihood of spelling variation. Regardless of a verb's weakness, however, the preformatives and sufformatives of the Imperfect conjugation do not change. For this reason, it is very important to have first memorized the Imperfect forms of the strong verb before working through this chapter. In this chapter, you are not required to memorize every weak verb paradigm. Rather, you will be required to memorize only four weak paradigms: II-Guttural verbs, III-ח/ע verbs (16.2), III-א verbs (16.4) and III-ה verbs (16.6). Only recognition of the remaining weak verb forms will be emphasized.

16.2 **II-Guttural and III-ח/ע Verbs.** Both II-Guttural and III-ח/ע weak verbs differ from the strong verb primarily in the stem vowel. Strong verbs have a Holem stem vowel (יִקְטֹל) but these two classes have Pathach (יִבְחַר).

	II-Guttural	III-ח/ע	Strong
3ms	יִבְחַר	יִשְׁלַח	יִקְטֹל
3fs	תִּבְחַר	תִּשְׁלַח	תִּקְטֹל
2ms	תִּבְחַר	תִּשְׁלַח	תִּקְטֹל
2fs	תִּבְחֲרִי	תִּשְׁלְחִי	תִּקְטְלִי
1cs	אֶבְחַר	אֶשְׁלַח	אֶקְטֹל
3mp	יִבְחֲרוּ	יִשְׁלְחוּ	יִקְטְלוּ
3fp	תִּבְחַרְנָה	תִּשְׁלַחְנָה	תִּקְטֹלְנָה
2mp	תִּבְחֲרוּ	תִּשְׁלְחוּ	תִּקְטְלוּ
2fp	תִּבְחַרְנָה	תִּשְׁלַחְנָה	תִּקְטֹלְנָה
1cp	נִבְחַר	נִשְׁלַח	נִקְטֹל

16.3 II-Guttural and III-ה/ע Notes.

1. Like the Qal Imperfect stative verbs studied in the last chapter, II-Guttural and III-ה/ע verbs take a Pathach stem vowel. This shift in stem vowel is due to the fact that guttural consonants prefer a-type vowels. Note that the vocalization of the Qal Imperfect stative (15.6) is identical to the vocalization of the Qal Imperfect III-ה/ע verb.

2. In the II-Guttural class, note the Hateph Pathach under the guttural in the 2fs (תִּבְחֲרִי), 3mp (יִבְחֲרוּ) and 2mp (תִּבְחֲרוּ) forms. You understand that the guttural in second root position cannot take the expected Vocal Shewa.

16.4 III-א Verbs.

Most of the changes that take place in this weak class result from the fact that the א in third root position is quiescent. This quiescent א changes the stem vowel in most forms of the paradigm when compared to the strong verb. Other than changes in the stem vowel, III-א verbs inflect just like the strong verb. Because the III-א class of weak verbs boasts some very high frequency vocabulary, it is important to memorize the following paradigm.

	III-א	Strong
3ms	יִמְצָא	יִקְטֹל
3fs	תִּמְצָא	תִּקְטֹל
2ms	תִּמְצָא	תִּקְטֹל
2fs	תִּמְצְאִי	תִּקְטְלִי
1cs	אֶמְצָא	אֶקְטֹל
3mp	יִמְצְאוּ	יִקְטְלוּ
3fp	תִּמְצֶּאנָה	תִּקְטֹלְנָה
2mp	תִּמְצְאוּ	תִּקְטְלוּ
2fp	תִּמְצֶּאנָה	תִּקְטֹלְנָה
1cp	נִמְצָא	נִקְטֹל

16.5   III-א Notes.

1. In those forms without a suffformative, the stem vowel is Qamets (יִמְצָא). The stem vowel of the strong verb is Holem (יִקְטֹל).

2. Those forms with suffformatives that consist of a vowel (2fs, 3mp and 2mp) are identical to their corresponding strong verb forms.

3. The twin 3fp and 2fp forms (תִּמְצֶאנָה) exhibit an unexpected Seghol stem vowel. This variation is unusual but will pose no difficulty for the identification of these two forms.

16.6   III-ה Verbs. The changes in this class of weak verb are considerable. As with the Perfect, the most significant change is the loss of the final ה root consonant in every form. For this reason, memorization of the following paradigm is required.

	III-ה	*Strong*
3ms	יִבְנֶה	יִקְטֹל
3fs	תִּבְנֶה	תִּקְטֹל
2ms	תִּבְנֶה	תִּקְטֹל
2fs	תִּבְנִי	תִּקְטְלִי
1cs	אֶבְנֶה	אֶקְטֹל
3mp	יִבְנוּ	יִקְטְלוּ
3fp	תִּבְנֶינָה	תִּקְטֹלְנָה
2mp	תִּבְנוּ	תִּקְטְלוּ
2fp	תִּבְנֶינָה	תִּקְטֹלְנָה
1cp	נִבְנֶה	נִקְטֹל

16.7   III-ה Notes.

1. Imperfect forms *without a suffformative* have an ה ֶ ending. This makes it seem as though the stem vowel of this weak class has shifted from Holem (יִקְטֹל) to Seghol (יִבְנֶה). The final ה in these forms is not, however, the original third root consonant but rather a vowel letter or *mater lectionis*. While this final ה is not

the original consonant, it does make identification of the verbal root easier in these forms. Even in the derived stems, the הָ ending will be diagnostic of most III-ה Imperfect forms.

2. The Imperfect forms *with a sufformative* have dropped this ה altogether. This is an important feature to recognize. When you are confronted by such a form, you will have only two of the three original root consonants. In order to determine the lexical form, therefore, you will have to reconstruct the original root consonants based upon your understanding of how III-ה verbal roots inflect.

3. In the twin 3fp and 2fp forms, the stem vowel is Seghol Yod (תִּבְנֶ֫ינָה). This is similar to the Hireq Yod stem vowel found in the Perfect conjugation of this weak verb class (compare the Perfect 2ms form בָּנִ֫יתָ). The similarity is in the fact that both the Perfect and Imperfect have unchangeable long stem vowels.

4. You will learn below that the Imperfect 3ms form of III-ה verbs (יִבְנֶה) may also occur without the final ה vowel letter (יִ֫בֶן). This form has a special use that will be treated in 18.14.

16.8   I-Guttural Verbs. There are two types of I-Guttural weak verbs. Each type is classified by the stem vowel. Type 1 has a Pathach stem vowel (יֶחֱזַק) and Type 2 has a Holem stem vowel (יַעֲמֹד). Recognition rather than memorization of these weak verbal forms is required. That is, you will not be required to reproduce these paradigms in Hebrew but you will need to be able to identify and parse each form.

	I-Guttural Type 1	I-Guttural Type 2	Strong
3ms	יֶחֱזַק	יַעֲמֹד	יִקְטֹל
3fs	תֶּחֱזַק	תַּעֲמֹד	תִּקְטֹל
2ms	תֶּחֱזַק	תַּעֲמֹד	תִּקְטֹל
2fs	תֶּחֶזְקִי	תַּעַמְדִי	תִּקְטְלִי
1cs	אֶחֱזַק	אֶעֱמֹד	אֶקְטֹל
3mp	יֶחֶזְקוּ	יַעַמְדוּ	יִקְטְלוּ
3fp	תֶּחֱזַ֫קְנָה	תַּעֲמֹ֫דְנָה	תִּקְטֹ֫לְנָה
2mp	תֶּחֶזְקוּ	תַּעַמְדוּ	תִּקְטְלוּ
2fp	תֶּחֱזַ֫קְנָה	תַּעֲמֹ֫דְנָה	תִּקְטֹ֫לְנָה
1cp	נֶחֱזַק	נַעֲמֹד	נִקְטֹל

16.9   I-Guttural Notes.

1. Type 1 verbs with the Pathach stem vowel exhibit a *Seghol preformative vowel* followed by a Hateph Seghol under the guttural in first root position (יֶחֱזַק). Note that in those forms having a sufformative consisting of a vowel (2fs, 3mp, 2mp), the vowel under the guttural is just Seghol in a closed syllable (תֶּחֶזְקוּ).

2. Type 2 verbs with the Holem stem vowel generally exhibit a *Pathach preformative vowel* and a Hateph Pathach under the guttural in first root position (יַעֲמֹד). The only exception to this pattern is the 1cs form אֶעֱמֹד with Seghol under the preformative and Hateph Seghol under the guttural. Note that the vowel under the guttural is just Pathach in a closed syllable in the 2fs (תַּעַמְדִי), 3mp (יַעַמְדוּ) and 2mp (תַּעַמְדוּ).

16.10   I-א Verbs. Although verbs with א in the first root position are to be classified as I-Guttural, weak verbs of this type require additional comment. While most I-א verbs inflect just like the Imperfect of חָזַק in 16.8 above, there are five I-א verbs that follow a different pattern.[1]

---

[1] The five I-א verbs that follow this Type 2 pattern are אָמַר (to say), אָכַל (to eat), אָבַד (to perish), אָפָה (to bake) and אָבָה (to be willing).

This alternate pattern is represented by the Type 2 paradigm below. Recognition rather than memorization of these weak verb forms is required.

	I-א *Type 1*	*I-א* *Type 2*	*Strong*
3ms	יֶאְסֹר	יֹאמַר	יִקְטֹל
3fs	תֶּאְסֹר	תֹּאמַר	תִּקְטֹל
2ms	תֶּאְסֹר	תֹּאמַר	תִּקְטֹל
2fs	תַּאַסְרִי	תֹּאמְרִי	תִּקְטְלִי
1cs	אֶאְסֹר	אֹמַר	אֶקְטֹל
3mp	יַאַסְרוּ	יֹאמְרוּ	יִקְטְלוּ
3fp	תֶּאֱסֹרְנָה	תֹּאמַֹרְנָה	תִּקְטֹלְנָה
2mp	תַּאַסְרוּ	תֹּאמְרוּ	תִּקְטְלוּ
2fp	תֶּאֱסֹרְנָה	תֹּאמַֹרְנָה	תִּקְטֹלְנָה
1cp	נֶאְסֹר	נֹאמַר	נִקְטֹל

16.11 I-א Notes.

1. It has already been noted that I-א verbs of the Type 1 class inflect just like the Type 1 verbs of the I-Guttural class (compare, for example, יֶחֱזַק with יֶאְסֹר). This should be easy to remember since א is a guttural consonant. Note the shift to a-type vowels in the 2fs (תַּאַסְרִי), 3mp (יַאַסְרוּ) and 2mp (תַּאַסְרוּ) Imperfect forms of אָסַר. These vowel changes and the differences in stem vowel should occasion no difficulty for identifying these forms.

2. Type 2 verbs of this class are very different in their inflection. The preformative vowel is Holem and the א is quiescent (יֹאמַר). While this pattern occurs in only five verbs, some of these verbs occur with a very high frequency. For example, the Qal Imperfect form of אָמַר (to say) occurs 2,973 times and אָכַל (to eat) occurs 382 times.

3. Note the unusual 1cs form of the Type 2 paradigm, אֹמַר (I will say). You would expect the א to be written twice, once for the

Imperfect preformative and once for the first consonant of the verbal root. Observe, however, that it is written only once. The א that is present is the Imperfect preformative for the 1cs. The first consonant of the verbal root is not written.

16.12 Geminate Verbs. You have already learned that a Geminate verb is one in which the second and third root consonants of the verbal root are identical as in סָבַב (to go around) or תָּמַם (to be complete). Recognition rather than memorization of these weak verbal forms is required.

	Geminate Type 1	Alternate Type 1	Geminate Type 2	Strong
3ms	יָסֹב	יִסֹב	יֵתַם	יִקְטֹל
3fs	תָּסֹב	תִּסֹב	תֵּתַם	תִּקְטֹל
2ms	תָּסֹב	תִּסֹב	תֵּתַם	תִּקְטֹל
2fs	תָּסֹבִּי	תִּסֹבִּי	תֵּתַמִּי	תִּקְטְלִי
1cs	אָסֹב	אֶסֹב	אֵתַם	אֶקְטֹל
3mp	יָסֹבּוּ	יִסֹבּוּ	יֵתַמּוּ	יִקְטְלוּ
3fp	תְּסֻבֶּינָה	תִּסֻבֶּינָה	תִּתַמֶּינָה	תִּקְטֹלְנָה
2mp	תָּסֹבּוּ	תִּסֹבּוּ	תֵּתַמּוּ	תִּקְטְלוּ
2fp	תְּסֻבֶּינָה	תִּסֻבֶּינָה	תִּתַמֶּינָה	תִּקְטֹלְנָה
1cp	נָסֹב	נִסֹב	נֵתַם	נִקְטֹל

16.13 Geminate Notes.

1. There are two types of Geminate verbs. Type 1 has the Holem stem vowel (יִסֹב) in most forms. Type 2 has the Pathach stem vowel (יֵתַם). Note also that Type 1 Geminate verbs have an alternate form that also has a Holem stem vowel (יִסֹב). Each type is further distinguished by the preformative vowel. Type 1 verbs have a Qamets (יָסֹב) or the alternate Hireq preformative vowel (יִסֹב). Type 2 verbs exhibit the Tsere preformative vowel (יֵתַם). Other minor variations also exist for which the lexicon will provide information.

2. In every form of both Geminate paradigms, only one of the Geminate consonants remains. In those forms with a sufformative, the presence of a Daghesh Forte in the remaining Geminate consonant should help you to identify the verbal root. In those forms without a sufformative, there is no Daghesh Forte in the Geminate consonant. This will make identification of the verbal root more difficult, as you will simply have to recognize the Geminate root as a possibility.

16.14 Biconsonantal Verbs. You learned in 14.12 that Biconsonantal verbs are composed of two rather than three root consonants (קָם, he rose up). You will also recall that Biconsonantal verbs are sometimes designated as II- י/ו verbs. It should be clear from the paradigms below why this weak class has been called II- י/ו. With the Imperfect and related conjugations, a medial vowel letter is found in every form. In the Imperfect, these Biconsonantal or II- י/ו verbs are further classified by their medial vowel letter.

	Qal Perfect 3ms	*Qal Imperfect 3ms*	*Lexical Entry*
ו - *Class*	קָם he arose	יָקוּם he will arise	קוּם to arise
ו - *Class*	בָּא he entered	יָבוֹא he will enter	בּוֹא to enter
י - *Class*	שָׂם he placed	יָשִׂים he will place	שִׂים to place

The vowel letters are an important feature of these verbs and should be memorized as a part of your vocabulary. Biconsonantal verbs are listed in the lexicon and vocabulary sections in the Infinitive Construct form (קוּם, שִׂים and בּוֹא).[2] Recognition rather than memorization of these weak verbal forms is suggested.

---

[2] The Infinitive Construct of Biconsonantal verbs will be studied in 20.7 below.

	וֹ Class קוּם	יְ Class שִׂים	וֹ Class בּוֹא	Strong
3ms	יָקוּם	יָשִׂים	יָבוֹא	יִקְטֹל
3fs	תָּקוּם	תָּשִׂים	תָּבוֹא	תִּקְטֹל
2ms	תָּקוּם	תָּשִׂים	תָּבוֹא	תִּקְטֹל
2fs	תָּקוּמִי	תָּשִׂימִי	תָּבוֹאִי	תִּקְטְלִי
1cs	אָקוּם	אָשִׂים	אָבוֹא	אֶקְטֹל
3mp	יָקוּמוּ	יָשִׂימוּ	יָבוֹאוּ	יִקְטְלוּ
3fp	תְּקוּמֶ֫ינָה	תְּשִׂימֶ֫ינָה	תָּבוֹאנָה[3]	תִּקְטֹ֫לְנָה
2mp	תָּקוּמוּ	תָּשִׂימוּ	תָּבוֹאוּ	תִּקְטְלוּ
2fp	תְּקוּמֶ֫ינָה	תְּשִׂימֶ֫ינָה	תָּבוֹאנָה	תִּקְטֹ֫לְנָה
1cp	נָקוּם	נָשִׂים	נָבוֹא	נִקְטֹל

16.15 Biconsonantal Notes.

1. In all forms (except 3fp and 2fp) and in every class, the preformative vowel is Qamets (יָקוּם, יָשִׂים and יָבוֹא).

2. The stem vowel of every form is determined by the Biconsonantal sub-class: Shureq (יָקוּם), Hireq Yod (יָשִׂים) or Holem Waw (יָבוֹא).

3. It should be noted that some mixing of the diagnostic stem vowel does occur. For example, יָשִׂים is sometimes rendered יָשׂוּם (Ex 4:11). It should also be noted that sometimes the unchangeable long stem vowel may be written defectively. For example, יָקוּם may appear as יָקֻם (Gen 27:31).

16.16 I-י Verbs. In terms of the Imperfect inflection, there are two types of I-י verbs. With Type 1 verbs, the first consonant of the verbal root drops off in every form. With Type 2 verbs, the first root consonant is seemingly preserved as a vowel letter. We have also included the verb הָלַךְ (to walk) in the following paradigms because it inflects just like I-י (Type 1) weak verbs. Recognition rather than memorization of these weak verbal forms is suggested.

---

[3] The alternate spellings תְּבֹאֶ֫ינָה and תָּבֹאנָה are also attested.

	I-י Type 1	הָלַךְ	I-י Type 2	Strong
3ms	יֵשֵׁב	יֵלֵךְ	יִירַשׁ	יִקְטֹל
3fs	תֵּשֵׁב	תֵּלֵךְ	תִּירַשׁ	תִּקְטֹל
2ms	תֵּשֵׁב	תֵּלֵךְ	תִּירַשׁ	תִּקְטֹל
2fs	תֵּשְׁבִי	תֵּלְכִי	תִּירְשִׁי	תִּקְטְלִי
1cs	אֵשֵׁב	אֵלֵךְ	אִירַשׁ	אֶקְטֹל
3mp	יֵשְׁבוּ	יֵלְכוּ	יִירְשׁוּ	יִקְטְלוּ
3fp	תֵּשַׁבְנָה	תֵּלַכְנָה	תִּירַשְׁנָה	תִּקְטֹלְנָה
2mp	תֵּשְׁבוּ	תֵּלְכוּ	תִּירְשׁוּ	תִּקְטְלוּ
2fp	תֵּשַׁבְנָה	תֵּלַכְנָה	תִּירַשְׁנָה	תִּקְטֹלְנָה
1cp	נֵשֵׁב	נֵלֵךְ	נִירַשׁ	נִקְטֹל

16.17 I-י Notes.

1. In every form of the Type 1 paradigm, the initial י root consonant has dropped and the Imperfect preformative vowel is Tsere throughout. You should also note that the stem vowel is Tsere in all forms without a sufformative. Verbs of this type can be difficult to recognize because the initial consonant (י) is lost, leaving only the second and third consonants of the verbal root. You should understand that the י in the 3ms and 3mp forms is the Imperfect preformative and not the first consonant of the verbal root. It is helpful to think of the Tsere preformative vowel as characteristic of this class of I-י verbs. Recognizing this feature should help you to properly reconstruct the full verbal root.

2. In the Type 2 paradigm, the initial י of the verbal root is seemingly preserved as the vowel letter Hireq Yod. The stem vowel is Pathach (יִירַשׁ), except in those forms that have a sufformative ending with a vowel. Identification of the verbal root in this class should not be as difficult as Type 1 verbs because of the additional י in the preformative vowel.

3. The verb הָלַךְ (to walk) inflects just like the Type 1 verb above with a loss of the initial root consonant. This verb occurs frequently and so it is important to be able to recognize these forms.

16.18 I-נ Verbs. As with I-י verbs, there are two types of I-נ verbs. Type 1 verbs have a Holem stem vowel (יִפֹּל). Type 2 verbs have the Pathach stem vowel (יִסַּע). An additional doubly weak paradigm is also included for study (I-נ and II-Guttural). Recognition rather than memorization of these weak verbal forms is suggested.

	I-נ Type 1	I-נ Type 2	I-נ Doubly Weak	Strong
3ms	יִפֹּל	יִסַּע	יִנְחַל	יִקְטֹל
3fs	תִּפֹּל	תִּסַּע	תִּנְחַל	תִּקְטֹל
2ms	תִּפֹּל	תִּסַּע	תִּנְחַל	תִּקְטֹל
2fs	תִּפְּלִי	תִּסְעִי	תִּנְחֲלִי	תִּקְטְלִי
1cs	אֶפֹּל	אֶסַּע	אֶנְחַל	אֶקְטֹל
3mp	יִפְּלוּ	יִסְעוּ	יִנְחֲלוּ	יִקְטְלוּ
3fp	תִּפֹּלְנָה	תִּסַּעְנָה	תִּנְחַלְנָה	תִּקְטֹלְנָה
2mp	תִּפְּלוּ	תִּסְעוּ	תִּנְחֲלוּ	תִּקְטְלוּ
2fp	תִּפֹּלְנָה	תִּסַּעְנָה	תִּנְחַלְנָה	תִּקְטֹלְנָה
1cp	נִפֹּל	נִסַּע	נִנְחַל	נִקְטֹל

16.19 I-נ Notes.

1. Type 1 verbs are distinguished from Type 2 verbs by their stem vowel. Type 1 has the Holem stem vowel and Type 2 exhibits the Pathach stem vowel. With both Type 1 and Type 2 verbs, the initial root consonant (נ) has assimilated into the second consonant of the verbal root and is represented by a Daghesh Forte. For example, יִנְפֹּל has become יִפֹּל with the assimilation of the נ. The presence of this Daghesh Forte should enable you to identify the verbal root as I-נ. Note, however, that the assimilated נ may be given up in the 2fs, 3mp and 2mp forms of the Type 2 class.

2. In the above doubly weak paradigm (I-נ and II-Guttural), you will notice that the נ that is the first root consonant does *not* assimilate into the second root consonant. The expected assimilation does not occur because the second root consonant is a guttural and, therefore, rejects the assimilation of the נ because it cannot take a Daghesh Forte.

3. The verb לָקַח (to take) inflects just like the Type 2 verb above with assimilation of the first root consonant (ל) into the second root consonant with a resulting Daghesh Forte (יִקַּח). This verb occurs frequently and so it is important to be able to recognize its Imperfect forms.

16.20 Doubly Weak Verbs. As you know, some verbal roots have more than one weak root consonant. For example, the verb יָצָא (to go or come out) is both I-י and III-א. When this occurs, the verb will exhibit the weak features of both weak verbal categories. Several doubly weak verbs that occur frequently are listed below for your study. You should not try to memorize these paradigms. Rather, work through the forms of each paradigm and identify the weak features. In other words, use the information that you have already learned in this chapter to analyze the following weak verbs.

	עָשָׂה	רָאָה	הָיָה	יָצָא	נָשָׂא	נָתַן
3ms	יַעֲשֶׂה	יִרְאֶה	יִהְיֶה	יֵצֵא	יִשָּׂא	יִתֵּן
3fs	תַּעֲשֶׂה	תִּרְאֶה	תִּהְיֶה	תֵּצֵא	תִּשָּׂא	תִּתֵּן
2ms	תַּעֲשֶׂה	תִּרְאֶה	תִּהְיֶה	תֵּצֵא	תִּשָּׂא	תִּתֵּן
2fs	תַּעֲשִׂי	תִּרְאִי	תִּהְיִי	תֵּצְאִי	תִּשְׂאִי	תִּתְּנִי
1cs	אֶעֱשֶׂה	אֶרְאֶה	אֶהְיֶה	אֵצֵא	אֶשָּׂא	אֶתֵּן
3mp	יַעֲשׂוּ	יִרְאוּ	יִהְיוּ	יֵצְאוּ	יִשְׂאוּ	יִתְּנוּ
3fp	תַּעֲשֶׂינָה	תִּרְאֶינָה	תִּהְיֶינָה	תֵּצֶאנָה	תִּשֶּׂאנָה	תִּתֵּנָּה
2mp	תַּעֲשׂוּ	תִּרְאוּ	תִּהְיוּ	תֵּצְאוּ	תִּשְׂאוּ	תִּתְּנוּ
2fp	תַּעֲשֶׂינָה	תִּרְאֶינָה	תִּהְיֶינָה	תֵּצֶאנָה	תִּשֶּׂאנָה	תִּתֵּנָּה
1cp	נַעֲשֶׂה	נִרְאֶה	נִהְיֶה	נֵצֵא	נִשָּׂא	נִתֵּן

16.21 Doubly Weak Notes.

1. In the three III-ה paradigms (עָשָׂה, רָאָה and הָיָה), note the ה֖
   ending, except in those forms with sufformatives. The ה֖ ending
   is diagnostic of III-ה Imperfect verbs in both the Qal and derived
   stems.

2. The verb עָשָׂה is both III-ה and I-Guttural. Note the vowel pattern
   of Pathach under the Imperfect preformative and Hateph Pathach
   under the guttural in first root position. This is the expected
   pattern in the Type 2 class of I-Guttural verbs (16.8). Even the
   Seghol/Hateph Seghol pattern is preserved in the 1cs form
   (אֶעֱשֶׂה).

3. Study the Imperfect forms of הָיָה with care. You will observe
   that this doubly weak verb inflects exactly like the Imperfect of
   בָּנָה (16.6). Careful study is required, however, because the
   presence of י in second root position creates certain forms that
   appear to be irregular in their inflection such as תְּהִי (2fs), יִהְיוּ
   (3mp), תִּהְיוּ (2mp) and even תִּהְיֶינָה (3fp and 2fp). In fact, these
   forms are inflected exactly like their counterparts in the בָּנָה
   paradigm above.

4. In the Imperfect of נָשָׂא, most forms preserve a Daghesh Forte
   in the second consonant of the verbal root as in יִשָּׂא (3ms). This
   Daghesh Forte represents the assimilated נ that is the first root
   consonant. Observe, however, that the Daghesh Forte is given
   up in the 2fs, 3mp and 2mp forms.

5. The Imperfect forms of נָתַן need careful study as did those of
   הָיָה above. In every form, the first consonant of the verbal root
   (נ) has assimilated into the second root consonant and remains
   as a Daghesh Forte. But there is another process of assimilation
   to be observed in this paradigm. In the two feminine plural
   forms that are identical (תִּתֵּנָּה), the final נ that is the third
   consonant of the verbal root has assimilated into the נ of the
   sufformative (נָה) and is represented as a Daghesh Forte.

16.22 Reconstructing Verbal Roots. As you know by now, some weak verbs
may lose one or more of their original root consonants. For example,
in the above paradigm of נָתַן (to give), the Imperfect 3ms form יִתֵּן (he
will give) exhibits the loss of the first root consonant. This type of loss

can make identification of the full verbal root a difficult task. How, therefore, do you identify a verbal root when one or more of the original root consonants is missing? The first step is to know your options. With the Imperfect, there are four major weak verb classes that drop a root consonant: I-י, I-נ, III-ה and Geminate. Secondly, after all else fails and if you are still lost in one of the standard lexicons, an analytical or computerized lexicon will provide the verbal root for any inflected form in the Hebrew Bible. There are, however, clues or diagnostic features for certain weak verbal roots that will make their identification easier.

1. With certain I-י verbs, the Yod consonant drops off in every form. For example, the Imperfect 3ms form of יָשַׁב (to sit, dwell) is יֵשֵׁב (I will sit, dwell). This weak form preserves only two of the three original root consonants. If you are unfamiliar with the verbal root, how do you know what has dropped off? Is this verb Biconsonantal (שָׁב or שׁוּב), Geminate (שָׁבַב), III-ה (שָׁבָה), I-י (יָשַׁב) or I-נ (נָשַׁב)? In this case, the key to identifying the verbal root is the Tsere preformative vowel (יֵשֵׁב). The Tsere preformative vowel is a diagnostic feature of the I-י Imperfect conjugation. By knowing this, you will be able to correctly identify the verbal root without having to look up numerous other verbal roots in a lexicon.

2. Most I-נ verbs (and לָקַח) assimilate their first root consonant into the second root consonant with a resulting Daghesh Forte. For example, the Imperfect 3ms form of נָפַל (to fall) is יִפֹּל (he will fall). In this case, the Daghesh Forte in the second root consonant (יִפֹּל) should alert you to the fact that this is a I-נ weak verbal root.

3. With III-ה weak verbal roots, the loss of the final ה root consonant occurs in every Imperfect form. In those forms without an Imperfect sufformative, a final ה vowel letter is present (יִבְנֶה). This is not, however, the third consonant of the verbal root. Fortunately, the presence of this vowel letter makes reconstructing the original verbal root much easier. In the remaining forms of the Imperfect having a sufformative, the final ה is altogether absent. For example, the Imperfect 3mp form of בָּנָה (to build) is יִבְנוּ (they will build). Note the absence

of the final root consonant. In this case, it is helpful to use a process of elimination: (1) there is no Daghesh Forte in the בּ of this form and so it is not I-נ; (2) the preformative vowel is not Tsere and so it is not I-י; and (3) it could be Geminate but the preformative vowel of a Geminate verb is usually Qamets or Tsere. The only other option is III-ה. This might seem like a complicated process at first but it is better than trying to look up numerous, possibly nonexistent, forms in a Hebrew lexicon in an attempt to discover the original root consonants.

4. With Geminate verbs, only one Geminate consonant remains in the Imperfect conjugation. For example, the Imperfect 3ms form of סָבַב (to surround) is יָסֹב (he will surround), with only one בּ. Some Geminate forms of the Imperfect exhibit a Daghesh Forte in the remaining Geminate consonant. In such instances, this clue should enable you to identify the weak verbal form as Geminate. In those forms without the Daghesh Forte, you will want to use the same process of elimination as with III-ה verbs, though it is more difficult with Geminate verbs because they exhibit considerable variation.

16.23 Summary.

1. Verbal paradigms to be memorized.

Strong	*II-Gutt*	*III-ח/ע*	*III-א*	*III-ה*
יִקְטֹל	יִבְחַר	יִשְׁלַח	יִמְצָא	יִבְנֶה
תִּקְטֹל	תִּבְחַר	תִּשְׁלַח	תִּמְצָא	תִּבְנֶה
תִּקְטֹל	תִּבְחַר	תִּשְׁלַח	תִּמְצָא	תִּבְנֶה
תִּקְטְלִי	תִּבְחֲרִי	תִּשְׁלְחִי	תִּמְצְאִי	תִּבְנִי
אֶקְטֹל	אֶבְחַר	אֶשְׁלַח	אֶמְצָא	אֶבְנֶה
יִקְטְלוּ	יִבְחֲרוּ	יִשְׁלְחוּ	יִמְצְאוּ	יִבְנוּ
תִּקְטֹלְנָה	תִּבְחַרְנָה	תִּשְׁלַחְנָה	תִּמְצֶאנָה	תִּבְנֶינָה
תִּקְטְלוּ	תִּבְחֲרוּ	תִּשְׁלְחוּ	תִּמְצְאוּ	תִּבְנוּ
תִּקְטֹלְנָה	תִּבְחַרְנָה	תִּשְׁלַחְנָה	תִּמְצֶאנָה	תִּבְנֶינָה
נִקְטֹל	נִבְחַר	נִשְׁלַח	נִמְצָא	נִבְנֶה

2. All other weak verbs that have been studied above are for recognition only. This means that you are not required to reproduce their paradigms in Hebrew. You must be able, however, to identify and parse these weak verb forms.

3. Verbal features to be memorized for reconstructing missing root consonants.

   a. I-י verbs normally drop their first root consonant but will be identifiable by the Tsere preformative vowel (and Tsere stem vowel) for Type 1 verbs. Type 2 verbs have the Hireq Yod preformative vowel and Pathach stem vowel (16.16). The verb הָלַךְ (to walk) also inflects like a I-י verb of the Type 1 class.

   b. I-נ verbs frequently assimilate the נ of the first root consonant into the second root consonant. The resulting Daghesh Forte will enable you to identify the missing consonant as I-נ. The verb לָקַח (to take) also inflects like a I-נ verb with assimilation of the ל.

   c. III-ה verbs drop their final root consonant but are identifiable by their distinctive הֶ ending (in those forms without a sufformative).

   d. Geminate verbs retain only one Geminate consonant in the Imperfect conjugation. In some forms, this weak class is identifiable by a Daghesh Forte in the remaining Geminate consonant. In those forms without a Daghesh Forte, it is identifiable by a process of elimination and a Qamets or Tsere preformative vowel in most forms.

16.24 Vocabulary.

Verbs

קָרַב	to draw near (280)
חָטָא	to miss (a mark), sin (241)
יָרַשׁ	to subdue, possess, dispossess, inherit (233)
רָבָה	to be(come) numerous, be great (229)
יָסַף	to add (213)

נָטָה   to turn, stretch out (216)

עָזַב   to leave, abandon (214)

גָּאַל   to redeem (104)

כָּפַר   to cover (102)

שָׁתָה   to drink (218)

תָּמַם   to be complete (64)

Nouns

כַּף   hand, palm (195); feminine

רֵעַ   friend, fellow, companion (188)

Other

נֶגֶד   before, opposite (151)

16.25 **The Iniquity of Us All.** There are few texts in the Old Testament as precious to Christians as the great promise of the Suffering Servant in Isa 53. No one doubts that this text was written hundreds of years before Jesus (eight centuries on a conservative dating and no less than six centuries even on the most critical view of this part of Isaiah). Here, in extraordinary detail, is a depiction of substitutionary atonement that, in the words of F. Delitzsch, "looks as if it had been written beneath the cross upon Golgotha."[4] But a question that plagues many new Christians is that if Isaiah intended to predict the sufferings of Jesus, why did he use past tenses (at least according to most English translations)? Why did he not write in 53:6, for example, "and the Lord *will lay* on him the iniquity of us all"?

A pastor who is privileged to hear this thoughtful question will be incapable of answering it apart from a knowledge of Hebrew. As is often the case with such basic questions, the commentaries offer no help. The pastor who has studied Hebrew, however, will readily recall what is perhaps the most intriguing feature of that language from the standpoint of English, its extraordinary tense system. For example, Hebrew employs two verbal forms (Perfect and Imperfect) to express

---

[4] F. Delitzsch, *Biblical Commentary on the Prophecies of Isaiah*, 2 vols. (Grand Rapids: Eerdmans, 1954) 2:303.

a range of meaning for which English requires twelve tenses and three moods. While many of the details of the Hebrew verbal system continue to challenge scholars, and while other explanations are possible for the use of the Perfects, Imperfects, and converted Imperfects in Isa 53, most of which are commonly translated with a past tense, it is undeniable that these same forms are often employed elsewhere in contexts that make clear a future reference. In particular, in Isa 9:5 (English 9:6), English Bibles regularly translate these same verb forms with the future tense, "For a child *will be born* [יֻלַּד a Perfect] to us, a son *will be given* [נִתַּן a Perfect] to us; and the government *will rest* [וַתְּהִי a converted Imperfect] on his shoulders; and his name *will be called* [וַיִּקְרָא a converted Imperfect] Wonderful Counselor, Mighty God, Eternal Father, Prince of Peace."

Gordon P. Hugenberger
Senior Pastor, Park Street Church
Boston, Massachusetts

16.26 Advanced Information. The Qal Imperfect of the stative verb יָכֹל (to be able) is irregular and occurs with some frequency.

	יָכֹל	*Translation*
3ms	יוּכַל	he is able
3fs	תּוּכַל	she is able
2ms	תּוּכַל	you are able
2fs	תּוּכְלִי	you are able
1cs	אוּכַל	I am able
3mp	יוּכְלוּ	they are able
3fp	תּוּכַלְנָה	they are able
2mp	תּוּכְלוּ	you are able
2fp	תּוּכַלְנָה	you are able
1cp	נוּכַל	we are able

Chapter 17

Waw Conversive[1]

17.1 **Introduction.** For the Qal stem, you have now completed the study of the Perfect and Imperfect verbal conjugations. You know that the Perfect conjugation is used to express a *completed action* and is usually translated by the English past, present perfect, past perfect or future perfect tenses. The completed action of the Perfect verb may occur in the past, present or future. The Imperfect is used to express *incomplete action* and is usually translated by the present or future tenses but it may also be used to express repeated or habitual action in the past, present or future. The Imperfect may also be rendered by various modal values (would, could, should, may, might, can, etc.).

In this chapter, you will study a special and complementary use of the Perfect and Imperfect conjugations. When used in the context of biblical narrative (though it also occurs in poetry), an Imperfect verb may be prefixed with a special form of the conjunction ו and translated with all the values of the Perfect. This special form of the conjunction ו is called the *Waw Conversive*. It is called "conversive" because when the Waw Conversive is prefixed to an Imperfect verb, the value of the verb is no longer Imperfect but Perfect. Because the verb is Imperfect in form but Perfect in translation value, it may be called a "converted" Imperfect. Similarly, when a Waw Conversive is prefixed to a Perfect verbal form, it is "converted" to the Imperfect in terms of its translation value and may be called a "converted" Perfect.

It is important to understand that the Waw Conversive and converted verbal forms are used primarily in narrative sequences to denote consecutive actions, that is, actions occurring in sequence. For example,

---

[1] The following discussion of Waw Conversive and the narrative sequences hardly betrays the complexity of the topic or the range of scholarly opinion on these issues. The nomenclature that has been utilized in this grammar (Waw Conversive, "converted" verbal forms; see also notes 3 and 10 below) will be regarded by some as archaic and a simplification of historical and linguistic realities. We agree on both counts. Nevertheless, despite its inadequacies, the terminology is descriptive for the beginning student and represents a helpful point of departure for the study of these very important but complex concepts.

"I sat down, and then I opened my book, and then I studied Hebrew" describes a sequence of consecutive actions occurring in the past. Similarly, "I will sit down, and I will open my book, and I will study Hebrew" describes consecutive or sequentially related actions occurring in the future. Because the converted verbal forms are used primarily to describe a sequence of consecutive actions, the alternate terminology Waw Consecutive is also acceptable. In this grammar, we have chosen to use the "conversive" and "converted" terminology throughout. You must not forget, however, that *converted verbal forms are used primarily to denote sequences of consecutive actions,* either in the past, present or future. Below you will study both the form and function of the Waw Conversive and converted verbal forms in a narrative context.

17.2   Form of Waw Conversive with the Imperfect.[2] When an Imperfect verbal form is prefixed with Waw Conversive, it will be translated with the values of a Perfect verbal form. A few examples illustrate its form and basic translation.

	Qal Imperfect without Waw Conversive	*Qal Imperfect with Waw Conversive*
יִשְׁמֹר he will observe	וַיִּשְׁמֹר and he observed
יִזְכֹּר he will remember	וַיִּזְכֹּר and he remembered

The Waw Conversive with the Imperfect is spelled with the conjunction וֹ with a Pathach vowel and a Daghesh Forte in the Imperfect preformative.

Imperfect with Waw Conversive

וַיִּקְטֹל

The pointing of the Waw Conversive with the Imperfect should remind you of the definite article (הַ·). Now study the full Qal Imperfect paradigm of the strong verb with Waw Conversive and the following important notes.

---

[2]   The Qal Imperfect verbal form occurs 10,466 times in the Hebrew Bible. The converted Imperfect marked with the Waw Conversive occurs 11,485 times.

Imperfect with Waw Conversive

3ms	וַיִּקְטֹל	and he killed
3fs	וַתִּקְטֹל	and she killed
2ms	וַתִּקְטֹל	and you killed
2fs	וַתִּקְטְלִי	and you killed
1cs	וָאֶקְטֹל	and I killed
3mp	וַיִּקְטְלוּ	and they killed
3fp	וַתִּקְטֹלְנָה	and they killed
2mp	וַתִּקְטְלוּ	and you killed
2fp	וַתִּקְטֹלְנָה	and you killed
1cp	וַנִּקְטֹל	and we killed

Notes:

1. Except for the addition of the Waw Conversive, the spelling of the Imperfect verbal forms is unchanged. Be certain to note how these forms are translated. Each is Imperfect in form but Perfect in translation. Because of the Waw Conversive, the Imperfect verbs are translated like Perfect verbs (English past tense).

2. Note the spelling of the Waw Conversive in the 1cs וָאֶקְטֹל (and I killed). Because the א preformative is a guttural, it rejects the Daghesh Forte and the Pathach vowel under the Waw undergoes compensatory lengthening to Qamets.

3. Imperfect verbs may also appear with the simple conjunction וְ as in וְיִכְתֹּב (and he will write). The "simple" or "regular" Waw conjunction has neither the form nor function of the Waw Conversive. In this case, the Imperfect is not "converted" and retains its normal Imperfect value. The spelling of the Waw Conversive on an Imperfect verb is very distinctive and cannot be missed (· וַ). Compare the two paradigms below and note how the spelling of the Waw Conversive on the Imperfect is distinct from that of the simple or regular Waw conjunction on the Imperfect.

	Qal Imperfect with Waw Conversive	Qal Imperfect with Regular Waw Conjunction	
3ms	וַיִּקְטֹל	וְיִקְטֹל	and he will kill
3fs	וַתִּקְטֹל	וְתִקְטֹל	and she will kill
2ms	וַתִּקְטֹל	וְתִקְטֹל	and you will kill
2fs	וַתִּקְטְלִי	וְתִקְטְלִי	and you will kill
1cs	וָאֶקְטֹל	וְאֶקְטֹל	and I will kill
3mp	וַיִּקְטְלוּ	וְיִקְטְלוּ	and they will kill
3fp	וַתִּקְטֹלְנָה	וְתִקְטֹלְנָה	and they will kill
2mp	וַתִּקְטְלוּ	וְתִקְטְלוּ	and you will kill
2fp	וַתִּקְטֹלְנָה	וְתִקְטֹלְנָה	and you will kill
1cp	וַנִּקְטֹל	וְנִקְטֹל	and we will kill

17.3   **The Use of the Converted Imperfect.** It has already been emphasized that converted verbal forms are used to describe a sequence of consecutive actions. In the context of Hebrew narrative, the converted Imperfect is normally used for the *past tense narrative sequence*.[3] In other words, when an author wanted to write about a series of actions in the past, he would use the Imperfect with Waw Conversive.

1.   Normally, the past tense narrative sequence will begin with a Perfect verb followed by any number of converted Imperfect verbs.[4] The Perfect verb that begins the sequence serves to signal the past tense narration. In this past tense narration, each converted Imperfect verb is temporally, logically, sequentially and (often) consequentially related to the preceding verb.

---

[3]   Though the terminology "past tense narrative sequence" is not commonly used, the term is descriptive of how the Imperfect with Waw Conversive functions in this type of biblical narration. The language will be used throughout because it is easily understood by the beginning student.

[4]   The past tense narrative sequence, also called the Perfect-Imperfect sequence, is often referred to by grammarians as the *qatal-wayyiqtol* sequence. This name derives from the transliteration of the Hebrew קָטַל וַיִּקְטֹל which represents the "classical" construction of the sequence, beginning with the Perfect (קָטַל) and followed by Imperfects with the Waw Conversive (וַיִּקְטֹל).

וְהָאָדָם יָדַע אֶת־חַוָּה אִשְׁתּוֹ וַתַּהַר וַתֵּלֶד אֶת־קַיִן

And Adam knew Eve his wife, *and then she
conceived, and then she bore* Cain (Gen 4:1).

וַתַּהַר Qal Imperfect 3fs הָרָה with Waw Conversive

וַתֵּלֶד Qal Imperfect 3fs יָלַד with Waw Conversive

וּמֹשֶׁה עָלָה אֶל־הָאֱלֹהִים וַיִּקְרָא אֵלָיו יְהוָה מִן־הָהָר

And Moses went up to God, *and then* Yahweh
called to him from the mountain (Ex 19:3).

וַיִּקְרָא Qal Imperfect 3ms קָרָא with Waw Conversive

2. Instead of a Perfect verbal form, the past tense narrative sequence
may also begin with the temporal modifier וַיְהִי followed by
Imperfect verbs with Waw Conversive. The form וַיְהִי is the Qal
Imperfect 3ms form of הָיָה (to be) with Waw Conversive.[5] It is
called a "temporal modifier" because it marks the beginning of
a *past tense* narrative sequence. This temporal modifier frequently
stands at the beginning of the sequence.

וַיְהִי אַחֲרֵי מוֹת אַבְרָהָם וַיְבָרֶךְ אֱלֹהִים אֶת־יִצְחָק בְּנוֹ

And after the death of Abraham
God blessed Isaac his son (Gen 25:11).

The form וַיְהִי may also appear at the beginning of a temporal
clause within the sequence. When beginning a temporal clause,
וַיְהִי is frequently followed by a preposition or conjunction like
כְּ or כַּאֲשֶׁר and the whole construction may be translated as
"and when." Words that designate time are commonly a part of
this type of construction.

וַיְהִי כְּמוֹת אַחְאָב וַיִּפְשַׁע מֶלֶךְ־מוֹאָב בְּמֶלֶךְ יִשְׂרָאֵל

And when Ahab died, the king of Moab
rebelled against the king of Israel (2 Kgs 3:5).

---

[5] וַיְהִי occurs 1,008 times in the Hebrew Bible. The Daghesh Forte that is
expected in the Imperfect preformative with the prefixing of the Waw Conversive
is absent because the verb begins with the syllable יְ.

3. The past tense narrative sequence may begin with either a Perfect verbal form or וַיְהִי followed by any number of converted Imperfect verbs. It is not uncommon, however, for this sequence to begin with the converted Imperfect itself.

וַיִּקְרָא אֶל־מֹשֶׁה וַיְדַבֵּר יְהוָה אֵלָיו מֵאֹהֶל מוֹעֵד

And Yahweh *called* to Moses and he spoke to him
from the tent of meeting (Lev 1:1).

וַיִּפְשַׁע מוֹאָב בְּיִשְׂרָאֵל אַחֲרֵי מוֹת אַחְאָב

Moab *rebelled* against Israel after the
death of Ahab (2 Kgs 1:1).

4. You now understand that the past tense narrative sequence is composed of a string of converted Imperfect verbs, each marked with the Waw Conversive. Occasionally, this string of converted forms may be interrupted by a regular Perfect in the place of an expected Imperfect with Waw Conversive. This interruption in the narrative sequence can happen for a number of reasons but it will happen frequently when a negative clause appears in the sequence. The negated verb interrupts the sequence in that the verb is no longer an Imperfect with Waw Conversive but now a regular Perfect following the negative particle. Note that the regular conjunction וְ is often prefixed to this negative particle (וְלֹא). After this interruption, the sequence may return to the string of converted Imperfect verbs. The following example illustrates a past tense narrative sequence that begins with a converted Imperfect (וַיֶּחֱזַק). The sequence is interrupted by a negative clause (וְלֹא־שָׁמַע) and then returns to converted Imperfect verbs (וַיָּבֹא and וַיִּפֶן).

וַיֶּחֱזַק לֵב־פַּרְעֹה וְלֹא־שָׁמַע אֲלֵהֶם כַּאֲשֶׁר דִּבֶּר יְהוָה
וַיִּפֶן פַּרְעֹה וַיָּבֹא אֶל־בֵּיתוֹ

And Pharaoh's heart became hard and he did not listen
to them just as Yahweh had said. And (so) Pharaoh
turned and went to his house (Ex 7:22-23).

17.4 **Changes in the Spelling of the Converted Imperfect Verb.** In most cases, the prefixing of the Waw Conversive does not change the spelling of the Imperfect verb. There are some weak verbs, however, that do experience minor changes. These changes should not give you too much trouble.

1. In I-א verbs of the אָמַר type and certain I-י verbs (including הָלַךְ), the stem vowel changes to Seghol.[6] Note the following examples:

יֹאמַר	he will say	➤	וַיֹּאמֶר	and he said
יֵשֵׁב	he will dwell	➤	וַיֵּשֶׁב	and he dwelt
יֵלֵךְ	he will walk	➤	וַיֵּלֶךְ	and he walked

2. With the prefixing of the Waw Conversive, Biconsonantal and III-ה verbs are "shortened" in those Imperfect forms without a sufformative (except the 1cs).[7] In Biconsonantal verbs, the medial vowel letter is lost. In III-ה verbs the final ה drops off. Note the following examples:

יָקוּם	he will rise up	➤	[8]וַיָּקָם	and he rose up
יָשִׂים	he will set	➤	וַיָּשֶׂם	and he set
יִבְנֶה	he will build	➤	וַיִּבֶן	and he built
יִגְלֶה	he will reveal	➤	וַיִּגֶל	and he revealed

17.5 **Form of Waw Conversive with the Perfect.**[9] When a Perfect verbal form is prefixed with Waw Conversive, it will be translated with the values of an Imperfect verb. A few examples will illustrate its form and basic translation.

---

[6] This type of change is occasioned by the retraction of the accent that occurs with the prefixing of the Waw Conversive to forms without a sufformative (except for the 1cs).

[7] This type of change is also occasioned by retraction of the accent.

[8] Note that the vowel under the ק is Qamets Hatuf and not Qamets.

[9] The Qal Perfect verb occurs 9,680 times in the Hebrew Bible. The Perfect prefixed with וְ (Waw Conversive or regular conjunction וְ) occurs 4,330 times. As you can see, the Qal Imperfect with Waw Conversive, occurring 11,485 times, is much more common than the Perfect with Waw Conversive.

Qal Perfect without Waw Conversive	*Qal Perfect with Waw Conversive*
שָׁמַר he observed	וְשָׁמַר and he will observe
זָכַר he remembered	וְזָכַר and he will remember

Note that the Waw Conversive with the Perfect is spelled differently than the Waw Conversive with the Imperfect.

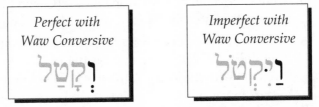

Perfect with Waw Conversive	*Imperfect with Waw Conversive*
וְקָטַל	וַיִּקְטֹל

With the Perfect, there is no difference in spelling between the Waw Conversive and the simple or regular conjunction וֹ (both are prefixed according to the rules of 5.7). Later in this chapter, we will discuss how to distinguish between the Waw Conversive and the regular conjunction on the Perfect. For now, study both the form and translation value of the Perfect with Waw Conversive.

Perfect with Waw Conversive

3ms	וְקָטַל	and he will kill
3fs	וְקָטְלָה	and she will kill
2ms	וְקָטַלְתָּ	and you will kill
2fs	וְקָטַלְתְּ	and you will kill
1cs	וְקָטַלְתִּי	and I will kill
3cp	וְקָטְלוּ	and they will kill
2mp	וּקְטַלְתֶּם	and you will kill
2fp	וּקְטַלְתֶּן	and you will kill
1cp	וְקָטַלְנוּ	and we will kill

Notes:

1. The spelling of the Perfect verb is not changed by the prefixing of the Waw Conversive.

2. On most forms, the Waw Conversive is spelled with Shewa (וְ). In the 2mp (וּקְטַלְתֶּם) and 2fp (וּקְטַלְתֶּן), the Waw Conversive is spelled וּ because it occurs before a consonant with Vocal Shewa (see 5.7).

3. In the Perfect with Waw Conversive, the accent usually shifts to the final syllable in the 1cs and 2ms forms. For example, קָטַלְתִּי (I killed) is accented on the second syllable but וְקָטַלְתִּי (and I will kill) is usually accented on the final syllable because it is prefixed with the Waw Conversive. This shift in accent does not occur, however, when the Perfect verb is prefixed with the regular conjunction as in וְקָטַלְתִּי (and I killed). The shift in accent can help you to distinguish between the Waw Conversive and the regular conjunction in the 1cs and 2ms forms. This point is illustrated with the beginning of Gen 9:15 which reads: וְזָכַרְתִּי אֶת־בְּרִיתִי. Given the similarity of spelling between the Waw Conversive and the regular conjunction on a Perfect, is the conjunction that is prefixed to זָכַרְתִּי the Waw Conversive or the regular conjunction? Should this text be translated as "I remembered my covenant" (regular conjunction) or "I will remember my covenant" (Waw Conversive)? Because the Hebrew Bible locates the accent on the final syllable (וְזָכַרְתִּי), the Waw should be identified as the Waw Conversive and translated "I will remember my covenant." Other contextual considerations, studied in the next section, will also help you to distinguish between the Waw Conversive and the regular conjunction on the Perfect.

17.6 **The Use of the Converted Perfect.** Like the converted Imperfect, the converted Perfect is also used in narrative sequences. The difference between the two, however, is that the converted Perfect is normally used for the *future tense narrative sequence*[10] (also habitual-durative)

---

[10] Though the terminology "future tense narrative sequence" is not commonly used, the term is descriptive of how the Perfect with Waw Conversive functions in this type of biblical narration. As with the designation "past tense narrative

rather than the *past tense narrative sequence* of the converted Imperfect.[11]
So, for example, Hebrew may use the converted Perfect for prophetic
revelations that look to the future. The first two uses detailed below
correspond to those of the converted Imperfect above.

1. Normally, the future tense narrative sequence begins with an
   Imperfect verb followed by any number of converted Perfect
   verbs. The Imperfect verb that begins this narrative sequence
   signals the future tense narration.

שֵׁשֶׁת יָמִים תַּעֲבֹד וְעָשִׂיתָ כָּל־מְלַאכְתֶּךָ

Six days you will labor *and (you will) do*
all your work (Deut 5:13).

לְמַעַן תִּזְכְּרוּ וַעֲשִׂיתֶם אֶת־כָּל־מִצְוֹתָי וִהְיִיתֶם קְדֹשִׁים לֵאלֹהֵיכֶם

So you will remember *and (you will) do* all my commandments
and (you will) be holy to your God (Num 15:40).

2. Recall from your study above that the temporal modifier וַיְהִי
   can mark the beginning of a past tense narrative sequence.
   Likewise, the temporal modifier וְהָיָה (Qal Perfect 3ms הָיָה with
   Waw Conversive) may mark the beginning of a future tense
   narrative sequence.[12]

וְהָיָה כִּי־יִקְרָא לָכֶם פַּרְעֹה וְאָמַר מַה־מַּעֲשֵׂיכֶם

When Pharaoh calls (to) you, *he will say,*
"What is your occupation?" (Gen 46:33).

וְהָיָה בַּיּוֹם הַהוּא וְשָׁבַרְתִּי אֶת־קֶשֶׁת יִשְׂרָאֵל

And in that day *I will break* the
bow of Israel (Hos 1:5).

---

sequence" above, this language will also be used throughout the discussion because
it is easily understood by the beginning student.

[11] On analogy with *qatal-wayyiqtol* (Perfect-Imperfect), the Imperfect-
Perfect sequence is often referred to as the *yiqtol-wᵉqatal* sequence. This designation
derives from the transliteration of the Hebrew יְקֹטֹל וְקָטַל which represents the
"classical" construction of this sequence, beginning with an Imperfect (יְקֹטֹל) and
followed by Perfects with Waw Conversive (וְקָטַל).

[12] וְהָיָה occurs 681 times in the Hebrew Bible.

3. The converted Perfect will frequently follow an Imperative verb.
In such cases, the converted Perfect verb will carry the full force
of the initial Imperative verb. Even though you have not yet
studied the Imperative verb form, the following examples should
be clear.

עֲמֹד בְּשַׁעַר בֵּית יְהוָה וְקָרָאתָ שָּׁם אֶת־הַדָּבָר הַזֶּה
וְאָמַרְתָּ שִׁמְעוּ דְבַר־יְהוָה

Stand (Imperative) in the gate of Yahweh's house *and*
(you will) proclaim there this word *and (you will) say,*
"Hear the word of Yahweh" (Jer 7:2).

שִׁמְעוּ אֶת־דִּבְרֵי הַבְּרִית הַזֹּאת וַעֲשִׂיתֶם אוֹתָם

Hear (Imperative) the words of this covenant
and (you will) do them (Jer 11:6).

17.7 **Translating the Temporal Modifiers and the Waw Conversive.** Because
of their frequency in certain contexts, the temporal modifiers וַיְהִי and
וְהָיָה are best not translated in most occurrences, though you can still
translate the conjunction as "and." Some will suggest, however, that
וַיְהִי be translated "and it came to pass that" and that וְהָיָה be translated
"and it will be that." Given the frequency with which these temporal
modifiers will sometimes appear in a narrative sequence, however, it is
often best to avoid these translations in the interest of good English
style.

17.8 **Parsing.** The parsing of converted verbal forms is just like the parsing
of regular Perfect or Imperfect verbs except that you must identify the
presence of the Waw Conversive as the following examples illustrate.

וַיִּשְׁמֹר Qal Imperfect 3ms שָׁמַר with Waw Conversive

וְזָכַר Qal Perfect 3ms זָכַר with Waw Conversive

17.9 Summary.

1. Converted verbal forms are used primarily to denote a sequence of consecutive actions, either in the past, present or future.

2. When an Imperfect verb is prefixed with the Waw Conversive, it will be translated with the values of the Perfect. The Waw Conversive on the Imperfect consists of the conjunction ו with a Pathach vowel beneath the conjunction and a Daghesh Forte in the Imperfect preformative (וַיִּקְטֹל).

3. The converted Imperfect is normally used for the past tense narrative sequence. This narrative sequence may begin with a Perfect verb followed by any number of converted Imperfects. It may also begin with וַיְהִי or a converted Imperfect.

4. Some weak verb classes experience minor spelling changes with the prefixing of the Waw Conversive. In I-א verbs of the אָמַר type and certain I-י verbs (including הָלַךְ), the stem vowel changes to Seghol. Biconsonantal and III-ה converted verbs are "shortened" in those forms without a sufformative (except the 1cs).

5. When a Perfect verb is prefixed with the Waw Conversive, it will be translated with the values of the Imperfect. The Waw Conversive with the Perfect is spelled just like the simple or regular conjunction (וְקָטַל). In order to distinguish between the Waw Conversive and the regular conjunction on the Perfect, you will need to rely upon certain issues of context (17.6). Additionally, a shift in accent in the Perfect 1cs and 2ms forms may provide you with the correct identification.

6. The converted Perfect is commonly used for the future tense narrative sequence (also habitual-durative). This narrative sequence may begin with an Imperfect verb followed by any number of converted Perfects. It may also begin with the temporal modifier וְהָיָה.

7. At first, you should probably translate every Waw Conversive and temporal modifier in order to reinforce their identification in translation. Later on, however, it is preferable not to translate every one of these forms.

17.10 Vocabulary.

Verbs

אָהַב	to love (216)
אָסַף	to gather, take in (200)
כָּלָה	to cease, come to an end, finish, complete (207)
שָׁפַט	to judge, enter into controversy (204)
אָבַד	to perish (185)
גָּלָה	to reveal, uncover (187)
רוּם	to be(come) high, exalted (197)
טָהֵר	to be clean, be pure (94)
בָּעַר	to consume, burn (94)

Nouns

אֱמֶת	truth, trustworthiness (127); feminine
כִּסֵּא	seat, throne (135)
מִסְפָּר	number (134)
עֶשֶׂר	(group of) ten, decade (259)
שֶׁמֶשׁ	sun (158)

17.11 Believing is Seeing. When Abraham is called in Gen 12, he is expected to trust God to take him "to a land *I will show you*" (אַרְאֶךָּ, Hiphil Imperfect 1cs of רָאָה with 2ms pronominal suffix). This is a radical call, to leave everything familiar without any knowledge of where he was going. His only source of confidence could be the promise of God "to show him." In a second episode of testing (Gen 22), Abraham is called to sacrifice his beloved son in "the land of Moriah" or הַמֹּרִיָּה (a name likely playing on the same root, רָאָה). Abraham set out promptly and on the third day he lifted up his eyes and *saw* (וַיַּרְא Qal Imperfect 3ms of רָאָה with Waw Conversive) the place to which God was leading him (22:4). In 22:8, when Isaac asks his father where the offering is, the answer is simply: "God will *reveal* it" אֱלֹהִים יִרְאֶה־לּוֹ (Qal Imperfect 3ms of רָאָה). As Abraham was about to slay his son, the angel's voice stopped him. The patriarch lifted up his eyes (again) and *saw* (וַיַּרְא Qal Imperfect 3ms of רָאָה with Waw Conversive) a ram caught in the thicket (22:13).

As a result of this divine provision, Abraham names the place יְהוָה יִרְאֶה (The Lord *will see*). In 22:13, the verb is again a Qal Imperfect of רָאָה. To this day, we are told in 22:14, the name is retained because, "on the mount of the Lord it shall be revealed" (יֵרָאֶה Niphal Imperfect 3ms of רָאָה).

Most of us know the name from this story as "Jehovah Jireh" which translates "The Lord [my] Provider." The root רָאָה certainly carries the nuance of providing in this context. But it is helpful to bear in mind its primary meaning, that of sight: The Lord "revealed" the sacrifice to Abraham.

In the Old Testament, faith is sometimes described as a form of sight. In 2 Chr 26:5, the faithful king Uzziah was commended for, literally, "learning how *to see* God" (רְאֹת Qal Infinitive Construct from רָאָה). One of the most common designations for an Old Testament prophet is רֹאֶה, a *seer*. A prophet was a person who could see divine things, and could see earthly things from God's perspective. Abraham would one day be honored in Hebrews 11 for a faith defined as the "conviction of things *not yet seen*."

Tim Laniak
Assistant Professor of Old Testament
Gordon-Conwell Theological Seminary
Charlotte, North Carolina

Chapter 18

Qal Imperative, Cohortative and Jussive

18.1 **Introduction.** In this chapter, we will study the Hebrew *volitional* conjugations known as Imperative, Cohortative and Jussive. The term "volitional" describes those conjugations used, as a general rule, *to express some type of command, wish or desire.* The various forms of the volitional conjugations are related to corresponding Imperfect forms. For this reason, you will want to have mastered the Imperfect forms of strong and weak verbs before working through this chapter.

18.2 **Imperative Conjugation.** The Imperative is the most frequently occurring volitional conjugation in the Hebrew Bible.[1] It is used primarily to express direct commands, demanding (immediate) action from the one being addressed. It can also be used to grant permission or to communicate a request. The Hebrew Imperative *occurs only in the second person, singular and plural.* For example, "*You* (second person) *defend* the cause of the weak!"

18.3 **Imperative Paradigm: Strong Verbs.** Because the Imperative conjugation occurs exclusively in the second person, there are only four forms to study: masculine singular and plural and feminine singular and plural. These forms will be easy to memorize because they are derived from their corresponding Imperfect forms. You should think of the Imperative verbal form as an Imperfect without the preformative. The following Imperative paradigm must be memorized.

	Imperative	Sufformative	Translation
2ms	קְטֹל		(you) kill!
2fs	קִטְלִי	ִי	(you) kill!
2mp	קִטְלוּ	וּ	(you) kill!
2fp	קְטֹלְנָה	נָה	(you) kill!

---

[1] The Imperative conjugation occurs 4,323 times in the Hebrew Bible. In the Qal stem it occurs 2,898 times, 67% of all Imperatives.

18.4 Imperative Paradigm Notes.

1. The most important observation to make is that the above forms of the Imperative are related to their corresponding Imperfect forms. Remove the Imperfect preformative (consonant and vowel) from the four second person forms, singular and plural, and you have the Imperative paradigm. This means that if you have memorized the Imperfect paradigm, then you already know the forms of the Imperative.

	Imperfect Form		*Subtract Preformative*		*Imperative Form*
2ms	תִּקְטֹל	⟩	תִּ|קְטֹל	⟩	קְטֹל
2fs	תִּקְטְלִי	⟩	תִּ|קְטְלִי	⟩	קְטְלִי
2mp	תִּקְטְלוּ	⟩	תִּ|קְטְלוּ	⟩	קְטְלוּ
2fp	תִּקְטֹלְנָה	⟩	תִּ|קְטֹלְנָה	⟩	קְטֹלְנָה

2. Both the 2fs and 2mp forms undergo a minor change based upon the rule that two Vocal Shewas cannot stand together at the beginning of a word (3.15). For example, begin with the Imperfect form תִּקְטְלוּ and subtract the preformative (consonant and vowel) for the Imperative and you are left with קְטְלוּ. Because two Vocal Shewas cannot stand together at the beginning of a word, the Imperative form is subsequently rendered קִטְלוּ after applying Rule of Shewa (3.15).

3. Frequently (245 times), the 2ms Imperative appears with an הָ ending as in קָטְלָה (kill!). Note that the vowel in the first syllable is Qamets Hatuf and not Qamets. Be careful not to confuse this alternate Imperative form with the Qal Perfect 3fs קָטְלָה. Context (and the Metheg) will enable you to distinguish between the two forms. It is important to note that this alternate form with הָ does not translate differently than the regular 2ms form. Below are three more examples of the 2ms Imperative with the הָ ending.

Verbal Root	*Regular 2ms Form*	*Alternate Form (הָ)*	*Translation*
שָׁמַר	שְׁמֹר	שָׁמְרָה	you (2ms) observe!
שָׁפַט	שְׁפֹט	שָׁפְטָה	you (2ms) judge!
שָׁמַע	שְׁמַע	שָׁמְעָה[2]	you (2ms) listen!

18.5 **Negation of the Imperative.** To produce a negative command, Hebrew does not negate an Imperative form. Prohibitions (negative commands) are expressed with the negative particles לֹא or אַל with the Imperfect (see 15.9). For review, the particle לֹא before the Imperfect can express an absolute and permanent prohibition. The particle אַל before an Imperfect expresses an immediate and specific prohibition (see also 18.15).

18.6 **The Particle נָא.** Frequently (242 times), Imperatives are followed by the particle נָא which may be translated as "please" or simply left untranslated. This particle may or may not be connected to the Imperative with a Maqqef. For example, both שְׁמֹר נָא and שָׁמָר־נָא occur and may be translated as either "observe!" or "please observe!" Note that when the Imperative is connected to the particle with a Maqqef, there is a vowel change in the Imperative (Holem to Qamets Hatuf). Do not be concerned since the presence of the נָא particle is often an indication of the Imperative, though it can signal other forms as well.

18.7 **Translating the Imperative.** When translating the Hebrew Imperative, it is not always necessary to use the second person pronoun (you). For example, שְׁמֹר may be translated as either "you observe!" or simply "observe!" English style normally prefers the shorter translation without the pronoun. Please note, however, that the Imperative is always second person even if you choose not to use the second person pronoun in your translation. The following examples illustrate both translation options.

---

[2] With relative frequency, the vowel under the first root consonant in these alternate Imperative forms will be Hireq instead of Qamets.

עִבְדוּ אֶת־יְהוָה[3]	You (2mp) serve Yahweh! (Ex 10:8)	
	Serve Yahweh!	
קְבֹר מֵתֶךָ	You (2ms) bury your dead! (Gen 23:6)	
	Bury your dead!	
שְׁמַע בְּקוֹלָם	You (2ms) heed their voice! (1 Sam 8:22)	
	Heed their voice!	

18.8 **Weak Forms of the Imperative: Part 1**. You have learned that strong verb Imperative forms are related to strong Imperfect forms. This also holds true for the weak verb forms of the Imperative. There are, however, some weak Imperative forms that do not correspond exactly to their Imperfect counterparts. These changes are minor and should not present any great difficulty in terms of recognizing the forms of the paradigm. It is important to note in the following weak verb Imperatives that no root consonants are lost and all of the expected sufformatives remain unchanged.

	I-Guttural			II-Guttural		
	Imperfect		*Imperative*	*Imperfect*		*Imperative*
2ms	תֶּחֱזַק	>	חֲזַק	תִּבְחַר	>	בְּחַר
2fs	תֶּחֶזְקִי	>	חִזְקִי	תִּבְחֲרִי	>	בַּחֲרִי
2mp	תֶּחֶזְקוּ	>	חִזְקוּ	תִּבְחֲרוּ	>	בַּחֲרוּ
2fp	תֶּחֱזַקְנָה	>	חֲזַקְנָה	תִּבְחַרְנָה	>	בְּחַרְנָה

---

[3] Frequently, in the 2fs and 2mp Imperative forms (such as עִבְדִי and עִבְדוּ), the Daghesh Lene that is expected in the *begadkephat* consonant after the Silent Shewa is given up. This loss of Daghesh Lene (in a *begadkephat* consonant after a closed syllable) was seen in 10.5.7 in the study of Segholate nouns. It occurs in other circumstances as well.

	I-א Type 1[4]			I-א Type 2	
	Imperfect	*Imperative*		*Imperfect*	*Imperative*
2ms	תֶּאֱסֹר	➤ אֱסֹר		תֹּאמַר	➤ אֱמֹר
2fs	תַּאַסְרִי	➤ אִסְרִי		תֹּאמְרִי	➤ אִמְרִי
2mp	תַּאַסְרוּ	➤ אִסְרוּ		תֹּאמְרוּ	➤ אִמְרוּ
2fp	תֶּאֱסֹרְנָה	➤ אֱסֹרְנָה		תֹּאמַרְנָה	➤ אֱמֹרְנָה

	III-ח/ע			III-א	
	Imperfect	*Imperative*		*Imperfect*	*Imperative*
2ms	תִּשְׁלַח	➤ שְׁלַח		תִּמְצָא	➤ מְצָא
2fs	תִּשְׁלְחִי	➤ שִׁלְחִי		תִּמְצְאִי	➤ מִצְאִי
2mp	תִּשְׁלְחוּ	➤ שִׁלְחוּ		תִּמְצְאוּ	➤ מִצְאוּ
2fp	תִּשְׁלַחְנָה	➤ שְׁלַחְנָה		תִּמְצֶאנָה	➤ מְצֶאנָה

18.9   **Weak Forms of the Imperative: Part 2**. In the above triconsonantal weak verb classes (18.8), you studied Imperative forms in which no root consonants were lost. Compared to the strong verb paradigm, some minor vowel changes were observed. Now we will study four triconsonantal weak verb classes in which a root consonant is lost. When encountering such a form, you will need to recover the missing consonant in order to identify the verbal root. Once again, the best way to begin reconstructing verbal roots is to know your options. As you will see from the following discussion, there are four major classes that drop a root consonant in the Imperative conjugation: III-ה, I-נ, I-י and Geminate. When you are attempting to reconstruct a triconsonantal verbal root from only two remaining consonants, use the order provided above. For example, if you were to encounter שַׁל־נְעָלֶיךָ (...your shoes!) in Exodus 3:5, you would need to reconstruct the verbal root of the Imperative שַׁל in order to determine its lexical meaning. Begin with

---

[4] You will recall that there are two types of I-א Imperfects. Type 1 has a Seghol preformative vowel as in יֶאֱסֹר and Type 2 has a Holem preformative vowel as in יֹאמַר. In the Imperative conjugation, however, only one type exists. Regardless of the Imperfect pattern, the Imperative conjugation follows only one pattern of vocalization.

the III-ה option, שָׁלָה (be quiet) and you will find from the lexicon that this does not work (Be quiet your shoes!). Next, try the I-נ option, נָשַׁל (to remove) and you will discover that this is the correct option (Remove your shoes!). Once you have correctly identified the full verbal root, you may want to check the other options in order to confirm your selection. In this case, neither the I-י form יָשַׁל (unattested) or the Geminate form שָׁלַל (Plunder your shoes!) provides a better option.

III-ה

	Imperfect		Imperative
2ms	תִּבְנֶה	⟩	בְּנֵה[5]
2fs	תִּבְנִי	⟩	בְּנִי
2mp	תִּבְנוּ	⟩	בְּנוּ
2fp	תִּבְנֶ֫ינָה	⟩	בְּנֶ֫ינָה

Geminate

	Imperfect		Imperative
2ms	תָּסֹב	⟩	סֹב
2fs	תָּסֹ֫בִּי	⟩	סֹ֫בִּי[6]
2mp	תָּסֹ֫בּוּ	⟩	סֹ֫בּוּ
2fp	תְּסֻבֶּ֫ינָה	⟩	סֻבְנָה

I-נ Type 1[7]

	Imperfect		Imperative
2ms	תִּפֹּל	⟩	נְפֹל
2fs	תִּפְּלִי	⟩	נִפְלִי
2mp	תִּפְּלוּ	⟩	נִפְלוּ
2fp	תִּפֹּ֫לְנָה	⟩	נְפֹ֫לְנָה

I-נ Type 2[8]

	Imperfect		Imperative
2ms	תִּסַּע	⟩	סַע
2fs	תִּסְעִי	⟩	סְעִי
2mp	תִּסְעוּ	⟩	סְעוּ
2fp	תִּסַּ֫עְנָה	⟩	סַ֫עְנָה

---

[5] The final ה in this form is a vowel letter and not the third root consonant. This vowel letter, however, does make identification of the verbal root a little easier. The ה ֶ ending is diagnostic of III-ה ms Imperative forms in the Qal and derived stems.

[6] The Daghesh Forte in the remaining Geminate consonant of the Imperative 2fs and 2mp forms is diagnostic of the Geminate class.

[7] In the Imperfect of this I-נ class, the נ (first consonant of the verbal root) has assimilated into the second root consonant and remains as a Daghesh Forte. It does not assimilate, however, in the Imperative forms of this type. In this type of I-נ verb, the Imperative preserves all three consonants of the verbal root, including the נ in first root position.

[8] In the Imperfect of this I-נ class, the second root consonant exhibits the Daghesh Forte, representing the assimilated נ that is the first consonant of the verbal root. The Imperative forms of this I-נ type (Type 2) simply drop the נ that is the first consonant of the verbal root. These are called short Imperative forms because only two root consonants remain.

	I-ʸ Type 1			I-ʸ Type 2[9]	
	Imperfect	*Imperative*		*Imperfect*	*Imperative*
2ms	תֵּשֵׁב	➤ שֵׁב		תִּירַשׁ	➤ רַשׁ
2fs	תֵּשְׁבִי	➤ שְׁבִי		תִּירְשִׁי	➤ רְשִׁי
2mp	תֵּשְׁבוּ	➤ שְׁבוּ		תִּירְשׁוּ	➤ רְשׁוּ
2fp	תֵּשַׁבְנָה	➤ שֵׁבְנָה		תִּירַשְׁנָה	➤ רַשְׁנָה

18.10 **Biconsonantal Imperative Forms.** Biconsonantal Imperatives are quite easy to recognize with only minor variation in the 2fp. Carefully study the Imperative forms of the three Biconsonantal classes. Note that the Imperatives, for the most part, retain the distinctive vowel letters of the corresponding Imperfect forms.

	קוּם			שִׂים	
	Imperfect	*Imperative*		*Imperfect*	*Imperative*
2ms	תָּקוּם	➤ קוּם[10]		תָּשִׂים	➤ שִׂים
2fs	תָּקֹוּמִי	➤ קֹוּמִי		תָּשִֽׂימִי	➤ שִֽׂימִי
2mp	תָּקֹוּמוּ	➤ קֹוּמוּ		תָּשִֽׂימוּ	➤ שִֽׂימוּ
2fp	תְּקוּמֶֽינָה	➤ קֹמְנָה		תְּשִׂימֶֽינָה	

	בּוֹא	
	Imperfect	*Imperative*
2ms	תָּבוֹא	➤ בּוֹא
2fs	תָּבֹואִי	➤ בֹּואִי
2mp	תָּבֹואוּ	➤ בֹּואוּ
2fp	תָּבֹואנָה	

---

[9] In the Imperfect of both I-ʸ types, the first consonant of the verbal root has been lost (though the Hireq Yod preformative vowel in Type 2 is helpfully reminiscent of this lost consonant). Both Type 1 and Type 2 have short Imperative forms, preserving only the second and third root consonants.

[10] The alternate form קוּמָה occurs 16 times.

18.11 Irregular or Doubly Weak Imperatives. The following six paradigms represent irregular or doubly verbs. For the most part, each Imperative form is related to its Imperfect counterpart. If you have mastered the Imperfect of these verbs, then the Imperative forms will present no significant difficulty.

נָתַן (to give)

	Imperfect		Imperative
2ms	תִּתֵּן	➤	תֵּן [12]
2fs	תִּתְּנִי	➤	תְּנִי
2mp	תִּתְּנוּ	➤	תְּנוּ
2fp	תִּתֵּנָּה	➤	תֵּנָּה

לָקַח [11] (to take)

	Imperfect		Imperative
2ms	תִּקַּח	➤	קַח
2fs	תִּקְחִי	➤	קְחִי
2mp	תִּקְחוּ	➤	קְחוּ
2fp	תִּקַּחְנָה	➤	קַחְנָה

הָלַךְ [13] (to walk)

	Imperfect		Imperative
2ms	תֵּלֵךְ	➤	לֵךְ [14]
2fs	תֵּלְכִי	➤	לְכִי
2mp	תֵּלְכוּ	➤	לְכוּ
2fp	תֵּלַכְנָה	➤	לֵכְנָה

הָיָה (to be)

	Imperfect		Imperative
2ms	תִּהְיֶה	➤	הֱיֵה
2fs	תִּהְיִי		
2mp	תִּהְיוּ	➤	הֱיוּ
2fp	תִּהְיֶינָה		

עָלָה (to go up)

	Imperfect		Imperative
2ms	תַּעֲלֶה	➤	עֲלֵה
2fs	תַּעֲלִי	➤	עֲלִי
2mp	תַּעֲלוּ	➤	עֲלוּ
2fp	תַּעֲלֶינָה	➤	עֲלֶינָה

נָטָה (to extend)

	Imperfect		Imperative
2ms	תִּטֶּה	➤	נְטֵה
2fs	תִּטִּי	➤	נְטִי
2mp	תִּטּוּ	➤	נְטוּ
2fp	תִּטֶּינָה	➤	נְטֶינָה

---

[11] This verb behaves just like the Type 2 verb of the I-נ class listed above (נָסַע), that is, the ל behaves just like the נ and is assimilated in selected Imperfect forms. There is no assimilation of the ל in the Imperative forms. It simply drops.

[12] The alternate form תְּנָה occurs 17 times.

[13] This verb behaves just like the Type 1 verb of the I-י class discussed above (16.16).

[14] The alternate form לְכָה occurs 17 times.

18.12 **Frequently Confused Forms.** Some forms of the Imperative are easily confused with other verb and noun forms. Five pairs of the most commonly confused words are listed below. In some instances, the different words are identical in form. In such cases, context will enable you to make the correct choice.

1. כָּתְבָה Qal Perfect 3fs from כָּתַב meaning "she wrote"

   כָּתְבָה Qal Imperative 2ms from כָּתַב (with the הָ ending) meaning "(you) write!"

2. כָּתְבוּ Qal Perfect 3cp from כָּתַב meaning "they wrote"

   כִּתְבוּ Qal Imperative 2mp from כָּתַב meaning "(you) write!"

3. בְּנִי Qal Imperative 2fs from בָּנָה meaning "(you) build!"

   בְּנִי Masculine singular noun בֵּן with 1cs pronominal suffix meaning "my son"

4. בָּנוּ Qal Perfect 3cp from בָּנָה meaning "they built"

   בְּנוּ Qal Imperative 2mp from בָּנָה meaning "(you) build!"

5. עָלוּ Qal Perfect 3cp from עָלָה meaning "they went up"

   עֲלוּ Qal Imperative 2mp from עָלָה meaning "(you) go up!"

18.13 **Cohortative.** The Cohortative conjugation is used much like the Imperative, to express a wish, request or command. It may also be used, however, to express purpose (in order to) or result (resulting in). The Cohortative *occurs only in the first person, singular and plural*. For example, "*Let* me (1cs) *honor* the Lord!" or "*May* we (1cp) *honor* the Lord!" When translating the Cohortative, use the key words "let" or "may" as in these two examples. Like the Imperative, the particle נָא also occurs with the Cohortative.

The Cohortative verbal form is constructed by adding הָ to a first person form of the Imperfect. This final הָ is the diagnostic indicator of the Cohortative conjugation. It might be helpful to think of the Cohortative as a lengthened form of the Imperfect.

Imperfect			Cohortative
אֶקְטֹל	+	הָ ַ =	אֶקְטְלָה
נִקְטֹל	+	הָ ַ =	נִקְטְלָה

In each of the above Cohortative forms, note that the stem vowel is reduced from Holem to Vocal Shewa as in אֶקְטְלָה. The following are additional examples of the Cohortative.

אֶשְׁמְרָה תוֹרָתְךָ   *May I observe* your law (Ps 119:44).
Let me observe your law.

נִכְרְתָה בְרִית   *Let us make* (cut) a covenant (Gen 26:28).
May we make (cut) a covenant.

18.14 Jussive. The Jussive conjugation is used to express either a mild command or a strong wish. It occurs *in the third person* (3ms, 3fs, 3mp, 3fp).[15] When translating the Jussive, you can use the same key words "let" or "may" as with the Cohortative. Like the Imperative and Cohortative above, the particle נָא also occurs with the Jussive.

With strong verbs, the Jussive is the same as its corresponding Imperfect form, as in יִכְתֹּב which may be translated as either "he will write" or "let him write." The Imperfect translation value is far more frequent than the Jussive translation. Context should suggest the correct identification, though there certainly are instances of ambiguity. The presence of the particle נָא will suggest the Jussive translation.

יִזְכָּר־נָא הַמֶּלֶךְ אֶת־יְהוָה   *Let* the king *remember* Yahweh (2 Sam 14:11).

יִשְׁפֹּט יְהוָה בֵּינִי וּבֵינֶיךָ   *May* Yahweh *judge* between me and between you (Gen 16:5).

יִסְלַח יְהוָה לְעַבְדֶּךָ   *May* Yahweh *forgive* your servant (2 Kgs 5:18).

It must be repeated that, unlike Imperative and Cohortative forms that are *inflected differently* than their Imperfect counterparts, Jussive verbal forms are *often the same* as the third person Imperfect forms (singular

---

[15] Infrequent by comparison, first and second person Jussives are also attested.

and plural). In other words, third person Imperfect forms may also be translated with the Jussive nuance in strong and many weak verbs.

With certain weak verbs, however, the Jussive is a shortened (or apocopated) form of the Imperfect. For example, these shortened forms are encountered with frequency in the III-הֹ class of weak verbs.[16] Study the following chart of III-הֹ Perfect, Imperfect and (short) Jussive forms. All forms are 3ms.

Perfect	*Imperfect*	*Jussive (short)*
בָּנָה he built	יִבְנֶה he will build	יִּבֶן let him build
עָשָׂה he made	יַעֲשֶׂה he will make	יַּעַשׂ let him make
עָלָה he went up	יַעֲלֶה he will go up	יַּעַל let him go up
רָאָה he saw	יִרְאֶה he will see	יֵּרְא let him see

It is obvious that the Imperfect and Jussive forms are spelled differently. The Imperfect forms have an הֹ ending. The Jussive forms *do not* have the הֹ ending. These distinctive Jussive forms are attested only in the singular. They are not attested in the plural because the plural Imperfect forms have sufformatives that cannot be dropped. Below study two biblical examples of III-הֹ Jussive verbs.

וְיִבֶן אֶת־בֵּית יְהוָה   And *let him build* the house of Yahweh (Ezra 1:3). יִבֶן is a shortened form of the Qal Imperfect 3ms יִבְנֶה from בָּנָה (to build).

וַיֹּאמֶר אֱלֹהִים יְהִי אוֹר   And God said, "*let there be* light" (Gen 1:3). יְהִי is a shortened form of the Qal Imperfect 3ms יִהְיֶה from הָיָה (to be).

Note that the Jussive form in each text (וְיִבֶן in Ezra 1:3 and יְהִי in Gen 1:3) is translated with the volitional nuance ("let him build" and "let there be"). Further note that the short Jussive form is the same form that occurs when prefixed with the Waw Conversive (17.4.2). When prefixed with Waw Conversive, the short Imperfect form will not be translated with a volitional nuance. In terms of frequency, the short

---

[16] Shortened forms are also attested with Geminate and Biconsonantal roots.

form with Waw Conversive is much more common. The primary importance of short III-ה Imperfect forms is that, in a past tense narrative sequence, the Waw Conversive is prefixed to the short form (יִּבֶן) and not to the long form (יִבְנֶה).The following examples illustrate the use of short Imperfect forms that are prefixed with the Waw Conversive and so they are not to be translated with the volitional nuance.

וַיִּבֶן נֹחַ מִזְבֵּחַ לַיהוָה	*And* Noah *built* an altar to Yahweh (Gen 8:20). וַיִּבֶן is Qal Imperfect 3ms from בָּנָה with Waw Conversive.
וַיְהִי־עֶרֶב וַיְהִי־בֹקֶר	*And it was* evening *and it was* morning (Gen 1:5). וַיְהִי is Qal Imperfect 3ms from הָיָה with Waw Conversive.
וַיַּעַל מֹשֶׁה אֶל־הַר הָאֱלֹהִים	*And* Moses *went up* to the mountain of God (Ex 24:13). וַיַּעַל is Qal Imperfect 3ms from עָלָה with Waw Conversive.

18.15 Negation of the Cohortative and Jussive. In general, Jussive and Co-hortative verbs are negated with אַל (15:9; 18:5). This construction ex-presses a negative wish or a milder form of prohibition than that ex-pressed by לֹא plus the Imperfect. The particle נָא is sometimes attached to אַל with the Maqqef (אַל־נָא). In most instances, you do not need to translate the particle נָא.

אַל־נָא נֹאבְדָה	Do not let us perish (Jonah 1:14).
וְאַל־יִחַר אַפְּךָ בְּעַבְדֶּךָ	Do not let your anger burn against your servant (Gen 44:18).

18.16 Important Sequences with Volitional Conjugations. There are many important sequences involving the volitional conjugations. Three of the more important sequences are described below.

1. Several Imperative verbs may occur in succession. They may or may not be linked with the conjunction (וְ). In this construction, context will determine whether or not they are related consequentially or sequentially.

עֲלֵה וּקְבֹר אֶת־אָבִיךְ   *Go up* and *bury* your father (Gen 50:6).

זֹאת עֲשׂוּ וִחְיוּ   *Do* this and *you will live* (Gen 42:18).

2. An Imperative may be followed by a Perfect verb with Waw Conversive. In this sequence, the Perfect verb may carry the full force of the preceding Imperative in its translation. In other words, the Perfect verb with Waw Conversive and the preceding Imperative are related in terms of consecution of action.

לֵךְ וְאָמַרְתָּ אֶל־עַבְדִּי   *Go* and *say* to my servant (2 Sam 7:5).

שָׁמֹר וְשָׁמַעְתָּ אֵת כָּל־הַדְּבָרִים הָאֵלֶּה   *Observe* and *obey* all of these these words (Deut 12:28).

3. An Imperative may be followed by an Imperfect or Cohortative, a construction that will create a purpose or result clause. In this sequence, the Imperfect will be marked with the conjunction וְ (not Waw Conversive) and may be translated as "so that."

רְדוּ־שָׁמָּה וְשִׁבְרוּ־לָנוּ מִשָּׁם וְנִחְיֶה   Go down there and buy grain for us from there *so that we might live* (Gen 42:2).

הוֹצֵא אֶת־בִּנְךָ וְיָמֹת   Bring out your son *so that he may die* (Judg 6:30). הוֹצֵא is Hiphil Imperative 2ms from יָצָא.

18.17 Summary.

1. A volitional conjugation is used to express some type of command, wish or desire. In Hebrew, the volitional conjugations are the Imperative (second person), Cohortative (first person) and Jussive (third person). By far, the Imperative is the most frequent volitional conjugation in the Hebrew Bible.

2. Each of the volitional conjugations is related to corresponding Imperfect forms. The Imperative and Jussive, in some instances, are shortened forms of the Imperfect. The Cohortative is a lengthened form of the Imperfect.

3. Memorization of the following Qal Imperative paradigm for the strong verb is required.

	Imperative	Sufformative	Translation
2ms	קְטֹל		(you) kill!
2fs	קִטְלִי	ִי	(you) kill!
2mp	קִטְלוּ	וּ	(you) kill!
2fp	קְטֹלְנָה	נָה	(you) kill!

4. In the strong verb, the Imperative forms are related to their corresponding Imperfect forms. Remove the Imperfect preformative from the four second person forms and you have the Imperative paradigm. Some variation in spelling does occur in certain weak verb classes.

5. The Cohortative conjugation occurs only in the first person, singular and plural. This verbal form is constructed by adding ָה to either first person form of the Imperfect. The final ָה is diagnostic of the Cohortative conjugation. When translating the Cohortative, use the key words "let" or "may."

6. The Jussive conjugation occurs in the third person, singular and plural. In most verb types, the Jussive verbal form is the same as its corresponding Imperfect form. In such cases, only context will make identification possible. The Jussive may also be a shortened form of the Imperfect. This is the case with III-ה, Geminate and Biconsonantal verbal roots. When translating the Jussive, you can use the same key words "let" or "may" as with the Cohortative.

7. To produce a negative command, the Imperative is not negated. Prohibitions (negative commands) are expressed with the negative particles לֹא and אַל followed by Imperfect, Jussive or Cohortative forms (15.9; 18.5, 15).

8. The נָא particle of entreaty may be translated as "please" or simply left untranslated. This particle may occur with or without the Maqqef (נָא־). It occurs with all three volitional forms and is a helpful marker of the volitional conjugations.

18.18   Vocabulary.

Verbs

בָּחַר	to choose (172)
בִּין	to understand, perceive (171)
דָּרַשׁ	to seek (165)
הָרַג	to kill (167)
קָדַשׁ	to be holy (171)
רָעָה	to feed, graze, tend flocks (164)
חָפֵץ	to please, delight, take pleasure (74)
טוֹב	to be good, pleasant (44)
שָׁאַל	to ask (for), demand (176)

Nouns

בַּעַל	owner, husband, Baal (210)
שֵׁבֶט	rod, staff, tribe (190)

Other

נָא	please, now (405); particle of entreaty often not translated
יַעַן	on account of, because (100)
בַּעַד	behind, through (104); also as בְּעַד

18.19   Choose for Yourselves Whom You Will Serve. Hebrew can use the construction of an Imperative verb followed by the preposition לְ with a suffix to emphasize the action of a particular subject, often in isolated contrast to the behavior of others. For example, when God calls Abraham, he says לֶךְ־לְךָ (literally, "go yourself" or "you go"). The construction is a Qal Imperative of הָלַךְ followed by the preposition לְ with 2ms pronominal suffix. Grammars sometimes refer to this use of לְ as an "ethical dative," not because other datives are unethical (!), but because of its reflexive emphasis on the subject's or object's independent, individual choice. Notice how the verse continues: "Go yourself from your land and your family and from the house of your father to a land I will show you." God is calling Abraham to a *determined disassociation* with his family and surroundings. The phrase is used again in Gen 22 when God calls Abraham to sacrifice his only son on Mt. Moriah.

In Josh 22:4, we find the same construction used when the Reubenites, the Gadites, and the half-tribe of Manasseh are summoned after the initial conquest to return to the eastern side of the Jordan: פְּנוּ וּלְכוּ לָכֶם לְאָהֳלֵיכֶם (literally, "turn and go yourselves to your tents"). Note the sequence of the Qal Imperative of פָּנָה followed by the Qal Imperative of הָלַךְ and, finally, the preposition לְ with a 2mp pronominal suffix. This was the time for the two and one half tribes to separate themselves from the other tribes and establish their independent identity in a different geographical location. In Joshua's final speech to all the people, he calls them to make a *spiritual* choice of distinction: "If serving the Lord seems useless to you, then choose for yourselves [בַּחֲרוּ לָכֶם; Qal Imperative of בָּחַר plus the preposition לְ with 2mp pronominal suffix] today whom you will serve ... but as for me and my household, we will serve the Lord" (Josh 24:15).

Tim Laniak
Assistant Professor of Old Testament
Gordon-Conwell Theological Seminary
Charlotte, North Carolina

Chapter 19

Pronominal Suffixes on Verbs

19.1 **Introduction.** In chapter 9, you learned how to identify pronominal suffixes on nouns, prepositions and the definite direct object marker. In this chapter, you will learn how to identify pronominal suffixes on Qal Perfect, Imperfect and Imperative verbs. You already know that when a pronoun is the direct object of a verb, it is commonly attached to the definite direct object marker אֵת or אֶת־ (9.14) as in the following examples.

יִשְׁמֹר אֹתָנוּ   he will keep us

שָׁפַט אֹתְךָ   he judged you

In each of these examples, the direct object is a pronoun and it is attached to the accusative particle. There is, however, another way of indicating this grammatical construction. Instead of adding the pronominal suffix to the definite direct object marker, it may be added directly to the verb.

יִשְׁמְרֵנוּ   he will keep us
(Qal Imperfect 3ms שָׁמַר with 1cp suffix)

שְׁפָטְךָ   he judged you
(Qal Perfect 3ms שָׁפַט with 2ms suffix)

Note that both grammatical constructions are translated in the same way. In this chapter, you will learn how to identify pronominal suffixes on verbs and some of the spelling changes that take place in the verbal stem with the addition of these suffixes.

19.2 **The Pronominal Suffixes.** The suffixes added to the definite direct object marker are the same suffixes that you will see on verbs. In general, verbs use Type 1 pronominal suffixes with an objective translation value. For your review, Type 1 pronominal suffixes with their objective translation values are listed below. Carefully study both the form and translation value for each suffix before continuing in this chapter.

	Type 1 Suffixes	Type 1 Alternate	Objective Translation
1cs	יִ	נִי	me
2ms	ךָ		you
2fs	ךְ		you
3ms	וֹ	הוּ	him (it)
3fs	הָ	הָ	her (it)
1cp	נוּ		us
2mp	כֶם		you
2fp	כֶן		you
3mp	הֶם	ם	them
3fp	הֶן	ן	them

19.3 **Pronominal Suffixes on the Perfect**. In the following chart, the Qal Perfect 3ms verb קָטַל (he killed) is listed with the full range of pronominal suffixes. Observe how the suffix is added to the verb and translated as the direct object of that verb.

	Qal Perfect 3ms	Translation
1cs	קְטָלַנִי	he killed me
2ms	קְטָלְךָ	he killed you
2fs	קְטָלֵךְ	he killed you
3ms	קְטָלוֹ	he killed him (it)
3fs	קְטָלָהּ	he killed her (it)
1cp	קְטָלָנוּ	he killed us
2mp	קְטָלְכֶם	he killed you
2fp	קְטָלְכֶן	he killed you
3mp	קְטָלָם	he killed them
3fp	קְטָלָן	he killed them

Notes:

1. The spelling of the Qal Perfect 3ms verbal stem has changed from קָטַל to קְטָל with the addition of pronominal suffixes. You should already be familiar with this type of change. The addition of a pronominal suffix to the verbal stem causes a shift in accent and syllable structure, resulting in a spelling change. The spelling קְטָל is due, therefore, to propretonic reduction in the first syllable (קְ) and lengthening of the pretonic vowel to Qamets (טָ).

2. In the Perfect conjugation, the alternate Type 1 pronominal suffixes are preferred for the 1cs (קְטָלַנִי), 3mp (קְטָלָם) and 3fp (קְטָלָן). Both forms of the 3ms suffix appear with some frequency (קְטָלָהוּ or קְטָלוֹ).

3. The 2mp, 2fp and 3fp pronominal suffixes appear infrequently or are not attested with the Perfect.

19.4　Spelling of the Perfect Conjugation with Pronominal Suffixes. It was noted above that the spelling of the Qal Perfect 3ms changed with the addition of pronominal suffixes (קָטַל to קְטָל). Unfortunately, similar types of changes occur in all forms of the Perfect conjugation. The changes in spelling depend on whether the suffix is added to a Perfect form that ends in a consonant or one that ends in a vowel. In the 3ms, for example, the suffixes are added to a form that ends in a consonant (קְטָל). The following chart shows how the various forms of the Qal Perfect strong verb are spelled before pronominal suffixes. Be especially careful to note any change in the spelling of the Perfect sufformative.

	Qal Perfect Without Suffixes	Qal Perfect Before Suffixes
3ms	קָטַל	קְטָל[1]
3fs	קָטְלָה	קְטָלַת
2ms	קָטַׁלְתָּ	קְטַלְתָּ
2fs	קָטַלְתְּ	קְטַלְתִּי
1cs	קָטַׁלְתִּי	קְטַלְתִּי
3cp	קָטְלוּ	קְטָלוּ
2mp[2]	קְטַלְתֶּם	
2fp	קְטַלְתֶּן	
1cp	קָטַׁלְנוּ	קְטַלְנוּ

Notes:

1. In the 3fs, the ה sufformative is replaced by either תַ or תַ
   before a pronominal suffix (קְטָלַת). The suffix is then added to
   the תַ or תַ ending. This type of change in feminine forms
   should be familiar by now.

   קְטָלַתְהוּ ‎‎‎ הוּ + (קְטָלַת) קָטְלָה ➤ קְטָלַתְהוּ she (it) killed him

   אֲכָלַתְנִי ‎‎ נִי + (אֲכָלַת) אָכְלָה ➤ אֲכָלַתְנִי she (it) devoured me

   מְצָאַתְנוּ ‎ נוּ + (מְצָאַת) מָצְאָה ➤ מְצָאַתְנוּ she (it) found us

2. When suffixes are added to the 2ms form (קָטַׁלְתָּ), the sufformative
   is simply תָּ before the suffix (קְטַלְתָּ).

   קְטַלְתָּהוּ ‎ הוּ + (קְטַלְתָּ) קָטַׁלְתָּ ➤ קְטַלְתָּהוּ you killed him

   יְדַעְתּוֹ ‎‎‎ וֹ + (יְדַעְתָּ) יָדַׁעְתָּ ➤ יְדַעְתּוֹ you knew him

   עֲבַדְתַּׁנִי ‎ נִי + (עֲבַדְתָּ) עָבַׁדְתָּ ➤ עֲבַדְתַּׁנִי you served me

---

[1] It is important to note that the vowel under the ט is Qamets and not Qamets
Hatuf.

[2] The 2mp occurs only 3 times with a pronominal suffix. It is spelled קְטַלְתּוּ
before a suffix. The 2fp is not attested in the Hebrew Bible with a pronominal
suffix.

3. The spelling of the 2fs and 1cs forms are identical before pronominal suffixes (קְטַלְתִּי). Note, however, that the 2fs form of the Perfect conjugation with a pronominal suffix occurs only sixteen times in the Hebrew Bible. In other words, when you encounter a form like קְטַלְתִּי with a pronominal suffix, you should expect the 1cs form. Note also that the Hireq Yod ending is frequently written defectively as Hireq before the pronominal suffix.

קָטַלְתִּי (קְטַלְתִּי)	+	וֹ	⪢	קְטַלְתִּיו	I killed him
נָתַתִּי (נְתַתִּי)	+	הָ	⪢	נְתַתִּיהָ	I gave her (it)
עָשִׂיתִי (עֲשִׂיתִי)	+	ם	⪢	עֲשִׂיתִם	I made them

4. The spelling of the 3cp before a pronominal suffix (קְטָלוּ) should be easy to recognize because the sufformative (וּ) is retained. The Shureq sufformative of the Perfect 3cp may be written defectively as Qibbuts before a pronominal suffix.

קָטְלוּ (קְטָלוּ)	+	הוּ	⪢	קְטָלוּהוּ	they killed him
סָבְבוּ (סְבָבֻ)	+	נִי	⪢	סְבָבֻנִי	they surrounded me
יָדְעוּ (יְדָעֻ)	+	ם	⪢	יְדָעֻם	they knew them

5. The Perfect 1cp form (קָטַלְנוּ) is spelled קְטַלְנוּ before a pronominal suffix, preserving the spelling of the sufformative (נוּ). It may also be spelled defectively (קְטַלְנֻ).

קָטַלְנוּ (קְטַלְנוּ)	+	הוּ	⪢	קְטַלְנוּהוּ	we killed him
דָּרַשְׁנוּ (דְּרַשְׁנֻ)	+	הוּ	⪢	דְּרַשְׁנֻהוּ	we sought him
יָדַעְנוּ (יְדַעְנֻ)	+	ם	⪢	יְדַעְנוּם	we knew them

6. Though infrequent (52 times), in the Perfect conjugation of III-ה verbs, the 3ms form drops the ה before the pronominal suffix as in the following example: רָאָהוּ ⪢ הוּ + רָאָה (he saw him).

19.5 Changes in the Spelling of a Suffix on the Perfect. To this point, our study has focused on how the verbal stem is spelled before a pronominal suffix. Additionally, there are slight variations in how the pronominal suffixes themselves are spelled when added to a Perfect form.

1. Some suffixes are spelled differently, depending on whether they are being added to a Perfect form that ends in a consonant

(3ms, 3fs or 2ms) or one that ends in a vowel (all other Perfect forms). For example, the alternate form of the 3fs suffix (הָ) is used if the verbal stem ends in a vowel as in קְטַלְתִּיהָ (I killed her). The 3ms suffix also exhibits some variation in spelling. Frequently, the 3ms suffix וֹ is spelled ו after a vowel as in נְתַתִּיו (I gave him). These types of changes are relatively minor and should not give you too much trouble.

2. The addition of certain pronominal suffixes to verb forms that end in a consonant will frequently require some type of *connecting vowel* between the verbal stem and pronominal suffix. For example, the form שְׁלָחֲךָ (he sent you) requires a connecting vowel (Tsere) between the verbal stem and suffix. A form like קְטַלְתִּיךָ (I killed you), however, does not require a connecting vowel because the verb form already ends in a vowel. You are not required to learn all the possible connecting vowels for each form. Rather, you simply must be aware that connecting vowels are used when required (see 19.13).

19.6 **Pronominal Suffixes on the Imperfect.** Like the Perfect, Type 1 pronominal suffixes are used with the Imperfect. There are, however, three additional suffixes that occur on the Imperfect with some frequency. These additional suffixes may be called Nun-suffixes because of their distinctive form.

	Type 1 Suffix	Nun- Suffix	Example	Translation
2ms	ךָ	ךָּ	יִלְכָּדְךָ	he will capture *you*
3ms	הוּ/וֹ	נּוּ	יִלְכָּדֶנּוּ	he will capture *him*
3fs	הָ/ָהּ	נָּה	יִלְכָּדֶנָּה	he will capture *her*

Notes:

1. As you can see, these suffixes are distinguished by the presence of an additional נ (Nun).[3] Note that in the 2ms form (ךָּ), the נ has been assimilated and appears as Daghesh Forte in the consonant of the pronominal suffix.

---

[3] Though infrequent, Nun-suffixes are also attested in the 1cs (נִי/נִּי) and 1cp (נוּ).

2. Despite the variety of forms for a particular type of suffix, its translation value is the same. For example, the 3ms suffixes וֹ, הוּ and נּוּ ֶ are all translated with the same objective value, "him."

19.7   Spelling of the Imperfect Conjugation with Pronominal Suffixes. The changes that take place in the Imperfect with the addition of pronominal suffixes are minor compared to those in the Perfect. The changes are minor for two reasons: (1) the spelling of the Imperfect preformative is unchanged in every form; and (2) most Imperfect forms that take a pronominal suffix do not have a sufformative. Compare below the regular spelling of the Qal Imperfect with its spelling before most pronominal suffixes.

	Qal Imperfect *Without Suffixes*	*Qal Imperfect* *Before Suffixes*
3ms	יִקְטֹל	יִקְטְל
3fs	תִּקְטֹל	תִּקְטְל
2ms	תִּקְטֹל	תִּקְטְל
2fs	תִּקְטְלִי	תִּקְטְלִי
1cs	אֶקְטֹל	אֶקְטְל
3mp	יִקְטְלוּ	יִקְטְלוּ
3fp	תִּקְטֹלְנָה	
2mp	תִּקְטְלוּ	תִּקְטְלוּ
2fp	תִּקְטֹלְנָה	
1cp	נִקְטֹל	נִקְטְל

Notes:

1. There is only one basic change in the spelling of the strong Imperfect verb before pronominal suffixes. This change is the reduction of the stem vowel (pretonic reduction) from Holem (יִקְטֹל) to Shewa (יִקְטְל). Of course, this reduction has already taken place in the 2fs, 3mp and 2mp Imperfect forms. Note the following examples.

יִקְטֹל	+	הוּ	＞	יִקְטְלֵהוּ	he will kill him
יִקְטְלוּ	+	נוּ	＞	יִקְטְלוּנוּ	they will kill us
וַיִּקְבְּרוּ	+	הוּ	＞	וַיִּקְבְּרֻהוּ	and they buried him

2. The reduction of the stem vowel from Holem to Shewa does not take place with the addition of the 2ms suffix (ךָ). In this case, the Holem is *shortened* to Qamets Hatuf.[4]

יִשְׁמֹר	+ ךָ	⪢	יִשְׁמָרְךָ	he will observe you
יִקְטֹל	+ ךָ	⪢	יִקְטָלְךָ	he will kill you

If the verb has a Pathach stem vowel, the Pathach is not reduced but *lengthened* to Qamets before the 2ms pronominal suffix.

יִשְׁלַח	+ ךָ	⪢	יִשְׁלָחֲךָ	he will send you
יִשְׁמַע	+ ךָ	⪢	יִשְׁמָעֲךָ	he will hear you

3. If the Imperfect form ends in a consonant, a connecting vowel may be used between the verb and pronominal suffix as in יִקְטְלֵהוּ (Tsere) and יִשְׁמְרֶהָ (Seghol). If the Imperfect form ends in a vowel, no connecting vowels are necessary (as in יִקְטְלוּנוּ and יִשְׁמְרוּם). As with the Perfect, you are not required to learn all the possible connecting vowels for each form.[5] Rather, you must be aware that connecting vowels are used when required (see 19.14).

4. In the Imperfect conjugation of III-ה verbs, forms that end in הֶ drop this ending before the pronominal suffix as in the following example: יִרְאֶה + ֶנָּה ⪢ יִרְאֶנָּה (he will see her).

5. The Imperfect forms of the weak verbs נָתַן (to give), לָקַח (to take) and שִׂים (to put, place) occur frequently with pronominal suffixes. These verbs can be difficult to identify at first and so we have included some examples below.

וַיִּתֵּן	+ ם	⪢	וַיִּתְּנֵם	and he gave them
וַיִּקַח	+ הָ	⪢	וַיִּקָּחֶהָ	and he took her (it)
יָשִׂים	+ ךָ	⪢	יְשִׂימְךָ	he will place you

---

[4] If the original Imperfect stem vowel is Tsere, then it is shortened to Seghol with the addition of the 2ms pronominal suffix.

[5] In general, Perfect verbs prefer a-class connecting vowels (Pathach and Qamets) and Imperfect verbs prefer e-class connecting vowels (Seghol and Tsere).

19.8   **Pronominal Suffixes on the Imperative.** The suffixes used on the Imperative are the same as those used on the Imperfect. A few observations will be helpful, however, in terms of understanding some of the minor spellings changes that take place in the verb stem.

1. The Qal Imperative 2ms form קְטֹל is spelled קָטְל before a pronominal suffix. The vowel beneath the ק is Qamets Hatuf.

שְׁמֹר	+	ם	➤	שָׁמְרֵם (You) observe them!
שְׁפֹט	+	נִי	➤	שָׁפְטֵנִי (You) judge me!

2. The Imperative 2fs (קִטְלִי) and 2mp (קִטְלוּ), both ending in a vowel, do not change before a pronominal suffix.[6]

תִּפְשׂוּ	+	ם	➤	תִּפְשׂוּם (You) seize them!
דִּרְשׁוּ	+	נִי	➤	דִּרְשׁוּנִי (You) seek me!

3. Like the Imperfect, Imperatives with a Pathach stem vowel (שְׁמַע) lengthen the Pathach to Qamets before the pronominal suffix.

שְׁמַע	+	נִי	➤	שְׁמָעֵנִי (You) hear me!
גְּאַל	+	הָ	➤	גְּאָלָהּ (You) redeem her (it)!

19.9   **Parsing.** When parsing verbs with pronominal suffixes, you will need to identify the verb and also the person, gender and number of the suffix.

נְתַתִּיךָ	Qal Perfect 1cs	נָתַן	with 2ms suffix
יִלְכְּדֶנּוּ	Qal Imperfect 3ms	לָכַד	with 3ms suffix

19.10 **Summary.**

1. When a pronoun is the direct object of a verb, it may be attached to either the definite direct object marker (נְתַתִּי אֹתְךָ) or directly to the verb (נְתַתִּיךָ).

2. In general, Perfect, Imperfect and Imperative verbs use Type 1 pronominal suffixes with an objective translation value. With

---

[6] Pronominal suffixes occurring on the Imperative 2fs form occur only in the Hiphil stem (8 times). Pronominal suffixes are not attested on the Imperative 2fp form.

the Imperfect, three additional suffixes must be memorized: ךָ֖֫
(2ms), נוּ֫ (3ms) and נָּה֫ (3fs). These are the so-called Nun-
suffixes. You must be able to recognize and identify the person,
gender and number of all pronominal suffixes.

3. You will need to become familiar with the spelling changes that
   occur in the verb stem with the addition of pronominal suffixes
   to the Perfect, Imperfect and Imperative.

4. The addition of certain pronominal suffixes to verbal forms that
   end in a consonant will frequently require some type of connecting
   vowel between the verbal stem and pronominal suffix. In general,
   Perfect verbs prefer a-class connecting vowels (Pathach or
   Qamets), whereas Imperfect and Imperative verbs prefer e-class
   connecting vowels (Seghol or Tsere).

19.11 Vocabulary.

Verbs

בָּטַח	to trust (118)
בָּכָה	to weep (114)
כָּבֵד	to be heavy, honored (114)
לָבַשׁ	to put on, clothe (112)
שָׁלֵם	to be whole, complete (116)
שָׂרַף	to burn (118)

Nouns

פֶּ֫תַח	gate, opening, entrance (165)
שָׂפָה	lip, shore, bank (178)
דּוֹר	generation, lifetime, lifespan (167)
פַּר	young bull, cow (133)
רֹב	multitude, abundance (149)
חוּץ	outside (164)
מְלָאכָה	work (167)

19.12 **The Wife of Uriah the Hittite.** Often the narrator's emphasis or viewpoint concerning a certain event(s) is expressed by the various ways that individuals are designated in the text, for example, "Bathsheba" or "wife of Uriah the Hittite." Likewise, the order of designations when clustered together and the repetition or preference of one designation over another is also important. These designations, in conjunction with other grammatical and narrative features, often signal the main idea driving the story line. When applying some of these observations to Bathsheba in 2 Sam 11-12, "The David and Bathsheba Tragedy," we can gain insight on the author's perspective and point(s) of emphasis.

The narrator uses five separate designations for Bathsheba in these chapters. On one occasion, her kinship tie as the "daughter of Eliam" is expressed (11:3). At the beginning and the end of the story, the proper name "Bathsheba" is used (11:3; 12:24). The common female designation "woman" occurs in four places (11:2 [2 times], 3, 5). The 3fs pronominal suffix (she/her) is used eight times (11:4 [3 times], 26 [2 times], 27; 12:24 [2 times]). And her rank in society as either Uriah's or David's "wife" appears ten times (11:3, 11, 26, 27; 12:9 [2 times], 10 [2 times], 15, 24).

These numbers reveal two important factors. First, the author favors her classification as "wife" above all other designations in the passage. Of the ten instances of אִשָּׁה, six speak of Uriah's wife and four refer to David taking as a wife someone who rightfully belonged to another. The narrator deliberately keeps the woman's intimate relationship with Uriah constantly before the reader. Secondly, generic designations feature strongly. This results in a limited use of the proper name "Bathsheba." In other words, a somewhat depersonalized individual continually appears before the reader. As a result of this, her social standing is emphasized while the person Bathsheba is not a point of emphasis. Bathsheba as a person is truly peripheral in the story. The author's choice of designations, especially "the wife of Uriah the Hittite," magnifies David's gross misconduct and undeniable guilt. This expressive choice in designation helps direct the narrative and serves to underscore David's sin and weakness as a man in contrast to his known strength(s) as king of Israel. As a result, David appears rather human to the reader.

In this manner, the narrator exposes purpose and viewpoint simply by the choice of a dominating designation and its repetition in the narrative.

Donna Petter
Ph.D. candidate
University of Toronto
Toronto, Canada

19.13 **Advanced Information: Pronominal Suffixes on the Perfect.** The following chart is given for your reference. It includes the basic and most frequently attested spellings of pronominal suffixes on Perfect verbs. In this chart, the connecting vowels are included and the suffixes are placed in one of two categories: (1) those attached to Perfect forms ending in a consonant; and (2) those attached to Perfect forms that end in a vowel.

	Suffixes after Consonant	*Suffixes after Vowel*	*Objective Translation*
1cs	נִי/נִֽי ָ/נִֽי ַ	נִי	me
2ms	ךָ/ךָ ְ/ךָ ֶ	ךָ	you
2fs	ךְ/ךְ ָ	ךְ	you
3ms	וֹ/וֹ/הוּ/הֽוּ ָ	וֹ/הוּ	him (it)
3fs	הָ ַ/הָ ָ	הָ	her (it)
1cp	נוּ/נֽוּ ָ	נוּ	us
2mp	כֶם	כֶם	you
2fp	–	–	you
3mp	ָם/ַם	ם	them
3fp	ָן	ן	them

19.14 Advanced Information: Pronominal Suffixes on the Imperfect. The following chart is given for your reference. It includes the basic and most frequently attested spellings of pronominal suffixes on Imperfect verbs. In this chart, the connecting vowels are included.

	Type 1 Suffixes with Imperfect	Nun-Suffixes with Imperfect	Objective Translation
1cs	נִי ֵ ֫ /נִי ֶ /נִי	נִי ֵ ֫	me
2ms	ךָ ֶ /ךָ ֶ /ךָ ֶ /ךָ	ךָ ֵ ֫	you
2fs	ךְ ֵ /ךְ		you
3ms	הוּ ֵ ֫ /הוּ	נּוּ ֵ ֫	him (it)
3fs	הָ/הָ ֵ ֫ /הָ ָ	נָּה ֵ ֫	her (it)
1cp	נוּ ֵ ֫ /נוּ	נּוּ ֵ ֫	us
2mp	כֶם ְ		you
2fp	–		you
3mp	ם ֵ /ם		them
3fp	ן ָ		them

Chapter 20

Qal Infinitive Construct

20.1 **Introduction**. In Hebrew, there are two Infinitive forms, the Infinitive Construct and the Infinitive Absolute. Infinitives are *verbal nouns* and, as such, have features in common with both verbs and nouns. The Infinitive Construct can function much like the English Infinitive, commonly translated with the preposition "to" plus a verb as in "to study" or "to learn." In this chapter, we will study both the form and function of the Qal Infinitive Construct. In the next chapter, we will cover the Qal Infinitive Absolute.

20.2 **The Form of the Infinitive Construct**. The Infinitive Construct form is not inflected for person, gender or number. There is one basic form and, therefore, no paradigm to memorize. The following graphic represents the standard vowel pattern for the Qal Infinitive Construct strong verb.

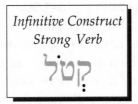

Infinitive Construct
Strong Verb

קְטֹל

Note that the Infinitive Construct form of the strong verb is identical to the Qal Imperative 2ms (also קְטֹל). There are, therefore, two possible identifications for קְטֹל (Qal Infinitive Construct or Qal Imperative 2ms). Context would likely resolve this ambiguity.

The vowel pattern for the Qal Infinitive Construct is consistent for all strong verbs and even for most weak verbs. Carefully study the following strong and weak verb Infinitive Constructs and note the consistency of this vowel pattern. Give special attention to how the Qal Infinitive Construct compares to the Qal Imperative 2ms, especially with the weak verbs.

	Imperative 2ms	Infinitive Construct	Translation
Strong	כְּתֹב	כְּתֹב	to write, writing
Strong	זְכֹר	זְכֹר	to remember, remembering
Strong	שְׁמֹר	שְׁמֹר	to keep, keeping
I-Gutt	עֲזֹב	עֲזֹב	to abandon, abandoning
I-א	אֱמֹר	אֱמֹר	to say, saying
II-Gutt	בְּחַר	בְּחֹר	to choose, choosing
III-ח	שְׁלַח	שְׁלֹחַ	to send, sending
III-ע	שְׁמַע	שְׁמֹעַ	to hear, hearing
III-א	קְרָא	קְרֹא[1]	to call, calling

20.3   Notes on the Form of the Infinitive Construct.

1. You will recall that Imperfect verbs with a-class stem vowels
    (such as II-Guttural, III-ח/ע and III-א) will preserve that same
    stem vowel in the Imperative. This a-class stem vowel is not
    preserved, however, in the Infinitive Construct form. For
    example, the Imperative 2ms of the II-Guttural verb בְּחַר is בָּחַר
    (choose!) and it preserves the Pathach stem vowel of the Imperfect
    2ms תִּבְחַר (you will choose). The Infinitive Construct form of
    this verb (בְּחֹר) does not preserve, however, the Pathach stem
    vowel. Rather, it follows the standard Shewa-Holem vowel
    pattern as in the strong verb. This same observation also applies
    to the III-ח/ע and III-א weak verbs as seen in the chart above.

2. I-Guttural and I-א verbal roots have a reduced vowel under the
    guttural in first root position (אֱמֹר and עֲזֹב). This should come
    as no surprise because you know that guttural consonants cannot
    take Vocal Shewa.

3. Note the Furtive Pathach in שְׁלֹחַ and שְׁמֹעַ (III-ח/ע verbs). Do
    not confuse this with the stem vowel. The stem vowel in these
    forms is still Holem.

---

[1] The alternate form קְרֹאת also occurs, especially with the לְ preposition as
לִקְרֹאת (2 times with קָרָא, "to call" and 119 times with קָרָא, "to meet, encounter").

20.4 **III-ה Infinitive Construct Forms.** The Infinitive Construct form of III-ה verbs ends in ות. For this class of weak verb, you will recall that Imperfect forms end in ה ֶ (except in those forms with suffformatives) and that Imperative forms end in ה ֵ (2ms). Now you must learn that the Infinitive Constructs of III-ה verbs end in ות.

Summary of III-ה Verbal Endings

	Ending	*Example*	*Translation*
Imperfect	ה ֶ	יִבְנֶה	he will build
Imperative	ה ֵ	בְּנֵה	you (2ms) build!
Infinitive Construct	ות	בְּנוֹת	to build, building

In the following chart, several III-ה verbs are listed in their Infinitive Construct form. Note that every form begins with a Vocal Shewa (or a Hateph vowel with gutturals) under the first root consonant. Additionally, every form ends in ות, the characteristic ending of III-ה Infinitive Constructs.

Verbal Root	*Infinitive Construct*	*Translation*
בָּנָה	בְּנוֹת	to build, building
בָּכָה	בְּכוֹת	to weep, weeping
עָלָה	עֲלוֹת	to go up, going up
עָנָה	עֲנוֹת	to answer, answering
עָשָׂה	עֲשׂוֹת	to do, doing
הָיָה	הֱיוֹת	to be, being
רָאָה	רְאוֹת	to see, seeing

20.5 **I-נ Infinitive Construct Forms.** Many verbs with נ in the first root position have Infinitive Constructs that conform to the strong verb pattern with preservation of the נ as in נְפֹל or נְסֹעַ. A number of I-נ verbs, however, have an alternate Infinitive Construct form in which the initial נ is lost and a ת is added to the end as in סַעַת (from נָסַע

meaning "to depart"). As seen in the chart below, there are other vocalization possibilities for the alternate form of the Infinitive Construct with נ. Recognizing the diagnostic final ת on these verbs is essential for identification of the verbal form and reconstruction of the verbal root.

Verbal Root	Infinitive Construct with נ	Alternate Form with ת
נָסַע	נְסֹעַ	סַעַת
נָגַע	נְגַע	גַּעַת
נָטַע	נְטֹעַ	טַעַת
נָשָׂא	נְשֹׂא	שְׂאֵת (שְׂאֵת)
נָגַשׁ		גֶּשֶׁת
נָתַן	נְתֹן	תֵּת[2]

20.6 I-י Infinitive Construct Forms. A few verbs of this class preserve the standard vowel pattern as in יְשֹׁן from יָשֵׁן (to sleep). Most I-י verbs, however, drop the initial י and add a final ת (similar to the alternate form of I-נ verbs above). The vowel pattern of these Infinitives with ת is generally reminiscent of Segholate nouns (with accent on the first syllable). There are, therefore, two weak verb classes that drop the initial weak consonant and add a final ת: I-י and I-נ weak verbs. The following examples illustrate the I-י weak class.

---

[2] This alternate Infinitive Construct form has lost both its first and third root consonants and it is very difficult to identify. Because this form occurs over 150 times in the Hebrew Bible, it is best to memorize it as a separate vocabulary word.

Verbal Root	Infinitive Construct
יָשַׁב	שֶׁבֶת
יָרַשׁ	רֶשֶׁת
יָלַד	לֶדֶת
יָרַד	רֶדֶת
יָדַע	דַּעַת[3]
יָצָא	צֵאת[4]
הָלַךְ	לֶכֶת[5]

20.7 **Biconsonantal Infinitive Construct Forms.** Recall that Biconsonantal verbs are divided into three classes based on the medial vowel letter: קוּם with Shureq, בּוֹא with Holem Waw and שִׂים with Hireq Yod. The forms that you have been memorizing for vocabulary (lexical form) are, in fact, the Infinitive Construct forms. These forms are also identical to the Biconsonantal Imperative 2ms verbal form. Once again, when confronted by one of these identical forms, context should enable you to distinguish between the Imperative and Infinitive Construct. The following examples illustrate the Infinitive Construct of this weak class.

Verbal Root	Infinitive Construct
שׁוּב	שׁוּב
מוּת	מוּת
בּוֹא	בּוֹא
בּוֹשׁ	בּוֹשׁ
דִּין	דִּין

20.8 **Parsing the Infinitive Construct.** The Infinitive Construct form is *not* inflected for person, gender or number. When parsing, therefore, you will be required to identify only stem, conjugation and lexical form.

---

[3] Variation in vowel pattern (Pathach instead of Seghol) is occasioned by the guttural consonant in third root position.

[4] Variation in vowel pattern is occasioned by the quiescent א in third root position.

[5] As you know by now, הָלַךְ inflects like a I-י verb.

The following examples illustrate how you should parse the Qal Infinitive Construct.

כְּתֹב   Qal Infinitive Construct   כָּתַב
אֱמֹר   Qal Infinitive Construct   אָמַר

20.9 **The Infinitive Construct with Pronominal Suffixes.**[6] Though the Infinitive Construct is not inflected, the form frequently appears with a pronominal suffix that can function as either the subject or object of the verbal idea.

The Infinitive Construct of the strong verb קָטַל with the full range of suffixes is listed below. Notice how the vocalization changes with the addition of pronominal suffixes. Each form now begins with a Qamets Hatuf in a closed syllable. This initial closed syllable with Qamets Hatuf is diagnostic of the strong verb Infinitive Construct with pronominal suffixes (variations can occur with the 2ms and 2mp suffixes). Note that two different translations are given below. The first represents the pronominal suffix functioning as the subject of the verbal idea. The second translation renders the subject as the object of the verbal action.

	Suffix PGN	Suffix As Subject	Suffix As Object
קָטְלִי	1cs	my killing	killing me
קָטְלְךָ[7]	2ms	your killing	killing you
קָטְלֵךְ	2fs	your killing	killing you
קָטְלוֹ	3ms	his killing	killing him
קָטְלָהּ	3fs	her killing	killing her
קָטְלֵנוּ	1cp	our killing	killing us
קָטְלְכֶם[8]	2mp	your killing	killing you
קָטְלְכֶן	2fp	your killing	killing you
קָטְלָם	3mp	their killing	killing them
קָטְלָן	3fp	their killing	killing them

[6] Pronominal suffixes occur on the Infinitive Construct 1,519 times, that is, on 23% of all Infinitive Construct forms.

[7] The alternate spelling קָטְלֶךָ is also attested.

[8] The alternate spelling קְטָלְכֶם is also attested.

20.10 **The Infinitive Construct with Inseparable Prepositions.** The inseparable prepositions בְּ, כְּ and לְ may be prefixed to the Infinitive Construct with a range of uses and translation values. In general, however, the Infinitive Construct with לְ is used to express purpose or result as in לִזְכֹּר (*in order to* remember). When prefixed to an Infinitive Construct, the inseparable prepositions בְּ and כְּ are used temporally and either preposition may translate as "when" or "while" as in בִּשְׁמֹר or כִּשְׁמֹר (*when* or *while* observing). Of all the verbal conjugations studied so far, only the Infinitive Construct will take a prepositional prefix. This means that, whenever you encounter a verbal form with a prepositional prefix, you can be confident that it is an Infinitive Construct. In addition, note that the Infinitive Construct form with a prefixed preposition can also take a pronominal suffix as in כְּשָׁמְעוֹ. This form should be parsed as a Qal Infinitive Construct of שָׁמַע with prefix כְּ and 3ms pronominal suffix.

20.11 **Negation of the Infinitive Construct.** The negative particles לֹא and אַל are not used to negate the Infinitive Construct. Rather, the Hebrew Infinitive is negated with בִּלְתִּי meaning "not" or "in order not." More frequently, it occurs as לְבִלְתִּי.[9] There is, however, no difference in meaning between the two forms. In other words, both בִּלְתִּי קְטֹל and לְבִלְתִּי קְטֹל mean the same thing ("in order not to kill" or "not to kill").

20.12 **The Use of the Infinitive Construct.** Of all the Hebrew conjugations, the Infinitive Construct poses the most difficulty in terms of translation. As noted earlier, it may occur with pronominal suffixes that can function as either the subject or the object, depending on context (20.9). In addition, the inseparable prepositions בְּ, כְּ or לְ may be prefixed to an Infinitive Construct with a range of uses and translation values (20.10). Though surely not the equivalent of an Infinitive in English, the Hebrew Infinitive Construct does share the essential characteristic of having both noun and verbal functions. Some of its more common uses are detailed below.

---

[9] This negative particle occurs 112 times, 26 times without לְ (בִּלְתִּי) and 86 times with לְ (לְבִלְתִּי).

1. *Purpose, Intention or Result.* When prefixed with the preposition
   לְ,[10] the Infinitive Construct may denote purpose, intention or
   result. When used in this way, the key words "to" or "in order
   to" may be used in your translation.

   לִרְאוֹת אֶת־עֶרְוַת הָאָרֶץ בָּאתֶם

   (In order) *to see* the nakedness of the land
   you have come (Gen 42:9).

   לִרְאוֹת Qal Infinitive Construct רָאָה with prefix לְ

   וַיִּקַּח אֶת־הַמַּאֲכֶלֶת לִשְׁחֹט אֶת־בְּנוֹ

   And he took the knife (in order)
   to slaughter his son (Gen 22:10).

   לִשְׁחֹט Qal Infinitive Construct שָׁחַט with prefix לְ

   וַיֵּשְׁבוּ לֶאֱכָל־לֶחֶם

   And they sat down (in order) *to eat* bread (Gen 37:25).

   לֶאֱכָל Qal Infinitive Construct אָכַל with prefix לְ

   וְלֹא־נָתַן יְהוָה לָכֶם לֵב לָדַעַת וְעֵינַיִם לִרְאוֹת
   וְאָזְנַיִם לִשְׁמֹעַ עַד הַיּוֹם הַזֶּה

   But Yahweh has not given to you a heart *to know* or eyes
   to see or ears *to hear* until this day (Deut 29:3 [English 29:4]).

   לָדַעַת Qal Infinitive Construct יָדַע with prefix לְ

   לִרְאוֹת Qal Infinitive Construct רָאָה with prefix לְ

   לִשְׁמֹעַ Qal Infinitive Construct שָׁמַע with prefix לְ

   כִּי הָאָרֶץ אֲשֶׁר אַתָּה בָא־שָׁמָּה לְרִשְׁתָּהּ לֹא כְאֶרֶץ מִצְרַיִם

   For the land which you are entering *to take possession of it* (to
   possess it) is not like the land of Egypt (Deut 11:10).

   לְרִשְׁתָּהּ Qal Infinitive Construct יָרַשׁ with prefix לְ
   and 3fs pronominal suffix functioning as the object

---

[10] The Infinitive Construct occurs 6,699 times in the Hebrew Bible. It appears
with the preposition לְ 4,530 times (68%).

2. *Inceptive.* When prefixed with the preposition לְ, the Infinitive Construct may denote an action about to take place. This construction frequently involves the use of הָיָה (to be) and an Infinitive Construct prefixed with the preposition לְ. When used in this way, the key words "about to" may be used in your translation.

וַיְהִי הַשֶּׁמֶשׁ לָבוֹא

The sun was *about to set* (Gen 15:12).

לָבוֹא Qal Infinitive Construct בּוֹא with prefix לְ

וַיְהִי הַשַּׁעַר לִסְגּוֹר

The gate was *about to shut* (Josh 2:5).

לִסְגּוֹר Qal Infinitive Construct סָגַר with prefix לְ

3. *Verbal Noun.* In this use, the Infinitive Construct functions like a noun, often as the subject or object of the verbal idea. It may or may not be prefixed with the preposition לְ when used in this way.

הִנֵּה שְׁמֹעַ מִזֶּבַח טוֹב

Behold, *to obey* (obeying) is better than sacrifice (1 Sam 15:22).

שְׁמֹעַ Qal Infinitive Construct שָׁמַע

טוֹב לְהֹדוֹת לַיהוָה

It is good to praise Yahweh, or Praising
Yahweh is good (Ps 92:2).

לְהֹדוֹת Hiphil Infinitive Construct יָדָה with prefix לְ

4. *Complementary.* Another use of the Infinitive Construct is to explain, clarify or complement a preceding action or statement. It may or may not be prefixed with the preposition לְ when used in this way.[11] When used in this way, you can translate the Infinitive Construct with "by" plus the "-ing" form of the verb as in the following examples.

וְשָׁמְרוּ בְנֵי־יִשְׂרָאֵל אֶת־הַשַּׁבָּת לַעֲשׂוֹת
אֶת־הַשַּׁבָּת לְדֹרֹתָם בְּרִית עוֹלָם

The people of Israel shall observe the Sabbath *by doing*
the Sabbath throughout their generations as an
everlasting covenant (Ex 31:16).

לַעֲשׂוֹת Qal Infinitive Construct עָשָׂה with prefix לְ

וְלֹא־הָיִיתָ כְּעַבְדִּי דָוִד אֲשֶׁר שָׁמַר מִצְוֹתַי וַאֲשֶׁר־הָלַךְ
אַחֲרַי בְּכָל־לְבָבוֹ לַעֲשׂוֹת רַק הַיָּשָׁר בְּעֵינָי

You were not (have not been) like my servant David
who observed my commandments and who walked
after me with all his heart *by doing* only what was
right in my eyes (1 Kgs 14:8).

לַעֲשׂוֹת Qal Infinitive Construct עָשָׂה with prefix לְ

וְשָׁמַרְתָּ אֶת־מִצְוֹת יְהוָה אֱלֹהֶיךָ לָלֶכֶת בִּדְרָכָיו

And you shall observe the commandments of Yahweh
your God *by walking* in his ways (Deut 8:6).

לָלֶכֶת Qal Infinitive Construct הָלַךְ with prefix לְ

5. *Temporal.* All of the above uses relate to the construction of the Infinitive Construct with prefixed לְ. Now we turn to another very common use of the Infinitive Construct. When prefixed with the prepositions בְּ or כְּ, the Infinitive Construct may be used in a temporal clause. When used in this way, the prepositions בְּ and כְּ are translated either "when" or "while." Frequently, in this construction, the Infinitive Construct will also have a pronominal suffix.[12]

---

[11] In addition to these four uses of the Infinitive Construct with לְ, there are several other less frequent uses. When prefixed with the preposition לְ, the Infinitive construct may also (1) complement a preceding verb and be translated like a finite (Perfect or Imperfect) verb, (2) denote consecution of verbal action(s) or (3) denote obligation or necessity.

[12] The Infinitive Construct is prefixed with the prepositions בְּ or כְּ 989 times in the Hebrew Bible. In 556 instances (56%), this construction appears with a pronominal suffix.

The operative phrase in the preceding paragraph is "temporal clause." Given that the Infinitive Construct is a form *without tense*, the temporal value (i.e., past, present or future) assigned to the Infinitive must be taken from context. For example, the form כְּשָׁמְעוֹ (Qal Infinitive Construct of שָׁמַע with prefix כְּ and 3ms pronominal suffix) may be translated as either "when he heard" or "when he hears (will hear)." Note the two possible translation values: one denoting action completed (when he heard) and the other indicating action not completed (when he hears or when he will hear). In the absence of context, the phrase can be translated either way. However, in the constructions וַיְהִי כְּשָׁמְעוֹ (and when he heard) or וְהָיָה כְּשָׁמְעוֹ (and when he hears [will hear]), the temporal modifiers provide the context for determining the temporal value of the Infinitive Construct. Remember that the temporal modifier וַיְהִי signals past tense narration (17.3.2) and the temporal modifier וְהָיָה signals future tense narration (17.6.2). Of course, there are other contextual considerations that will determine tense value such as recognition of the narrative sequence in which the Infinitive Construct appears. Study the following biblical examples of how the Infinitive Construct is used in a temporal clause, especially with וַיְהִי and וְהָיָה.

וַיְהִי בִּשְׁכֹּן יִשְׂרָאֵל בָּאָרֶץ הַהִוא

When (while) Israel *dwelt* in that land ... (Gen 35:22)

בִּשְׁכֹּן Qal Infinitive Construct שָׁכַן with prefix בְּ

וַיְהִי בִּהְיוֹתָם בַּשָּׂדֶה

When they were in the field ... (Gen 4:8)

בִּהְיוֹתָם Qal Infinitive Construct הָיָה
with prefix בְּ and 3mp pronominal suffix

וְהָיָה כְּצֵאת מֹשֶׁה אֶל־הָאֹהֶל יָקוּמוּ כָּל־הָעָם
וְנִצְּבוּ אִישׁ פֶּתַח אָהֳלוֹ

Whenever Moses *went out* to the tent, all the people rose up
and every man stood at the door of his tent (Ex 33:8).

כְּצֵאת Qal Infinitive Construct יָצָא with prefix כְּ

וְהָיָה בְּעָבְרְכֶם אֶת־הַיַּרְדֵּן תָּקִימוּ אֶת־הָאֲבָנִים הָאֵלֶּה

And *when you pass* (have passed) over the Jordan,
you shall set up these stones (Deut 27:4).

בְּעָבְרְכֶם Qal Infinitive Construct עָבַר with prefix בְּ
and 2mp pronominal suffix

וְהָיָה כְשִׁבְתּוֹ עַל כִּסֵּא מַמְלַכְתּוֹ וְכָתַב לוֹ אֶת־מִשְׁנֵה
הַתּוֹרָה הַזֹּאת עַל־סֵפֶר

And *when he sits* on the throne of his kingdom, he will write
for himself a copy of this law in (upon) a book (Deut 17:18).

כְשִׁבְתּוֹ Qal Infinitive Construct יָשַׁב with prefix כְּ
and 3ms pronominal suffix

אֵלֶּה הָעֵדֹת וְהַחֻקִּים וְהַמִּשְׁפָּטִים אֲשֶׁר דִּבֶּר מֹשֶׁה אֶל־בְּנֵי
יִשְׂרָאֵל בְּצֵאתָם מִמִּצְרָיִם

These are the testimonies and the statutes and the
judgements which Moses spoke to the people of Israel
when they came out from Egypt (Deut 4:45).

בְּצֵאתָם Qal Infinitive Construct יָצָא with prefix בְּ and 3mp
pronominal suffix functioning as the subject

20.13 Summary.

1. The Infinitive Construct is not inflected for person, gender or
   number. In strong and many weak verbal roots, its basic form
   is identical to the Qal Imperative 2ms.

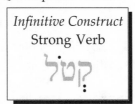

Infinitive Construct
Strong Verb

קְטֹל

2. Three weak verbs classes have Infinitive Construct forms that
   vary significantly from the vowel pattern of the strong verb.

   a. The Infinitive Construct of III-ה verbs drops the final ה
      and adds וֹת as in בְּנוֹת from בָּנָה.

b. The Infinitive Construct of some I-נ verbs drops the initial נ and adds ת as in סַעַת from נָסַע.

c. The Infinitive Construct of some I-י verbs drops the initial י and adds ת as in שֶׁבֶת from יָשַׁב.

3. The Infinitive Construct may occur with prepositional prefixes, pronominal suffixes or both. In other words, you must be familiar with the following four options:

קְטֹל	basic form
קָטְלִי	basic form with pronominal suffix (1cs)
לִקְטֹל	basic form with prepositional prefix (לְ)
כְּקָטְלוֹ	basic form with prepositional prefix (כְּ) and pronominal suffix (3ms)

4. The Infinitive Construct may occur with a pronominal suffix that can function as either the subject of object of the verbal idea.

5. The Infinitive Construct is negated with בִּלְתִּי or לְבִלְתִּי ("not" or "in order not").

6. There are five common uses of the Infinitive Construct.

a. Occurring with לְ to express purpose, intention or result.

b. Occurring with לְ to denote an action about to take place.

c. Occurring with or without לְ to explain, clarify or complement a preceding action or statement.

d. Occurring with or without לְ as a verbal noun.

e. Occurring with בְּ or כְּ in a temporal clause with or without pronominal suffixes.

20.14 Vocabulary.

Verbs

אָחַז	to seize (63)
טָמֵא	to be unclean (162)
יָצַר	to form, shape, fashion (63)
נוּס	to flee (160)

נָגַע	to touch, reach (150)
סָבַב	to turn around, surround (163)
סָפַר	to write, count, number (107)
שָׁבַר	to break (148)
שָׂמַח	to rejoice (156)

Nouns

עֲבוֹדָה	service (145)
עֵדָה	congregation (146)
יַחַד	community, union; (adverb) together, at the same time (145); most frequently as יַחְדָּו
יַיִן	wine (141)

Other

בִּלְתִּי	not, in order not (112); usually appears as לְבִלְתִּי

20.15 **A Life Centered on Torah.** The priest/scribe Ezra was a man whose life provided a model of godly leadership to a people in desperate need of hearing God's Word and seeing God's will lived out in practical ways.

You have learned that the Infinitive Construct with the preposition לְ often complements the main verb by expressing the purpose, goal, or result to which the main verb points. In Ezra 7:10, there are three Infinitive Construct forms that are used in this way in a verse that highlights Ezra's personal commitments.

The narrator has already introduced Ezra as a minister with the right pedigree (7:1-5) and the right professional abilities: he was a סֹפֵר, a "scribe," "skilled in the Torah of Moses" (7:6; cf. 7:11). Ezra's every request was granted him by the Persian king and his ministry flourished "because the (good) hand of Yahweh his God was on him" (7:6, 9). Ezra 7:10 then provides the reason for this divine favor.

כִּי עֶזְרָא הֵכִין לְבָבוֹ לִדְרוֹשׁ אֶת־תּוֹרַת יְהוָה
וְלַעֲשֹׂת וּלְלַמֵּד בְּיִשְׂרָאֵל חֹק וּמִשְׁפָּט

> For Ezra set his heart *to study* the Torah of Yahweh,
> and *to practice* (it), and *to teach* (its) statutes
> and ordinances in Israel.

Here we find the main verb הֵכִין (to set, establish)[13] followed by three Infinitive Constructs with the preposition לְ (לְדְרוֹשׁ, לַעֲשֹׂת, לְלַמֵּד[14]), each of which clarifies the purpose to which Ezra committed himself: study → practice → teach. This progression of action, grounded in God's Word, characterized Ezra's life and ministry and we are perhaps wise to follow his example. Sound study of the Scriptures must give rise to personal practice. Only then can we have a basis for effective teaching. But as Daniel I. Block emphasizes, far too often preachers and teachers either lose the centrality of the Word in their ministry or confuse the order of Ezra's resolve. Some focus on teaching technique at the expense of quality time in the Word, thus substituting the shape of the message for its essence. Others are quick to proclaim God's truth but are slow to apply it to their own lives, resulting in hypocritical leaders who have forgotten that only the pure in heart will see God (Matt 5:8; Ps 24:3-5; Heb 12:13). Still others apply before having studied, allowing their own definitions of right and wrong to guide conduct rather than the revealed divine will in the Scriptures.[15]

Ezra was serious about understanding God's Word, applying it and proclaiming it - in that order! This personal commitment generated a ministry blessed by God. We would do well to follow the pattern of Ezra today. "The hand of our God works for good on all who seek him, but his powerful wrath is against all who forsake him" (Ezra 8:22).

Jason S. DeRouchie
Ph.D. candidate
The Southern Baptist Theological Seminary
Louisville, Kentucky

---

[13] Hiphil Perfect 3ms of כּוּן

[14] Piel Infinitive Construct of לָמַד with לְ preposition

[15] Daniel I. Block, "Training Scribes and Pastors in the Tradition of Ezra," *Southern Seminary Magazine* (June, 1999) 6.

Chapter 21

Qal Infinitive Absolute

21.1 **Introduction.** The Infinitive Absolute occurs less frequently than any other Hebrew conjugation with only 872 total occurrences. Like the Infinitive Construct, the Infinitive Absolute is also a verbal noun. With regard to function, however, there is no English equivalent to the Hebrew Infinitive Absolute.

21.2 **Qal Infinitive Absolute of the Strong Verb.** The Infinitive Absolute is not inflected for person, gender or number. There is, therefore, only one form to memorize. This form is easy to identify and varies little with weak verbal roots. The following graphic represents the Qal Infinitive Absolute form for the strong verb.

Infinitive Absolute
Strong Verb
קָטוֹל

21.3 **Notes on the Form of the Qal Infinitive Absolute.**

1. The vowel pattern of the strong verb also occurs in most weak verb types (see 21.4 below).

2. Frequently, the Holem Waw stem vowel is written defectively as Holem. In other words, קָטוֹל is also spelled קָטֹל. This variation in spelling should not present any difficulty.

3. Be careful not to confuse the alternate form of the Infinitive Absolute (קָטֹל) with the Imperative 2ms or Infinitive Construct verb forms (קְטֹל). The Qamets under the first root consonant will distinguish the Infinitive Absolute from these two forms.

4. Unlike the Infinitive Construct, the Infinitive Absolute does not occur with prepositional prefixes or pronominal suffixes.

21.4 **Weak Forms of the Qal Infinitive Absolute.** Most weak verb forms follow the strong verb pattern as the following examples illustrate.

	Qal Perfect *3ms*	*Infinitive* *Absolute*
I-Guttural	הָלַךְ	הָלוֹךְ
I-Guttural	עָבַר	עָבוֹר
I-א	אָכַל	אָכוֹל
II-Guttural	גָּאַל	גָּאוֹל
II-Guttural	בָּחַר	בָּחוֹר
III-ח	שָׁכַח	שָׁכוֹחַ
III-ע	שָׁמַע	שָׁמוֹעַ
III-א	יָצָא	יָצוֹא
I-נ	נָפַל	נָפוֹל
I-י	יָדַע	יָדוֹעַ
Geminate	סָבַב	סָבוֹב

As you can see, the weak verbs above follow the standard pattern of vocalization. Despite this consistency, however, a few weak verb forms deserve comment.

1. Note the Furtive Pathach in שָׁכוֹחַ and שָׁמוֹעַ (III-ח/ע verbs). Do not confuse this with the stem vowel. The stem vowel in these forms is still Holem Waw.

2. With III-ה verbs, the Infinitive Absolute may appear in one of two forms.

Verbal Root		*Infinitive Absolute*
עָשָׂה	➤	עָשֹׂה or עָשׂוֹ
שָׁתָה	➤	שָׁתֹה or שָׁתוֹ
רָאָה	➤	רָאֹה or רָאוֹ
חָיָה	➤	חָיֹה or חָיוֹ

3. With Biconsonantal verbs, the Infinitive Absolute appears with a Holem Waw (or Holem) stem vowel in every class. In other words, שִׂים (with Hireq Yod) and קוּם (with Shureq) appear as שׂוֹם and קוֹם in the Infinitive Absolute.

Verbal Root		Infinitive Absolute
בּוֹא	➤	בּוֹא or בֹּא
שִׂים	➤	שׂוֹם
קוּם	➤	קוֹם
מוּת	➤	מוֹת

Note the similarity between the Infinitive Absolute of מוּת and the construct form of מָוֶת (מוֹת).

21.5 **Parsing the Infinitive Absolute.** The Infinitive Absolute form is *not* inflected for person, gender or number. When parsing, therefore, you will be required to identify only stem, conjugation and lexical form. The following examples illustrate how you should parse the Qal Infinitive Absolute.

| הָלוֹךְ | Qal Infinitive Absolute | הָלַךְ |
| מוֹת | Qal Infinitive Absolute | מוּת |

21.6 **The Use of the Infinitive Absolute.** The Infinitive Absolute is a verbal noun. With regard to function, however, there is no English equivalent to the Hebrew Infinitive Absolute. It may be used in conjunction with other verbs to emphasize or intensify the verbal meaning. It may also be used in the place of an Imperative to express a command. In special instances, it can be used with other verbs to express two verbal actions occurring at the same time. Once again, remember that the Infinitive Absolute does not occur with prepositional prefixes or pronominal suffixes. The four most common uses are detailed below.

1. *Emphatic.* Frequently, the Infinitive Absolute will immediately precede (or rarely follow) a Perfect or Imperfect verbal form of the same root in order to emphasize the verbal meaning. Study the following examples and note how the translations give emphasis to the verbal meaning.

שָׁמוֹעַ תִּשְׁמְעוּ	you (2mp) will *indeed* listen (Ex 19:5)
מוֹת תָּמוּת	you (2ms) will *certainly* die (2 Kings 1:16)
אָמוֹר אָמַרְתִּי	I have *surely* said (1 Sam 2:30)
יָדֹעַ תֵּדַע כִּי מוֹת תָּמוּת	know *for certain* that you (2ms) will *surely* die (1 Kgs 2:37)

2. *Imperatival.* The Infinitive Absolute can stand by itself and function as an Imperative.

זָכוֹר אֶת־הַיּוֹם הַזֶּה   *Remember* this day! (Ex 13:3)

שָׁמוֹר אֶת־יוֹם הַשַּׁבָּת   *Observe* the sabbath day! (Deut 5:12)

3. *Contemporaneous Action.* With some frequency, two Infinitive Absolutes may be used together with a Perfect or Imperfect verb for the purpose of expressing two verbal actions occurring simultaneously.

וַיֵּלֶךְ הָלוֹךְ וְאָכֹל   (literally) and he walked, *walking* and *eating*; (idiomatically) and he walked, *eating as he went* (Judg 14:9)

וְעָלוּ עָלֹה וּבָכֹה   (literally) and they went up, *going up* and *weeping*; (idiomatically) and they went up, *weeping as they went* (2 Sam 15:30)

4. *Complementary.* An Infinitive Absolute may complement the main verb of a sentence and carry the temporal value of that main verb. In this usage, the Infinitive will translate just like a Perfect or Imperfect even though it is not an inflected form.

רָגוֹם אֹתוֹ בָאֲבָנִים כָּל־הָעֵדָה   All of the congregation *shall stone him* with stones (Num 15:35).

נָתוֹן אֹתוֹ עַל כָּל־אֶרֶץ מִצְרָיִם   *He set him* over all the land of Egypt (Gen 41:43).

21.7   **The Particles** יֵשׁ **and** אֵין. Hebrew may express *the existence of someone or something* by using the particle יֵשׁ (also spelled יֶשׁ־) which translates either "(there) is" or "(there) are." This particle does not change its spelling to indicate gender or number.

יֵשׁ מֶלֶךְ   "there is a king" or "a king is"

יֵשׁ מְלָכִים   "there are kings" or "kings are"

אָכֵן יֵשׁ יְהוָה בַּמָּקוֹם הַזֶּה   Surely the Lord is in this place (Gen 28:16).

The particle יֵשׁ may also be used to express possession when followed by the preposition לְ (to).

יֶשׁ־לִי תִקְוָה   Literally: There is to me hope.
Idiomatically: I have hope (Ruth 1:12).

הֲיֵשׁ לָכֶם אָח   Literally: Is there to you a brother?
Idiomatically: Do you have a brother?
(Gen 43:7)

יֶשׁ־לָנוּ אָב זָקֵן   Literally: There is to us an elderly father.
Idiomatically: We have an elderly father
(Gen 44:20).

Hebrew may express *the non-existence or absence of someone or something*
by using the particle אֵין (also spelled אַיִן) which translates either "(there)
is not" or "(there) are not." This particle is the negative counterpart of
יֵשׁ and it also is not inflected for gender or number.

אֵין־יוֹסֵף בַּבּוֹר   Joseph was not in the cistern (Gen 37:29).

וְאֵין־דַּעַת אֱלֹהִים בָּאָרֶץ   (And) there is no knowledge of God in
the land (Hosea 4:1).

אֵין לוֹ בֵּן   He did not have a son (Num 27:4).

With some frequency, the particle אֵין will appear with pronominal
suffixes as in אֵינֶנּוּ (3ms or 1cp) and אֵינָם (3mp).[1] Finally, the particle
אֵין may be used to negate a verbless clause or sentences with Participles
used predicatively.

אֵינָם יְרֵאִים אֶת־יְהוָה   They do not fear the Lord (2 Kgs 17:34).

אָמַר נָבָל בְּלִבּוֹ אֵין אֱלֹהִים   The fool says in his heart, "There is no
God" (Ps 53:2 [English 53:1]).

אֵין עֹשֵׂה־טוֹב אֵין גַּם־אֶחָד   There is no one who does good, there is
not even one (Ps 53:4 [English 53:3]).

אֲנִי יְהוָה וְאֵין עוֹד זוּלָתִי   I am Yahweh and there is no other;
אֵין אֱלֹהִים   apart from me there is no God (Isa 45:5).

---

[1] Pronominal suffixes on יֵשׁ (9 times) are rare by comparison with the frequency
of their appearance on אֵין (104 times).

21.8 Summary.

1. The Infinitive Absolute is not inflected for person, gender or number. The following graphic represents the Qal Infinitive Absolute form for the strong verb.

> *Infinitive Absolute*
> *Strong Verb*
>
> קָטוֹל

2. The stem vowel of the Infinitive Absolute may be written defectively as Holem (קְטֹל).

3. Most weak verb forms follow the standard קָטוֹל pattern. Remember, however, that III-ח/ע verbs have Furtive Pathach (שָׁמוֹעַ), III-ה verbs occur in one of two forms (בָּכֹה or בָּכוֹ) and Biconsonantal verbs typically have the Holem Waw (or Holem) stem vowel (קוֹם or שׂוֹם).

4. The Infinitive Absolute is a verbal noun with a variety of uses. The four most common uses are: (1) emphatic; (2) imperatival; (3) contemporaneous action; and (4) complementary.

5. Hebrew may express the existence of someone or something by using the particle יֵשׁ (also spelled יֶשׁ־) which translates either "(there) is" or "(there) are." Hebrew may express the non-existence or absence of someone or something by using the particle אַיִן (also spelled אֵין) which translates either "(there) is not" or "(there) are not."

21.9 Vocabulary.

Verbs

נָסַע	to depart (146)
זָבַח	to slaughter, sacrifice (134)
חָנָה	to encamp (143)
נוּחַ	to rest, settle down (140)
פָּנָה	to turn about, turn aside (134)

פָּתַח	to open (136)
רָדַף	to pursue, persecute (144)
שָׂנֵא	to hate (150)
שָׁאַר	to remain (133)

Nouns

בָּמָה	high place, funerary installation (106)
חֻקָּה	statute, prescription (104); חֻקּוֹת or חֻקֹת (plural)
יָמִין	right, right side (141); feminine
מִשְׁכָּן	dwelling, tabernacle (139)
נַחַל	stream, wadi (137)
רָעָב	hunger, famine (101)

21.10 **What a Difference a Pronoun Makes.** You know that, in addition to functioning as the subject of a non-verbal sentence, the independent personal pronoun can also be used with (finite) verbs for a number of reasons, one of which is to emphasize the subject. If the author places no particular stress on the subject, he would simply state: יָשַׁב בָּעִיר (He lived in the city). But if the author wanted to indicate that it was *he*, and not someone else who lived in the city, the 3ms independent personal pronoun could be added: הוּא יָשַׁב בָּעִיר or יָשַׁב הוּא בָּעִיר (*He* or *He himself* lived in the city). This particular use of the independent personal pronoun is referred to as the "emphatic use." Although it may seem to be a minor grammatical point, the emphatic use of the independent personal pronoun is employed by the authors of the Old Testament at various points to make important theological statements. For example, in Deut 4:35, Moses asserts:

יְהוָה הוּא הָאֱלֹהִים אֵין עוֹד מִלְּבַדּוֹ

Yahweh (Yahweh himself) is God; there is none beside him.

Similarly, in 1 Kgs 18:39, when the people witnessed the power of the Lord in contrast to the power of Baal, they cried out:

יְהוָה הוּא הָאֱלֹהִים יְהוָה הוּא הָאֱלֹהִים

Yahweh (Yahweh, he) is God! Yahweh (Yahweh, he) is God!

As a final example, the emphatic use of the independent personal pronoun appears in Isa 46 to make the same claim to the Lord's supremacy and matchlessness. The chapter opens in Isa 46:1-2 with a description of the idols of two Babylonian deities:

> Bel has bowed down, Nebo stoops over;
> their images are assigned to the beasts and to the cattle.
> The things that you carry are burdensome,
> a load for the weary beast.
> They stoop over, they have bowed down together,
> they could not rescue the burden,
> but have themselves gone into captivity.

In striking contrast, verses 3-4 emphasize that Israel has been carried not by animals, but *by Yahweh himself*, from the very beginning of her existence. She has been lifted up *by Yahweh* from birth. The theme continues, with an intentional emphasis on Yahweh as the means of Israel's support:

Until old age, *I* am he.	אֲנִי הוּא
Until your hair is grey, *I myself* will bear you.	אֲנִי אֶסְבֹּל
I myself have done (it),	אֲנִי עָשִׂיתִי
and *I myself* will lift (you) up,	אֲנִי אֶשָּׂא
and *I myself* will bear (you),	אֲנִי אֶסְבֹּל
and I will deliver you.	

With the emphatic use of the personal pronoun, Isaiah asserts one of the most important theological concepts in the Bible, that there is no God but Yahweh. Tragically, this emphatic sense is often lost in English translations. It is not missed, however, by those who read biblical Hebrew! These subtle, but significant, features of Hebrew are the very reasons why we learn to read the Bible in its original languages. What a difference a pronoun makes!

Catherine Beckerleg
Ph.D. candidate
Harvard University
Cambridge, Massachusetts

Chapter 22

Qal Participle

22.1 **Introduction.** In English, Participles are formed by adding "-ing" to a verb as in "walking," "eating" or "sleeping." Because a Participle is a verbal adjective, it shares the characteristics of both verbs and adjectives. As a verb, the Participle has stem (Qal) and voice (active or passive) and expresses some type of verbal action such as "running" or "studying." As an adjective, the Participle has gender (masculine or feminine) and number (singular or plural) and is used much like an adjective: attributively ("the *sleeping* student"), predicatively ("the student is *sleeping*") and substantively ("*studying* requires discipline"). When translating the Hebrew Participle, begin by using the "-ing" form of the verb as in the above examples.

22.2 **The Qal Active Participle Paradigm: Strong Verbs.** The Participle inflects like an adjective, with both gender and number. It is not inflected for person. Having already memorized the endings for nouns and adjectives, the inflection of the Participle should look familiar. The following paradigm must be memorized. Note that there are two feminine singular forms.

	Active Participle		Inflectional Endings	
	Singular	*Plural*	*Singular*	*Plural*
Masculine	קֹטֵל	קֹטְלִים		◌ִים
Feminine	קֹטֶלֶת	קֹטְלוֹת	◌ֶת	וֹת
Feminine	קֹטְלָה		◌ָה	

22.3 **Notes on the Qal Active Participle Paradigm: Strong Verbs.**

1. As you can see from the paradigm above, Participles are not inflected for person, only for gender and number. The inflectional endings for the Participle are the same as those you have memorized for adjectives and nouns. Note, however, that there are two feminine singular forms.

2. In terms of inflection, the feminine singular קֹטֶלֶת is more irregular than קֹטְלָה but it occurs more frequently. Nevertheless, both forms must be memorized.

3. The Holem vowel in the first syllable of all Participle forms is diagnostic of the Qal active Participle (קֹטֵל). Recognition of this diagnostic vowel is very important. Do not be surprised to see this vowel written as Holem Waw (קוֹטֵל). The Holem-Tsere vowel pattern is distinctive of the masculine singular Qal active Participle.

> **Qal Active Participle**
> **Strong Verb**
>
> קֹטֵל

22.4 **The Qal Active Participle: Weak Verbs.** In the Qal stem, all I-Guttural, I-נ, I-י and Geminate weak verbs follow the strong verb pattern as the following paradigms illustrate:

	Singular	Plural	Singular	Plural
Masculine	עֹמֵד	עֹמְדִים	נֹפֵל	נֹפְלִים
Feminine	עֹמֶדֶת	עֹמְדוֹת	נֹפֶלֶת	נֹפְלוֹת
Feminine	עֹמְדָה		נֹפְלָה	

	Singular	Plural	Singular	Plural
Masculine	יֹשֵׁב	יֹשְׁבִים	סֹבֵב	סֹבְבִים
Feminine	יֹשֶׁבֶת	יֹשְׁבוֹת	סֹבֶבֶת	סֹבְבוֹת
Feminine	יֹשְׁבָה		סֹבְבָה	

Other weak verb roots, however, deviate from this strong verb pattern. Note below that in every weak verb class except one (Biconsonantal), the diagnostic Holem vowel and inflectional endings are unchanged.

1. *II-Guttural Verbal Roots.* The presence of a guttural consonant in second root position will create only minor spelling differences

compared to the strong verb. In the feminine singular and both plural forms, a Vocal Shewa is expected under the second root consonant (קֹטְלָה). With II-Guttural verbal roots, the Vocal Shewa cannot stand under the guttural consonant and so the guttural takes Hateph Pathach (בֹּחֲרָה or שֹׁאֲלִים). This minor change should not pose any problem as the diagnostic Holem vowel is preserved in every form. Note the Holem-Tsere vowel pattern in the masculine singular form of both weak verb types.

	Singular	*Plural*	*Singular*	*Plural*
Masculine	בֹּחֵר	בֹּחֲרִים	שֹׁאֵל	שֹׁאֲלִים
Feminine	בֹּחֶרֶת	בֹּחֲרוֹת	שֹׁאֶלֶת	שֹׁאֲלוֹת
Feminine	בֹּחֲרָה		שֹׁאֲלָה	

2. **III-ח/ע** *Verbal Roots.* In this weak verb class, only the feminine singular form, שֹׁלַחַת or שֹׁמַעַת, varies from the strong verb pattern (קֹטֶלֶת). As you know, this change in vowel pattern is due to the fact that gutturals prefer a-class vowels. Note the Furtive Pathach in the masculine singular form.

	Singular	*Plural*	*Singular*	*Plural*
Masculine	שֹׁלֵחַ	שֹׁלְחִים	שֹׁמֵעַ	שֹׁמְעִים
Feminine	שֹׁלַחַת	שֹׁלְחוֹת	שֹׁמַעַת	שֹׁמְעוֹת
Feminine	שֹׁלְחָה		שֹׁמְעָה	

3. **III-א** *Verbal Roots.* Once again, it is only the feminine singular מֹצֵאת that varies from the strong verb pattern. In this form, the א is quiescent. The remaining III-א forms follow the strong verb pattern.

	Singular	*Plural*
Masculine	מֹצֵא	מֹצְאִים
Feminine	מֹצֵאת	מֹצְאוֹת
Feminine	מֹצְאָה	

4. *III-ה Verbal Roots.* In this weak class, the final root consonant (ה) is lost in every form. In the singular forms, however, the presence of the ה vowel letter (*mater lectionis*) helps with identification. Be careful to distinguish between the masculine singular בֹּנֶה and the feminine singular בֹּנָה. Note also that the feminine singular בֹּנִיָּה is not well-attested, occurring only ten times. It has been included to complete the paradigm but not for memorization. Like the singular forms, only two root consonants remain in the masculine and feminine plural forms. There is no ה vowel letter, however, with either plural form to help with identification. Only mastery of the paradigm will enable you to recognize these forms, though it helps to remember that III-ה verbs will drop the final consonant in all forms of the Participle.

	Singular	*Plural*
Masculine	בֹּנֶה	בֹּנִים
Feminine	בֹּנָה	בֹּנוֹת
Feminine	בֹּנִיָּה	

5. *Biconsonantal Verbal Roots.* This weak class is the only one without a diagnostic Holem vowel. For this reason, memorization of the following paradigm is required. Note that the masculine singular Participle קָם (rising) is identical to the Qal Perfect 3ms form קָם (he rose). Likewise, the feminine singular Participle קָמָה (rising) is distinguished from the Qal Perfect 3fs form קָמָה (she rose) only by the accent. In both cases, context (and accent) will enable you to make the correct choice.

	Singular	*Plural*
Masculine	קָם	קָמִים
Feminine	קָמָה	קָמוֹת

22.5 **The Use of the Qal Active Participle.** In Hebrew, Participles function just like adjectives. As such, the three uses of the Participle are attributive, predicative and substantive.

1. *Attributive Use.* When a Participle directly modifies a noun, it is
being used attributively. In the examples, *"sleeping* giant" and
"running water," the Participle directly modifies a noun. In the
attributive usage, the Participle follows, or comes after, the noun
that it modifies. The modifying Participle must also match the
noun in gender, number *and definiteness*. As with nouns and
adjectives, the term "definiteness" refers to the presence (definite)
or absence (indefinite) of the definite article. Note that the
attributive Participle may also be translated with a relative clause
as in "the giant *who is sleeping*" or "the water *that is running*."
The following examples illustrate the attributive use of the
Participle.

הָעָם הַיּשֵׁב בָּאָרֶץ	the people *who dwell* (who are dwelling) in the land (Num 13:28)
הַמַּלְאָךְ הַדֹּבֵר בִּי	the angel *who was speaking* with me (Zech 2:2 [English 2:3])
יְהוָה אֱלֹהֶיךָ אֵשׁ אֹכְלָה	Yahweh your God is a *consuming* fire (Deut 4:24).

2. *Predicative Use.* This use of the Participle does not directly modify
a noun but rather asserts something about it and creates a
predication as in "the giant *is sleeping*" or "the water *is running*."
In English, a form of the verb "to be" is used to indicate the
predicative relationship. In Hebrew, the predicative relationship
is indicated when an adjective matches the noun in gender and
number *but not definiteness*. In this usage, the Participle never
takes the definite article. With regard to word order, the Participle
usually follows the noun. Finally, note that the Participle is a
"tenseless" verb form and so must take its tense from context
(past tense, present tense, future tense, etc.). The following
examples illustrate the predicative use of the Participle.

הָהָר בֹּעֵר בָּאֵשׁ	The mountain *was burning* with fire (Deut 4:11).
וּשְׁמוּאֵל שֹׁכֵב בְּהֵיכַל	And Samuel *was lying down* in (the) temple (1 Sam 3:3).

3. *Substantive Use.* A Participle may be used independently as a noun, indicating the "one who" performs a certain action. In Hebrew, when a Participle is used substantively, it behaves just like a noun. As such it may function as the subject or object of a verb, take a definite article, appear in a construct chain or take pronominal suffixes and prepositional prefixes. In fact, several Hebrew Participles are used with such frequency as substantives that they are commonly listed as nouns. For example, the nouns כֹּהֵן (priest), אֹיֵב (enemy) and שֹׁפֵט (judge) are technically masculine singular Participles functioning substantively (each noun retains the Holem-Tsere vowel pattern of the masculine singular Participle). This same phenomenon occurs in English as well. For example, the "one who teaches" is called a "teacher" and the "one who studies" is called a "student." The following examples illustrate the substantive use of the Participle.

הַיוֹשֶׁבֶת בַּגַּנִּים   *you who dwell* in the gardens (Song 8:13)

וְלֹא יִישָׁן שׁוֹמֵר יִשְׂרָאֵל   and *the one who keeps* Israel will not sleep (Ps 121:4)

22.6 **The Qal Passive Participle.** In addition to the active Participle that you have just studied, there is also a passive Participle in Hebrew. The terms *active* and *passive* (voice) are used to describe the relationship between subject and verb. With verbs having an active voice, the subject of the verb performs the action of the verb (David killed Goliath). With verbs having a passive voice, the subject of the verb receives or is the object of the verbal action (Goliath was killed by David). When translating a passive Participle, the "-ing" ending appears on the helping verb as in *"being* killed" or *"being* written." Additionally, an English form like "blessed" may be used as in *"Blessed* is the person who studies Hebrew."

22.7 **The Qal Passive Participle Paradigm.** The passive Participle, like the active Participle, is inflected in four forms. Unlike the active Participle, however, there is only one feminine singular form. Remember that neither Participle (active or passive) is inflected for person, only gender and number.

	Passive Participle		Inflectional Endings	
	Singular	*Plural*	*Singular*	*Plural*
Masculine	קָטוּל	קְטוּלִים		ִים.
Feminine	קְטוּלָה	קְטוּלוֹת	ָה	וֹת

22.8   Notes on the Qal Passive Participle Paradigm.

1. The diagnostic feature of the Qal passive Participle is the Qamets-Shureq vowel pattern (קָטוּל). It may also be spelled defectively with Qibbuts as in קָטֻל.

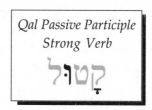

Qal Passive Participle
Strong Verb

קָטוּל

2. In those forms with inflectional endings (fs, mp, fp), a Vocal Shewa appears under the first root consonant as in קְטוּלָה.[1] With I-Guttural verbal roots, this Vocal Shewa changes to Hateph Pathach as in עֲזוּבָה (from עָזַב, to leave, forsake, abandon). As you know, this occurs because gutturals cannot take Vocal Shewa but take reduced vowels, usually Hateph Pathach.

3. You should be able to recognize the passive Participle of most weak verbs without difficulty. In the following weak verb examples, the strong verb vowel pattern is present in every form. Only the masculine singular forms are given.

עָזוּב	abandoned	פָּתוּחַ	opened
שָׂנוּא	hated	יָדוּעַ	known
שָׁאוּל	asked	נָטוּעַ	planted
שָׁחוּט	slaughtered	אָרוּר	cursed
אָכוּל	eaten	יָעוּץ	advised

---

[1] With the addition of inflectional endings (fs, mp, fp), the Qamets under the first root consonant reduces to Shewa according to the principle of propretonic reduction (קָטוּל + ָה ‹ קְטוּלָה).

4. The form of the III-ה passive Participle is quite unusual at first glance. In every form, the consonant י stands in the place of the third root consonant, reminiscent of the fact that III-ה verbs were originally III-י (see 14.7.4). For example, נְטוּיָה is the feminine singular Qal passive Participle from נָטָה (to stretch out). You should think of this י as indicative of the III-ה class of weak verbs. Knowing this will help you to reconstruct the lexical form of the verb.

	Singular	Plural
Masculine	בָּנוּי	בְּנוּיִים
Feminine	בְּנוּיָה	בְּנוּיוֹת

22.9 **The Use of the Qal Passive Participle**. The passive Participle is used just like the active Participle: attributively, predicatively or substantively.

1. *Attributive Use.* The passive Participle follows the noun it modifies and agrees in gender, number and definiteness.

   הַבְּרִית הַכְּתוּבָה בְּסֵפֶר the covenant *written* in this book
   הַתּוֹרָה הַזֶּה of the law (Deut 29:20 [English 29:21])

   וַיִּבֶן אֶת־כָּל־הַחוֹמָה (And) he (re)built all of the *broken*
   הַפְּרוּצָה wall (2 Chr 32:5).

2. *Predicative Use.* The passive Participle either precedes or follows the noun it modifies and agrees in gender and number only (not definiteness).

   בָּרוּךְ יְהוָה לְעוֹלָם *Blessed* is Yahweh forever (Ps 89:53 [English 89:52]).

   בָּרוּךְ הַגֶּבֶר אֲשֶׁר יִבְטַח *Blessed* is the man who trusts (will
   בַּיהוָה trust) in Yahweh (Jer 17:7).

   בָּרוּךְ הַבָּא בְּשֵׁם יְהוָה *Blessed* is he who comes in the name of Yahweh (Ps 118:26).

   אֲרוּרָה הָאֲדָמָה בַּעֲבוּרֶךָ *Cursed* is the ground because of you (Gen 3:17).

3. *Substantive Use.* In the examples below, the passive Participles are used independently as nouns, indicating the "one who" performs a certain action. When a Participle is used substantively, it behaves just like a noun.

וְהֶחָלוּץ יַעֲבֹר לִפְנֵי   And *the one equipped* (for battle)

אֲרוֹן יְהוָה   will pass before the ark of Yahweh (Josh 6:7).

וְתַחַת הֲרוּגִים יִפֹּלוּ   And they will fall among *the slain ones* (Isa 10:4).

22.10 **Parsing the Participle.** Like a verb, the Participle has stem and voice. Like an adjective, it is inflected for gender and number. When parsing, therefore, you will be required to identify stem, conjugation, gender, number and lexical form. The following examples illustrate how you should parse Qal Participles.

| יָשַׁב | Qal Active Participle | ms | יֹשֵׁב |
| בָּרַךְ | Qal Passive Participle | ms | בָּרוּךְ |

22.11 **Participles with Prefixes and Suffixes.** Because Participles behave like nouns, they may take the definite article, prepositional prefixes or pronominal suffixes. They may also be found in the construct state. Study the following examples and be certain that you understand how each Participle is used.

הַהֹלֵךְ בַּשָּׂדֶה   "*the one who walks* in the field" (Gen 24:65). Note the definite article on the Participle.

לְשֹׁמְרֵי בְרִיתוֹ   "*to those who keep (who are keeping)* his covenant" (Ps 103:18). Literally, the phrase translates "to the keepers of his covenant." Note the לְ preposition that is prefixed to the Participle. Observe also that the Participle is in the construct state.

אֲנִי יְהוָה רֹפְאֶךָ   "I am Yahweh *who heals you*" (Ex 15:26). Note the 2ms object suffix (ךָ) on the Participle.

יֹדְעֵי טוֹב וָרָע "*knowing* good and evil" (Gen 3:5). The Participle is in the construct state. Note the diagnostic construct ending (ֵי) as in Ps 103:18 above.

22.12 Summary.

1. Participles are verbal adjectives. Like a verb, Participles have stem (Qal) and voice (active or passive). Like an adjective, they have gender and number. Participles do not have person.

2. The Qal active Participle paradigm for the strong verb must be memorized. The inflectional endings are the same as those that you have memorized for adjectives and nouns (except for the irregular feminine singular form קֹטֶלֶת).

	Active Participle		**Inflectional Endings**	
	Singular	*Plural*	*Singular*	*Plural*
Masculine	קֹטֵל	קֹטְלִים		ִים
Feminine	קֹטֶלֶת	קֹטְלוֹת	ֶת	וֹת
Feminine	קֹטְלָה		ָה	

3. The Holem-Tsere vowel pattern is distinctive of the masculine singular Qal active Participle.

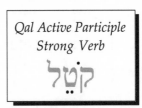

Qal Active Participle
Strong Verb

קֹטֵל

4. The only class of Qal active Participles without the Holem vowel is the Biconsonantal weak verb class. These weak verbs have a Qamets throughout (22.4.5).

5. The Qal passive Participle paradigm for the strong verb must be memorized. The inflectional endings are the same as those you have memorized for adjectives and nouns.

| | **Passive Participle** | | **Inflectional Endings** | |
	Singular	*Plural*	*Singular*	*Plural*
Masculine	קָטוּל	קְטוּלִים		ים.
Feminine	קְטוּלָה	קְטוּלוֹת	ה ָ	וֹת

6. The diagnostic feature for the Qal passive Participle is the Shureq stem vowel in every form, though you must memorize the Qamets-Shureq vowel pattern of the masculine singular form.

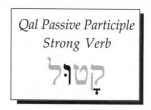

Qal Passive Participle
Strong Verb

קָטוּל

7. Most weak verbs inflect like the strong verb in the active and passive Participle. However, III-ה weak verbs exhibit a number of irregularities. In both active and passive forms, the final root consonant (ה) has been lost. Both paradigms must be memorized.

| | **Active Participle** | | **Passive Participle** | |
	Singular	*Plural*	*Singular*	*Plural*
Masculine	בֹּנֶה	בֹּנִים	בָּנוּי	בְּנוּיִים
Feminine	בֹּנָה	בֹּנוֹת	בְּנוּיָה	בְּנוּיוֹת
Feminine	בֹּנִיָּה			

8. The three uses of the Participle (active and passive) are attributive, predicative and substantive.

   a. *Attributive Use.* In the attributive use, the Participle follows the noun that it modifies and agrees in gender, number and definiteness.

   b. *Predicative Use.* In the predicative use, the Participle either precedes or follows the noun that it modifies and agrees in gender and number only (not definiteness).

c. *Substantive Use.* These Participles are used independently as nouns, indicating the "one who" performs a certain action. When a Participle is used substantively, it behaves just like a noun and may take the definite article, prepositional prefixes or pronominal suffixes.

22.13 Vocabulary.

Verbs

אָרַר	to curse (64)
בּוֹשׁ	to be ashamed (125)
גָּדַל	to be(come) strong, great (117)
חָשַׁב	to account, regard, value, think (124)
יָטַב	to be good (117)
לָכַד	to seize, capture (121)
נָגַשׁ	to draw near, approach (125)
קָבַץ	to gather (127)
קָבַר	to bury (133)
שָׁכַן	to dwell, settle, tent (130)
שָׁפַךְ	to pour out (117)

Nouns

חוֹמָה	(city) wall (133)
חֹק	statute, prescription, ordinance (131)
כֶּבֶשׂ	young ram, lamb (107)

22.14 The Name אֲדֹנָי. The term אֲדֹנָי appears 449 times in the Old Testament, each time with reference to the God of Israel. It is often claimed that אֲדֹנָי means "my Lord," and that its form may be explained as a pausal spelling (36.3) of an intensive plural (non-pausal form would be אֲדֹנַי). This proposal seems plausible, especially in contexts where God is directly addressed. It appears less likely in other contexts, however, such as those where there is a plurality of speakers (cf. Ps 44:24). This evidence is not decisive, however, since there are significant parallels, such as "Rabbi" רַבִּי (literally "my great one"), where a title originated from a pronominal form, which subsequently became frozen (i.e., the pronominal reference was lost). Perhaps more problematic, however, are texts where God employs אֲדֹנָי with reference to himself (Ezek 13:9; 23:49; Job 28:28).

An alternative explanation, which is perhaps preferable, is that the ָי suffix is a substantival afformative that emphasizes the root, not a pronominal suffix. On this view the meaning of אֲדֹנָי is "Lord par excellence" or "Lord of all." In support of this interpretation, scholars note the presence of a similar afformative in Ugaritic, which has this same emphasizing effect. Also, it is observed that the Septuagint normally renders אֲדֹנָי as κύριος (Lord) without a pronoun. Furthermore, it may be noted that in poetry אֲדֹנָי is frequently set in parallel to אֱלֹהִים (God) or יהוה (Yahweh) but never to a pronominal form, such as אֱלֹהַי (my God). Finally, it is notable that the regular 1cs pronominal forms of אָדוֹן, namely אֲדֹנִי (my lord) and אֲדֹנַי ("my lords" or "my Lord" as a plural of intensification), are used only with reference to people. They never appear with reference to God.

Gordon P. Hugenberger
Senior Pastor, Park Street Church
Boston, Massachusetts

Chapter 23

Issues of Sentence Syntax

23.1   **Introduction.** Before we move on to study the derived stems, we will pause to treat more fully the issue of normal word order in verbal sentences along with a selection of other issues relating to sentence syntax. Because you have already encountered numerous verbal sentences in your study of the Qal stem, the following discussion should simply make explicit what you probably already know implicitly. In other words, the point of the following discussion is to organize and clarify many issues of verbal syntax[1] with which you should already be familiar.

In English, normal word order is subject-verb-object. For example, in the sentence "Jacob loved Rachel," *Jacob* is the subject of the verb because his name precedes the verb. Additionally, *Rachel* is the object of the verb because her name follows the verb. If the sentence read "Rachel loved Jacob," then *Rachel* would be the subject and *Jacob* the object because of their positions in the sentence. In Hebrew, normal word order for a verbal sentence is *verb-subject-object*. The following examples illustrate this basic and general guideline.

וַיִּזְכֹּר אֱלֹהִים אֶת־נֹחַ

(And) God remembered Noah (Gen 8:1).

וַיַּחֲלֹם יוֹסֵף חֲלוֹם

(And) Joseph dreamed a dream (Gen 37:5).

וַיִּקְרָא מֹשֶׁה אֶל־כָּל־יִשְׂרָאֵל

(And) Moses called to all Israel (Ex 24:16).

---

[1] The study of Hebrew generally falls into three categories: phonology (the study of the sounds of the language); morphology (the study of how words are formed) and syntax (the study of sentence structure and the ordering of words into meaningful semantic units). All three are important for a working knowledge of the language but syntax is often the area of study that produces the most fruit in terms of exegetical insight. This brief study of normal word order in verbal sentences, along with other selected issues of sentence syntax, is just the first basic step in the study of Hebrew syntax.

In the above examples, the verbs are in the first position, the subjects are in second position, and the objects follow the subject (verb-subject-object). You should also understand, however, that it is not uncommon to encounter variations from this pattern, especially in poetic material. You can also expect certain particles, prepositional phrases or other sentence components to occur regularly in the midst of the basic verb-subject-object pattern. In the following discussion, only the most basic issues of sentence structure are presented.[2]

23.2 **The Syntax of the Verb**. In the syntax of the verbal sentence, the verb is normally at the beginning. In each of the following examples, the verb is in the first position.

$$\text{וַיָּ֥קָם מֶֽלֶךְ־חָדָ֖שׁ עַל־מִצְרָ֑יִם}$$

(And) a new king *arose* over Egypt (Ex 1:8).

$$\text{בָּטַ֥חְתִּי בְחֶֽסֶד־אֱלֹהִ֗ים עוֹלָ֥ם וָעֶֽד}$$

I *trust* in the steadfast love of God forever and ever
(Ps 52:10 [English 52:8]).

$$\text{שִׁ֣ירוּ לַ֭יהוָה שִׁ֣יר חָדָ֑שׁ}$$

Sing to Yahweh a new song (Ps 96:1).

23.3 **Exceptions to Word Order with Verb First**. While the verb does usually stand first in a sentence or clause, it may also be preceded by an adverb of time, an adverbial phrase, the word הִנֵּה (behold), a temporal modifier (וַיְהִי or וְהָיָה), an expression that provides context or circumstantial information or an independent personal pronoun for emphasis. A verb that is negated will be preceded immediately by a negative particle.[3] Each of these circumstances will be illustrated below but it is important to emphasize that, in normal word order, the verb is usually first or, at least, close to the beginning of its clause. Additionally, the presence of any of the sentence components listed above does not necessarily alter the verb-subject-object sentence arrangement.

---

[2] For a clear and insightful study of Hebrew syntax, see R. B. Chisholm, Jr., *From Exegesis to Exposition* (Grand Rapids: Baker, 1998) 57-117.

[3] These are only some of the most common exceptions to word order with verb first. There are others as well.

1. The verb may be preceded by an adverb (23.7).

עַתָּה יָדַעְתִּי כִּי־גָדוֹל יְהוָה מִכָּל־הָאֱלֹהִים

Now I know that Yahweh is greater
than all gods (Ex 18:11).

וְעַתָּה הִנֵּה יָדַעְתִּי כִּי מָלֹךְ תִּמְלוֹךְ

And now, behold, I know that you shall
surely be king (1 Sam 24:21).

רַק הִשָּׁמֶר⁴ לְךָ וּשְׁמֹר נַפְשְׁךָ מְאֹד

Only take heed to yourself and keep
your soul diligently (Deut 4:9).

2. The verb may be preceded by an expression that provides context, circumstantial information or a connection with the preceding clause or verse.

אַחַר הַדְּבָרִים הָאֵלֶּה הָיָה דְבַר־יְהוָה אֶל־אַבְרָם

After these things, the word of Yahweh
came (was) to Abram (Gen 15:1).

בַּיּוֹם הַהוּא כָּרַת יְהוָה אֶת־אַבְרָם בְּרִית

In that day, Yahweh made (cut) a covenant
with Abram (Gen 15:18).

עַל־כֵּן יַעֲזָב־אִישׁ אֶת־אָבִיו וְאֶת־אִמּוֹ

Therefore, a man shall leave his father
and his mother (Gen 2:24).

בְּרֵאשִׁית בָּרָא אֱלֹהִים אֵת הַשָּׁמַיִם וְאֵת הָאָרֶץ

In the beginning, God created the heavens
and the earth (Gen 1:1).

3. The verb may be preceded by הִנֵּה (behold). As noted earlier (13.13), the word הִנֵּה (also הֵן or ־הֶן) should not always be translated as "behold."[5]

---

⁴ הִשָּׁמֶר לְךָ "take heed to yourself"

⁵ The particle הִנֵּה may also be used in several important grammatical constructions, notably in the context of direct discourse and in clauses with Imperatives or Perfects with Waw Conversive.

וְהִנֵּה נָפְלוּ אֲבוֹתֵינוּ בֶּחָרֶב

And *behold*, our fathers have fallen
by the sword (2 Chr 29:9).

וַיֹּאמֶר הִנֵּה שָׁמַעְתִּי כִּי יֶשׁ־שֶׁבֶר בְּמִצְרָיִם

And he said, "*Behold*, I have heard that
there is grain in Egypt" (Gen 42:2).

הִנְנִי נֹתֵן לוֹ אֶת־בְּרִיתִי שָׁלוֹם

Behold, I am giving to him my covenant
of peace (Num 25:12).

4. The verb may be preceded by a *temporal clause* beginning with
וַיְהִי or וְהָיָה. Each of the examples below also illustrates the
frequent use of the Infinitive Construct following a temporal
modifier.

וַיְהִי בִּהְיוֹתָם בַּשָּׂדֶה וַיָּקָם קַיִן אֶל־הֶבֶל אָחִיו וַיַּהַרְגֵהוּ

When they were in the field, Cain rose up against
Abel his brother and he killed him (Gen 4:8).

וַיְהִי כְּבוֹא אַבְרָם מִצְרָיְמָה וַיִּרְאוּ הַמִּצְרִים
אֶת־הָאִשָּׁה כִּי־יָפָה הִוא מְאֹד

When Abraham came to Egypt, the Egyptians saw that
the woman was very beautiful (Gen 12:14).

5. The verb may be preceded by a negative particle.

אַל־תִּבְטְחוּ לָכֶם אֶל־דִּבְרֵי הַשֶּׁקֶר

Do *not* trust in deceptive words (Jer 7:4).

לֹא־אִירָא רָע

I will *not* fear evil (Ps 23:4).

לֹא תַעֲשֶׂה־לְךָ פֶסֶל

You shall *not* make for yourself
an idol (Ex 20:4).

6. The verb may be preceded by an independent personal pronoun for emphasis.

וְאַתֶּם תִּהְיוּ־לִי מַמְלֶכֶת כֹּהֲנִים

And *you* will be to me a kingdom
of priests (Ex 19:6).

וְאַתָּה תָּבוֹא אֶל־אֲבֹתֶיךָ בְּשָׁלוֹם

And *you* will go to your fathers
in peace (Gen 15:15).

אַתֶּם רְאִיתֶם אֲשֶׁר עָשִׂיתִי לְמִצְרָיִם

You have seen what I did
to Egypt (Ex 19:4).

7. The verb may also be preceded by a number of other modifiers or grammatical constructions. A few examples are given below.

אֵלִי אֵלִי לָמָה עֲזַבְתָּנִי

My God, my God, why have you
forsaken me? (Ps 22:2 [English 22:1]).

זֶה־הַיּוֹם עָשָׂה יְהוָה

This is the day Yahweh has made (Ps 118:24).

זֹאת הַבְּרִית אֲשֶׁר אֶכְרֹת אֶת־בֵּית יִשְׂרָאֵל

This is the covenant that I will make with
the house of Israel (Jer 31:33).

בֵּאלֹהִים בָּטַחְתִּי לֹא אִירָא מַה־יַּעֲשֶׂה אָדָם לִי

In God I trust; I will not be afraid. What
can man do to me? (Ps 56:12 [English 56:11]).

23.4 **The Syntax of the Subject.** You know that Perfect, Imperfect and Imperative verbs have an implied subject (12.3). This means that you will not always need an explicit subject to complete a sentence in Hebrew. When you do have an explicit subject, however, it will normally follow the verb.

1. In the syntax of the verbal sentence, the verb is normally followed immediately by its subject if one is specified.

וַיַּחֲלֹם יוֹסֵף חֲלוֹם

(And) *Joseph* dreamed a dream (Gen 37:5).

וַיֹּאמֶר הַנָּחָשׁ אֶל־הָאִשָּׁה

The *serpent* said to the woman (Gen 3:4).

וַיִּשְׁכֹּן כְּבוֹד־יְהוָה עַל־הַר סִינַי

The *glory of Yahweh* dwelt upon Mount Sinai (Ex 24:16).

2. The verb may be preceded by its subject to emphasize that subject, though there are other reasons for this type of variation.

יְהוָה יִמְלֹךְ לְעֹלָם וָעֶד

Yahweh will reign forever
and ever (Ex 15:18).

יְהוָה אֱלֹהֵינוּ כָּרַת עִמָּנוּ בְּרִית בְּחֹרֵב

Yahweh our God made (cut) with us
a covenant in Horeb (Deut 5:2).

כָּל עַצְמוֹתַי תֹּאמַרְנָה יְהוָה מִי כָמוֹךָ

All of my bones say, "Yahweh, who
is like you?" (Ps 35:10).

וּמֹשֶׁה עָלָה אֶל־הָאֱלֹהִים

And *Moses* went up to God (Ex 19:3).

וְנֹחַ מָצָא חֵן בְּעֵינֵי יְהוָה

And *Noah* found favor in the
eyes of Yahweh (Gen 6:8).

23.5 **The Syntax of the Object.** There are a number of different types of "objects" in Hebrew. For this discussion, the most important are the indirect (dative) and the direct (accusative) objects.

1. The indirect object is the person or thing that is indirectly affected by the action of the verb. It is usually marked with either the preposition לְ (to, for) or אֶל־ (to, for) and may either precede or follow the direct object (if any).

יָדַעְתִּי כִּי־נָתַן יְהוָה לָכֶם אֶת־הָאָרֶץ

I know that Yahweh has given *to you* the land (Josh 2:9).

וַיִּתֶּן־לוֹ צֹאן וּבָקָר וְכֶסֶף וְזָהָב

(And) he gave *to him* flocks and herds,
silver and gold (Gen 24:35).

וַיִּקְרָא מֹשֶׁה אֶל־כָּל־יִשְׂרָאֵל

(And) Moses called *to all Israel* (Deut 5:1).

2. A direct object (if any) will frequently stand immediately after the verb or its subject. As discussed in the grammar (6.7), definite direct objects are usually marked with אֵת or אֶת־. A direct object may precede or follow an indirect object.

בָּרָא אֱלֹהִים אֵת הַשָּׁמַיִם וְאֵת הָאָרֶץ

God created *the heavens and
the earth* (Gen 1:1).

וְזָכַרְתִּי אֶת־בְּרִיתִי אֲשֶׁר בֵּינִי וּבֵינֵיכֶם

(And) I will remember *my covenant* that is
between me and between you (Gen 9:15).

וְיִתֶּן־לְךָ מִשְׁאֲלֹת לִבֶּךָ

(And) he will give to you *the desires of your heart* (Ps 37:4).

3. The verb may be preceded by its object to emphasize that object, though there are other reasons for this type of variation.

אֶת־יְהוָה אֱלֹהֶיךָ תִּירָא

Yahweh your God you shall fear (Deut 10:20).

וְאֶת־אֲחִיכֶם קָחוּ וְקוּמוּ שׁוּבוּ אֶל־הָאִישׁ

Your brother take and arise; return
to the man (Gen 43:13).

אֶת־הַצַּדִּיק וְאֶת־הָרָשָׁע יִשְׁפֹּט הָאֱלֹהִים

The righteous and the wicked God
will judge (Eccl 3:17).

23.6   **Conditional Sentences.**[6] A conditional sentence consists of two clauses. The first clause states the condition and is called the *protasis* (the "if-clause"). The second clause states the consequence of the condition and is called the *apodosis* (the "then-clause"). The protasis of a conditional sentence will often begin with אִם (if) as in the following example.

וַיֹּאמֶר אֵלֶיהָ בָּרָק אִם־תֵּלְכִי עִמִּי וְהָלָכְתִּי וְאִם־לֹא תֵלְכִי עִמִּי לֹא אֵלֵךְ

Barak said to her, "*If* you will go with me, *then* I will go;
but *if* you will not go with me, (*then*) I will not go" (Judg 4:8).

Condition (Protasis)	Consequence (Apodosis)
"if (אִם) you will go"	"then I will go"
"but if (אִם) you will not go"	"(then) I will not go"

In addition to אִם, the *protasis* may also begin with אֲשֶׁר, הֵן or כִּי followed by a Perfect, Imperfect or Participle.[7] The *apodosis* will often begin with the conjunction וְ. Finally, note that in rare circumstances, both the protasis and apodosis may be unmarked. The following examples illustrate a number of different types of conditional clauses.

4 אִם־יֶשְׁךָ מְשַׁלֵּחַ אֶת־אָחִינוּ אִתָּנוּ נֵרְדָה וְנִשְׁבְּרָה לְךָ אֹכֶל
5 וְאִם־אֵינְךָ מְשַׁלֵּחַ לֹא נֵרֵד

If you send our brother with us, (*then*) we will go down and buy
food for you; but *if* you do not send him, (*then*) we will not
go done (Gen 43:4-5).

כִּי־תַעֲלֶה בָבֶל הַשָּׁמַיִם וְכִי תְבַצֵּר מְרוֹם עֻזָּהּ מֵאִתִּי יָבֹאוּ שֹׁדְדִים לָהּ

If Babylon were to reach up to heaven and *if* she were to fortify
the height of her strength, (*then*) I would bring destroyers
against her (Jer 51:53).

וְעָזַב אֶת־אָבִיו וָמֵת

If he leaves his father, *then* he (his father)
will die (Gen 44:22).

---

[6] For a more detailed study of conditional sentences and other clause sequences, see B. K. Waltke and M. O'Connor, *An Introduction to Biblical Hebrew Syntax* (Winona Lake: Eisenbrauns, 1990) 632-646.

[7] Though less frequent, there is another type of conditional sentence (clause) that may begin with לוּ (if) or וְלוּלֵי (if not). For examples, see Num 14:2 and Ps 119:92.

23.7 **Adverbs.** An adverb is a word that is used to modify, describe, limit or qualify a verb, adjective or another adverb. In the example, "he *continually* seeks the Lord," the adverb "continually" modifies the verb "seeks." In the example, "the king seemed *genuinely* pleased," the adverb "genuinely" modifies the adjective "pleased." Adverbs are generally divided into four categories: adverbs of time (then, now), place (here, there), degree (very, extremely) and manner (swiftly, gently). For the purpose of illustration, a few Hebrew adverbs are categorized below with examples.

1. *Adverbs of Time.*[8]

   עַתָּה (now)

   עַתָּה יָדַעְתִּי כִּי־יְרֵא אֱלֹהִים אַתָּה

   Now I know that you fear God (Gen 22:12).

   אָז (then, at that time)

   אָז יַקְהֵל שְׁלֹמֹה אֶת־זִקְנֵי יִשְׂרָאֵל

   Then Solomon assembled the elders of Israel (1 Kgs 8:1).

   טֶרֶם (before, not yet)[9]

   וַיָּלִינוּ שָׁם טֶרֶם יַעֲבֹרוּ

   They camped there *before* they crossed over (Josh 3:1).

2. *Adverbs of Place.*

   פֹּה (here)

   וַיֹּאמֶר שְׁבוּ־פֹה וַיֵּשֵׁבוּ

   And he said, "Sit *here*," and they sat (Ruth 4:2).

   הֵנָּה (here)

   וַיֹּאמֶר יְהוֹשֻׁעַ אֶל־בְּנֵי יִשְׂרָאֵל גֹּשׁוּ הֵנָּה וְשִׁמְעוּ

   And Joshua said to the people of Israel, "Approach *here* and listen" (Josh 3:9).

---

[8] It is important to note that certain adverbs of time, such as אָז (then, at that time) and טֶרֶם (before, not yet), may be followed by an Imperfect verb that should be translated as a Perfect. The examples above, following אָז and טֶרֶם, illustrate this special use of these adverbs with the Imperfect conjugation.

[9] This adverb will also appear with the preposition בְּ (בְּטֶרֶם) with the same meaning.

שָׁם   (there)

וַיָּשֶׂם שָׁם אֶת־הָאָדָם אֲשֶׁר יָצָר

And he placed *there* the man whom he had formed (Gen 2:8).

חוּץ   (outside)

וְשַׂמְתָּ אֶת־הַשֻּׁלְחָן מִחוּץ[10]

You will place the table *outside* (Ex 26:35).

3. *Adverbs of Degree.*

מְאֹד   (very)

וַיַּרְא אֱלֹהִים אֶת־כָּל־אֲשֶׁר עָשָׂה וְהִנֵּה־טוֹב מְאֹד

And God saw everything that he had made and, behold, (it was) *very* good (Gen 1:31).

עוֹד   (again)

וַתַּהַר עוֹד וַתֵּלֶד בֵּן

And she conceived *again* and bore a son (Gen 29:33).

תָּמִיד   (continually)

עֵינַי תָּמִיד אֶל־יְהוָה

My eyes are *continually* on the Lord (Ps 25:15).

4. *Adverbs of Manner.*

יַחְדָּו   (together)

וַיַּעֲנוּ כָל־הָעָם יַחְדָּו

And all the people answered *together* (Ex 19:8).

פִּתְאֹם   (suddenly)

וַיָּבֹא אֲלֵיהֶם יְהוֹשֻׁעַ פִּתְאֹם

And Joshua came upon them *suddenly* (Josh 10:9).

23.8   **Disjunctive Waw.** Even a casual exposure to biblical Hebrew will yield the striking impression that sentences are often composed of numerous clauses connected by a form of the conjunction וְ. You have probably noticed by now that this conjunction should not be translated as "and" in every occurrence. In Hebrew, there are two different types of the

---

[10] מִחוּץ = חוּץ with the preposition מִן

conjunction, identified as *conjunctive* and *disjunctive*. The conjunctive Waw is usually *prefixed to a verb* and links clauses sequentially, temporally, logically and often consequentially. You have had some exposure to this usage in chapter 17 (Waw Conversive).[11] The disjunctive Waw is *prefixed to a non-verbal form* and is non-sequential, that is, it introduces some kind of a break or interruption in the narrative. The disjunctive Waw may be used in a number of different ways. Four of the major uses are described below: parenthetical, circumstantial, contrastive and introductory.

1. *Parenthetical.* In this use, the disjunctive clause interrupts the narrative flow in order to provide some explanatory information that is important for understanding the narrative.

   וְהֵם לֹא יָדְעוּ כִּי שֹׁמֵעַ יוֹסֵף כִּי הַמֵּלִיץ בֵּינֹתָם

   Now they did not know that Joseph was understanding
   them because there was an interpreter between
   them (Gen 42:23).

   The disjunctive Waw (וְהֵם) introduces a parenthetical comment that explains why Joseph's brothers spoke openly with one another.

2. *Circumstantial.* In this use, the disjunctive clause introduces or identifies circumstantial information that relates to the main action of the narrative. These disjunctive clauses are often helpful for understanding or visualizing the action of the narrative. As the following example illustrates, the distinction between the parenthetical and circumstantial uses can be subtle.

   וַיְהִי כְּהַיּוֹם הַזֶּה וַיָּבֹא הַבַּיְתָה לַעֲשׂוֹת מְלַאכְתּוֹ
   וְאֵין אִישׁ מֵאַנְשֵׁי הַבַּיִת שָׁם בַּבָּיִת

   (And) one day, he went into the house to do his work
   and none of the household servants were there
   in the house (Gen 39:11).

---

[11] For an in-depth study of the conjunctive Waw, see B. K. Waltke and M. O'Connor, *An Introduction to Biblical Hebrew Syntax* (Winona Lake: Eisenbrauns, 1990) 519-563; 647-673.

The disjunctive Waw (וְאֵין) introduces a circumstantial comment that is important by way of setting up the attempted seduction of Joseph by Potiphar's wife.

3. *Contrastive.* In this use, the disjunctive Waw introduces a contrastive idea and is often translated as "but."

וַיִּשַׁע יְהוָה אֶל־הֶבֶל וְאֶל־מִנְחָתוֹ
וְאֶל־קַיִן וְאֶל־מִנְחָתוֹ לֹא שָׁעָה

The Lord looked favorably on Abel and his offering
but on Cain and his offering he did not look
favorably (Gen 4:4b-5a).

The disjunctive Waw (וְאֶל־קַיִן) contrasts the Lord's response to the two men and their offerings.

4. *Introductory.* In this use, the disjunctive Waw may begin a new narrative or introduce a new idea or theme within a narrative.

וְהַנָּחָשׁ הָיָה עָרוּם מִכֹּל חַיַּת הַשָּׂדֶה
אֲשֶׁר עָשָׂה יְהוָה אֱלֹהִים

Now the serpent was more crafty than any of the
creatures that the Lord God had made (Gen 3:1).

The disjunctive Waw in this text (וְהַנָּחָשׁ) introduces the temptation narrative of Adam and Eve. One could also view this disjunctive Waw as introducing a "parenthetical" comment that is essential for understanding the serpent's question that follows (Did God really say …?). Again, the various uses of the disjunctive Waw will often overlap.

23.9 Summary.

1. The normal word order for a Hebrew verbal sentence is verb-subject-object. Note, however, that neither an explicit subject nor an object is required in every instance. Conversely, a verbal clause may have multiple subjects or objects.

2. The verb may be preceded by an adverb of time, an adverbial phrase, the word הִנֵּה (behold), a temporal clause, an expression that provides context or circumstantial information or an

independent personal pronoun for emphasis. Additionally, a verb that is negated will be preceded immediately by a negative particle.

3. It is not uncommon for either the subject or the object to precede the verb. In such cases, the element placed before the verb is usually emphatic, though there are other reasons for this type of variation.

4. A conditional sentence consists of two clauses: (1) the first clause which states the condition (*protasis* or "if-clause") and (2) the second clause which states the consequence of the condition (*apodosis* or "then-clause"). The protasis with often begin with אִם (if).

5. An adverb is a word that is used to modify, describe, limit or qualify a verb, adjective or another adverb. Adverbs are generally divided into four categories: adverbs of time, place, degree and manner.

6. A disjunctive Waw is prefixed to a non-verbal form and is non-sequential, that is, it introduces some kind of break or interruption in the narrative. Four of the major uses of disjunctive Waw are parenthetical, circumstantial, contrastive and introductory.

23.10 Vocabulary.

Nouns

נְחֹשֶׁת	copper, bronze (139)
נָשִׂיא	chief, prince (130)
עֶרֶב	evening (134)
אוֹר	light (120)
בְּכֹר	firstborn (120); also as בְּכוֹר
חֵמָה	heat, rage, wrath (125)
חֲצִי	half (125)
כֹּחַ	strength, power (126)
עֶצֶם	bone (126)
קָהָל	assembly, congregation (123)

פְּרִי   fruit (119)

רֶכֶב   chariot, chariotry (120)

לָשׁוֹן   tongue (117)

תּוֹעֵבָה   abomination (118)

23.11 **Train Up a Child.** Students who are preparing for youth work or pastoral counseling sometimes wonder about the benefit of investing the time and effort required to gain a working knowledge of Hebrew. In reality, however, the biblical texts which are most relevant for these areas of ministry are often the very ones where a knowledge of the original language is of greatest advantage. Proverbs 22:6 is a case in point.

חֲנֹךְ לַנַּעַר עַל־פִּי דַרְכּוֹ גַּם כִּי־יַזְקִין לֹא־יָסוּר מִמֶּנָּה

The Authorized Version translates it, "Train up a child in the way he should go: and when he is old, he will not depart from it." As desirable as such a promise would be, experience contradicts it far too often to be attributable solely to deficient parenting. Indeed, in spite of the best parenting in the universe, namely God's own, many of his children departed from the way they should have gone, and they continued in their rebellion to the bitter end (cf. Isa 1:2, "I reared children and brought them up, but they have rebelled against me").

A second difficulty with the traditional understanding of Prov 22:6 is the likelihood that the final clause, which begins in Hebrew with גַּם כִּי, rather than merely כִּי, should be rendered "*even* when he is old he will not depart from it," as in many recent translations (NASB; cf. ASV, NEB, JPS, NAB). If this is correct, it implies not just an eventual return, perhaps after a period of waywardness as illustrated by the prodigal son in Luke 15, but a lifelong adherence to the way one should go.

The most serious difficulty with the traditional rendering of Proverbs 22:6, however, is the startling fact that in the Hebrew text there is virtually no basis to justify the all-important qualifier "should" in the phrase, "the way he *should* go." The Hebrew merely has עַל־פִּי דַרְכּוֹ, which is literally, "according to *his way*," as is correctly indicated in the margin of the *New American Standard Bible*. Although in theory, דַרְכּוֹ (his way) could be an elliptical means for expressing "the way *he should go,"* there are, in fact, no biblical examples which support this interpretative expansion. Forms of דֶּרֶךְ with a pronominal suffix, such as דַּרְכּוֹ (his way), are well-attested in the Bible; there are 25 examples in the book of Proverbs alone. None of these requires a rendering similar to "the way he should go." Instead, in each case, "his way" (8:22; 11:5; 14:8; 16:9, 17; 19:3; 20:24; 21:29), "his ways" (3:31; 10:9; 14:2, 14; 19:16), "her ways" (3:17; 6:6; 7:25), "their way" (1:31), etc., refer to the way these persons actually go. The evidence is similar for analogous expressions, such as "the way of wicked men" (2:12), "a man's ways" (5:21), "the way of a fool" (12:15), etc.

Accordingly, Prov 22:6 is not so much a promise, as it is a solemn warning. Parents, if you train up your child "according to *his* way" – in other words, if you quit the hard work of loving discipline and just give in and let your child have his own way – you will reinforce his sinful proclivities to such a degree that, apart from supernatural intervention, "even when he is old he will not depart from it." The book of Proverbs elsewhere places similar urgency on the discipline of children and the danger of being left to follow one's own way.

> Discipline your son, for in that there is hope;
> do not be a willing party to his death (19:18).

> Folly is bound up in the heart of a child,
> but the rod of discipline will drive it far from him (22:15).

> The rod of correction imparts wisdom,
> a child left to himself disgraces his mother (29:15).

It is likely that earlier translators missed this understanding of the text as a warning not because of any difficulty in the Hebrew, but because it construes the first clause as an ironic command. It tells the reader to do something he should not do: "train up a child according to his way." Actually, such a rhetorical device is entirely at home in wisdom literature such as Proverbs, which uses sarcasm to good effect. Compare Proverbs 19:27, "Stop listening to instruction, my son, and you will stray from the words of knowledge."

Gordon P. Hugenberger
Senior Pastor, Park Street Church
Boston, Massachusetts

Chapter 24

The Niphal Stem - Strong Verbs

24.1 **Introduction**. Having studied the Qal stem, you are now equipped to identify over sixty-nine percent of all verb forms in the Hebrew Bible. It is now time to begin our study of the derived stems and their conjugations. You will find it helpful to review the introduction to verbal stems in 12.5-10. The good news is that no further paradigm memorization is required. The "diagnostic" approach to the derived stems does assume, however, that you have mastered the Qal stem and all of its paradigms.

24.2 **The Meaning of the Niphal Stem**. The Niphal stem is used to express *simple* action with either a *passive* or *reflexive* voice.[1] Frequently, whatever a verb means in the Qal stem, it becomes passive or reflexive in the Niphal stem. For example, שָׁמַע in the Qal stem is translated "he heard," while נִשְׁמַע in the Niphal stem is translated as either "he *was* heard" (passive) or "he heard *himself*" (reflexive). The Niphal may also be used with a reciprocal meaning as in נִשְׁמְעוּ, "they heard *one another*."[2] The name "Niphal" (נִפְעַל) *will remind you* that every verb in the Niphal stem takes a נ prefix. This prefix is unique to the Niphal stem and so distinguishes it from the other verbal stems.

24.3 **The Conjugations of the Niphal Stem**. In the Niphal paradigms throughout this chapter, you will notice that a נ is present in the verbal stem of every form. This is the נ of the Niphal. In the Perfect, Participle and one form of the Infinitive Absolute, this prefixed נ makes identification of the Niphal stem easy. In the Imperfect, Imperative, Infinitive Construct

---

[1] The Niphal stem occurs 4,142 times in the Hebrew Bible. It occurs in the Perfect 1,434 times, Imperfect 1,545 times, Imperative 118 times, Infinitive Construct 206 times, Infinitive Absolute 36 times and Participle 803 times.

[2] Though infrequent by comparison with its passive, reflexive or reciprocal uses, the Niphal may also be used to express a "middle" meaning. The middle nuance describes an action where agency is not implied. That is, the object of the action is also remotely the subject of the action. For example, the Niphal as passive is translated "the gate was opened," whereas the Niphal as middle is translated "the gate opened," where "gate" is both the subject and object of the verbal idea.

286

and the other Infinitive Absolute form, however, the נ prefix assimilates into the first consonant of the verbal root and remains as a Daghesh Forte. In other words, the prefixed נ of the Niphal will be present either as the actual consonant or as a Daghesh Forte representing the assimilation of that נ. We will study the various conjugations of the Niphal stem with the strong verb קָטַל (to kill) even though it will produce some awkward translations in selected forms. The following Niphal strong verb paradigms are presented with the corresponding Qal paradigms for the purpose of comparison. Please note that you are not required to memorize any of these Niphal paradigms. You must, however, memorize the diagnostic points of spelling for each of the Niphal conjugations.

24.4 **Niphal Perfect**. The Niphal Perfect is formed with the Niphal prefix (נִ), the verbal stem and the Perfect sufformatives. For now, translate the Niphal Perfect passively with a form of the helping verb "to be" as in "he *was* killed."

	Qal	*Niphal*	*Translation*
3ms	קָטַל	נִקְטַל	he was killed
3fs	קָטְלָה	נִקְטְלָה	she was killed
2ms	קָטַֽלְתָּ	נִקְטַֽלְתָּ	you were killed
2fs	קָטַלְתְּ	נִקְטַלְתְּ	you were killed
1cs	קָטַֽלְתִּי	נִקְטַֽלְתִּי	I was killed
3cp	קָטְלוּ	נִקְטְלוּ	they were killed
2mp	קְטַלְתֶּם	נִקְטַלְתֶּם	you were killed
2fp	קְטַלְתֶּן	נִקְטַלְתֶּן	you were killed
1cp	קָטַֽלְנוּ	נִקְטַֽלְנוּ	we were killed

24.5 **Niphal Perfect Diagnostics.**

1. נ prefix in every form. This is the נ of the Niphal stem and it will enable you to distinguish between the Niphal Perfect and the Qal Perfect. This prefix will also distinguish the Niphal Perfect from all other derived stem Perfects.

2. Pathach stem vowel in all forms, except the 3fs (נִקְטְלָה) and 3cp
(נִקְטְלוּ). The inflection of these two forms exhibits a Vocal Shewa
in the stem vowel position. This vocalization is occasioned by
the fact that these forms have a sufformative that either begins
with a vowel or consists of a vowel.

Niphal Perfect
Strong Verb

נִקְטַל

24.6   **Niphal Imperfect.** The Niphal Imperfect is formed with the Imperfect
preformatives, the verbal stem with assimilated נ of the Niphal and the
Imperfect sufformatives. It must be emphasized that with the Imperfect,
the נ of the Niphal will assimilate into the first consonant of the verbal
root and be represented by a Daghesh Forte. Translate the Niphal
Imperfect passively with a form of the helping verb "to be" as in "he
will *be* killed."

	Qal	*Niphal*	*Translation*
3ms	יִקְטֹל	יִקָּטֵל	he will be killed
3fs	תִּקְטֹל	תִּקָּטֵל	she will be killed
2ms	תִּקְטֹל	תִּקָּטֵל	you will be killed
2fs	תִּקְטְלִי	תִּקָּטְלִי	you will be killed
1cs	אֶקְטֹל	אֶקָּטֵל	I will be killed
3mp	יִקְטְלוּ	יִקָּטְלוּ	they will be killed
3fp	תִּקְטֹלְנָה	תִּקָּטַלְנָה	they will be killed
2mp	תִּקְטְלוּ	תִּקָּטְלוּ	you will be killed
2fp	תִּקְטֹלְנָה	תִּקָּטַלְנָה	you will be killed
1cp	נִקְטֹל	נִקָּטֵל	we will be killed

24.7   **Niphal Imperfect Diagnostics.**

1. Hireq preformative vowel in all forms, except the 1cs (אֶקָּטֵל)
which has Seghol like the Qal.

2. Daghesh Forte in the first consonant of the verbal root (יִקָּטֵל). This is the נ of the Niphal but it has been assimilated into the first consonant of the verbal root. Note that this assimilation also occurs in the Imperative, Infinitive Construct and one form of the Infinitive Absolute.

3. Qamets under the first consonant of the verbal root in every Imperfect form. Note that the stem vowel is not considered to be diagnostic.

4. Be careful not to confuse the Qal Imperfect 1cp form (נִקְטֹל) with the Niphal Imperfect 1cp form (נִקָּטֵל).

Niphal Imperfect
Strong Verb

יִקָּטֵל

24.8   **Niphal Imperative.** The Niphal Imperative and Infinitive Construct forms may be studied together in terms of their diagnostics because their basic forms are identical. The Niphal Imperative is formed with a ה prefix, verbal stem with assimilated נ of the Niphal and the Imperative sufformatives. It must be emphasized again that the נ prefix of the Niphal will assimilate into the first consonant of the verbal root. For now, translate the Niphal Imperative passively with a form of the helping verb "to be" as in *"be* killed!"[3]

	Qal	*Niphal*	*Translation*
2ms	קְטֹל	הִקָּטֵל	be killed!
2fs	קִטְלִי	הִקָּטְלִי	be killed!
2mp	קִטְלוּ	הִקָּטְלוּ	be killed!
2fp	קְטֹלְנָה	הִקָּטַלְנָה	be killed!

---

[3] The translation value of the Niphal Imperative will often lose the passive nuance as in הִשָּׁמֶר לְךָ פֶּן־תִּשְׁכַּח אֶת־יְהוָה "take heed to yourself lest you forget the Lord" (Deut 6:12).

24.9   **Niphal Infinitive Construct**. The masculine singular Imperative
(הִקָּטֵל) and the basic Infinitive Construct form (הִקָּטֵל) are identical.

24.10 **Niphal Imperative and Infinitive Construct Diagnostics**.

1. הִ prefix in every form of the Imperative and in the Infinitive
    Construct.

2. Daghesh Forte in the first consonant of the verbal root. This is
    the assimilated נ of the Niphal stem.

3. Qamets under the first consonant of the verbal root in every
    form of the Imperative and in the Infinitive Construct.

4. The stem vowel is variable in both the Imperative and Infinitive
    Construct forms but it is not considered to be diagnostic.

Niphal Imperative/
Inf Construct

הִקָּטֵל

24.11 **Niphal Infinitive Absolute**. There are two forms for the Niphal Infinitive
Absolute. The first form preserves the נ of the Niphal in the spelling.
The second form has the ה prefix and assimilates the נ of the Niphal
into the first consonant of the verbal root.

Qal	Niphal
קָטוֹל	נִקְטוֹל
	הִקָּטוֹל

24.12 **Niphal Infinitive Absolute Diagnostics**.

1. The Niphal Infinitive Absolute occurs only thirty-six times in the
    Hebrew Bible. The two forms (נִקְטוֹל and הִקָּטוֹל) are evenly
    attested.

2. Both forms preserve the Holem Waw stem vowel, like the Qal
    Infinitive Absolute. The Holem Waw may also be written
    defectively as Holem (הִקָּטֵל). Frequently, the stem vowel is
    Tsere (הִקָּטֵל) and thus identical in form to the 2ms Imperative
    and Infinitive Construct forms.

*Niphal Inf Absolute
Strong Verb*

נִקְטוֹל
הִקָּטוֹל

24.13 Niphal Participle. The Niphal Participle is formed with the Niphal prefix (נִ), the verbal stem and the same inflectional endings that were seen on the Qal Participle. Remember that Participles are verbal adjectives and inflect for gender and number but not for person.

	Qal	*Niphal*	*Translation*
ms	קֹטֵל	נִקְטָל	being killed
fs	קֹטֶלֶת	נִקְטֶלֶת⁴	being killed
mp	קֹטְלִים	נִקְטָלִים	being killed
fp	קֹטְלוֹת	נִקְטָלוֹת	being killed

24.14 Niphal Participle Diagnostics.

1. נ prefix in all forms of the Participle.

2. Qamets stem vowel in all forms, except one form of the feminine singular (נִקְטֶלֶת).

3. Note that the only difference between the Niphal Perfect 3ms (נִקְטַל) and the masculine singular Niphal Participle (נִקְטָל) is the stem vowel. It is Pathach in the Perfect and Qamets in the Participle.

*Niphal Participle
Strong Verb*

נִקְטָל

---

⁴ Like the Qal Participle, the Niphal Participle also occurs with the הָ ending as in נִקְטָלָה.

24.15 **Summary**. At this point in the grammar, chapter summaries will consist primarily of diagnostic reviews. It is very important that you memorize the basic diagnostic features of each conjugation since this will prevent having to memorize numerous paradigms.

1. The Niphal stem is used to express *simple action* with either a *passive* or *reflexive* voice. It may also express a *reciprocal* type of action.

2. In the Niphal stem, the נ prefix is added to every form of every conjugation. In the Perfect, Participle and one form of the Infinitive Absolute, the נ appears as a consonant in the spelling. In the Imperfect, Imperative, Infinitive Construct and one form of the Infinitive Absolute, the נ assimilates into the first consonant of the verbal root and remains as a Daghesh Forte.

3. It is not necessary that you memorize the paradigms in this chapter. Rather, you should memorize the diagnostic features of spelling that are presented in the following summary chart for each conjugation. A version of this summary chart, with the diagnostics marked in red, is located on the CD-ROM.

Niphal Stem - Strong Verb

Perfect	Imperfect	Imperative	Infinitive Construct	Infinitive Absolute	Participle
נִקְטַל	יִקָּטֵל	הִקָּטֵל	הִקָּטֵל	נִקְטוֹל הִקָּטוֹל	נִקְטָל
נִקְטַל	יִקָּטֵל	הִקָּטֵל	הִקָּטֵל	נִקְטוֹל	נִקְטָל
נִקְטְלָה	תִּקָּטֵל	הִקָּטְלִי		הִקָּטוֹל	נִקְטֶלֶת
נִקְטַלְתָּ	תִּקָּטֵל	הִקָּטְלוּ			נִקְטָלִים
נִקְטַלְתְּ	תִּקָּטְלִי	הִקָּטַלְנָה			נִקְטָלוֹת
נִקְטַלְתִּי	אֶקָּטֵל				
נִקְטְלוּ	יִקָּטְלוּ				
נִקְטַלְתֶּם	תִּקָּטַלְנָה				
נִקְטַלְתֶּן	תִּקָּטְלוּ				
נִקְטַלְנוּ	תִּקָּטַלְנָה				
	נִקָּטֵל				

24.16 Vocabulary. Note that verbal meanings other than those of the Niphal have been included in the vocabulary, even though you have not yet studied the other derived stems in depth (12.7).

Verbs

אָמֵן	(Niphal) to be steady, firm, trustworthy, faithful; (Hiphil) believe (97)
יָשַׁע	(Niphal) to be saved; (Hiphil) save (205)
יָתַר	(Niphal) to be left, remain (106)
כּוּן	(Niphal) to be firm, established (219)
לָחַם	(Niphal) to fight (171)
מָלַט	(Niphal) to escape (94)
נָחַם	(Niphal) to be sorry, repent; (Piel) comfort, console (108)

נָכָה   (Niphal) to be hit; (Hiphil) smite (501)

נָצַב   (Niphal) to take one's stand, be stationed (75)

נָצַל   (Niphal) to be delivered; (Hiphil) snatch away (213)

סָתַר   (Niphal) to conceal, hide; (Hiphil) hide someone (82)

פָּלָא   (Niphal) to be extraordinary, wonderful (71)

רוּץ   to run (104)

שָׁחַת   (Niphal) to be corrupt, spoiled; (Hiphil) destroy (152)

שָׁמַד   (Niphal) to be destroyed, exterminated; (Hiphil) exterminate (90)

24.17 Hebrew Reading: The Call and Commission of Moses at the Burning Bush. The narrative of Moses' call at the burning bush (Ex 3) is mesmerizing and captures the imagination. In the mountainous desert of the Sinai, God identifies himself to the fearful shepherd in this way (Ex 3:6).

וַיֹּאמֶר אָנֹכִי אֱלֹהֵי אָבִיךָ אֱלֹהֵי אַבְרָהָם אֱלֹהֵי יִצְחָק וֵאלֹהֵי יַעֲקֹב
וַיַּסְתֵּר מֹשֶׁה פָּנָיו כִּי יָרֵא מֵהַבִּיט אֶל־הָאֱלֹהִים

As Moses hides his face, the Lord speaks (Ex 3:7-8).

7 וַיֹּאמֶר יְהוָה רָאֹה רָאִיתִי אֶת־עֳנִי עַמִּי אֲשֶׁר בְּמִצְרָיִם וְאֶת־צַעֲקָתָם
שָׁמַעְתִּי מִפְּנֵי נֹגְשָׂיו כִּי יָדַעְתִּי אֶת־מַכְאֹבָיו 8 וָאֵרֵד לְהַצִּילוֹ מִיַּד
מִצְרַיִם וּלְהַעֲלֹתוֹ מִן־הָאָרֶץ הַהִוא אֶל־אֶרֶץ טוֹבָה וּרְחָבָה אֶל־אֶרֶץ
זָבַת חָלָב וּדְבָשׁ

The converted Imperfect verb וָאֵרֵד (and so I have come down) at the beginning of 3:8 reveals that God has witnessed the dire plight of his people in Egypt and he now acts to meet their need in faithfulness to the covenant promises that he made to the patriarchal fathers (Ex 2:24). For his part, Moses now learns that he will play a prophet's role in God's deliverance (Ex 3:10).

וְעַתָּה לְכָה וְאֶשְׁלָחֲךָ אֶל־פַּרְעֹה וְהוֹצֵא אֶת־עַמִּי בְנֵי־יִשְׂרָאֵל מִמִּצְרָיִם

Moses poses a question that betrays his sense of inadequacy and lack of credentials for the mission to which God has called him, though some have suggested that his question is prompted out of a sense of humility (Ex 3:11).

וַיֹּאמֶר מֹשֶׁה אֶל־הָאֱלֹהִים מִי אָנֹכִי כִּי אֵלֵךְ אֶל־פַּרְעֹה וְכִי אוֹצִיא
אֶת־בְּנֵי יִשְׂרָאֵל מִמִּצְרָיִם

The reluctant prophet is given divine assurance that he will not be on his own: אֶהְיֶה עִמָּךְ (Ex 3:12). In the early stages of his call to this seemingly impossible mission, Moses' greatest fear was the prospect that the people would believe neither the message nor the divine messenger (Ex 3:13).

וַיֹּאמֶר מֹשֶׁה אֶל־הָאֱלֹהִים הִנֵּה אָנֹכִי בָא אֶל־בְּנֵי יִשְׂרָאֵל וְאָמַרְתִּי לָהֶם
אֱלֹהֵי אֲבוֹתֵיכֶם שְׁלָחַנִי אֲלֵיכֶם וְאָמְרוּ־לִי מַה־שְּׁמוֹ מָה אֹמַר אֲלֵהֶם

In asking for the deliverer's name, the people are seeking to understand his character, authority and credential to accomplish their release from bondage. Is the God of the patriarchal fathers (Ex 2:24; 3:6) up to the task of confronting the god-king of Egypt and a pantheon of many gods? After all, Egypt is not the desert region of Abraham, Isaac and Jacob with its provincial gods but one of the world empires of the day with cosmic deities. In order to convince Israel to listen and Pharaoh to obey, Moses needed to give the people a name but, more importantly, the character and authority behind it.

It is in the context of the call of Moses and his commission to mediate Israel's release from bondage in Egypt that the divine name and the character behind it are revealed afresh to the prophet and to the oppressed nation. In its fullest scope within the book of Exodus, the divine self-revelation is contained in three texts (3:13-15; 6:2-8; 34:5-7). Each of these texts will be the subject of a brief study in the coming chapters.

Gary D. Pratico
Professor of Old Testament
Gordon-Conwell Theological Seminary
South Hamilton, Massachusetts

Chapter 25

The Niphal Stem - Weak Verbs

25.1 **Introduction.** We will now study weak verbs in the Niphal stem. The study of weak verb diagnostics will build upon your familiarity with strong verb diagnostics. For this reason, you will need to have memorized the Niphal strong verb diagnostics in the previous chapter before working through this chapter. Remember, you should be memorizing diagnostics and *not paradigms*. You should also note that many weak verbs in the Niphal will preserve the diagnostics of the Niphal strong verb. For example, III-ה/ע verbs exhibit all of the Niphal strong verb diagnostics.

25.2 **III-א Verbs: Diagnostics and Paradigms.**

Perfect	Imperfect	Imperative	Infinitive Construct	Infinitive Absolute	Participle
נִמְצָא	יִמָּצֵא	הִמָּצֵא	הִמָּצֵא	נִמְצוֹא	נִמְצָא
נִמְצָא	יִמָּצֵא	הִמָּצֵא	הִמָּצֵא	נִמְצוֹא	נִמְצָא
נִמְצְאָה	תִּמָּצֵא	הִמָּצְאִי			נִמְצָאָה[1]
נִמְצֵאתָ	תִּמָּצֵא	הִמָּצְאוּ			נִמְצָאִים
נִמְצֵאת	תִּמָּצְאִי	הִמָּצֶאנָה			נִמְצָאוֹת
נִמְצֵאתִי	אֶמָּצֵא				
נִמְצְאוּ	יִמָּצְאוּ				
נִמְצֵאתֶם	תִּמָּצֶאנָה				
נִמְצֵאתֶן	תִּמָּצְאוּ				
נִמְצֵאנוּ	תִּמָּצֶאנָה				
	נִמָּצֵא				

---

[1] An alternative form, נִמְצֵאת, occurs only two times. While the form נִמְצָאָה is more frequent, it only occurs four times.

25.3   **III-א Verbs: Notes**. Most of the diagnostics for the Niphal strong verb are retained in the III-א Niphal forms. The diagnostics are identical in the Imperfect, Imperative, Infinitive Construct and Infinitive Absolute. The diagnostics of the Perfect and Participle, however, exhibit only minor changes.

1. The נ prefix, characteristic of the Niphal stem, remains in both the Perfect and Participle. No other stem has this prefix and it is a sure indicator of the Niphal stem.

2. In the Perfect, it is the stem vowel that has changed compared to the strong verb. In the strong verb, the stem vowel is normally Pathach as in נִקְטַל. In III-א forms, however, the stem vowel is Qamets as in נִמְצָא. It should be noted, however, that the Qamets stem vowel occurs only in the 3ms form. It is more frequently Tsere as in נִמְצֵאתִי and Vocal Shewa in the 3fs and 3cp forms. These minor changes in the stem vowel should not pose any great difficulty. Your knowledge of the strong verb diagnostics should be sufficient for identification of most III-א Niphal forms.

25.4   **III-ה Verbs: Diagnostics and Paradigms**.

Perfect	Imperfect	Imperative	Infinitive Construct	Infinitive Absolute	Participle
נִבְנָה נִבְנֵית	יִבָּנֶה	הִבָּנֶה	הִבָּנוֹת	נִבְנֹה הִבָּנֵה	נִבְנֶה
נִבְנָה	יִבָּנֶה	הִבָּנֶה	הִבָּנוֹת	נִבְנֹה	נִבְנֶה
נִבְנְתָה	תִּבָּנֶה	הִבָּנִי		הִבָּנֵה	נִבְנָה
נִבְנֵיתָ	תִּבָּנֶה	הִבָּנוּ			נִבְנִים
נִבְנֵית	תִּבָּנִי	הִבָּנֶינָה			נִבְנוֹת
נִבְנֵיתִי	אֶבָּנֶה				
נִבְנוּ	יִבָּנוּ				
נִבְנֵיתֶם	תִּבָּנֶינָה				
נִבְנֵיתֶן	תִּבָּנוּ				
נִבְנֵינוּ	תִּבָּנֶינָה				
	נִבָּנֶה				

25.5 **III-ה Verbs: Notes**. Once again, the majority of the diagnostics for the Niphal strong verb are retained in the III-ה forms of the Niphal. The diagnostics are the same in every conjugation except the Perfect and Participle.

1. The stem vowel of the Perfect varies between Qamets in the 3ms form (נִבְנָה) and Tsere Yod in the remaining forms (נִבְנֵיתָ), except in the 3fs and 3cp forms as usual. The stem vowel of the masculine singular Participle is Seghol. The reason for this is explained in the next point.

2. In the chart of Niphal III-ה diagnostics (25.4), you should note the endings that are highlighted in dark gray. With the exception of the Infinitive Construct, all of the other conjugations end with the consonant ה. You will recall from your study of Qal III-ה verbs that this is not the third consonant of the verbal root but a vowel letter. The shading of these vowel letters (and their associated vowels) is for the purpose of identifying them as unique and diagnostic endings of the III-ה class of verbs. These endings are not diagnostic, however, of the various stems because they are attested in all stems (Qal through Hithpael). The following chart lists the III-ה endings for your review.

Diagnostic Endings for III-ה
Verbs in All Stems

Conjugation	Ending
Perfect	הָ
Imperfect	הֶ
Imperative	הֵ
Infinitive Construct	וֹת
Participle	הֶ

You will also need to remember that these endings do not appear in verb forms with sufformatives. For example, the הֵ ending of the Imperative appears only in the masculine singular form because all other Imperative forms have a sufformative. Similarly, the הֶ ending of the Participle will occur only in the masculine singular because the other Participle forms have inflectional endings.

25.6 I-Guttural Verbs: Diagnostics and Paradigms.

Perfect	Imperfect	Imperative	Infinitive Construct	Infinitive Absolute	Participle
נֶעֱזַב	יֵעָזֵב	הֵעָזֵב	הֵעָזֵב	נַעֲזוֹב הֵעָזוֹב	נֶעֱזָב
נֶעֱזַב	יֵעָזֵב	הֵעָזֵב	הֵעָזֵב	נַעֲזוֹב	נֶעֱזָב
נֶעֶזְבָה	תֵּעָזֵב	הֵעָזְבִי		הֵעָזוֹב	נֶעֱזֶבֶת
נֶעֱזַבְתָּ	תֵּעָזֵב	הֵעָזְבוּ			נֶעֱזָבִים
נֶעֱזַבְתְּ	תֵּעָזְבִי	הֵעָזַבְנָה			נֶעֱזָבוֹת
נֶעֱזַבְתִּי	אֵעָזֵב				
נֶעֶזְבוּ	יֵעָזְבוּ				
נֶעֱזַבְתֶּם	תֵּעָזַבְנָה				
נֶעֱזַבְתֶּן	תֵּעָזְבוּ				
נֶעֱזַבְנוּ	תֵּעָזַבְנָה				
	נֵעָזֵב				

25.7 I-Guttural Verbs: Notes. The changes that occur in the Niphal forms of I-Guttural verbal roots, while appearing drastic at first, are explained by rules that you have already learned.

1. With those forms where the נ of the Niphal normally assimilates into the first consonant of the verbal root (Imperfect, Imperative, Infinitive Construct and one form of the Infinitive Absolute), the guttural consonant rejects the Daghesh Forte associated with the assimilating נ. This results in the *compensatory lengthening* of the prefix vowel, Hireq to Tsere in every form of these conjugations. Remember that in the rules of compensatory lengthening, Hireq lengthens to Tsere. For example, in the Imperfect form יֵעָזֵב (3ms), the presence of the Tsere under the Imperfect preformative is due to the fact that the ע has rejected the Daghesh Forte of the assimilating נ and caused the Hireq preformative vowel to lengthen to Tsere. Note that the diagnostic Qamets under the first consonant of the verbal root is preserved in each of these conjugations (Imperfect, Imperative, Infinitive Construct and one form of the Infinitive Absolute).

2. Memorizing the diagnostic forms of the Niphal Perfect and Participle should be easy since you are already familiar with the pattern. The Perfect and Participle forms of Niphal I-Guttural verbs behave just like the I-Guttural forms of the Qal Imperfect of חָזַק (16.8). Compare the diagnostics below.

Qal Imperfect	*Niphal Perfect*	*Niphal Participle*
יֶחֱזַק	נֶעֱזַב	נֶעֱזָב

In every form of the Niphal Perfect and Participle, the prefix vowel is Seghol. In most forms, this is followed by the Hatef Seghol under the guttural that is the first consonant of the verbal root. In the Niphal Perfect forms, the stem vowel is Pathach (except in the 3fs and 3cp). In the Niphal Participle, the stem vowel is Qamets, except in the feminine singular form.

25.8   **I-נ Verbs: Diagnostics and Paradigms.**

Perfect	*Imperfect*	*Imperative*	*Infinitive Construct*	*Infinitive Absolute*	*Participle*
נִצֵּל	יִנָּצֵל	הִנָּצֵל	הִנָּצֵל	הִנָּצֵל / נִצּוֹל	נִצָּל
נִצַּל	יִנָּצֵל	הִנָּצֵל	הִנָּצֵל	הִנָּצֵל	נִצָּל
נִצְּלָה	תִּנָּצֵל	הִנָּצְלִי		נִצּוֹל	נִצֶּלֶת
נִצַּלְתָּ	תִּנָּצֵל	הִנָּצְלוּ			נִצָּלִים
נִצַּלְתְּ	תִּנָּצְלִי	הִנָּצַלְנָה			נִצָּלוֹת
נִצַּלְתִּי	אֶנָּצֵל				
נִצְּלוּ	יִנָּצְלוּ				
נִצַּלְתֶּם	תִּנָּצַלְנָה				
נִצַּלְתֶּן	תִּנָּצְלוּ				
נִצַּלְנוּ	תִּנָּצַלְנָה				
	נִנָּצֵל				

25.9   **I-נ Verbs: Notes.** All of the diagnostics for the Niphal strong verb are retained in the Niphal I-נ conjugations.

1. Our concern for the I-נ Niphal forms relates not to the diagnostics but rather to the need for recognizing the assimilation of the first root consonant in the Perfect, one form of Infinitive Absolute (נִצּוֹל) and the Participle forms. The נ that appears at the beginning of each form in these three conjugations is the נ of the Niphal stem and not the נ that is the first consonant of the verbal root. The נ of the verbal root has assimilated into the second root consonant and remains as a Daghesh Forte.

2. In the Imperfect, Imperative, Infinitive Construct and one form of the Infinitive Absolute (הִנָּצֵל), the נ of the verbal root is retained while the נ of the Niphal stem has assimilated into the first consonant of the verbal root. This is the regular pattern of assimilation characteristic of the Niphal stem. Knowing when a נ is part of the I-נ verbal root or part of the Niphal stem is essential for the proper identification of the stem and verbal root. Carefully study each paradigm of 25.8 and be certain that you understand which נ has assimilated, the first consonant of the verbal root or the נ of the Niphal stem.

25.10 I-י Verbs: Diagnostics and Paradigms.

Perfect	Imperfect	Imperative	Infinitive Construct	Infinitive Absolute[2]	Participle
נוֹשָׁב	יִוָּשֵׁב	הִוָּשֵׁב	הִוָּשֵׁב		נוֹשָׁב
נוֹשַׁב	יִוָּשֵׁב	הִוָּשֵׁב	הִוָּשֵׁב	הִוָּשֵׁב	נוֹשָׁב
נוֹשְׁבָה	תִּוָּשֵׁב	הִוָּשְׁבִי			נוֹשֶׁבֶת
נוֹשַׁבְתָּ	תִּוָּשֵׁב	הִוָּשְׁבוּ			נוֹשָׁבִים
נוֹשַׁבְתְּ	תִּוָּשְׁבִי	הִוָּשַׁבְנָה			נוֹשָׁבוֹת
נוֹשַׁבְתִּי	אִוָּשֵׁב				
נוֹשְׁבוּ	יִוָּשְׁבוּ				
נוֹשַׁבְתֶּם	תִּוָּשַׁבְנָה				
נוֹשַׁבְתֶּן	תִּוָּשְׁבוּ				
נוֹשַׁבְנוּ	תִּוָּשַׁבְנָה				
	נִוָּשֵׁב				

---

[2] The Niphal Infinitive Absolute is not attested in I-י verbs.

25.11 I-ʼ Verbs: Notes. While the vowel changes in the above diagnostics and paradigms appear drastic at first glance, most of the Niphal strong verb diagnostics are still evident.

1. Most of the verbs that we now identify as I-ʼ were originally I-ו. In the conjugations of the Niphal stem, this original ו reappears and replaces the ʼ that is in the first root position. In the Imperfect, Imperative and Infinitive Construct, the Waw appears as the first root consonant with the Daghesh Forte (וּ),[3] representing the assimilated נ of the Niphal stem. Knowing this, the diagnostics of the Imperfect, Imperative and Infinitive Construct forms are identical to the strong Niphal diagnostics.

2. In the Perfect and Participle forms, the original ו appears as a Holem Waw (וֹ). The נ of the Niphal stem is still present and the stem vowel of each form is also unchanged from the strong diagnostics (Pathach in the Perfect and Qamets in the Participle). In other words, the only change in diagnostics in the Perfect and Participle forms of I-ʼ verbs is the presence of the Holem Waw prefix vowel rather than the Hireq of the strong verb.

3. The difficulty with I-ʼ verbs is not the recognition of diagnostics but rather the identification of the verbal root. In order to correctly identify these verbs, you will need to remember that I-ʼ verbs were originally I-ו and that the original ו consonant reappears in the Niphal stem as either a consonant (Imperfect, Imperative and Infinitive Construct) or a vowel (Perfect and Participle).

25.12 Other Weak Forms. There are several other weak verb classes that are attested in the Niphal stem. The diagnostics of III-ח/ע weak verbs are identical to the strong verb. Biconsonantal, Geminate and various doubly weak forms occur infrequently and do not warrant attention here. Mastery of the diagnostics for the strong and weak verbs already presented will be sufficient to enable you to successfully identify these more infrequent weak forms of the Niphal stem.

---

[3] You must understand that this is the consonant Waw with a Daghesh Forte (וּ) and not the vowel Shureq (וּ).

25.13 Summary: Niphal Diagnostics.

	Perfect	Imperfect	Imperative	Infinitive Construct	Infinitive Absolute	Participle
Strong	נָקְטַל נִקְטַל	יִקָּטֵל	הִקָּטֵל	הִקָּטֵל	נִקְטוֹל הִקָּטוֹל	נִקְטָל
III-א	נִמְצָא נִמְצָא	יִמָּצֵא	הִמָּצֵא	הִמָּצֵא	נִמְצוֹא	נִמְצָא
III-ה	נִבְנָה נִבְנָה נִבְנֵיתָ	יִבָּנֶה	הִבָּנֶה	הִבָּנוֹת	נִבְנֹה הִבָּנֵה	נִבְנֶה
I-Gutt	נֶעֱזַב נֶעֱזַב	יֵעָזֵב	הֵעָזֵב	הֵעָזֵב	נַעֲזוֹב הֵעָזוֹב	נֶעֱזָב
I-נ	נִצַּל נִצַּל	יִנָּצֵל	הִנָּצֵל	הִנָּצֵל	הִנָּצֵל נִצּוֹל	נִצָּל
I-י	נוֹשַׁב נוֹשַׁב	יִוָּשֵׁב	הִוָּשֵׁב	הִוָּשֵׁב		נוֹשָׁב

25.14 Vocabulary.

Verbs

הָפַךְ	to turn, overturn (95)
זָנָה	to commit fornication, play the harlot (95)
חָרָה	to become hot, angry (94)
רָעַע	to be wicked, evil (97)
שָׁכַח	to forget (102)
שָׁמֵם	to be astonished, be desolate (92)

שָׂבַע   to satisfy, be satiated (98)

Nouns

זָכָר   man, male (82)

חֹשֶׁךְ   darkness (80)

מִגְרָשׁ   pasture, untilled ground (114)

מַמְלָכָה   kingdom (117)

נָהָר   river, stream (119)

צֶדֶק   righteousness, what is right, just (123)

רֹעֶה   shepherd (84)

25.15 What Is His Name? Exodus 3:13-15 is the first of three biblical texts that are essential for a provisional understanding of the revelation and meaning of God's personal name, יהוה, the name that defines his relationship as covenant Lord of his people. In Ex 3:13, Moses asks God how he is to respond to the community in bondage when they ask about the name and authority of the one in whose name Moses mediates the message of deliverance.

הִנֵּה אָנֹכִי בָא אֶל־בְּנֵי יִשְׂרָאֵל וְאָמַרְתִּי לָהֶם אֱלֹהֵי אֲבוֹתֵיכֶם
שְׁלָחַנִי אֲלֵיכֶם וְאָמְרוּ־לִי מַה־שְּׁמוֹ מָה אֹמַר אֲלֵהֶם

Suppose I go to the people of Israel and I say to them,
"The God of your fathers has sent me to you," and they ask me,
"What is his name?" Then what shall I say to them?

This verse makes clear the intention of Moses to identify the God of Exodus events with the God of the patriarchal fathers. This is how God revealed himself to Moses at the burning bush (Ex 3:6), in the context of his self-revelation in this text (Ex 3:15-16), in the preparation of Moses for his mission (Ex 4:5) and in the reiteration of his promise of deliverance (Ex 6:2, 8). In fact, the destination of the delivered people will be the land promised to the fathers (Ex 6:8).

וְהֵבֵאתִי אֶתְכֶם אֶל־הָאָרֶץ אֲשֶׁר נָשָׂאתִי אֶת־יָדִי לָתֵת אֹתָהּ לְאַבְרָהָם
לְיִצְחָק וּלְיַעֲקֹב וְנָתַתִּי אֹתָהּ לָכֶם מוֹרָשָׁה אֲנִי יְהוָה

The narrative is burdened to establish the unbroken continuity and identity between the God of the fathers and the God of Exodus events.

The question of the people in Ex 3:13 (מַה־שְּׁמֹו) is supremely theological. In its Old Testament usage, and especially in 3:13 and 6:3, the noun שֵׁם (name) often communicates immeasurably more than a simple label by which one is known. The concept of a personal name includes personhood, character, reputation and authority. The concept of a name can signify and encompass the whole person. A name can express theological meaning or signify one's hopes or expectations for a person. This explains the significance of naming and name changes in the Old Testament (Gen 17:5, 15; 32:28; 35:10; Hos 1:2-8; Isa 8:3). In some contexts, the name of God is tantamount to his being (Ex 20:24; 23:21; Deut 12:5). In their question, the people are seeking to know the character, authority and reputation of the divine messenger behind the message. God identifies himself to Moses and instructs him how to respond to the people (Ex 3:14).

וַיֹּאמֶר אֱלֹהִים אֶל־מֹשֶׁה אֶהְיֶה אֲשֶׁר אֶהְיֶה וַיֹּאמֶר כֹּה תֹאמַר לִבְנֵי
יִשְׂרָאֵל אֶהְיֶה שְׁלָחַנִי אֲלֵיכֶם

Here God declares that his name is אֶהְיֶה אֲשֶׁר אֶהְיֶה (traditionally, "I am who I am"). The two verbs are Qal Imperfect 1cs from הָיָה with the relative pronoun אֲשֶׁר between them. This construction allows for "I am who/what I am" or "I will be who/what I will be." Moses is further instructed in 3:14 to identify the God of their fathers as אֶהְיֶה ("I am" or "I will be"). The context clearly links the אֶהְיֶה אֲשֶׁר אֶהְיֶה with God's statement to Moses in Ex 3:12 (אֶהְיֶה עִמָּךְ) and also with the *tetragrammaton* in 3:15. The divine self-revelation continues in 3:15, creating a seamless connection between the God of the fathers (3:13, 15), אֶהְיֶה אֲשֶׁר אֶהְיֶה (3:14a), אֶהְיֶה (3:14b), and the *tetragrammaton* (3:15), which also derives from היה (originally הוה).

How then does this divine self-revelation answer the people's question in 3:13, validating the mission of Moses and disclosing the authority of the divine deliverer? The answer is in the verb "to be" (הָיָה) which floods this narrative. Clearly, the use of this verb in Ex 3:10-15 implies more than just ontological being. The use of הָיָה in the context of God's mighty and miraculous deliverance of Israel from Egypt and the exercise of his judgement on the oppressing nation implies both his dynamic presence and his dynamic activity. The arena of human history is about to experience a dynamic intrusion of the divine.[4]

Gary D. Pratico
Professor of Old Testament
Gordon-Conwell Theological Seminary
South Hamilton, Massachusetts

---

[4] This study will continue in 26.15.

Chapter 26

The Piel Stem - Strong Verbs

26.1 **Introduction.** In this chapter, we will study the second of the derived stems, the Piel.[1] As in your study of the Niphal stem, paradigm memorization is not required for the Piel stem. Rather, you will study certain diagnostic points of spelling that are unique to the Piel stem. The most important diagnostic features include: (1) Vocal Shewa under all Imperfect and Participle preformatives and prefixes; (2) Pathach under the first root consonant of every conjugation, except the Perfect; and (3) Daghesh Forte in the second root consonant of every form.

26.2 **The Meaning of the Piel Stem.**[2]

1. *Intensive.* The Piel stem is used to express an *intensive* type of action with an *active* voice.[3] In other words, the simple action of the Qal stem will take on some type of intensive nuance in the Piel stem. For example, the verb שָׁבַר means "he broke" in the Qal stem. The Piel form, however, is שִׁבֵּר and means "he smashed" or "he shattered." This intensive type of action, however, is only one of several different types of "intensive" action denoted by the Piel stem. Some of the more common types of action are detailed below.

2. *Factitive.* The factitive use of the Piel makes an intransitive Qal verb transitive. In other words, if a Qal verb is intransitive (does not take a direct object), it will become transitive (can take a direct object) in the Piel stem. The following examples illustrate

---

[1] The Piel stem occurs 6,808 times in the Hebrew Bible. It appears in the Perfect 2,215 times, Imperfect 2,565 times, Imperative 444 times, Infinitive Construct 725 times, Infinitive Absolute 85 times and Participle 774 times.

[2] Some Piel verbs do not fall into any of the following categories. You will need to consult a standard lexicon when you are not certain of a verb's meaning in a given derived stem.

[3] We recognize the difficulty of characterizing the varieties of action denoted by the Piel stem (also Pual and Hithpael) with a single designation like "intensive." Such a designation is a helpful starting point, however, for the beginning student. Additionally, it is legitimate to think of the factitive and iterative as "types" of intensive action.

how an intransitive Qal verb becomes transitive in the Piel.

Qal (Intransitive)			*Factitive Piel (Transitive)*	
קָדַשׁ	to be holy	>	קִדַּשׁ	to sanctify
אָבַד	to perish	>	אִבַּד	to destroy
טָמֵא	to be unclean	>	טִמֵּא	to defile

3. *Denominative*. Verbs that are derived from a noun or adjective are often inflected in the Piel stem, not the Qal. When this occurs, the type of verbal action is simple and not intensive.

Noun			*Denominative Piel*	
דָּבָר	word	>	דִּבֶּר	to speak
כֹּהֵן	priest	>	כִּהֵן	to serve as priest
עָפָר	dust	>	עִפֵּר	to throw dirt

4. *Iterative*. The iterative action of the Piel expresses the nuance of repeated action. This use occurs primarily with verbs that express physical movement, effort or voice projection. This type of action is often difficult to translate into English.

Qal			*Iterative Piel*	
הָלַךְ	to go, walk	>	הִלֵּךְ	to pace, walk around
צָעַק	to cry	>	צִעֵק	to weep over and over, keep crying

26.3 **Piel Perfect**. It is the vocalization (vowel pattern) that will distinguish the Piel stem from the Qal stem. In the Piel Perfect, the distinguishing features are a Hireq under the first root consonant and a Daghesh Forte in the second root consonant.

	Qal	Piel	Translation[4]
3ms	קָטַל	קִטֵּל	he slaughtered
3fs	קָטְלָה	קִטְּלָה	she slaughtered
2ms	קָטַלְתָּ	קִטַּלְתָּ	you slaughtered
2fs	קָטַלְתְּ	קִטַּלְתְּ	you slaughtered
1cs	קָטַלְתִּי	קִטַּלְתִּי	I slaughtered
3cp	קָטְלוּ	קִטְּלוּ	they slaughtered
2mp	קְטַלְתֶּם	קִטַּלְתֶּם	you slaughtered
2fp	קְטַלְתֶּן	קִטַּלְתֶּן	you slaughtered
1cp	קָטַלְנוּ	קִטַּלְנוּ	we slaughtered

26.4 Piel Perfect Diagnostics.

1. Hireq under the first consonant of the verbal root.

2. Daghesh Forte in the second consonant of the verbal root.

3. The stem vowel is variable between Tsere and Pathach, except in the 3fs and 3cp, where the expected Vocal Shewa is present. Note that the Tsere stem vowel occurs only in the 3ms.

Piel Perfect
Strong Verb

קִטֵּל

26.5 Piel Imperfect.
Once again, it is the vowel pattern that will distinguish the Piel Imperfect from the Qal Imperfect. In the Piel Imperfect, the distinguishing features include: Vocal Shewa under the preformative, Pathach under the first root consonant and Daghesh Forte in the second root consonant.

---

[4] The verb קַטַל is not attested in the Piel stem. The translation "to slaughter" would be the intensive rendering of the Qal meaning "to kill."

	Qal	Piel	Translation
3ms	יִקְטֹל	יְקַטֵּל	he will slaughter
3fs	תִּקְטֹל	תְּקַטֵּל	she will slaughter
2ms	תִּקְטֹל	תְּקַטֵּל	you will slaughter
2fs	תִּקְטְלִי	תְּקַטְּלִי	you will slaughter
1cs	אֶקְטֹל	אֲקַטֵּל	I will slaughter
3mp	יִקְטְלוּ	יְקַטְּלוּ	they will slaughter
3fp	תִּקְטֹלְנָה	תְּקַטֵּלְנָה	they will slaughter
2mp	תִּקְטְלוּ	תְּקַטְּלוּ	you will slaughter
2fp	תִּקְטֹלְנָה	תְּקַטֵּלְנָה	you will slaughter
1cp	נִקְטֹל	נְקַטֵּל	we will slaughter

26.6   Piel Imperfect Diagnostics.

1. Vocal Shewa under the Imperfect preformative (Hateph Pathach in the 1cs since gutturals cannot take Vocal Shewa).

2. Pathach under the first consonant of the verbal root. This is the most important diagnostic feature since it occurs in every other Piel conjugation, except the Perfect. Note that the stem vowels are not considered to be diagnostic, though it is helpful to observe the presence of Tsere throughout the conjugations of the Piel (see summary chart in 26:13).

3. Daghesh Forte in the second consonant of the verbal root.

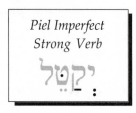

Piel Imperfect
Strong Verb

26.7   Piel Imperative, Infinitive Construct and Infinitive Absolute. These forms may be studied together in terms of their diagnostics because their basic forms are identical. There are two diagnostic features that characterize all three forms.

1. Pathach under the first consonant of the verbal root.

2. Daghesh Forte in the second consonant of the verbal root.

Piel Imperative/
Infinitive Construct
and Absolute

קַטֵּל

26.8 **Piel Imperative.** As in the Qal, all four forms of the Piel Imperative are derivable from their corresponding Imperfect forms by simply removing the Imperfect preformatives. When studying the Piel Imperative paradigm, note the similarity between the Imperative forms and the corresponding forms of the Imperfect.

	Piel Imperfect	*Piel Imperative*	*Translation*
2ms	תְּקַטֵּל	קַטֵּל	(you) slaughter!
2fs	תְּקַטְּלִי	קַטְּלִי	(you) slaughter!
2mp	תְּקַטְּלוּ	קַטְּלוּ	(you) slaughter!
2fp	תְּקַטֵּלְנָה	קַטֵּלְנָה	(you) slaughter!

26.9 **Piel Infinitive Construct.** The basic form of the Piel Infinitive Construct is identical to the 2ms form of the Piel Imperative. The following chart compares the Qal and Piel Infinitive Construct forms.

Qal	*Piel*	*Translation*
קְטֹל	קַטֵּל	to slaughter, slaughtering

26.10 **Piel Infinitive Absolute.** The Piel Infinitive Absolute of קָטַל is קַטֵּל. The Qal and Niphal forms of the Infinitive Absolute normally exhibit an o-class stem vowel, Holem or Holem Waw. In the Piel, Hiphil and Hithpael stems, however, an e-class stem vowel is present, usually Tsere (but sometimes Tsere Yod or Seghol).[5]

---

[5] In five instances, the Piel Infinitive Absolute will have an o-class stem vowel (Holem Waw or Holem).

26.11 Piel Participle. The Piel Participle is formed with a מ prefix and has diagnostics similar to those of the Piel Imperfect. Remember that Participles are verbal adjectives and inflect for gender and number but not person.

	Qal	*Piel*	*Translation*
ms	קֹטֵל	מְקַטֵּל	slaughtering
fs	קֹטֶלֶת	מְקַטֶּלֶת[6]	slaughtering
mp	קֹטְלִים	מְקַטְּלִים	slaughtering
fp	קֹטְלוֹת	מְקַטְּלוֹת	slaughtering

26.12 Piel Participle Diagnostics.

1. מְ prefix. A מ prefix will characterize the Participles of the Piel, Pual, Hiphil and Hophal stems. In the Piel and Pual Participles, this prefix appears with Shewa (מְ).

2. Pathach under the first consonant of the verbal root.

3. Daghesh Forte in the second consonant of the verbal root.

*Piel Participle
Strong Verb*

מְקַטֵּל

26.13 Summary.

1. The most important diagnostic features for the strong verb of the Piel stem include: (1) Daghesh Forte in the second root consonant of every form; (2) Pathach under the first root consonant of every conjugation, except the Perfect; and (3) Vocal Shewa under all Imperfect and Participle preformatives and prefixes. Though not considered to be diagnostic, it is helpful to note the Tsere stem vowel throughout the conjugations.

---

[6] Like the Qal Participle, the Piel Participle may also end in הָ as in מְקַטְּלָה.

2. Looking ahead, note that the Daghesh Forte in the second consonant of the verbal root will also characterize the strong verb inflections of the Pual and Hithpael stems.

3. Note the distinctive מ prefix in the forms of the Piel Participle. This same prefix also occurs with the Participles of the Pual, Hiphil and Hophal stems.

Piel Stem - Strong Verbs

Perfect	Imperfect	Imperative	Infinitive Construct	Infinitive Absolute	Participle
קָטַל	יְקַטֵּל	קַטֵּל	קַטֵּל	קַטֵּל	מְקַטֵּל
קִטֵּל	יְקַטֵּל	קַטֵּל	קַטֵּל	קַטֵּל	מְקַטֵּל
קִטְּלָה	תְּקַטֵּל	קַטְּלִי			מְקַטֶּלֶת
קִטַּלְתָּ	תְּקַטֵּל	קַטְּלוּ			מְקַטְּלִים
קִטַּלְתְּ	תְּקַטְּלִי	קַטֵּלְנָה			מְקַטְּלוֹת
קִטַּלְתִּי	אֲקַטֵּל				
קִטְּלוּ	יְקַטְּלוּ				
קִטַּלְתֶּם	תְּקַטֵּלְנָה				
קִטַּלְתֶּן	תְּקַטְּלוּ				
קִטַּלְנוּ	תְּקַטֵּלְנָה				
	נְקַטֵּל				

26.14 Vocabulary.

Verbs

בָּקַשׁ	(Piel) to seek (225)
דָּבַר	(Piel) to speak (1,136)
הָלַל	(Piel) to praise (146)
יָדָה	(Piel) to throw, cast; (Hiphil) to praise (111)
כָּסָה	(Piel) to cover, conceal (153)
מָהַר	(Piel) to hasten (81)

נָבָא   (Niphal) to prophesy (115)

נָבַט   (Piel) to look at, regard (70)

סָגַר   to shut, close (91)

צָוָה   (Piel) to command (496)

קָטַר   (Piel) to send an offering up in smoke; (Hiphil) make smoke
            (115)

שִׁיר   to sing (88)

שִׁית   to put, set, place (86)

שָׁרַת   (Piel) to minister, to serve (98)

26.15 Hebrew Reading: I Am the Lord. Exodus 6:2-8 is the second text that is
essential for understanding the revelation and meaning of God's
covenant name (יהוה). It complements Ex 3:13-15, repeating some
aspects of the earlier divine self-revelation but adding new elements.
The intervening narrative is devoted to Moses' resistance to God's call
with God's continued encouragement and equipping of the reluctant
prophet (4:1-17). In Ex 5:1-23, we witness the initial failures of Moses'
mission before both Pharaoh and the deliverer's own people.

Moses demands (Ex 5:1):

וְאַחַר בָּאוּ מֹשֶׁה וְאַהֲרֹן וַיֹּאמְרוּ אֶל־פַּרְעֹה כֹּה־אָמַר יְהוָה אֱלֹהֵי
יִשְׂרָאֵל שַׁלַּח אֶת־עַמִּי וְיָחֹגּוּ לִי בַּמִּדְבָּר

Pharaoh responds (Ex 5:2):

וַיֹּאמֶר פַּרְעֹה מִי יְהוָה אֲשֶׁר אֶשְׁמַע בְּקֹלוֹ לְשַׁלַּח אֶת־יִשְׂרָאֵל לֹא
יָדַעְתִּי אֶת־יְהוָה וְגַם אֶת־יִשְׂרָאֵל לֹא אֲשַׁלֵּחַ

Pharaoh's statement is both profound and amusing. With his declaration
(לֹא יָדַעְתִּי אֶת־יְהוָה), he is about to embark on a graduate-level
education. This deficiency in his cosmopolitan schooling was about to
be remedied. Initially, neither the message nor the messenger were
accorded any respect by the god-king of Egypt but, with time, Pharaoh
would come to know, fear and obey the God of Moses.

Early on, Moses' greatest fears were realized. Deliverance was not immediately forthcoming and his first efforts only increased the burden of his people. He complains to God (Ex 5:22-23).

22 וַיָּשָׁב מֹשֶׁה אֶל־יְהוָה וַיֹּאמַר אֲדֹנָי לָמָה הֲרֵעֹתָה לָעָם הַזֶּה לָמָּה זֶּה שְׁלַחְתָּנִי 23 וּמֵאָז בָּאתִי אֶל־פַּרְעֹה לְדַבֵּר בִּשְׁמֶךָ הֵרַע לָעָם הַזֶּה וְהַצֵּל לֹא־הִצַּלְתָּ אֶת־עַמֶּךָ

The promise of deliverance is reiterated (Ex 6:1).

וַיֹּאמֶר יְהוָה אֶל־מֹשֶׁה עַתָּה תִרְאֶה אֲשֶׁר אֶעֱשֶׂה לְפַרְעֹה כִּי בְיָד חֲזָקָה יְשַׁלְּחֵם וּבְיָד חֲזָקָה יְגָרְשֵׁם מֵאַרְצוֹ

Notice the use of verbs and verbal stem. Pharaoh won't just "let them go" (יְשַׁלְּחֵם Piel Imperfect 3ms of שָׁלַח with 3mp pronominal suffix); "he will drive them from his land" (יְגָרְשֵׁם Piel Imperfect 3ms of גָּרַשׁ with 3mp pronominal suffix). The divine declaration אֲנִי יְהוָה (I am Yahweh) is used like bookends in Ex 6:2-8. The passage begins and ends with this divine self-identification and it occurs twice more within the passage. Throughout the text, the divine name is connected with a torrent of verbs and phrases that describe the Lord's redemptive activity on behalf of his people.

אֲנִי שָׁמַעְתִּי אֶת־נַאֲקַת בְּנֵי יִשְׂרָאֵל

I have heard ...

וָאֶזְכֹּר אֶת־בְּרִיתִי

I have remembered ...

וְהוֹצֵאתִי אֶתְכֶם מִתַּחַת סִבְלֹת מִצְרַיִם

I will bring you out ...

וְהִצַּלְתִּי אֶתְכֶם מֵעֲבֹדָתָם

I will deliver you ...

וְגָאַלְתִּי אֶתְכֶם בִּזְרוֹעַ נְטוּיָה

I will redeem you ...

In fulfillment of his promises to the fathers (Ex 3:6, 13, 15, 16; 4:5; 6:3, 8), God will mightily, dynamically and miraculously break into human history for the purpose of redeeming his people from bondage and creating with them an intimate relationship (Ex 6:7).[7]

וְלָקַחְתִּי אֶתְכֶם לִי לְעָם וְהָיִיתִי לָכֶם לֵאלֹהִים וִידַעְתֶּם כִּי אֲנִי יְהוָה
אֱלֹהֵיכֶם הַמּוֹצִיא אֶתְכֶם מִתַּחַת סִבְלוֹת מִצְרָיִם

Gary D. Pratico
Professor of Old Testament
Gordon-Conwell Theological Seminary
South Hamilton, Massachusetts

26.16 **Advanced Information: Loss of Daghesh Forte.** There are a number of circumstances in which an expected Daghesh Forte is lost. You have already encountered this phenomenon (5.5) when, for example, the definite article is prefixed to words that begin with יְ or מְ as in הַיְלָדִים (the boys) or הַמְרַגְּלִים (the spies). Similarly, the consonants נ, מ, ל, ו, י, ‏‎ ק and ש, שׂ, ס, צ (the sibilants) will frequently lose an expected Daghesh Forte when a Vocal Shewa occurs under that consonant. Note that this phenomenon is especially common with the Piel stem as the following examples illustrate.

הַמְדַבֵּר	Piel Participle ms with the definite article. The expected Daghesh Forte of the definite article is lost because the syllable begins with מְ.
וַיְדַבֵּר	Piel Imperfect 3ms with Waw Conversive. The expected Daghesh Forte of the Waw Conversive is lost because the syllable begins with יְ.
וַיְקַנְאוּ	Piel Imperfect 3mp with Waw Conversive. The expected Daghesh Forte of the Waw Conversive is lost because the syllable begins with יְ. Additionally, the expected Daghesh Forte in the second root consonant of the Piel stem is absent because נ is one of the consonants that may give up a Daghesh Forte when occurring with Vocal Shewa (נְ).
מִלְאוּ	Piel Perfect 3cp. The expected Daghesh Forte in the second root consonant of the Piel stem is lost because the ל occurs with Vocal Shewa (לְ).

---

[7] This study will continue in section 27.14.

26.17 **Advanced Information: Conjunctive Daghesh**. A conjunctive Daghesh is a *Daghesh Forte that has been placed in the initial consonant of a word* to connect it to the previous word in order to smooth out the pronunciation. The use of the conjunctive Daghesh often takes place when the first word ends in an unaccented הָ or הָ and the following word begins with an accented syllable. Two examples include וְזֶה־שְּׁמוֹ (and this is his name) and לְכָה־נָּא (come then). The Daghesh Forte in the שׁ of שְּׁמוֹ and in the נ of נָּא is the conjunctive Daghesh.

Chapter 27

The Piel Stem - Weak Verbs

27.1 **Introduction**. Most weak verbs in the Piel stem maintain the diagnostic features of the strong verb. It is only II-Guttural weak verbs that exhibit any major changes.

27.2 **Weak Verbal Roots with Strong Diagnostic Features**. Most weak verbal roots maintain the strong verb diagnostics in the Piel stem. The following four weak verb classes (III-ה/ע, III-א, III-ה and Geminate) are given for your study and observation but not for memorization.

27.3 **III-ה/ע Verbs: Diagnostics and Paradigms**. The paradigm verb שָׁלַח is translated "to send off, send away" in the Piel stem. Note that the Tsere stem vowel of the Piel strong verb is replaced by a Pathach stem vowel in this weak verb class. This change is due to the fact that gutturals prefer a-class vowels. With the exception of this stem vowel change, all of the diagnostics of the Piel strong verb are present.

Perfect	Imperfect	Imperative	Infinitive Construct	Infinitive Absolute	Participle
שַׁלֵּחַ	יְשַׁלֵּחַ	שַׁלֵּחַ	שַׁלֵּחַ[1]	שַׁלֵּחַ	מְשַׁלֵּחַ
שִׁלַּח	יְשַׁלַּח	שַׁלַּח	שַׁלַּח	שַׁלַּח	מְשַׁלֵּחַ
שִׁלְּחָה	תְּשַׁלַּח	שַׁלְּחִי			מְשַׁלַּחַת
שִׁלַּחְתָּ	תְּשַׁלַּח	שַׁלְּחוּ			מְשַׁלְּחִים
שִׁלַּחַתְּ	תְּשַׁלְּחִי	שַׁלַּחְנָה			מְשַׁלְּחוֹת
שִׁלַּחְתִּי	אֲשַׁלַּח				
שִׁלְּחוּ	יְשַׁלְּחוּ				
שִׁלַּחְתֶּם	תְּשַׁלַּחְנָה				
שִׁלַּחְתֶּן	תְּשַׁלְּחוּ				
שִׁלַּחְנוּ	תְּשַׁלַּחְנָה				
	נְשַׁלַּח				

---

[1] Even though the stem vowel is not diagnostic, a Tsere stem vowel occurs with the same frequency as Pathach.

318

27.4 **III-א Verbs: Diagnostics and Paradigms.** In the paradigm verb מָצָא, note that the stem vowel in the Perfect is Tsere and not Pathach. Nevertheless, all of the Piel strong verb diagnostics are present in this weak verb class.

Perfect	Imperfect	Imperative	Infinitive Construct	Infinitive Absolute	Participle
מַצֵּא	יְמַצֵּא	מַצֵּא	מַצֵּא	מַצֵּא [2]	מְמַצֵּא
מִצֵּא	יְמַצֵּא	מַצֵּא	מַצֵּא	מַצֹּא	מְמַצֵּא
מִצְּאָה	תְּמַצֵּא	מַצְּאִי			מְמַצֵּאת
מִצֵּאתָ	תְּמַצֵּא	מַצְּאוּ			מְמַצְּאִים
מִצֵּאת	תְּמַצְּאִי	מַצֶּאנָה			מְמַצְּאוֹת
מִצֵּאתִי	אֲמַצֵּא				
מִצְּאוּ	יְמַצְּאוּ				
מִצֵּאתֶם	תְּמַצֶּאנָה				
מִצֵּאתֶן	תְּמַצְּאוּ				
מִצֵּאנוּ	תְּמַצֶּאנָה				
	נְמַצֵּא				

27.5 **III-ה Verbs: Diagnostics and Paradigms.** The paradigm verb גָּלָה is translated "to uncover," "disclose" or "make known" in the Piel. All of the Piel strong verb diagnostics are present in this weak verb class. Note, however, the stem vowels in the Piel Perfect (Qamets and Hireq Yod). Additionally, note the III-ה diagnostic endings that are highlighted in dark gray. These are the same III-ה endings that appear in all stems, Qal through Hithpael.

---

[2] The Piel Infinitive Absolute form of III-א verbs occurs only four times: one time with the Tsere stem vowel (טַמֵּא) and three times with the Holem stem vowel (קַנֹּא and רַפֹּא). Nevertheless, the stem vowel is not considered to be diagnostic.

Perfect	Imperfect	Imperative	Infinitive Construct	Infinitive Absolute	Participle
גָּ_לָה	יְגַ_לֶּה	גַּ_לֵּה	גַּלּוֹת	גַּ_לֵּה	מְגַ_לֶּה
גִּלָּה	יְגַלֶּה	גַּלֵּה	גַּלּוֹת	גַּלֵּה	מְגַלֶּה
גִּלְּתָה	תְּגַלֶּה	גַּלִּי			מְגַלָּה
גִּלִּיתָ	תְּגַלֶּה	גַּלּוּ			מְגַלִּים
גִּלִּית	תְּגַלִּי	גַּלֶּינָה			מְגַלּוֹת
גִּלִּיתִי	אֲגַלֶּה				
גִּלּוּ	יְגַלּוּ				
גִּלִּיתֶם	תְּגַלֶּינָה				
גִּלִּיתֶן	תְּגַלּוּ				
גִּלִּינוּ	תְּגַלֶּינָה				
	נְגַלֶּה				

27.6 **Geminate Verbs: Diagnostics and Paradigms.** The paradigm verb הָלַל is translated "to praise" in the Piel. All of the Piel strong verb diagnostics are present in this weak verb class. Note the absence of the Daghesh Forte in selected forms of the Perfect (3fs, 3cp), Imperfect (2fs, 3mp, 2mp) and Imperative (fs, mp).

Perfect	Imperfect	Imperative	Infinitive Construct	Infinitive Absolute	Participle
הָ_לַל	יְהַ_לֵּל	הַ_לֵּל	הַ_לֵּל	הַ_לֵּל	מְהַ_לֵּל
הִלֵּל	יְהַלֵּל	הַלֵּל	הַלֵּל	הַלֵּל	מְהַלֵּל
הִלְּלָה	תְּהַלֵּל	הַלְלִי			מְהַלֶּלֶת
הִלַּלְתָּ	תְּהַלֵּל	הַלְלוּ			מְהַלְלִים
הִלַּלְתְּ	תְּהַלְלִי	הַלֵּלְנָה			מְהַלְלוֹת
הִלַּלְתִּי	אֲהַלֵּל				
הִלְּלוּ	יְהַלְלוּ				
הִלַּלְתֶּם	תְּהַלֵּלְנָה				
הִלַּלְתֶּן	תְּהַלְלוּ				
הִלַּלְנוּ	תְּהַלֵּלְנָה				
	נְהַלֵּל				

27.7 **II-Guttural Verbs**. With the previous weak verbal roots, the strong verb diagnostics are retained. In the Piel stem, only II-Guttural verbs exhibit any major changes compared to the diagnostics of the strong verb. These changes occur because the guttural consonant in second root position rejects the Daghesh Forte of the Piel stem and this results in either virtual doubling or compensatory lengthening (see 5.4 for a review of these concepts). With virtual doubling, the guttural consonant rejects the Daghesh Forte but the preceding vowel is *not* lengthened. With compensatory lengthening, the guttural consonant rejects the Daghesh Forte and the preceding vowel is lengthened. The following graphic illustrates these two patterns with the Piel Perfect 3ms.

Strong Verb	*II-Guttural Virtual Doubling*	*II-Guttural Compensatory Lengthening*
קִטֵּל	בֵּעֵר	מֵאֵן

In the form בֵּעֵר the ע rejects the Daghesh Forte but the preceding vowel is *not* lengthened. In the form מֵאֵן the א rejects the Daghesh Forte and the Tsere under the מ is the result of compensatory lengthening. In the patterns of compensatory lengthening, the vowel Hireq lengthens to Tsere. Most verbs exhibit either virtual doubling or compensatory lengthening. Some verbs, however, may exhibit both patterns.

27.8 **II-Guttural Verbs with Virtual Doubling: Diagnostics and Paradigms**. The paradigm verb נָחַם is translated "to comfort" or "to console" in the Piel. This verb exhibits virtual doubling in the Piel conjugations.

Perfect	*Imperfect*	*Imperative*	*Infinitive Construct*	*Infinitive Absolute*	*Participle*
נִחַם	יְנַחֵם	נַחֵם	נַחֵם	נַחֵם	מְנַחֵם
נִחַם	יְנַחֵם	נַחֵם	נַחֵם	נַחֵם	מְנַחֵם
נִחֲמָה	תְּנַחֵם	נַחֲמִי			מְנַחֶמֶת
נִחַמְתָּ	תְּנַחֵם	נַחֲמוּ			מְנַחֲמִים
נִחַמְתְּ	תְּנַחֲמִי	נַחֵמְנָה			מְנַחֲמוֹת
נִחַמְתִּי	אֲנַחֵם				
נִחֲמוּ	יְנַחֲמוּ				
נִחַמְתֶּם	תְּנַחֵמְנָה				
נִחַמְתֶּן	תְּנַחֲמוּ				
נִחַמְנוּ	תְּנַחֵמְנָה				
	נְנַחֵם				

27.9 **II-Guttural Verbs with Virtual Doubling: Notes.** All of the Piel strong verb diagnostics are present in this weak class, except the Daghesh Forte in the second root consonant.

   1. You should now understand that when the Daghesh Forte is rejected by the guttural consonant in the second root position and the preceding vowel is *not* lengthened, it is called *virtual doubling*.

   2. In the II-Guttural class of weak verbs in the Piel, the stem vowel may be either Tsere (בֵּעֵר) or Pathach (נִחַם). Though it is important to be aware of this distinction, the stem vowel is not a diagnostic feature of the Piel stem.

27.10 **II-Guttural Verbs with Compensatory Lengthening: Diagnostics and Paradigms.** The paradigm verb בָּרַךְ is translated "to bless" in the Piel. This verb exhibits compensatory lengthening in the Piel conjugations.

Perfect	Imperfect	Imperative	Infinitive Construct	Infinitive Absolute	Participle
בֵּרֵךְ	יְבָרֵךְ	בָּרֵךְ	בָּרֵךְ	בָּרֵךְ	מְבָרֵךְ
בֵּרֵךְ	יְבָרֵךְ	בָּרֵךְ	בָּרֵךְ	בָּרֵךְ	מְבָרֵךְ
בֵּרְכָה	תְּבָרֵךְ	בָּרְכִי			מְבָרֶכֶת
בֵּרַכְתָּ	תְּבָרֵךְ	בָּרְכוּ			מְבָרְכִים
בֵּרַכְתְּ	תְּבָרְכִי	בָּרֵכְנָה			מְבָרְכוֹת
בֵּרַכְתִּי	אֲבָרֵךְ				
בֵּרְכוּ	יְבָרְכוּ				
בֵּרַכְתֶּם	תְּבָרֵכְנָה				
בֵּרַכְתֶּן	תְּבָרְכוּ				
בֵּרַכְנוּ	תְּבָרֵכְנָה				
	נְבָרֵךְ				

27.11 **II-Guttural Verbs with Compensatory Lengthening: Notes.** In the verb בָּרַךְ (to bless), the consonant ר in second root position is functioning like a guttural in that it rejects the Daghesh Forte of the Piel. The result is compensatory lengthening of the preceding vowel. In the Perfect, Hireq is lengthened to Tsere under the first root consonant (בֵּרֵךְ). In all other conjugations, Pathach is lengthened to Qamets under the first root consonant (יְבָרֵךְ). Be certain that you understand where compensatory lengthening takes place in each conjugation.

27.12 **Summary: Piel Diagnostics.** Once again, the major diagnostic features of the Piel stem include: (1) Daghesh Forte in the second root consonant; (2) Pathach under the first consonant of the verbal root in every conjugation, except the Perfect; and (3) Vocal Shewa under all Imperfect and Participle preformatives and prefixes. The only weak verbs to experience any significant change in these diagnostics are II-Guttural weak verbs. The following chart summarizes all Piel stem diagnostics, both strong and weak.

	Perfect	Imperfect	Imperative	Infinitive Construct	Infinitive Absolute	Participle
Strong	קִטֵּל	יְקַטֵּל	קַטֵּל	קַטֵּל	קַטֵּל	מְקַטֵּל
III-ח/ע	שִׁלַּח	יְשַׁלַּח	שַׁלַּח	שַׁלַּח	שַׁלֵּחַ	מְשַׁלֵּחַ
III-א	מִצֵּא	יְמַצֵּא	מַצֵּא	מַצֵּא	מַצֵּא	מְמַצֵּא
III-ה	גִּלָּה	יְגַלֶּה	גַּלֵּה	גַּלּוֹת	גַּלֵּה	מְגַלֶּה
Geminate	הִלֵּל	יְהַלֵּל	הַלֵּל	הַלֵּל	הַלֵּל	מְהַלֵּל
II-Gutt[3]	נִחַם	יְנַחֵם	נַחֵם	נַחֵם	נַחֵם	מְנַחֵם
II-Gutt[4]	בֵּרַךְ	יְבָרֵךְ	בָּרֵךְ	בָּרֵךְ	בָּרֵךְ	מְבָרֵךְ

27.13 Vocabulary.

Verbs

גּוּר	to sojourn (82)
יָעַץ	to give counsel, give advice (81)
לָמַד	to learn; (Piel) teach (87)
מָשַׁל	to govern, rule (81)
מָכַר	to sell (80)
עָזַר	to help, assist (82)
עָנָה	(Piel) to oppress, humiliate (79)
קָלַל	to be slight, trifling, swift; (Piel) declare cursed; (Hiphil) make light (82)
קָנָה	to acquire, buy (85)
רָכַב	to ride (78)
שָׁחַט	to slaughter, kill (81)

---

[3] II-Guttural verbs with virtual doubling
[4] II-Guttural verbs with compensatory lengthening

Nouns

עַמּוּד	pillar, column (112)	
שֶׁקֶר	lie, falsehood, deception (113)	
אָחוֹת	sister (119); feminine	
כָּנָף	wing, corner, edge (111)	

27.14 But By My Name Yahweh. Few verses in the Old Testament have generated the scholarly attention received by Ex 6:2-3.

2 וַיְדַבֵּר אֱלֹהִים אֶל־מֹשֶׁה וַיֹּאמֶר אֵלָיו אֲנִי יְהוָה

3 וָאֵרָא אֶל־אַבְרָהָם אֶל־יִצְחָק וְאֶל־יַעֲקֹב בְּאֵל שַׁדָּי

וּשְׁמִי יְהוָה לֹא נוֹדַעְתִּי לָהֶם

2 God said to Moses, "I am Yahweh.

3 I appeared[5] to Abraham, to Isaac and to Jacob as El Shaddai[6] but by my name Yahweh I did not make myself known to them."[7]

Based on these verses, many scholars deny to the patriarchs any knowledge of the divine name (יהוה), contrary to its appearance nearly 170 times in the book of Genesis and the first three chapters of Exodus. In dozens of instances, the name יהוה is spoken by the patriarchs or used by God and others in speaking to the fathers. It is argued, nevertheless, that the patriarchal fathers worshipped El Shaddai and had no knowledge of the name יהוה. On this view, the name יהוה was first revealed in the setting of these Exodus events.[8] In its most extreme expression, this understanding of Ex 6:2-3 severs the historical and theological continuity between the religion of the patriarchal fathers and that of Moses and early Israel at the time of the Exodus. This disjuncture has important implications for one's understanding of early Israelite origins and the composition of the early biblical writings.

---

[5] וָאֵרָא (Niphal Imperfect 1cs of רָאָה with Waw Conversive) may also be translated with the reflexive nuance (I revealed myself).

[6] El Shaddai (אֵל שַׁדָּי) is traditionally translated "God Almighty," but its etymology is uncertain.

[7] נוֹדַעְתִּי is the Niphal Perfect 1cs of יָדַע (to know). In the Niphal stem, the verb means "to make oneself known."

[8] Proponents of this view argue that the name יהוה was written into the text of Genesis anachronistically.

Contrary to this view is the interpretation that does not deny knowledge of the name יהוה to the patriarchs as is clearly suggested by the narratives of Genesis and early Exodus. The fathers knew the name but they did not understand the fullness of its revelation of the divine character. Ex 6:2-8 is not a new revelation of the name; it is a nuanced revelation of the name. The name is now being revealed afresh in the setting of God's dynamic and miraculous intrusion into human history for the primary purpose of redeeming his people from bondage in Egypt. Understanding the use of the noun שֵׁם (name) as detailed earlier, Ex 6:2 may be interpretively translated as follows.

> I appeared to Abraham, to Isaac, and to Jacob as El Shaddai,
> but in the character expressed by my name Yahweh
> I did not make myself known to them.[9]

With regard to the etymology of the tetragrammaton (יהוה), there is general agreement that it derives from the verb "to be" (הָיָה originally הָוָה) and that it is also associated with an Imperfect 3ms form. Uncertainty and disagreement abound, however, as to whether the name derives from the Qal or Hiphil stem or whether the Imperfect derivation should be translated by the present or future tense. Though some will protest, an analysis of historical and textual context will contribute more to an understanding of the name than etymological analysis. The context of Ex 3:14-15 would appear to favor the Qal derivation. But whether translated by the present or future, this much is clear. The name is not metaphysical but dynamic. The "new" revelation of the divine character is that of dynamic activity. Mightily and miraculously (Ex 7:3), the Lord intervenes in time and space in order to effect his redemptive purposes for his covenant people and he brings judgement on Egypt and its gods in the process. Ex 3:13-15 and 6:2-8 record a new stage in the progressive self-revelation of God's name and character to his people. One cannot help but recall that in the sacramental setting of Jesus' last meal with his disciples, he said, "I have manifested your name" (John 17:6). Implicit in "your name" is the person, character, authority and the redemptive work of God.[10]

---

[9] J. A. Motyer, *The Revelation of the Divine Name* (London: Tyndale, 1959) 11-17.

[10] This study will continue in section 28.11.

Gary D. Pratico
Professor of Old Testament
Gordon-Conwell Theological Seminary
South Hamilton, Massachusetts

27.15 Advanced Information: The Polel Stem. In chapter 12, you were introduced to the seven "major" stems of the Hebrew verbal system (Qal and the six derived stems). There are, however, a number of additional stems that are considered "minor" because of their relative infrequency. In this grammar, we will cover four of the "minor" verbal stems in certain "Advanced Information" sections. These stems include the Polel, Polal (29.13), Hithpolel (35.13) and Hishtaphel (35.14).[11]

Biconsonantal verbs occur infrequently in the Piel, Pual and Hithpael stems. Instead, they occur in the Polel, Polal and Hithpolel stems. Geminate roots may also appear in these stems. In general, the meaning of the Piel corresponds to the meaning of the Polel, the Pual to the Polal and the Hithpael to the Hithpolel. With Biconsonantal verbs, these stems are characterized by a Holem Waw after the first consonant and the duplication of the second root consonant. For your reference, the Polel forms of the verb רוּם (to exalt, lift up) are presented below.

Perfect	Imperfect	Imperative	Infinitive Construct	Infinitive Absolute	Participle
רוֹמֵם	יְרוֹמֵם	רוֹמֵם	רוֹמֵם		מְרוֹמֵם
רוֹמְמָה	תְּרוֹמֵם	רוֹמְמִי			מְרוֹמֶמֶת
רוֹמַ֫מְתָּ	תְּרוֹמֵם	רוֹמְמוּ			מְרוֹמְמִים
רוֹמַמְתְּ	תְּרוֹמְמִי	רוֹמֵ֫מְנָה			מְרוֹמְמוֹת
רוֹמַ֫מְתִּי	אֲרוֹמֵם				
רוֹמְמוּ	יְרוֹמְמוּ				
רוֹמַמְתֶּם	תְּרוֹמֵ֫מְנָה				
רוֹמַמְתֶּן	תְּרוֹמְמוּ				
רוֹמַ֫מְנוּ	תְּרוֹמֵ֫מְנָה				
	נְרוֹמֵם				

---

[11] There are several other "minor" verbal stems found in the Hebrew Bible. For a more thorough discussion, see B. K. Waltke and M. O'Connor, *Introduction to Biblical Hebrew Syntax* (Winona Lake: Eisenbrauns, 1990) 359-361.

Chapter 28

The Pual Stem - Strong Verbs

28.1 **Introduction**. In this chapter, we will study the Pual stem.[1] It is the passive counterpart of the Piel stem. Once again, paradigm memorization is not required in this chapter. Instead, the diagnostic features of the Pual stem are presented for study. The most significant diagnostic features of the Pual stem include: (1) Vocal Shewa under all Imperfect and Participle preformatives and prefixes; (2) Qibbuts under the first root consonant of every form; and (3) Daghesh Forte in the second root consonant of every form. Note that the first and third diagnostic features are identical to the Piel stem. Therefore, it is the second diagnostic feature (Qibbuts under the first root consonant) that will distinguish Pual forms from Piel forms. Given the infrequency of certain Pual forms, we will study only the Perfect, Imperfect and Participle.

28.2 **The Meaning of the Pual Stem**. The Pual stem is the passive counterpart of the Piel stem. The Pual stem is used, therefore, to express an *intensive* type of action with a *passive* voice. For example, the Piel Perfect verb שִׁבַּר means "he smashed." The Pual form, however, would be שֻׁבַּר and it would be translated "he (it) *was* smashed." Notice how a form of the English verb "to be" (was) is used to make the translation passive.

28.3 **Pual Perfect**. In the following paradigms, the Pual Perfect is listed with the Piel Perfect for comparison. The vowel under the first root consonant of each form will distinguish the Pual from the Piel. Translate the Pual Perfect passively with a form of the helping verb "to be" as in "he (it) *was* slaughtered."

---

[1] The Pual stems occurs 448 times in the Hebrew Bible: 160 times in the Perfect, 96 times in the Imperfect, 1 time in the Infinitive Construct, 1 time in the Infinitive Absolute, and 196 times in the Participle.

	Piel	*Pual*	*Translation*
3ms	קֻטַּל	קֻטַּל	he (it) was slaughtered
3fs	קֻטְּלָה	קֻטְּלָה	she (it) was slaughtered
2ms	קֻטַּלְתָּ	קֻטַּלְתָּ	you were slaughtered
2fs	קֻטַּלְתְּ	קֻטַּלְתְּ	you were slaughtered
1cs	קֻטַּלְתִּי	קֻטַּלְתִּי	I was slaughtered
3cp	קֻטְּלוּ	קֻטְּלוּ	they were slaughtered
2mp	קֻטַּלְתֶּם	קֻטַּלְתֶּם	you were slaughtered
2fp	קֻטַּלְתֶּן	קֻטַּלְתֶּן	you were slaughtered
1cp	קֻטַּלְנוּ	קֻטַּלְנוּ	we were slaughtered

28.4   Pual Perfect Diagnostics.

1. The important diagnostic is Qibbuts under the first consonant of the verbal root. This feature distinguishes the Pual Perfect from the Piel Perfect. The Piel Perfect has Hireq under the first root consonant.

2. As in the Piel, there is a Daghesh Forte in the second consonant of the verbal root. As noted above, this diagnostic feature is characteristic of the Piel, Pual and Hithpael stems. Though not diagnostic, the stem vowel is Pathach (except in the 3fs and 3cp).

*Pual Perfect
Strong Verb*

קֻטַּל

28.5   Pual Imperfect. The vowel under the first root consonant will distinguish the Pual Imperfect from the Piel Imperfect. Translate the Pual Imperfect passively with a form of the helping verb "to be" as in "he (it) will *be* slaughtered."

	Piel	*Pual*	*Translation*
3ms	יְקַטֵּל	יְקֻטַּל	he (it) will be slaughtered
3fs	תְּקַטֵּל	תְּקֻטַּל	she (it) will be slaughtered
2ms	תְּקַטֵּל	תְּקֻטַּל	you will be slaughtered
2fs	תְּקַטְּלִי	תְּקֻטְּלִי	you will be slaughtered
1cs	אֲקַטֵּל	אֲקֻטַּל	I will be slaughtered
3mp	יְקַטְּלוּ	יְקֻטְּלוּ	they will be slaughtered
3fp	תְּקַטֵּלְנָה	תְּקֻטַּלְנָה	they will be slaughtered
2mp	תְּקַטְּלוּ	תְּקֻטְּלוּ	you will be slaughtered
2fp	תְּקַטֵּלְנָה	תְּקֻטַּלְנָה	you will be slaughtered
1cp	נְקַטֵּל	נְקֻטַּל	we will be slaughtered

28.6 Pual Imperfect Diagnostics.

1. Vocal Shewa under the Imperfect preformative as in the Piel Imperfect.

2. Qibbuts under the first consonant of the verbal root. This diagnostic feature distinguishes the Pual Imperfect from the Piel Imperfect. The Piel has a Pathach under the first root consonant.

3. Daghesh Forte in the second consonant of the verbal root as in the Piel.

Pual Imperfect Strong Verb

יְקֻטַּל

28.7 Pual Participle. Like the Piel, the Pual Participle is formed with a מ prefix. Translate the Pual Participle passively with a form of the helping verb "to be" as in *"being slaughtered."*

	Piel	*Pual*	*Translation*
ms	מְקֻטָּל	מְקֻטָּל	being slaughtered
fs	מְקֻטֶּלֶת	מְקֻטֶּלֶת[2]	being slaughtered
mp	מְקֻטָּלִים	מְקֻטָּלִים	being slaughtered
fp	מְקֻטָּלוֹת	מְקֻטָּלוֹת	being slaughtered

28.8 Pual Participle Diagnostics.

1. As with the Piel, the Pual Participle has the מְ prefix. As noted above, a מ prefix is used with the Piel, Pual, Hiphil and Hophal Participles.

2. Qibbuts under the first consonant of the verbal root. This diagnostic feature distinguishes the Pual Participle from the Piel Participle. The Piel has a Pathach under the second root consonant.

3. Daghesh Forte in the second consonant of the verbal root .

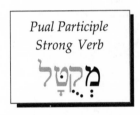

> *Pual Participle*
> *Strong Verb*
>
> מְקֻטָּל

28.9 Summary. The following chart summarizes the Pual strong verb diagnostics studied in this chapter. Be sure that you understand the diagnostic feature that will distinguish a Pual strong verb from a Piel strong verb, namely, the Qibbuts under the first consonant of the verbal root.

---

[2] The Pual Participle may also end in הָ as in the form מְקֻטָּלָה.

Pual Stem - Strong Verbs

Perfect	*Imperfect*	*Participle*
קֻטַּל	יְקֻטַּל	מְ קֻטָּל
קֻטַּל	יְקֻטַּל	מְקֻטָּל
קֻטְּלָה	תְּקֻטַּל	מְקֻטֶּלֶת
קֻטַּלְתָּ	תְּקֻטַּל	מְקֻטָּלִים
קֻטַּלְתְּ	תְּקֻטְּלִי	מְקֻטָּלוֹת
קֻטַּלְתִּי	אֲקֻטַּל	
קֻטְּלוּ	יְקֻטְּלוּ	
קֻטַּלְתֶּם	תְּקֻטַּלְנָה	
קֻטַּלְתֶּן	תְּקֻטְּלוּ	
קֻטַּלְנוּ	תְּקֻטַּלְנָה	
	נְקֻטַּל	

28.10 Vocabulary.

Verbs

אָסַר	to bind; (Niphal, Pual) be fettered, imprisoned (73)
זָעַק	to cry out (73)
חָזָה	to see, perceive (55)
חָלָה	to be(come) weak, sick (75)
חָנַן	to be gracious to, favor (78)
מָאַס	to reject (74)
עוּר	to arouse, awake (79)
עָרַךְ	to arrange, set in order (75)
רָחַץ	to wash, wash off (72)
שָׂכַל	to have success, prosper; (Hiphil) cause to consider, teach (60)

Nouns

מַרְאֶה	sight, appearance (115)
נֶגֶב	the dry country, south, Negev (112)
עָפָר	dry earth, dust (110)
פַּעַם	foot, step, time (118); feminine

28.11 **The Lord Proclaimed**. By the hand of Moses, God performed signs and wonders in the land of Egypt (Ex 7:3; Ps 78:42-51; 105:26-36), and by his chosen prophet, God led his people like a flock through the wilderness (Ps 77:11-20; 78:52-54). The psalmist remembered (Ps 77:14-16, 21 [English 77:13-15, 20]):

14 אֱלֹהִים בַּקֹּדֶשׁ דַּרְכֶּךָ מִי־אֵל גָּדוֹל כֵּאלֹהִים
15 אַתָּה הָאֵל עֹשֵׂה פֶלֶא הוֹדַעְתָּ בָעַמִּים עֻזֶּךָ
16 גָּאַלְתָּ בִּזְרוֹעַ עַמֶּךָ בְּנֵי־יַעֲקֹב וְיוֹסֵף
21 נָחִיתָ כַצֹּאן עַמֶּךָ בְּיַד־מֹשֶׁה וְאַהֲרֹן

Moses was truly a remarkable figure in Old Testament history. Between the Nile and Nebo, he wore many mantles, but perhaps none was more important for the people of Israel than that of intercessor (Ps 106:23). It is in the context of Israel's faithlessness and Moses' intercession on behalf of God's delivered people that we encounter the third text that is essential for understanding the meaning of the name יהוה and the character behind it (Ex 34:5-7).

Even God's "signs and wonders" in Egypt were not sufficient to ensure Israel's faithfulness in the wilderness of Sinai. While still on the sacred mountain, Moses receives this instruction from God (Ex 32:7-8).

7 וַיְדַבֵּר יְהוָה אֶל־מֹשֶׁה לֶךְ־רֵד כִּי שִׁחֵת עַמְּךָ אֲשֶׁר הֶעֱלֵיתָ מֵאֶרֶץ
מִצְרָיִם 8 סָרוּ מַהֵר מִן־הַדֶּרֶךְ אֲשֶׁר צִוִּיתִם עָשׂוּ לָהֶם עֵגֶל מַסֵּכָה
וַיִּשְׁתַּחֲווּ־לוֹ וַיִּזְבְּחוּ־לוֹ וַיֹּאמְרוּ אֵלֶּה אֱלֹהֶיךָ יִשְׂרָאֵל אֲשֶׁר הֶעֱלוּךָ
מֵאֶרֶץ מִצְרָיִם

Note the use of the 2ms pronominal suffix on עַם in 32:7 (your people). Addressing Moses, God here refers to this people as Moses' people (עַמְּךָ). In the intimate language of covenant relationship, God always uses a language construction that claims Israel as his own (Ex 6:7; Lev 26:12; Jer 7:23; Ezek 11:20). God then declares his intention to consume this stiff-necked people and make a great nation through Moses (Ex 32:10). Moses intercedes (Ex 32:11, 13).

11 וַיְחַל מֹשֶׁה אֶת־פְּנֵי יְהוָה אֱלֹהָיו וַיֹּאמֶר לָמָה יְהוָה יֶחֱרֶה אַפְּךָ בְּעַמֶּךָ אֲשֶׁר הוֹצֵאתָ מֵאֶרֶץ מִצְרַיִם בְּכֹחַ גָּדוֹל וּבְיָד חֲזָקָה

13 זְכֹר לְאַבְרָהָם לְיִצְחָק וּלְיִשְׂרָאֵל עֲבָדֶיךָ אֲשֶׁר נִשְׁבַּעְתָּ לָהֶם בָּךְ וַתְּדַבֵּר אֲלֵהֶם אַרְבֶּה אֶת־זַרְעֲכֶם כְּכוֹכְבֵי הַשָּׁמָיִם וְכָל־הָאָרֶץ הַזֹּאת אֲשֶׁר אָמַרְתִּי אֶתֵּן לְזַרְעֲכֶם וְנָחֲלוּ לְעֹלָם

The people are spared but at heavy cost (Ex 32:19; 30-35; 36:1-6). In the midst of this narrative, we are given a special glimpse of Moses' stature before the Lord (Ex 33:11).

וְדִבֶּר יְהוָה אֶל־מֹשֶׁה פָּנִים אֶל־פָּנִים כַּאֲשֶׁר יְדַבֵּר אִישׁ אֶל־רֵעֵהוּ

With this background, we now come to one of the most remarkable texts in the Old Testament (Ex 34:5-7). The Lord declares his intention to show his glory and to proclaim the name יהוה (Ex 33:18-19). Moses is instructed to return to the mountain with a new set of tablets, and then we read in 34:5-6:

5 וַיֵּרֶד יְהוָה בֶּעָנָן וַיִּתְיַצֵּב עִמּוֹ שָׁם וַיִּקְרָא בְשֵׁם יְהוָה

6 וַיַּעֲבֹר יְהוָה עַל־פָּנָיו וַיִּקְרָא יְהוָה יְהוָה אֵל רַחוּם וְחַנּוּן אֶרֶךְ אַפַּיִם וְרַב־חֶסֶד וֶאֱמֶת

Inherent in the repeated declaration of the name יהוה in verse 6 are those dynamic aspects of the divine character that have already been revealed in Ex 3:13-15 and 6:2-8. But then, almost by way of apposition, we read: אֵל רַחוּם וְחַנּוּן אֶרֶךְ אַפַּיִם וְרַב־חֶסֶד וֶאֱמֶת. With these words, God himself reveals those attributes of his character that define his relationship with his chosen people. With rare exception, the word רַחוּם (compassionate, merciful) is used only of God and refers to his deep compassion and mercy. The essential quality of this divine attribute is perhaps best understood with reference to a mother's tender love for her child. The word חַנּוּן (gracious) is used only with reference to God and in most of its occurrences it appears in combination with רַחוּם. In terms of the relationship between divine grace and divine mercy, grace is that aspect of God's character that gives what is not deserved; mercy withholds what is deserved. In other words, in his grace God gives redemption to those who don't deserve it. In his mercy, he does not give the judgement that is deserved. The construct אֶרֶךְ אַפַּיִם (literally, "long of nose") is used in the majority of its occurrences with reference to God; only four times in connection with man. The phrase is usually translated "longsuffering" or "slow to anger" and refers to God's seemingly inexhaustible patience. His patience is demonstrated principally with reference to his mercy. It is the "not yet" timing of the dispensing of his judgement. God's חֶסֶד is all of the above and so much more. With reference to God, it is a divine love that is forgiving, redeeming and relentless in its pursuit of those to whom it is to be given. The word חֶסֶד has been translated "lovingkindness," "steadfast love," "unfailing love," "mercy," and more. Some have attempted to associate the term with fidelity and loyalty to covenant obligation. No single word in English encompasses the range or complexity of its nuances in biblical usage. In the context of Ex 34:6, God's faithfulness (אֱמֶת) carries the underlying certainty and assurance that the attributes of this divine self-revelation will never fail.

Moses responds to the Lord's revelation with worship and he again intercedes for the people (Ex 34:9).

וַיֹּאמֶר אִם־נָא מָצָאתִי חֵן בְּעֵינֶיךָ אֲדֹנָי יֵלֶךְ־נָא אֲדֹנָי בְּקִרְבֵּנוּ כִּי עַם־קְשֵׁה־עֹרֶף הוּא וְסָלַחְתָּ לַעֲוֹנֵנוּ וּלְחַטָּאתֵנוּ וּנְחַלְתָּנוּ

Moses asks that the Lord would manifest his presence in the midst of this undeserving people. The Lord promises to do wonders on their behalf, wonders never done before in any nation in all of the world (34:10). The book of Exodus now concludes (Ex 35-40) with the building of the tabernacle, the portable tent-shrine that represented the earthly dwelling of יהוה in the midst of his people during their wilderness sojourn. Little wonder that the Lord's own revelation of his name and his character would echo throughout later Old Testament history (Neh 9:17; Ps 103:8; 145:8; Joel 2:13; Jonah 4:2) as, for example, in Ps 86:15:

וְאַתָּה אֲדֹנָי אֵל־רַחוּם וְחַנּוּן אֶרֶךְ אַפַּיִם וְרַב־חֶסֶד וֶאֱמֶת

Gary D. Pratico
Professor of Old Testament
Gordon-Conwell Theological Seminary
South Hamilton, Massachusetts

Chapter 29

The Pual Stem - Weak Verbs

29.1 **Introduction.** Before studying weak verbs in the Pual stem, be certain that you have mastered the Pual strong verb diagnostics in the previous chapter.

29.2 **Weak Verbal Roots with Strong Diagnostic Features.** Like the Piel, most weak verbal roots in the Pual stem maintain the strong verb diagnostics. Only II-Guttural verbs exhibit significant changes in the Pual. The following III-א and III-ה paradigms are given for your study and observation but not for memorization. Both of these weak verb classes maintain all of the Pual strong verb diagnostics. Those diagnostics will not be repeated below. Be certain, however, that you can identify each diagnostic feature.

29.3 **III-א Verbs: Diagnostics and Paradigms.** The paradigm verb מָצָא is translated "to be found" in the Pual.

Perfect	*Imperfect*	*Participle*
מֻצָּא	יְמֻצָּא	מְמֻצָּא
מֻצָּא	יְמֻצָּא	מְמֻצָּא
מֻצְּאָה	תְּמֻצָּא	מְמֻצָּאָה
מֻצֵּאתָ	תְּמֻצָּא	מְמֻצָּאִים
מֻצֵּאת	תְּמֻצְּאִי	מְמֻצָּאוֹת
מֻצֵּאתִי	אֲמֻצָּא	
מֻצְּאוּ	יְמֻצְּאוּ	
מֻצֵּאתֶם	תְּמֻצֶּאנָה	
מֻצֵּאתֶן	תְּמֻצְּאוּ	
מֻצֵּאנוּ	תְּמֻצֶּאנָה	
	נְמֻצָּא	

336

29.4 **III-ה Verbs: Diagnostics and Paradigms.** As you know, the final ה that is present in selected forms below is not the ה of the verbal root but rather a vowel letter or *mater lectionis*. Here, as above, the identification of these vowel letters with dark gray text recognizes that this is a unique feature of III-ה verbs. This is something that you are already familiar with from your study of III-ה roots in the Qal, Niphal and Piel stems. The paradigm verb גָּלָה is translated "to be uncovered," "disclosed" or "made known" in the Pual. All of the strong verb diagnostics are present in every form of each conjugation.

Perfect	*Imperfect*	*Participle*
גֻּלְּה	יְגֻלֶּה	מְגֻלֶּה
גֻּלָּה	יְגֻלֶּה	מְגֻלֶּה
גֻּלְּתָה	תְּגֻלֶּה	מְגֻלָּה
גֻּלֵּית	תְּגֻלֶּה	מְגֻלִּים
גֻּלֵּית	תְּגֻלִּי	מְגֻלּוֹת
גֻּלֵּיתִי	אֲגֻלֶּה	
גֻּלּוּ	יְגֻלּוּ	
גֻּלֵּיתֶם	תְּגֻלֶּינָה	
גֻּלֵּיתֶן	תְּגֻלּוּ	
גֻּלֵּינוּ	תְּגֻלֶּינָה	
	נְגֻלֶּה	

29.5 **II-Guttural Verbs.** Only II-Guttural verbs exhibit any significant changes in the Pual stem. These changes occur because the guttural consonant in second root position rejects the Daghesh Forte of the Pual stem and this results in either virtual doubling or compensatory lengthening. The following graphic illustrates these two patterns with the Pual Perfect 3ms.

Strong Verb	*II-Guttural Virtual Doubling*	*II-Guttural Compensatory Lengthening*
קֻטַּל	נֻחַם	בֹּרַךְ

In the patterns of compensatory lengthening, the vowel Qibbuts lengthens to Holem. In the form בֹּרַךְ, the Holem is the result of compensatory lengthening.

29.6 II-Guttural Verbs with Virtual Doubling: Diagnostics and Paradigms. The paradigm verb נֻחַם is translated "to be comforted" or "to be consoled" in the Pual.

Perfect	*Imperfect*	*Participle*
נֻחַם	יְנֻחַם	מְנֻחָם
נֻחַם	יְנֻחַם	מְנֻחָם
נֻחֲמָה	תְּנֻחַם	מְנֻחֶמֶת
נֻחַמְתָּ	תְּנֻחַם	מְנֻחָמִים
נֻחַמְתְּ	תְּנֻחֲמִי	מְנֻחָמוֹת
נֻחַמְתִּי	אֲנֻחַם	
נֻחֲמוּ	יְנֻחֲמוּ	
נֻחַמְתֶּם	תְּנֻחַמְנָה	
נֻחַמְתֶּן	תְּנֻחֲמוּ	
נֻחַמְנוּ	תְּנֻחַמְנָה	
	נְנֻחַם	

29.7 II-Guttural Verbs with Virtual Doubling: Notes. All of the Pual strong verb diagnostics are present in this weak verb class, except the Daghesh Forte in the second root consonant. This verb exhibits virtual doubling.

29.8 II-Guttural Verbs with Compensatory Lengthening: Diagnostics and Paradigms. The paradigm verb בָּרַךְ is translated "to be blessed" in the Pual.

Perfect	Imperfect	Participle
בֹּרַךְ	יְבֹרַךְ	מְבֹרָךְ
בֹּרַךְ	יְבֹרַךְ	מְבֹרָךְ
בֹּרְכָה	תְּבֹרַךְ	מְבֹרֶכֶת
בֹּרַ֫כְתָּ	תְּבֹרַךְ	מְבֹרָכִים
בֹּרַכְתְּ	תְּבֹרְכִי	מְבֹרָכוֹת
בֹּרַ֫כְתִּי	אֲבֹרַךְ	
בֹּרְכוּ	יְבֹרְכוּ	
בֹּרַכְתֶּם	תְּבֹרַ֫כְנָה	
בֹּרַכְתֶּן	תְּבֹרְכוּ	
בֹּרַ֫כְנוּ	תְּבֹרַ֫כְנָה	
	נְבֹרַךְ	

29.9 **II-Guttural Verbs with Compensatory Lengthening: Notes**. This verb exhibits compensatory lengthening because the ר rejects the Daghesh Forte of the Pual. As noted above, in the patterns of compensatory lengthening, the vowel Qibbuts lengthens to Holem. In the Pual Perfect, Imperfect and Participle of בָּרַךְ, the Holem vowel with the first consonant of the verbal root is the result of compensatory lengthening.

29.10 **Summary: Pual Diagnostics**. Once again, the diagnostic features of the Pual stem include: (1) Qibbuts under the first root consonant of every form; (2) Daghesh Forte in the second root consonant of every form; and (3) Vocal Shewa under all Imperfect and Participle preformatives and prefixes. Remember that the Qibbuts under the first root consonant distinguishes the Pual from the Piel. Also, like the Piel, only II-Guttural weak verbs exhibit any significant changes in the Pual. The following chart summarizes the Pual stem diagnostics studied in this chapter.

	Perfect	*Imperfect*	*Participle*
Strong	קֻטַּל	יְקֻטַּל	מְקֻטָּל
III-א	מֻצָּא	יְמֻצָּא	מְמֻצָּא
III-ה	גֻּלָּה	יְגֻלֶּה	מְגֻלֶּה
II-Gutt[1]	נֻחַם	יְנֻחַם	מְנֻחָם
II-Gutt[2]	בֹּרַךְ	יְבֹרַךְ	מְבֹרָךְ

29.11 Vocabulary.

Verbs

לִין	to spend the night, lodge (71)
מָשַׁח	to anoint (70); מָשִׁיחַ anointed one (38)
נָצַר	to watch, guard (63)

Nouns

תָּמִים	whole, entire, blameless (91)
חֵלֶב	fat (92)
פֶּשַׁע	rebellion, revolt, transgression (93)
קָצֶה	end, border, extremity (92)
חַיָּה	(wild) animal (93)
חֲמוֹר	(male) ass, donkey (96)
יֶתֶר	remainder, remnant (97)
עוֹר	skin, leather (99)

---

[1] II-Guttural with virtual doubling
[2] II-Guttural with compensatory lengthening

עֹז   strength, power, might (76)

שִׂמְחָה   joy, rejoicing (94)

גֵּר   sojourner, alien (92)

29.12 Hebrew Reading: Jonah and the Character of God.[3] Contrary to how Jonah is often preached, this book is not about the prophet. It is not about a great fish. It is about God and the character of God. Jonah's first commission (1:1-2) provided him with the opportunity to be, in the tradition of the patriarchs, a mediator of blessing and, in the tradition of the prophets, a conduit for the word of God. The recipient of both was to be Nineveh, the capital of the world empire of Assyria (Jonah 1:1-2).

1 וַיְהִי דְּבַר־יְהוָה אֶל־יוֹנָה בֶן־אֲמִתַּי לֵאמֹר 2 קוּם לֵךְ אֶל־נִינְוֵה הָעִיר
הַגְּדוֹלָה וּקְרָא עָלֶיהָ כִּי־עָלְתָה רָעָתָם לְפָנָי

Jonah would have been pleased to deliver Nahum's message of divine judgement against Assyria (Nahum 3:1-7) but he was a century and a half too early. His commission was to proclaim God's word with a view to repentance. His resistance to the possibility that this hated nation would be the recipient of divine blessing was so great that he would flee even the presence of the Lord, or so he thought (Jonah 1:3).

וַיָּקָם יוֹנָה לִבְרֹחַ תַּרְשִׁישָׁה מִלִּפְנֵי יְהוָה וַיֵּרֶד יָפוֹ וַיִּמְצָא אֳנִיָּה בָּאָה
תַרְשִׁישׁ וַיִּתֵּן שְׂכָרָהּ וַיֵּרֶד בָּהּ לָבוֹא עִמָּהֶם תַּרְשִׁישָׁה מִלִּפְנֵי יְהוָה

His flight from the presence of the Lord (מִלִּפְנֵי יְהוָה) is a point of emphasis (1:3, 10). In fact, flight and disobedience were his very first thought. That is the implication of קִדַּמְתִּי לִבְרֹחַ (I was quick to flee) in 4:2. The prophet did indeed understand the gracious and merciful character of God (4:2). That was why he fled, because he understood the qualities of divine grace. Given this divine character, repentance and redemption for this hated enemy just might be a possibility. But escape was impossible because God is present even "in the uttermost parts of the sea" (Ps 139:7-9). Jonah's God is the Creator and Lord of the sea (Gen 1:10; Ex 14:21) and he pursues his prophet in a great

---

[3] All biblical references in Jonah refer to the numbering of the Hebrew text.

windstorm. Jonah's fellow-passengers suspect that he is the cause of their plight (Jonah 1:8-10, 15).

וַיֹּאמְרוּ אֵלָיו הַגִּידָה־נָּא לָנוּ בַּאֲשֶׁר לְמִי־הָרָעָה הַזֹּאת לָנוּ 8
מַה־מְּלַאכְתְּךָ וּמֵאַיִן תָּבוֹא מָה אַרְצֶךָ וְאֵי־מִזֶּה עַם אָתָּה 9 וַיֹּאמֶר
אֲלֵיהֶם עִבְרִי אָנֹכִי וְאֶת־יְהוָה אֱלֹהֵי הַשָּׁמַיִם אֲנִי יָרֵא אֲשֶׁר־עָשָׂה
אֶת־הַיָּם וְאֶת־הַיַּבָּשָׁה 10 וַיִּירְאוּ הָאֲנָשִׁים יִרְאָה גְדוֹלָה וַיֹּאמְרוּ אֵלָיו
מַה־זֹּאת עָשִׂיתָ כִּי־יָדְעוּ הָאֲנָשִׁים כִּי־מִלִּפְנֵי יְהוָה הוּא בֹרֵחַ
כִּי הִגִּיד לָהֶם

וַיִּשְׂאוּ אֶת־יוֹנָה וַיְטִלֻהוּ אֶל־הַיָּם וַיַּעֲמֹד הַיָּם מִזַּעְפּוֹ 15

There is a dimension to Jonah's call that is unique (Jonah 2:1-2).

וַיְמַן יְהוָה דָּג גָּדוֹל לִבְלֹעַ אֶת־יוֹנָה וַיְהִי יוֹנָה בִּמְעֵי הַדָּג שְׁלֹשָׁה 1
יָמִים וּשְׁלֹשָׁה לֵילוֹת 2 וַיִּתְפַּלֵּל יוֹנָה אֶל־יְהוָה אֱלֹהָיו מִמְּעֵי הַדָּגָה

Jonah's psalm of thanksgiving and celebration of the Lord's deliverance and mercy in 2:3-10 is a literary jewel in the Old Testament.

The prophet is commissioned a second time (Jonah 2:11; 3:1-3).

וַיֹּאמֶר יְהוָה לַדָּג וַיָּקֵא אֶת־יוֹנָה אֶל־הַיַּבָּשָׁה 11

וַיְהִי דְבַר־יְהוָה אֶל־יוֹנָה שֵׁנִית לֵאמֹר 2 קוּם לֵךְ אֶל־נִינְוֵה הָעִיר 1
הַגְּדוֹלָה וּקְרָא אֵלֶיהָ אֶת־הַקְּרִיאָה אֲשֶׁר אָנֹכִי דֹּבֵר אֵלֶיךָ 3 וַיָּקָם יוֹנָה
וַיֵּלֶךְ אֶל־נִינְוֵה כִּדְבַר יְהוָה

Jonah's first and worst fear was realized (Jonah 3:5, 10).

וַיַּאֲמִינוּ אַנְשֵׁי נִינְוֵה בֵּאלֹהִים וַיִּקְרְאוּ־צוֹם וַיִּלְבְּשׁוּ שַׂקִּים מִגְּדוֹלָם 5
וְעַד־קְטַנָּם

וַיַּרְא הָאֱלֹהִים אֶת־מַעֲשֵׂיהֶם כִּי־שָׁבוּ מִדַּרְכָּם הָרָעָה וַיִּנָּחֶם הָאֱלֹהִים 10
עַל־הָרָעָה אֲשֶׁר־דִּבֶּר לַעֲשׂוֹת־לָהֶם וְלֹא עָשָׂה

Jonah wasn't just displeased at the success of his preaching. He was outraged, morally outraged and angry at the enemy's response (Jonah 4:1-3).

1 וַיֵּרַע אֶל־יוֹנָה רָעָה גְדוֹלָה וַיִּחַר לוֹ 2 וַיִּתְפַּלֵּל אֶל־יְהוָה וַיֹּאמַר אָנָּה
יְהוָה הֲלוֹא־זֶה דְבָרִי עַד־הֱיוֹתִי עַל־אַדְמָתִי עַל־כֵּן קִדַּמְתִּי לִבְרֹחַ
תַּרְשִׁישָׁה כִּי יָדַעְתִּי כִּי אַתָּה אֵל־חַנּוּן וְרַחוּם אֶרֶךְ אַפַּיִם וְרַב־חֶסֶד
וְנִחָם עַל־הָרָעָה 3 וְעַתָּה יְהוָה קַח־נָא אֶת־נַפְשִׁי מִמֶּנִּי
כִּי טוֹב מוֹתִי מֵחַיָּי

God's lifeline to Nineveh was a noose around the neck of the prophet (4:3). Jonah was outraged that the compassion of the Lord was not provincial but that it stretched far beyond the boundaries of his world and that it embraced even his worst enemy. The text does not disclose the resolution of Jonah's anger but, after all, this book is not about Jonah. It is not about a great fish. It is about God and the character of God (Jonah 4:2).

> That is why I was so quick to flee to Tarshish.
> I knew that you are a gracious and merciful God,
> slow to anger and abounding in steadfast love.

Gary D. Pratico
Professor of Old Testament
Gordon-Conwell Theological Seminary
South Hamilton, Massachusetts

29.13 Advanced Information: The Polal Stem. The Polal stem is the passive counterpart of the Polel stem (27.15). It is the equivalent of the Pual stem for certain Biconsonantal (and Geminate) verbal roots. With Biconsonantal verbs, you will recall that these stems are characterized by a Holem Waw after the first consonant and the duplication of the second root consonant. For your reference, the Polal forms of the verb רוּם (to raise, lift up, exalt) are presented below. In the Perfect, note that the forms of the Polal are identical to the Polel, except in the 3ms (רוֹמַם). In the Imperfect, there are also a number of identical forms (2fs, 3mp, 2mp).

Perfect	Imperfect	Participle
רוֹמַם	יְרוֹמַם	מְרוֹמָם
רוֹמְמָה	תְּרוֹמַם	מְרוֹמֶ֫מֶת
רוֹמַ֫מְתָּ	תְּרוֹמַם	מְרוֹמָמִים
רוֹמַמְתְּ	תְּרוֹמְמִי	מְרוֹמָמוֹת
רוֹמַ֫מְתִּי	אֲרוֹמַם	
רוֹמְמוּ	יְרוֹמְמוּ	
רוֹמַמְתֶּם	תְּרוֹמַ֫מְנָה	
רוֹמַמְתֶּן	תְּרוֹמְמוּ	
רוֹמַ֫מְנוּ	תְּרוֹמַ֫מְנָה	
	נְרוֹמַם	

Chapter 30

The Hiphil Stem - Strong Verbs

30.1 **Introduction.** In this chapter, we will study the Hiphil stem. The Hiphil stem occurs more frequently than any other derived stem.[1] As you know by now, the name "Hiphil" (הִפְעִיל) preserves certain diagnostic features of the Hiphil Perfect (הַ prefix and the Hireq Yod stem vowel).

30.2 **The Meaning of the Hiphil Stem.**

1. *Causative.* The Hiphil stem is used to express a *causative* type of action with an *active* voice. For example, the verb מָלַךְ means "he was king" or "he reigned" in the Qal stem. The Hiphil form is הִמְלִיךְ and it means "he *caused* to reign" or "he *made* (someone) king." Notice how the key words "caused" and "made" are used to express the causative action of the Hiphil stem. Study the following additional examples that illustrate how a Qal verb takes on a causative nuance in the Hiphil stem.

Qal Stem	*Hiphil Stem*
זָכַר he remembered	הִזְכִּיר he caused to remember he reminded
שָׁמַע he heard	הִשְׁמִיעַ he caused to hear he proclaimed
קָרַב he approached	הִקְרִיב he caused to approach he presented

In the translation of the Hiphil forms above, notice that there are both literal (he caused to remember) and then more idiomatic translations (he reminded). In terms of good English style, the more idiomatic translation is to be preferred. At first, however, you might want to use the more literal type of translation in

---

[1] The Hiphil stem occurs 9,483 times in the Hebrew Bible. It appears in the Perfect 2,680 times, Imperfect 4,058 times, Imperative 741 times, Infinitive Construct 948 times, Infinitive Absolute 221 times and Participle 835 times.

order to reinforce the causative nuance of the Hiphil stem. In addition to causative action, the Hiphil stem may also express other types of action.

2. *Simple Action*. Some verbs in the Hiphil stem can preserve the simple action of the Qal stem. In this case, the Hiphil verb would be translated like a Qal verb. This is frequently the case with verbal roots that are common in the Hiphil stem but are not attested (or rarely attested) in the Qal stem. The following examples illustrate this usage.

Qal Stem	Hiphil Stem	Translation
שָׁכַם	הִשְׁכִּים	he arose early
שָׁלַךְ	הִשְׁלִיךְ	he threw (down)
שָׁמַד	הִשְׁמִיד	he exterminated

3. *Declarative*. Hiphil verbs sometimes carry a declarative nuance, meaning that the subject of the verb declares someone (or something) to be in a certain condition or state of being. For example, the verb רָשַׁע means "to be guilty" in the Qal stem. In the Hiphil stem, however, it means "to declare guilty" or "to pronounce guilty."

4. *Factitive*. Like the Piel stem, the Hiphil stem may be used to make an intransitive verb into a transitive verb. That is, if a Qal verb is intransitive (does not take a direct object), it will become transitive (can take a direct object) in the Hiphil stem. For example, the verb גָּדַל means "to be great" in the Qal stem. In the Hiphil stem, however, it means "to make someone (something) great."

There are a few other categories of verbal meaning in the Hiphil stem, such as denominative and permissive, but these are infrequent. Additionally, the meaning of some Hiphil verbs cannot be categorized. In such cases, you will need to check the lexicon in order to determine meaning.

30.3 **Hiphil Perfect**. The Hiphil Perfect is formed with the Hiphil prefix (הִ), the verbal root (with a stem vowel that is variable between Hireq Yod and Pathach) and the Perfect sufformatives.

	Qal	Hiphil	Translation
3ms	קָטַל	הִקְטִיל	he caused to kill[2]
3fs	קָטְלָה	הִקְטִילָה	she caused to kill
2ms	קָטַ֫לְתָּ	הִקְטַ֫לְתָּ	you caused to kill
2fs	קָטַלְתְּ	הִקְטַלְתְּ	you caused to kill
1cs	קָטַ֫לְתִּי	הִקְטַ֫לְתִּי	I caused to kill
3cp	קָטְלוּ	הִקְטִ֫ילוּ	they caused to kill
2mp	קְטַלְתֶּם	הִקְטַלְתֶּם	you caused to kill
2fp	קְטַלְתֶּן	הִקְטַלְתֶּן	you caused to kill
1cp	קָטַ֫לְנוּ	הִקְטַ֫לְנוּ	we caused to kill

30.4 Hiphil Perfect Diagnostics.

1. הִ prefix in every form.

2. The stem vowel is variable between Hireq Yod (הִקְטִיל) and Pathach (הִקְטַ֫לְתָּ). All third person forms have Hireq Yod and all first and second person forms have Pathach.

Hiphil Perfect
Strong Verb

הִקְטִיל

הִקְטַ֫לְתָּ

3. Remember that the הִ prefix also characterizes the Niphal Imperative and Infinitive Construct (הִקָּטֵל). These forms should not be confused, however, because the vowel pattern of each is distinctive. Note especially the assimilated נ of the Niphal stem

---

[2] Though these translations are awkward, the intention is to reinforce the essential causative nuance of the Hiphil stem with our standard paradigm verb קָטַל.

in the Niphal Imperative and Infinitive Construct forms. In fact, the הַ prefix is the only feature that these two forms have in common.

Niphal Imperative/ Infinitive Construct	Hiphil Perfect 3ms
הִקָּטֵל	הִקְטִיל

30.5 **Hiphil Imperfect**. The Hiphil Imperfect is formed with the Imperfect preformatives, the verbal root (with Hireq Yod stem vowel) and the Imperfect sufformatives.

	Qal	Hiphil	Translation
3ms	יִקְטֹל	יַקְטִיל	he will cause to kill
3fs	תִּקְטֹל	תַּקְטִיל	she will cause to kill
2ms	תִּקְטֹל	תַּקְטִיל	you will cause to kill
2fs	תִּקְטְלִי	תַּקְטִ֫ילִי	you will cause to kill
1cs	אֶקְטֹל	אַקְטִיל	I will cause to kill
3mp	יִקְטְלוּ	יַקְטִ֫ילוּ	they will cause to kill
3fp	תִּקְטֹ֫לְנָה	תַּקְטֵ֫לְנָה	they will cause to kill
2mp	תִּקְטְלוּ	תַּקְטִ֫ילוּ	you will cause to kill
2fp	תִּקְטֹ֫לְנָה	תַּקְטֵ֫לְנָה	you will cause to kill
1cp	נִקְטֹל	נַקְטִיל	we will cause to kill

30.6 **Hiphil Imperfect Diagnostics**.

1. Pathach preformative vowel in every form. This same preformative vowel also occurs in the I-Guttural (Type 2) Qal Imperfect verbs (יַעֲמֹד). In such cases, the stem vowel will distinguish between the Qal (Holem stem vowel) and Hiphil (Hireq Yod stem vowel).

2. Hireq Yod stem vowel in every form, except the 3fp and 2fp forms in which it is Tsere (תַּקְטֵ֫לְנָה).

Hiphil Imperfect
Strong Verb

יַקְטִיל

30.7 **Hiphil Imperative.** The Hiphil Imperative is formed with the Hiphil prefix (הַ), the verbal root (with a stem vowel that is variable between Tsere and Hireq Yod) and the Imperative sufformatives.

	Qal	*Hiphil*	*Translation*
2ms	קְטֹל	הַקְטֵל	cause to kill!
2fs	קִטְלִי	הַקְטִֽילִי	cause to kill!
2mp	קִטְלוּ	הַקְטִֽילוּ	cause to kill!
2fp	קְטֹֽלְנָה	הַקְטֵֽלְנָה	cause to kill!

30.8 **Hiphil Imperative Diagnostics.**

1. הַ prefix in every form. This same prefix is also used with the Hiphil Infinitive Construct and Infinitive Absolute (30.9-12).

2. The stem vowel is either Tsere (2ms, 2fp) or Hireq Yod (2fs, 2mp). Those forms with sufformatives consisting of a vowel take the Hireq Yod stem vowel.

Hiphil Imperative
Strong Verb

הַקְטֵל
הַקְטִֽילִי

30.9 **Hiphil Infinitive Construct.** The Hiphil Infinitive Construct is formed with the Hiphil prefix (הַ) and the verbal root (with a Hireq Yod stem vowel). There are no sufformatives because the Infinitive Construct is not an inflected form. Remember, however, that an Infinitive Construct can take pronominal suffixes as in הַקְטִילִי (Hiphil Infinitive Construct with 1cs suffix).

Qal	Hiphil	Translation
קְטֹל	הַקְטִיל	to cause to kill, killing

30.10 Hiphil Infinitive Construct Diagnostics.

    1. הַ prefix.

    2. Hireq Yod stem vowel. It is the stem vowel that will distinguish the Infinitive Construct (הַקְטִיל) from the Hiphil Imperative ms (הַקְטֵל).

Hiphil Infinitive Construct

הַקְטִיל

30.11 Hiphil Infinitive Absolute. The Infinitive Absolute is formed with the Hiphil prefix (הַ) and the verbal root (with Tsere stem vowel). The stem vowel will distinguish the Infinitive Absolute (הַקְטֵל) from the Infinitive Construct (הַקְטִיל).

30.12 Hiphil Infinitive Absolute Diagnostics.

    1. הַ prefix.

    2. Tsere stem vowel. Note that the masculine singular Imperative and the Infinitive Absolute forms are identical. Context should enable you to identify the form correctly.

Hiphil Infinitive Absolute

הַקְטֵל

30.13 Hiphil Participle. The Hiphil Participle is formed with the Participle prefix (מ), the verbal root (with a Hireq Yod stem vowel) and the inflectional endings of the Participle.

	Qal	Hiphil	Translation
ms	קֹטֵל	מַקְטִיל	causing to kill
fs	קֹטֶלֶת	[3]מַקְטֶלֶת	causing to kill
mp	קֹטְלִים	מַקְטִילִים	causing to kill
fp	קֹטְלוֹת	מַקְטִילוֹת	causing to kill

30.14 Hiphil Participle Diagnostics.

1. מַ prefix in every form. Again, remember that a מ prefix characterizes the Participle in the Piel, Pual, Hiphil and Hophal stems.

2. Hireq Yod stem vowel throughout, except in one of the feminine singular forms (מַקְטֶלֶת).

Hiphil Participle
Strong Verb

מַקְטִיל

30.15 Summary.

1. The Hiphil stem is used to express *causative* action with an *active* voice. The key words "cause" and "make" may be used to change the simple action of the Qal into the causative action of the Hiphil. Oftentimes, however, the more idiomatic translations are to be preferred.

2. The most important diagnostic features of the Hiphil stem include: (1) ה prefix in all conjugations, except the Imperfect and Participle; (2) Pathach under all preformatives and prefixes, except in the Perfect, where it is Hireq; (3) Hireq Yod or Tsere stem vowel in all forms, except the second and first person forms of the Perfect where it is Pathach.

---

[3] Like the Qal Participle, the Hiphil Participle may also end in ה, as an alternative form (מַקְטִילָה).

Hiphil Stem - Strong Verbs

Perfect	Imperfect	Imperative	Infinitive Construct	Infinitive Absolute	Participle
הִקְטִיל הִקְטַלְתְּ	יַקְטִיל	הַקְטֵל הַקְטִילִי	הַקְטִיל	הַקְטֵל	מַקְטִיל
הִקְטִיל	יַקְטִיל	הַקְטֵל	הַקְטִיל	הַקְטֵל	מַקְטִיל
הִקְטִילָה	תַּקְטִיל	הַקְטִילִי			מַקְטֶלֶת
הִקְטַלְתָּ	תַּקְטִיל	הַקְטִילוּ			מַקְטִילִים
הִקְטַלְתְּ	תַּקְטִילִי	הַקְטֵלְנָה			מַקְטִילוֹת
הִקְטַלְתִּי	אַקְטִיל				
הִקְטִילוּ	יַקְטִילוּ				
הִקְטַלְתֶּם	תַּקְטֵלְנָה				
הִקְטַלְתֶּן	תַּקְטִילוּ				
הִקְטַלְנוּ	תַּקְטֵלְנָה				
	נַקְטִיל				

30.16 Vocabulary.

Verbs

חָלַל   (Niphal) to be defiled; (Piel) pollute, profane; (Hiphil) begin (135)

נָגַד   (Hiphil) to make known, report, tell (371)

שָׁבַע   (Niphal, Hiphil) to swear (186)

שָׁלַךְ   (Hiphil) to throw, cast (125)

Nouns

הָמוֹן   tumult, turmoil, multitude (86)

דַּעַת   knowledge (89); feminine

דֶּלֶת   door (88); feminine

זְרוֹעַ   arm, forearm (91); feminine

כֶּרֶם   vineyard (93)

כְּרוּב   cherub (93)

מַלְכוּת   kingdom, dominion, reign (91)

עֵצָה   advice, counsel (87)

Other

חָלָל   (adjective) slain (94)

טָמֵא   (adjective) unclean (88)

30.17   **The Promises to the Fathers.** God's promises to Abraham, Isaac and Jacob are central to the book of Genesis. One aspect of these promises is that Abraham will have many descendants. They will be "as numerous as the stars of the heaven and the sand of the seashore." Yet ironically, the wife of Abraham is barren (Gen 11:30). Isaac's wife, Rebekah, is also barren (Gen 25:21) and so is Rachel, the wife of Jacob (Gen 29:31). The infertility of Sarah, Rebekah and Rachel highlights an important theological truth: that God himself will bring about what he has promised. Thus God provides a son for Sarah, in spite of her barrenness and old age (Gen 21:1-2); Rebekah gives birth to twins in answer to the prayer of Isaac (Gen 25:21-26); and God opens Rachel's womb which previously had produced no "fruit" (Gen 30:22-24). The theological truth that God himself will accomplish what he has promised is clearly reflected in the common use of the Hiphil verbal stem in the context of God's promises.

This theological truth is not only seen in the patriarchal narratives but also in the grammar, since it is the Hiphil verb form that is commonly used in God's promises. The Hiphil stem is important in this context because it expresses "causative" action. Let us consider, for example, the verb פָּרָה (to be fruitful) and רָבָה (to multiply). God said to Abraham, "I will multiply you exceedingly" (Gen 17:2) and "I will cause you to be exceedingly fruitful" (Gen 17:6). The Hiphil forms of רָבָה and פָּרָה in these two passages could be translated: "I will *cause* you to multiply exceedingly" and "I will *cause* you to be exceedingly fruitful." Notice that in both cases, God is the subject of the verbs. We also read that

God appeared to Jacob and said to him, "I will multiply your descendants as the stars of the heavens" (Gen 26:4). Towards the end of Jacob's life, he recalled the promise that God had made to him: "I will *make* you fruitful and *make* you numerous" (Gen 48:4). The Hiphil verbal forms in these two texts, with God as the subject, once again underscore the causative action of God. The book of Genesis then concludes with Jacob's descendants numbering seventy when they entered Egypt (Gen 46:27; Ex 1:5). Yet when the Israelites left Egypt, they numbered in the thousands! Moses acknowledges that it was God who brought this to pass, recalling his covenant with Abraham: "The Lord your God has multiplied you, and behold, you are this day as the stars of heaven for a multitude" (Deut 1:10). The Hiphil form of רָבָה once again highlights that God caused Israel to multiply in Egypt (cf. Ps 105:23-24). God brought to fruition his promise of increase! In the New Testament, we read that God continues to bring forth children, for we, like Isaac, are children of promise (Gal 4:28).

Carol M. Kaminski
Ph.D. candidate
Cambridge University
Cambridge, England

Chapter 31

The Hiphil Stem - Weak Verbs

31.1 **Introduction.** In this chapter, we will study weak verbs in the Hiphil stem. Before working through this chapter, however, be certain that you have first mastered the strong verb diagnostics of the Hiphil stem. By way of review, the diagnostics for the strong verb of the Hiphil stem include: (1) הֿ prefix in all conjugations, except the Imperfect and Participle; (2) Pathach under all preformatives and prefixes, except in the Perfect, where it is Hireq; (3) Hireq Yod or Tsere stem vowel in all forms, except the second and first person forms of the Perfect where it is Pathach.

31.2 **I-Guttural Paradigms and Diagnostics.**

Perfect	Imperfect	Imperative	Infinitive Construct	Infinitive Absolute	Participle
הֶעֱמִיד הֶעֱמַ֫דְתָּ	יַעֲמִיד	הַעֲמֵד הַעֲמִ֫ידִי	הַעֲמִיד	הַעֲמֵד	מַעֲמִיד
הֶעֱמִיד	יַעֲמִיד	הַעֲמֵד	הַעֲמִיד	הַעֲמֵד	מַעֲמִיד
הֶעֱמִ֫ידָה	תַּעֲמִיד	הַעֲמִ֫ידִי			מַעֲמֶ֫דֶת[1]
הֶעֱמַ֫דְתָּ	תַּעֲמִיד	הַעֲמִ֫ידוּ			מַעֲמִידִים
הֶעֱמַדְתְּ	תַּעֲמִ֫ידִי	הַעֲמֵ֫דְנָה			מַעֲמִידוֹת
הֶעֱמַ֫דְתִּי	אַעֲמִיד				
הֶעֱמִ֫ידוּ	יַעֲמִ֫ידוּ				
הֶעֱמַדְתֶּם	תַּעֲמֵ֫דְנָה				
הֶעֱמַדְתֶּן	תַּעֲמִ֫ידוּ				
הֶעֱמַ֫דְנוּ	תַּעֲמֵ֫דְנָה				
	נַעֲמִיד				

---

[1] The alternate form מַעֲמִידָה is also attested.

31.3   I-Guttural Notes.

1. In every conjugation, except the Perfect, the strong verb diagnostics of the Hiphil stem are preserved in this weak verb class.

2. The Perfect has a Seghol prefix vowel (הֶעֱמִיד) rather than the Hireq of the strong verb (הִקְטִיל). You have encountered this same vowel pattern in both the Qal Imperfect (יֶחֱזַק) and Niphal Perfect (נֶעֱזַב) of I-Guttural verbs (16.8-9; 25.6-7).

3. While it is not diagnostic, it is helpful to note that the guttural consonant in first root position takes a reduced vowel in every form of every conjugation: Hateph Seghol in the Perfect and Hateph Pathach in all other conjugations.

31.4   III-ח/ע Paradigms and Diagnostics.

Perfect	Imperfect	Imperative	Infinitive Construct	Infinitive Absolute	Participle
הִשְׁלִיחַ הִשְׁלַחְתָּ	יַשְׁלִיחַ	הַשְׁלַח הַשְׁלִיחִי	הַשְׁלִיחַ	הַשְׁלֵחַ	מַשְׁלִיחַ
הִשְׁלִיחַ	יַשְׁלִיחַ	הַשְׁלַח	הַשְׁלִיחַ	הַשְׁלֵחַ	מַשְׁלִיחַ
הִשְׁלִיחָה	תַּשְׁלִיחַ	הַשְׁלִיחִי			מַשְׁלַחַת
הִשְׁלַחְתָּ	תַּשְׁלִיחַ	הַשְׁלִיחוּ			מַשְׁלִיחִים
הִשְׁלַחַתְּ	תַּשְׁלִיחִי	הַשְׁלַחְנָה			מַשְׁלִיחוֹת
הִשְׁלַחְתִּי	אַשְׁלִיחַ				
הִשְׁלִיחוּ	יַשְׁלִיחוּ				
הִשְׁלַחְתֶּם	תַּשְׁלַחְנָה				
הִשְׁלַחְתֶּן	תַּשְׁלִיחוּ				
הִשְׁלַחְנוּ	תַּשְׁלַחְנָה				
	נַשְׁלִיחַ				

31.5   III-ח/ע Notes.

1. Most of the Hiphil strong verb diagnostics are preserved in this weak verb class. The only variations are in the stem vowel of a few forms.

2. In the Imperfect 3fp and 2fp (תַּשְׁלַחְנָה), the stem vowel is Pathach rather than Tsere. This minor change is occasioned by the fact that gutturals prefer a-class vowels.

3. In the Imperative 2ms (הַשְׁלַח) and 2fp (הַשְׁלַחְנָה), the stem vowel is also Pathach rather that Tsere, just like the forms of the Imperfect mentioned above. Such minor variations should not present any difficulty in terms of identifying these Hiphil forms.

31.6   III-א Paradigms and Diagnostics.

Perfect	Imperfect	Imperative	Infinitive Construct	Infinitive Absolute	Participle
הַמְצִיא הִמְצֵאת	יַמְצִיא	הַמְצֵא הַמְצִיאִי	הַמְצִיא	הַמְצֵא	מַמְצִיא
הִמְצִיא	יַמְצִיא	הַמְצֵא	הַמְצִיא	הַמְצֵא	מַמְצִיא
הִמְצִיאָה	תַּמְצִיא	הַמְצִיאִי			מַמְצֵאת
הִמְצֵאתָ	תַּמְצִיא	הַמְצִיאוּ			מַמְצִיאִים
הִמְצֵאת	תַּמְצִיאִי	הַמְצֶאנָה			מַמְצִיאוֹת
הִמְצֵאתִי	אַמְצִיא				
הִמְצִיאוּ	יַמְצִיאוּ				
הִמְצֵאתֶם	תַּמְצֶאנָה				
הִמְצֵאתֶן	תַּמְצִיאוּ				
הִמְצֵאנוּ	תַּמְצֶאנָה				
	נַמְצִיא				

31.7   III-א Notes.

1. Most of the Hiphil strong verb diagnostics are preserved in this weak verb class. All prefix and preformative consonants and vowels follow the pattern of the Hiphil strong verb. The stem vowel variations that do occur should be familiar to you as changes characteristic of the III-א weak verb class.

2. In all second and first person forms of the Perfect, the stem vowel is Tsere (הִמְצֵאת). The stem vowel of the Hiphil strong verb is Pathach (הִקְטַלְתָּ).

3. In the Imperfect, the stem vowel in the 3fp and 2fp forms is
   Seghol (תִּמְצֶּאנָה) rather than Tsere (תִּקְטֹלְנָה). This same variation
   also occurs in the Imperative 2fp form (הַמְצֶּאנָה).

31.8 III-ה Paradigms and Diagnostics.

Perfect	Imperfect	Imperative	Infinitive Construct	Infinitive Absolute	Participle
הִגְלָה הִגְלִיתָ	יַגְלֶה	הַגְלֵה	הַגְלוֹת	הַגְלֵה	מַגְלֶה
הִגְלָה	יַגְלֶה	הַגְלֵה	הַגְלוֹת	הַגְלֵה	מַגְלֶה
הִגְלְתָה	תַּגְלֶה	הַגְלִי			מַגְלָה
הִגְלִיתָ	תַּגְלֶה	הַגְלוּ			מַגְלִים
הִגְלִית	תַּגְלִי	הַגְלֶינָה			מַגְלוֹת
הִגְלִיתִי	אַגְלֶה				
הִגְלוּ	יַגְלוּ				
הִגְלִיתֶם	תַּגְלֶינָה				
הִגְלִיתֶן	תַּגְלוּ				
הִגְלִינוּ	תַּגְלֶינָה				
	נַגְלֶה				

31.9 III-ה Notes.

1. In Hiphil III-ה verbs, all prefix and preformative consonants and
   vowels retain the Hiphil strong verb diagnostics. Variation from
   the strong verb diagnostics occurs mainly in the stem vowels of
   the various conjugations. In most instances, however, the
   distinctive preformatives and prefixes should be sufficient for
   identifying Hiphil III-ה verbs.

2. Note the III-ה diagnostic endings that are highlighted in dark
   gray in the above chart (31.8). These are the same endings that
   appear on all III-ה verbs in the Qal and derived stems.

3. In the Perfect, the Hired Yod stem vowel may also occur as
   Tsere Yod (הִגְלֵיתָ).

4. In the Imperfect, the Hireq Yod stem vowel of the Hiphil strong verb does not occur in any form. Note, however, that the הָ ending is characteristic of Imperfect III-ה forms that do not take a sufformative.

5. As expected in III-ה verbs, the Infinitive Construct has the וֹת ending.

31.10 I-נ Paradigms and Diagnostics.

Perfect	Imperfect	Imperative	Infinitive Construct	Infinitive Absolute	Participle
הִצִּיל הִצַּלְתָּ	יַצִּיל	הַצֵּל הַצִּילִי	הַצִּיל	הַצֵּל	מַצִּיל
הִצִּיל	יַצִּיל	הַצֵּל	הַצִּיל	הַצֵּל	מַצִּיל
הִצִּילָה	תַּצִּיל	הַצִּילִי			מַצֶּלֶת
הִצַּלְתָּ	תַּצִּיל	הַצִּילוּ			מַצִּילִים
הִצַּלְתְּ	תַּצִּילִי	הַצֵּלְנָה			מַצִּילוֹת
הִצַּלְתִּי	אַצִּיל				
הִצִּילוּ	יַצִּילוּ				
הִצַּלְתֶּם	תַּצֵּלְנָה				
הִצַּלְתֶּן	תַּצִּילוּ				
הִצַּלְנוּ	תַּצֵּלְנָה				
	נַצִּיל				

31.11 I-נ Notes.

1. All Hiphil strong verb diagnostics are preserved in this weak verb class.

2. The difficulty with I-נ Hiphil verbs is not with the recognition of stem diagnostics but rather with the identification of the verbal root. This difficulty is due to the fact that in every form of every conjugation above, the first root consonant (נ) has assimilated into the second root consonant (צ) and remains as a Daghesh Forte. In order to correctly identify the verbal root, you will need to recognize that the Daghesh Forte in the צ represents the assimilated נ of the verbal root.

31.12 I-י Paradigms and Diagnostics.

Perfect	Imperfect	Imperative	Infinitive Construct	Infinitive Absolute	Participle
הוֹשִׁיב הוֹשַׁבְתְּ	יוֹשִׁיב	הוֹשֵׁב הוֹשִׁיבִי	הוֹשִׁיב	הוֹשֵׁב	מוֹשִׁיב

Perfect	Imperfect	Imperative	Infinitive Construct	Infinitive Absolute	Participle
הוֹשִׁיב	יוֹשִׁיב	הוֹשֵׁב	הוֹשִׁיב	הוֹשֵׁב	מוֹשִׁיב
הוֹשִׁיבָה	תּוֹשִׁיב	הוֹשִׁיבִי			מוֹשֶׁבֶת
הוֹשַׁבְתָּ	תּוֹשִׁיב	הוֹשִׁיבוּ			מוֹשִׁיבִים
הוֹשַׁבְתְּ	תּוֹשִׁיבִי	הוֹשֵׁבְנָה			מוֹשִׁיבוֹת
הוֹשַׁבְתִּי	אוֹשִׁיב				
הוֹשִׁיבוּ	יוֹשִׁיבוּ				
הוֹשַׁבְתֶּם	תּוֹשֵׁבְנָה				
הוֹשַׁבְתֶּן	תּוֹשִׁיבוּ				
הוֹשַׁבְנוּ	תּוֹשֵׁבְנָה				
	נוֹשִׁיב				

31.13 I-י Notes.

Recall from your study of the Niphal stem that most I-י verbs were originally I-ו (25.10-11). In the Niphal, Hiphil, Hophal and Hithpael stems, the original ו will reappear as either a vowel letter or as a consonant, replacing the י root consonant.

1. In each of the above forms, note that the י in first root position has been replaced with Holem Waw. In every conjugation, this Holem Waw follows the prefix or preformative consonant. As in the Niphal Perfect and Participle, this Holem Waw represents the reappearance of the ו that was originally in first root position. Knowing that this Holem Waw is indicative of the I-י verb class will enable you to correctly identify the verbal root.

2. Apart from the presence of the Holem Waw discussed above, all of the other Hiphil strong verb diagnostics are preserved in the Hiphil stem of I-י verbs. The preformative and prefix consonants are exactly the same as in the strong verb and the stem vowels are as expected in all conjugations.

31.14 Biconsonantal Paradigms and Diagnostics.

Perfect	Imperfect	Imperative	Infinitive Construct	Infinitive Absolute	Participle
הֵקִים הֲקִימוֹת	יָקִים הָקִימִי	הָקֵם הָקִימִי	הָקִים	הָקֵם	מֵקִים
הֵקִים	יָקִים	הָקֵם	הָקִים	הָקֵם	מֵקִים
הֲקִימָה	תָּקִים	הָקִימִי			מְקִימָה
הֲקִימֹוֹתָ	תָּקִים	הָקִימוּ			מְקִימִים
הֲקִימוֹת	תָּקִימִי	הָקֵמְנָה			מְקִימוֹת
הֲקִימֹוֹתִי	אָקִים				
הֲקִימוּ	יָקִימוּ				
הֲקִימוֹתֶם	תְּקִימֶֽינָה²‎				
הֲקִימוֹתֶן	תָּקִימוּ				
הֲקִימֹוֹנוּ	תְּקִימֶֽינָה				
	נָקִים				

31.15 Biconsonantal Notes.

1. As you know, there are three Biconsonantal verb classes, each distinguished by their medial vowel letter. These classes are represented by the verbs קוּם (with Shureq), שִׂים (with Hireq Yod) and בּוֹא (with Holem Waw). In the Hiphil stem, however, Biconsonantal verbs exhibit the diagnostic Hireq Yod stem vowel in most forms, regardless of the Biconsonantal verb class. For example, the Hiphil Imperfect 3ms form for each class is יָקִים (קוּם), יָשִׂים (שִׂים) and יָבִיא (בּוֹא). Notice how each Imperfect form takes the Hireq Yod stem vowel, regardless of its original medial vowel letter. For this reason, the diagnostics for קוּם will suffice for all three classes of Biconsonantal verbs.

2. In the Perfect, the prefix vowel is variable between Tsere in the third person forms and Hateph Pathach in the second and first person forms. There is also a Holem Waw "connecting" vowel

---

² The spelling תָּקִימְנָה is also attested.

between the verbal root and Perfect sufformatives in all second
and first person forms (הֲקִימֹ֫ותָ). You have already encountered
this same connecting vowel in the Qal Perfect forms of Geminate
verbs (סַבֹּ֫ותָ 2ms from סָבַב). You should also note, however,
that the Holem Waw connecting vowel also appears simply as
Holem. For example, הֲקִימֹ֫ותִי is spelled defectively as הֲקִימֹתִי.

3. In the Imperfect, Imperative, Infinitive Construct and Infinitive
Absolute, the prefix and preformative vowels are Qamets rather
than the Pathach of the strong verb pattern. You should also
note that the prefix vowel for the Participle is variable between
Tsere (masculine singular) and Vocal Shewa.

4. The inflection of Hiphil Biconsonantal verbs can exhibit further
variation. Due to the relative infrequency of these variant
spellings, however, they will not be studied.

31.16 Summary: Hiphil Diagnostics. With weak verbs of the Hiphil stem, most of the strong verb diagnostics are retained. These should be sufficient for the identification of Hiphil weak verbs.

	Perfect	*Imperfect*	*Imperative*	*Infinitive Construct*	*Infinitive Absolute*	*Participle*
Strong	הִקְטִיל הִקְטַלְתָּ	יַקְטִיל	הַקְטֵל הַקְטִילִי	הַקְטִיל	הַקְטֵל	מַקְטִיל
I-Gutt	הֶעֱמִיד הֶעֱמַדְתָּ	יַעֲמִיד	הַעֲמֵד הַעֲמִידִי	הַעֲמִיד	הַעֲמֵד	מַעֲמִיד
III-ח/ע	הִשְׁלִיחַ הִשְׁלַחְתָּ	יַשְׁלִיחַ	הַשְׁלַח הַשְׁלִיחִי	הַשְׁלִיחַ	הַשְׁלֵחַ	מַשְׁלִיחַ
III-א	הִמְצִיא הִמְצֵאת	יַמְצִיא	הַמְצֵא הַמְצִיאִי	הַמְצִיא	הַמְצֵא	מַמְצִיא
III-ה	הִגְלָה הִגְלִיתָ	יַגְלֶה	הַגְלֵה	הַגְלוֹת	הַגְלֵה	מַגְלֶה
I-נ	הִצִּיל הִצַּלְתָּ	יַצִּיל	הַצֵּל הַצִּילִי	הַצִּיל	הַצֵּל	מַצִּיל
I-י	הוֹשִׁיב הוֹשַׁבְתָּ	יוֹשִׁיב	הוֹשֵׁב הוֹשִׁיבִי	הוֹשִׁיב	הוֹשֵׁב	מוֹשִׁיב
Bicon	הֵקִים הֲקִימֹות	יָקִים	הָקֵם הָקִימִי	הָקִים	הָקֵם	מֵקִים

31.17 Vocabulary.

Nouns

קֶדֶם	east, in front (87)
שֶׁקֶל	shekel, unit of weight (88)
אָוֶן	wickedness, iniquity (81)
אוֹצָר	supply, storehouse, treasure (79)
אוֹת	sign (79)
גּוֹרָל	lot, allotment (77)
יְשׁוּעָה	deliverance, salvation (78)
מִשְׁמֶרֶת	obligation, service (78); feminine
נֶגַע	blow, assault, plague (78)
קָרְבָּן	offering, gift (80)
צַר	adversary, foe (70)
מִקְנֶה	possessions, land, cattle (76)

31.18 Yes, I Will Remember. Measuring the emotional and volitional intensity of a writer can be a tricky matter. Unfortunately, it can degenerate into a wholly subjective exercise if we try to read our own feelings or volition into the text in order to wring something from the text. Yet this is precisely where the presence of the Cohortative verb assists the exegete and expositor. It signals the express direction and clear intention of the author's will. By it we can discern some of the emotional and volitional freight laden on the text.

For instance, in Ps 77 there are no less than eight Cohortative verbs. These are most strikingly conveyed in verses 12-13 (English 77:11-12) in two pairs of first common singular verbs, with the second in each set being Cohortative.

אַזְכִּיר מַעַלְלֵי־יָהּ כִּי־אֶזְכְּרָה מִקֶּדֶם פִּלְאֶךָ
וְהָגִיתִי בְכָל־פָּעֳלֶךָ וּבַעֲלִילוֹתֶיךָ אָשִׂיחָה

I will remember the deeds of the Lord; *yes, I will remember* your wonders
of old. *I will meditate* on all of your works and
I will consider all of your deeds.

The positioning of these Cohortative verbs emphasizes the author's personal intensity and intentionality as he wrestles with his faith amid trying circumstances.

"I will remember"	אַזְכִּיר	Hiphil Imperfect 1cs זָכַר
"Yes, I will remember"	אֶזְכְּרָה	Qal Cohortative 1cs זָכַר
"I will meditate"	וְהָגִיתִי	Qal Perfect 1cs הָגָה
"I will consider"	אָשִׂיחָה	Qal Cohortative 1cs שִׂיחַ

The piling up of such verbs is not superfluous verbiage. Rather, in the context of the psalm, this is how the author communicates his own deliberate action with respect to God's actions on behalf of his people. He will remember and he will muse on what God has done. This intentional, upward incline of his will is how he battles his own downward decline into depression and doubt. This is a tactic both for himself and for his audience. The use of Cohortative verbs underscores his desire to let God dominate his view, first and foremost. The author knows that only then will he be able to correctly assess his situation without numbing fear. This is the way faith fights.

Dorington G. Little
Senior Pastor, First Congregational Church of Hamilton
Hamilton, Massachusetts

31.19 **Advanced Information: The Verb יָדָה.** The verb יָדָה (to thank, praise) is well-attested in the Hiphil stem (100 times), especially in the Psalms (67 times). Given that this verb is doubly weak, both I-י and III-ה, certain of its forms merit special attention. Note that as a I-י verb in the Hiphil stem, the original ו will reappear as Holem Waw, replacing the י root consonant. You will also want to remember that III-ה verbs have their own distinctive endings. Some of the more common forms of this verb are presented below.

Perfect	הוֹדִינוּ	1cp	we give thanks
	הוֹדוּ	3cp	they give thanks
Imperfect	אוֹדֶה	1cs	I will give thanks
	יוֹדוּ	3mp	they will give thanks
Imperative	הוֹדוּ	2mp	(you) give thanks!
Inf Construct	הוֹדוֹת [3]		to give thanks
Participle	מוֹדֶה	ms	giving thanks

A few biblical examples with the Hiphil of יָדָה are presented below.

טוֹב לְהֹדוֹת לַיהוָה

(It is) good *to give thanks* to the Lord.
(Ps 92:2 [English 92:1])

הוֹדוּ לַיהוָה כִּי־טוֹב כִּי לְעוֹלָם חַסְדּוֹ

Give thanks to the Lord, for he is good;
for his steadfast love endures forever!
(Ps 118:1)

אוֹדֶה יְהוָה בְּכָל־לִבִּי

I *will give thanks* to the Lord with all my heart.
(Ps 9:2 [English 9:1])

---

[3] This form is most often spelled defectively as הֹדוֹת.

Chapter 32

The Hophal Stem - Strong Verbs

32.1 **Introduction.** In this chapter, we will study the Hophal stem. The Hophal stem occurs less frequently than any other derived stem.[1] Because certain forms of the Hophal stem occur with such infrequency, we will study only the Perfect, Imperfect and Participle in this chapter. The stem name "Hophal" (הָפְעַל) preserves certain diagnostic features of the Perfect (הָ prefix with Qamets Hatuf and Pathach stem vowel). In this case, the prefix vowel and the stem vowel will distinguish the Hophal from most Hiphil forms. In modern Hebrew, the name of this stem is spelled "Huphal," denoting the frequent presence of a u-class vowel with either the prefix or preformative in certain verbs.

32.2 **The Meaning of the Hophal Stem.** For the most part, the Hophal is the passive of the Hiphil. The Hophal stem, therefore, is used to express *causative* action with a *passive* voice. For example, the Hiphil verb הִמְלִיךְ means "he made (someone) king." The Hophal form is הָמְלַךְ and it is translated "he *was* made king."

32.3 **Hophal Perfect.** The Hophal Perfect of a strong verb may occur with either a Qibbuts (u-class) or Qamets Hatuf (o-class) prefix vowel, though Qamets Hatuf is more frequent in the strong verb.[2] For this reason, two Hophal Perfect paradigms are given below, each with a different prefix vowel. The Hophal Perfect is formed with the Hophal prefix (הָ), the verbal stem (with Pathach stem vowel) and the Perfect sufformatives. Translate the Hophal Perfect passively with a form of the helping verb "to be" as in "he caused to *be* killed."[3]

---

[1] The Hophal stem occurs 396 times in the Hebrew Bible. It appears in the Perfect 109 times, Imperfect 163 times, Imperative 2 times, Infinitive Construct 8 times, Infinitive Absolute 6 times and Participle 108 times.

[2] In Hophal weak verbs, u-class vowels are more frequent. The Hophal occurs 109 times in the Perfect (strong and weak verbs). In only 37 instances does the o-class stem vowel appear under the הָ prefix. In the remaining 72 instances, the u-class vowels Qibbuts or Shureq are present under the הָ. With the Hophal Imperfect, the o-class vowel occurs only 10 out of the 163 total occurrences.

[3] As with the Hiphil strong verb, we acknowledge the inadequacy and

	Hophal u-class	Hophal o-class	Translation
3ms	הָקְטַל	הָקְטַל	he caused to be killed
3fs	הָקְטְלָה	הָקְטְלָה	she caused to be killed
2ms	הָקְטַֿלְתָּ	הָקְטַֿלְתָּ	you caused to be killed
2fs	הָקְטַלְתְּ	הָקְטַלְתְּ	you caused to be killed
1cs	הָקְטַֿלְתִּי	הָקְטַֿלְתִּי	I caused to be killed
3cp	הָקְטְלוּ	הָקְטְלוּ	they caused to be killed
2mp	הָקְטַלְתֶּם	הָקְטַלְתֶּם	you caused to be killed
2fp	הָקְטַלְתֶּן	הָקְטַלְתֶּן	you caused to be killed
1cp	הָקְטַֿלְנוּ	הָקְטַֿלְנוּ	we caused to be killed

32.4   Hophal Perfect Diagnostics.

1. הֻ (u-class) or הָ (o-class) prefix in every form of their respective paradigms.

2. Pathach stem vowel in both classes, except in the 3fs and 3cp forms.

Hophal Perfect Strong Verb

הֻקְטַל

הָקְטַל

32.5   Hophal Imperfect. The Hophal Imperfect is formed with Imperfect preformatives, the verbal stem (with a Pathach stem vowel) and the Imperfect sufformatives. Like the Perfect above, the Imperfect

---

awkwardness of this translation and those for the other Hophal conjugations below. Nevertheless, in the interest of consistency, it is preferable to retain the paradigm verb קַטַל to illustrate the Hophal patterns. It is also helpful for the beginning student to retain the nuance of causation in these Hophal translations. Oftentimes, however, Hophal translations will not preserve the "cause to" value as in הָשְׁלַךְ, meaning "he was cast down."

preformative vowel is variable between Qibbuts and Qamets Hatuf. Translate the Hophal Imperfect passively with a form of the verb "to be" as in "he will cause to *be* killed."

	Hophal u-class	Hophal o-class	Translation
3ms	יָקְטַל	יָקְטַל	he will cause to be killed
3fs	תָּקְטַל	תָּקְטַל	she will cause to be killed
2ms	תָּקְטַל	תָּקְטַל	you will cause to be killed
2fs	תָּקְטְלִי	תָּקְטְלִי	you will cause to be killed
1cs	אָקְטַל	אָקְטַל	I will cause to be killed
3mp	יָקְטְלוּ	יָקְטְלוּ	they will cause to be killed
3fp	תָּקְטַלְנָה	תָּקְטַלְנָה	they will cause to be killed
2mp	תָּקְטְלוּ	תָּקְטְלוּ	you will cause to be killed
2fp	תָּקְטַלְנָה	תָּקְטַלְנָה	you will cause to be killed
1cp	נָקְטַל	נָקְטַל	we will cause to be killed

32.6 Hophal Imperfect Diagnostics.

1. Qibbuts preformative vowel (u-class) as in יָקְטַל or Qamets Hatuf preformative vowel (o-class) as in יָקְטַל in their respective paradigms.

2. Pathach stem vowel in both classes, except in those forms with sufformatives that consist of a vowel (2fs, 3mp, 2mp).

Hophal Imperfect
Strong Verb
יָקְטַל
יָקְטַל

32.7 Hophal Participle. The Hophal Participle is formed with the Participle prefix (מ), the verbal stem (with Qamets stem vowel) and the inflectional endings of the Participle. Once again, both prefix vowels, Qibbuts and

Qamets Hatuf, are attested in the Participle. Translate the Hophal
Participle passively with a form of the verb "to be" as in "causing to *be*
killed."

	Hophal u-class	Hophal o-class
ms	מָקְטָל	מֻקְטָל
fs	מָקְטֶלֶת	מֻקְטֶלֶת
mp	מָקְטָלִים	מֻקְטָלִים
fp	מָקְטָלוֹת	מֻקְטָלוֹת

32.8   Hophal Participle Diagnostics.

1. מָ or מֻ prefix. You will recall that the Piel, Pual, Hiphil and
   Hophal Participles have a מ prefix. The Piel and Pual have a
   Vocal Shewa under the prefix (מְ). The Hiphil has a Pathach
   under the prefix (מַ).

2. Qamets stem vowel in every form with the exception of the
   feminine singular.

Hophal Participle
Strong Verb

32.9   Summary.

1. The Hophal stem is used to express *causative* action with a *passive*
   voice. In most of its occurrences, the Hophal is the passive of
   the Hiphil.

2. The Hophal conjugations are distinguished from other derived
   stem conjugations by their prefix or preformative vowels, Qibbuts
   or Qamets Hatuf. It is perhaps best to think of the Hophal prefix
   vowels in terms of vowel class rather than particular vowels. As
   such, you should learn that the Hophal prefix vowel is variable
   between u-class and o-class vowels. With u-class vowels, Qibbuts

appears most frequently but Shureq also occurs in many weak verbs. With o-class vowels, Qamets Hatuf occurs most frequently but Holem and Holem Waw also appear. Thinking of the Hophal prefix vowel in terms of vowel classes will prevent confusion when you encounter variation, especially in the weak verb forms.

3. In the Perfect and Imperfect conjugations, the stem vowel is Pathach, except in those forms with sufformatives that begin with or consist of a vowel. In the Participle, the stem vowel is Qamets, except in the feminine singular.

Hophal Stem - Strong Verbs

Perfect u-class	Perfect o-class	Imperfect u-class	Imperfect o-class	Participle u-class	Participle o-class
הֻקְטַל	הָקְטַל	יֻקְטַל	יָקְטַל	מֻקְטָל	מָקְטָל
הֻקְטַל	הָקְטַל	יֻקְטַל	יָקְטַל	מֻקְטָל	מָקְטָל
הֻקְטְלָה	הָקְטְלָה	תֻּקְטַל	תָּקְטַל	מֻקְטֶלֶת	מָקְטֶלֶת
הֻקְטַלְתָּ	הָקְטַלְתָּ	תֻּקְטַל	תָּקְטַל	מֻקְטָלִים	מָקְטָלִים
הֻקְטַלְתְּ	הָקְטַלְתְּ	תֻּקְטְלִי	תָּקְטְלִי	מֻקְטָלוֹת	מָקְטָלוֹת
הֻקְטַלְתִּי	הָקְטַלְתִּי	אֻקְטַל	אָקְטַל		
הֻקְטְלוּ	הָקְטְלוּ	יֻקְטְלוּ	יָקְטְלוּ		
הֻקְטַלְתֶּם	הָקְטַלְתֶּם	תֻּקְטַלְנָה	תָּקְטַלְנָה		
הֻקְטַלְתֶּן	הָקְטַלְתֶּן	תֻּקְטְלוּ	תָּקְטְלוּ		
הֻקְטַלְנוּ	הָקְטַלְנוּ	תֻּקְטַלְנָה	תָּקְטַלְנָה		
		נֻקְטַל	נָקְטַל		

32.10 Vocabulary.

Nouns

צוּר	rock, boulder (76)
קֶשֶׁת	bow (weapon), rainbow (76); feminine
קֶרֶן	horn (76); feminine
אֶרֶז	cedar (73)

32.11 A Word Is Worth a Thousand Pictures. One of the great benefits of learning to read biblical Hebrew is that you will be able to do "word studies" in the original language in order to determine precisely what a given term means in a particular passage. Although many wonderful English translations are available, doing your own word studies on key terms in a passage often provides you with tremendous insight into a text's meaning that cannot be gained from the English alone. In the context of Ps 137:1-9, let's look at verses 5-6 as an example.

> 5 If I forget you, O Jerusalem, may my right hand wither.
> 6 May my tongue cling to the roof of my mouth,
> if I do not remember you,
> if I do not exalt Jerusalem above my chief joy.

What does it mean to "forget" Jerusalem? Why do many English translations render verse 5b as "may my right hand *forget its skill*" and why does the author refer to malfunctioning body parts in verses 5-6? A word study on שָׁכַח (to forget) reveals that while this term can mean simply a temporary or permanent lapse of memory, it can also refer to abandonment. Biblically, to forget God is to abandon him (Isa 49:14), to pervert one's ways (Jer 3:21) and to commit idolatry (Judg 3:7; Deut 4:23; Ps 44:17). In essence, to forget God is to break the covenant (for example, see Deut 8:2). This is precisely what is meant in verse 5. To forget Jerusalem would be to assimilate into Babylonian culture into which Judah had been exiled and to adopt her pagan religion.

Secondly, why do many English translations render verse 5b as "may my right hand forget its skill" rather than "may my right hand wither" as it has been translated above? This is where knowing Hebrew is particularly useful. The text of verse 5b reads תִּשְׁכַּח יְמִינִי with the verb שָׁכַח (to forget). Some argue, however, that a scribal mistake known as "graphic confusion" occurred, where כָּחַשׁ (to grow lean, wither) was mistaken for the previous verb in verse 5, שָׁכַח (to forget), and that the original text actually read תִּכְחַשׁ יְמִינִי ("may my right hand grow lean" or "may my right hand wither"). The Greek version of the Old Testament, the Septuagint, also attests to the confusion by rendering the active Hebrew verb with a passive Greek verb. How is one to determine the correct reading? One possible interpretation, and the one followed here, is based upon the context of Ps 137:5-6 and the author's reference to a malfunctioning tongue as a consequence of "forgetting" Jerusalem. Again, a brief word study on terms in the Old Testament, not only for "tongue" but also for body parts generally (eye, ear, tongue, hand, nose, etc.), demonstrates that mute tongues, dim eyes, deaf ears and withering hands are often linked to idol worship! This is the message of Ps 115:4-8.

4   Their idols are silver and gold,
    The work of man's hands.
5   They have mouths, but they cannot speak;
    They have eyes, but they cannot see;
6   They have ears, but they cannot hear;
    They have noses, but they cannot smell;
7   They have hands, but they cannot feel;
    They have feet, but they cannot walk;
    They cannot make a sound with their throat.
8   Those who make them will become like them,
    Everyone who trusts in them. (NASB)

The operative principle here is that you are what you worship! Thus the translation, "may my right hand wither" in Ps 137:5 better fits the context of idolatry in Ps 137. It also complements the following verse "may my tongue cling to the roof of my mouth," with which it stands in parallel. In other words, the psalmist is saying, "may I become like an immobile and mute idol if I worship one ever again!" While much can be learned by reading Ps 137 in English, without a knowledge of biblical Hebrew, textual problems like the one above cannot be examined. Additionally, by studying the text in English only, the reader may fail to see the connections between malfunctioning body parts and idolatry and, therefore, miss the force of the author's message.

Catherine Beckerleg
Ph.D. candidate
Harvard University
Cambridge, Massachusetts

32.12 **Advanced Information: Verbal Hendiadys**. Hebrew can express a single concept or idea by using two independent words that are connected by the conjunction וְ (and). An example of this type of construction in English is the expression "nice and warm" to communicate the single idea of extreme comfort. This coordination of two independent words with the conjunction is called *hendiadys*.[4] It is especially common with verbs as the following examples illustrate.

וּמִהַרְתֶּם וְהוֹרַדְתֶּם אֶת־אָבִי הֵנָּה

And you will *quickly (soon) bring* my
father *down* here (Gen 45:13).

The coordination in the above example is with the verbs מָהַר (Piel: to do something quickly or in a hurry) and יָרַד (Hiphil: to bring down).

וַיּוֹסִפוּ עוֹד שְׂנֹא אֹתוֹ

And they *hated* him even *more* (Gen 37:5).

In the above example, the two verbs יָסַף (Hiphil: to increase, enhance) and שָׂנֵא (to hate) are linked.

וַיְמַהֲרוּ וַיַּשְׁכִּימוּ וַיֵּצְאוּ אַנְשֵׁי־הָעִיר לִקְרַאת־יִשְׂרָאֵל לַמִּלְחָמָה

The men of the city *went out quickly, early in the morning,*
to meet Israel in battle (Josh 8:14).

In this example, the coordination is with the three verbs מָהַר (Piel: to do something quickly or in a hurry), שָׁכַם (Hiphil: to arise or do something early) and יָצָא (to go out).

---

[4] This is a Greek term meaning "one (ἕν) through (διά) two (δύο)," that is, the expression of one idea through two words.

וַיֹּאכַל וַיֵּשְׁתְּ וַיָּשָׁב וַיִּשְׁכָּב

And he ate and he drank and (then) he *lay*
down again (1 Kgs 19:6).

The last two verbs in this example are coordinated with the conjunction:
שׁוּב (to do something again) and שָׁכַב (to lay down).

In each of the above examples, the verbs are not translated independently
but are coordinated in translation with the use of an adverb (quickly,
more, again). In these constructions, the second verb usually expresses
the main idea with the first verb translated adverbially. Verbs commonly
used in this type of construction include:

מָהַר	to do something quickly (Piel)
יָסַף	to do something again, increase (Hiphil)
שׁוּב	to do something again (Qal)
שָׁכַם	to do something early (Hiphil)
רָבָה	to do something many times (Hiphil)

Chapter 33

The Hophal Stem - Weak Verbs

33.1   **Introduction.** The weak verb forms of the Hophal stem occur much more frequently than the strong verb forms. In fact, there are only about fifty Hophal strong verb forms in the Hebrew Bible, compared to about 250 weak verb forms. In spite of this fact, however, you must first master the strong verb diagnostics before studying Hophal weak verbs. Having memorized the strong verb diagnostics, you will be prepared to understand the weak verb variations of the Hophal stem. Once again, due to the infrequency of certain forms, only the Perfect, Imperfect and Participle of selected weak verbs will be studied.

33.2   **I-Guttural Paradigms and Diagnostics.**

Perfect	*Imperfect*	*Participle*
הָעֳמַד	יָעֳמַד	מָעֳמָד
הָעֳמַד	יָעֳמַד	מָעֳמָד
הָעֳמְדָה	תָּעֳמַד	מָעֳמֶדֶת
הָעֳמַדְתָּ	תָּעֳמַד	מָעֳמָדִים
הָעֳמַדְתְּ	תָּעֳמְדִי	מָעֳמָדוֹת
הָעֳמַדְתִּי	אָעֳמַד	
הָעֳמְדוּ	יָעֳמְדוּ	
הָעֳמַדְתֶּם	תָּעֳמַדְנָה	
הָעֳמַדְתֶּן	תָּעֳמְדוּ	
הָעֳמַדְנוּ	תָּעֳמַדְנָה	
	נָעֳמַד	

33.3   **I-Guttural Notes.**

1. I-Guttural verbs in the Hophal stem prefer the Qamets Hatuf (o-class) prefix or preformative vowel. However, Qibbuts (u-class) is also attested (7 times).

376

2. I-Guttural verbs maintain all strong verb diagnostics. Based on your study of I-Guttural verbs in the Qal and other derived stems, the presence of a reduced vowel (Hateph Qamets) under the guttural in first root position is expected (see 16.8-9).

33.4 **III-ה Paradigms and Diagnostics.**

Perfect	Imperfect	Participle
הָגְלָה	יָגְלֶה	מָגְלֶה
הָגְלָה	יָגְלֶה	מָגְלֶה
הָגְלְתָה	תָּגְלֶה	מָגְלָה
הָגְלֵיתָ	תָּגְלֶה	מָגְלִים
הָגְלֵית	תָּגְלִי	מָגְלוֹת
הָגְלֵיתִי	אָגְלֶה	
הָגְלוּ	יָגְלוּ	
הָגְלֵיתֶם	תָּגְלֶינָה	
הָגְלֵיתֶן	תָּגְלוּ	
הָגְלֵינוּ	תָּגְלֶינָה	
	נָגְלֶה	

33.5 **III-ה Notes.**

1. Like I-Guttural verbs above, III-ה verbs in the Hophal stem prefer the o-class (Qamets Hatuf) prefix or preformative vowel.

2. Remember that the verbs of this weak class will drop the final ה in the Perfect, Imperfect and Participle. In those forms that do show a final ה, it is the *mater lectionis* and not the final consonant of the verbal root.

33.6   I-נ Paradigms and Diagnostics.

Perfect	Imperfect	Participle
הֻצַּל	יֻצַּל	מֻצָּל

הֻצַּל	יֻצַּל	מֻצָּל
הֻצְּלָה	תֻּצַּל	מֻצֶּלֶת
הֻצַּלְתָּ	תֻּצַּל	מֻצָּלִים
הֻצַּלְתְּ	תֻּצְּלִי	מֻצָּלוֹת
הֻצַּלְתִּי	אֻצַּל	
הֻצְּלוּ	יֻצְּלוּ	
הֻצַּלְתֶּם	תֻּצַּלְנָה	
הֻצַּלְתֶּן	תֻּצְּלוּ	
הֻצַּלְנוּ	תֻּצַּלְנָה	
	נֻצַּל	

33.7   I-נ Notes.

1. I-נ Hophal verbs prefer the u-class prefix or preformative vowel, Qibbuts.

2. In verbs of this weak class, the נ in first root position assimilates into the second root consonant and remains as a Daghesh Forte. With only two root consonants remaining, the Daghesh Forte is your clue for the identification of the I-נ verbal root.

33.8　I-' Paradigms and Diagnostics.

Perfect	*Imperfect*	*Participle*
הוּשַׁב	יוּשַׁב	**מוּשָׁב**
הוּשַׁב	יוּשַׁב	מוּשָׁב
הוּשְׁבָה	תּוּשַׁב	מוּשֶׁבֶת
הוּשַׁבְתָּ	תּוּשַׁב	מוּשָׁבִים
הוּשַׁבְתְּ	תּוּשְׁבִי	מוּשָׁבוֹת
הוּשַׁבְתִּי	אוּשַׁב	
הוּשְׁבוּ	יוּשְׁבוּ	
הוּשַׁבְתֶּם	תּוּשַׁבְנָה	
הוּשַׁבְתֶּן	תּוּשְׁבוּ	
הוּשַׁבְנוּ	תּוּשַׁבְנָה	
	נוּשַׁב	

33.9　I-' Notes.

1. The last three weak verb classes to be studied in the Hophal stem are I-', Biconsonantal and Geminate. Each of these weak verb types prefers the u-class vowel (frequently Shureq but sometimes Qibbuts) in the various conjugations of the Hophal. In the I-נ paradigms above, note that Shureq appears as the prefix or preformative vowel in each of the conjugations (see also 33.10 and 33.12 below).

2. Remember that most I-' verbs were originally I-ו. In the Hophal stem, the original ו reappears as the vowel letter Shureq (וּ) in the Perfect (הוּשַׁב), Imperfect (יוּשַׁב) and Participle (מוּשָׁב). Since only two root consonants remain, it is important that you are able to recognize the Shureq as diagnostic of the I-' class of verbs. You will recall from previous chapters that the original ו also reappears in the Niphal (25.10-11) and Hiphil (31.12-13) stems.

33.10 Biconsonantal Paradigms and Diagnostics.

Perfect	Imperfect	Participle
הוּקַם	יוּקַם	מוּקָם
הוּקַם	יוּקַם	מוּקָם
הוּקְמָה	תּוּקַם	מוּקֶמֶת
הוּקַ֫מְתָּ	תּוּקַם	מוּקָמִים
הוּקַמְתְּ	תּוּקְמִי	מוּקָמוֹת
הוּקַ֫מְתִּי	אוּקַם	
הוּקְמוּ	יוּקְמוּ	
הוּקַמְתֶּם	תּוּקַ֫מְנָה	
הוּקַמְתֶּן	תּוּקְמוּ	
הוּקַ֫מְנוּ	תּוּקַ֫מְנָה	
	נוּקַם	

33.11 Biconsonantal Notes.

1. Shureq prefix or preformative vowel in every form (33.9.1).

2. The medial vowel letters of the Biconsonantal verb classes do not appear in the Hophal stem. The Perfect and Imperfect have a Pathach stem vowel, except in those forms that have sufformatives that begin with or consist of a vowel. The Participle has the Qamets stem vowel, except in the feminine singular form.

33.12 Geminate Paradigms and Diagnostics.

Perfect	*Imperfect*	*Participle*
הוּסַב	יוּסַב	מוּסָב
הוּסַב	יוּסַב	מוּסָב
הוּסַבָּה	תּוּסַב	מוּסֶבֶת
הוּסַבּוֹת	תּוּסַב	מוּסַבִּים
הוּסַבּוֹת	תּוּסַבִּי	מוּסַבּוֹת
הוּסַבּוֹתִי	אוּסַב	
הוּסַבּוּ	יוּסַבּוּ	
הוּסַבּוֹתֶם	תּוּסַבֶּינָה	
הוּסַבּוֹתֶן	תּוּסַבּוּ	
הוּסַבּוֹנוּ	תּוּסַבֶּינָה	
	נוּסַב	

33.13 Geminate Notes.

1. Shureq prefix or preformative vowel in every form (33.9.1), though some Geminate forms do show a Qibbuts prefix vowel.

2. With the Hophal forms of this weak class, only two root consonants are present because only one Geminate consonant is preserved. In some forms, however, the Daghesh Forte in the remaining Geminate consonant will aid in your identification of this weak verbal root. Additionally, the Holem Waw connecting vowel in the Perfect is another indicator of the Geminate class (14.10-11).

33.14 Summary: Hophal Diagnostics.

In the following summary chart, observe that five weak verb classes preserve only two root consonants. With III-ה verbs, the final ה is lost. With I-נ verbs, the נ assimilates into the second root consonant and remains as a Daghesh Forte. With I-י verbs (originally I-ו), the vowel letter Shureq replaces the י as the prefix or preformative vowel in the Perfect, Imperfect and Participle. With Geminate verbs, only one Geminate consonant is preserved, though it is represented as a Daghesh Forte in some forms. With Biconsonantal verbs, both root consonants remain and the prefix or preformative vowel is Shureq in every form of the Perfect, Imperfect and Participle.

	Perfect	*Imperfect*	*Participle*
Strong (u-class)	הָקְטַל	יָקְטַל	מָקְטָל
Strong (o-class)	הָקְטַל	יָקְטַל	מָקְטָל
I-Guttural	הָעֳמַד	יָעֳמַד	מָעֳמָד
III-ה	הָגְלָה	יָגְלֶה	מָגְלֶה
I-נ	הֻצַּל	יֻצַּל	מֻצָּל
I-י	הוּשַׁב	יוּשַׁב	מוּשָׁב
Biconsonantal	הוּקַם	יוּקַם	מוּקָם
Geminate	הוּסַב	יוּסַב	מוּסָב

33.15 Vocabulary.

בֶּטֶן	belly, womb (72); feminine
הֶבֶל	breath, vanity, idol (73)
הֶרְפָּה	reproach, disgrace (73)
מִזְרָח	sunrise, east (74)

33.16 Elijah's Destination in Sinai. In the prophet's despondency, Elijah ran away from Queen Jezebel to Beersheba (1 Kgs 19:1-3). In the nearby wilderness, he was ministered to by the angel of the Lord and fortified for the journey to Mt. Sinai or Horeb. In 1 Kgs 19:9 we read:

וַיָּבֹא־שָׁם אֶל־הַמְּעָרָה וַיָּלֶן שָׁם

And there he went into *the* cave and spent the night.

But no cave has been mentioned in this immediate context, so why does the Hebrew text use the article and the English translators use only "a" cave? The reason is because the article can be used to reflect a person or thing previously mentioned. But how far back can we extend that rule, since there is no cave mentioned previously in this context? So why does the biblical writer use the article here?

Elijah had journeyed to Mt. Sinai or Horeb, where Moses had also met the Lord. The context for Moses' encounter with God on Mt. Sinai is far removed from 1 Kgs 19, but in Ex 33:21-22, the Lord told Moses that "There is a place near me where you may stand on a rock. When my glory passes by [בַּעֲבֹר כְּבֹדִי], I will put you in a cleft in the rock." Even though the word "cave" (הַמְּעָרָה "the cave") does not appear in the Exodus passage, what makes the 1 Kgs 19 reference to this passage in Exodus certain is the similar phraseology used in 1 Kgs 19:11 ("the Lord is about to pass by" with the verb עֹבֵר as in Ex 33:22 above). There is a similar allusion in Ex 33:19 ("I will cause all of my goodness to pass in front of you" with the verb אַעֲבִיר). The expressions are rather unique in both places (1 Kgs 19 and Ex 33) and thus become markers of similar contexts.

For other cases of the article indicating a previous reference, but not as far removed, see Num 11:25b-26; 1 Kgs 19:11; Ezek 1:12, 20; 37:9-10.

Walter C. Kaiser, Jr.
President
Colman M. Mockler Distinguished Professor of Old Testament
Gordon-Conwell Theological Seminary
South Hamilton, Massachusetts

Chapter 34

The Hithpael Stem - Strong Verbs

34.1 **Introduction.** The Hithpael is the easiest of the derived stems to recognize because of the distinctive preformatives and prefixes in each of the conjugations.[1] The diagnostic features of the Hithpael stem include: (1) a distinctive prefix in all of the conjugations (for example, הִתְ in the Perfect); (2) Pathach under the first consonant of the verbal root; and (3) Daghesh Forte in the second consonant of the verbal root. With expected variations, these diagnostic features appear in every conjugation of the Hithpael strong verb. At this point, it is helpful to recall that Piel, Pual and Hithpael verbs have a Daghesh Forte in the second consonant of the verbal root.

34.2 **The Meaning of the Hithpael Stem.**

1. The Hithpael stem is used to express an *intensive* type of action with a *reflexive* voice. The reflexive voice is used when the subject of the verb performs the verbal action upon itself. For example, the verb קָדַשׁ means "he was holy" in the Qal. The Hithpael form is הִתְקַדַּשׁ and it means "he sanctified *himself*." Notice how the reflexive pronoun "himself" is used to render the reflexive nuance of the Hithpael. Other examples of English reflexive pronouns include: (singular) herself, yourself, myself and (plural) themselves, yourselves, ourselves. When translating Hithpael verbs with a reflexive nuance, the verbal subject and the reflexive pronoun must agree in both gender and number. In addition to the reflexive nuance, the Hithpael stem may also express the reciprocal or iterative types of action.

2. *Reciprocal.* This type of action expresses the notion of reciprocity. For example, "they looked *at each other*" is an illustration of

---

[1] The Hithpael stem occurs 984 times in the Hebrew Bible. It appears in the Perfect 161 times, Imperfect 491 times, Imperative 78 times, Infinitive Construct 104 times, Infinitive Absolute 3 times and Participle 147 times.

reciprocal action. The notion of "at each other" indicates that the action of looking by one party was returned or reciprocated by the other party.

הִתְרָאוּ they looked *at each other*
(Hithpael Perfect 3cp from רָאָה)

הִתְקַשְׁרוּ they conspired *with each other*
(Hithpael Perfect 3cp from קָשַׁר)

3. *Iterative.* The iterative expresses the notion of repeated action. For example, "he walked *back and forth*" is an illustration of iterative action. The notion of "back and forth" expresses the fact that the action of the verb occurred repeatedly.

הִתְהַלֵּךְ he walked *back and forth*
(Hithpael Perfect 3ms from הָלַךְ)

הִתְהַפֵּךְ he turned *this way and that*
(Hithpael Perfect 3ms from הָפַךְ)

4. It must also be noted that the Hithpael, in some instances, is translated just like the Qal, simple action with an active voice.

הִתְפַּלֵּל he prayed
(Hithpael Perfect 3ms from פָּלַל)

הִתְיַצֵּב he stood firm
(Hithpael Perfect 3ms from יָצַב)

34.3 **Hithpael Perfect**. The Hithpael Perfect is formed with the Hithpael prefix (הִת), the verbal stem (with a Daghesh Forte in the second root consonant) and the Perfect sufformatives.

	Qal	Hithpael	Translation
3ms	קָטַל	הִתְקַטֵּל	he killed himself[2]
3fs	קָטְלָה	הִתְקַטְּלָה	she killed herself
2ms	קָטַֽלְתָּ	הִתְקַטַּֽלְתָּ	you killed yourself
2fs	קָטַלְתְּ	הִתְקַטַּלְתְּ	you killed yourself
1cs	קָטַֽלְתִּי	הִתְקַטַּֽלְתִּי	I killed myself
3cp	קָטְלוּ	הִתְקַטְּלוּ	they killed themselves
2mp	קְטַלְתֶּם	הִתְקַטַּלְתֶּם	you killed yourselves
2fp	קְטַלְתֶּן	הִתְקַטַּלְתֶּן	you killed yourselves
1cp	קָטַֽלְנוּ	הִתְקַטַּֽלְנוּ	we killed ourselves

34.4 **Hithpael Perfect Diagnostics**.

1. הִת prefix in every form. This prefix is hard to miss and makes identification of the Hithpael Perfect an easy matter.

2. Pathach under the first consonant of the verbal root.

3. Daghesh Forte in the second consonant of the verbal root.

Hithpael Perfect Strong Verb

הִתְקַטֵּל

34.5 **Hithpael Imperfect**. The Hithpael Imperfect is formed with the Hithpael Imperfect preformatives (נִת/אֶת/תִּת/יִת), the verbal stem (with a Daghesh Forte in the second root consonant) and the Imperfect sufformatives.

---

[2] The rationale for preserving the paradigm verb קָטַל (despite the awkward translations) has been explained in sections 30.3 and 32.3.

	Qal	Hithpael	Translation
3ms	יִקְטֹל	יִתְקַטֵּל	he will kill himself
3fs	תִּקְטֹל	תִּתְקַטֵּל	she will kill herself
2ms	תִּקְטֹל	תִּתְקַטֵּל	you will kill yourself
2fs	תִּקְטְלִי	תִּתְקַטְּלִי	you will kill yourself
1cs	אֶקְטֹל	אֶתְקַטֵּל	I will kill myself
3mp	יִקְטְלוּ	יִתְקַטְּלוּ	they will kill themselves
3fp	תִּקְטֹלְנָה	תִּתְקַטֵּלְנָה	they will kill themselves
2mp	תִּקְטְלוּ	תִּתְקַטְּלוּ	you will kill yourselves
2fp	תִּקְטֹלְנָה	תִּתְקַטֵּלְנָה	you will kill yourselves
1cp	נִקְטֹל	נִתְקַטֵּל	we will kill ourselves

34.6 **Hithpael Imperfect Diagnostics**.

1. The preformatives for the Imperfect are יִתְ, תִּתְ, אֶתְ and נִתְ. These Hithpael Imperfect preformatives are unique and easy to identify.

2. Pathach under the first consonant of the verbal root.

3. Daghesh Forte in the second consonant of the verbal root.

Hithpael Imperfect Strong Verb

יִתְקַטֵּל

34.7 **Hithpael Imperative**. The Hithpael Imperative, Infinitive Construct and Infinitive Absolute may be studied together because the diagnostics for these three forms are identical (הִתְקַטֵּל). In fact, their diagnostics are the same as those for the Hithpael Perfect. Because the spelling of these four basic forms is identical, you will need to rely upon context for correct identification. The Hithpael Imperative is formed with the Hithpael prefix (הִתְ), the verbal stem (with a Daghesh Forte in the second root consonant) and the Imperative suffformatives.

	Qal	*Hithpael*	*Translation*
2ms	קְטֹל	הִתְקַטֵּל	kill yourself!
2fs	קִטְלִי	הִתְקַטְּלִי	kill yourself!
2mp	קִטְלוּ	הִתְקַטְּלוּ	kill yourselves!
2fp	קְטֹלְנָה	הִתְקַטֵּלְנָה	kill yourselves!

34.8 **Hithpael Infinitive Construct and Infinitive Absolute.**[3] The Infinitive Construct and Infinitive Absolute are identical (הִתְקַטֵּל) and are formed with the Hithpael prefix (הִת) and the verbal stem (with a Daghesh Forte in the second root consonant).

34.9 **Hithpael Imperative, Infinitive Construct and Infinitive Absolute Diagnostics.** As noted above, these same diagnostic features are also present in the Hithpael Perfect.

    1. הִת prefix in every form.

    2. Pathach under the first consonant of the verbal root.

    3. Daghesh Forte in the second consonant of the verbal root.

Hithpael Imperative, Infinitive Construct and Absolute

הִתְקַטֵּל

34.10 **Hithpael Participle.** The Hithpael Participle is formed with the Hithpael Participle prefix (מִת), the verbal stem (with a Daghesh Forte in the second root consonant) and the inflectional endings of the Participle.

	Qal	*Hithpael*
ms	קֹטֵל	מִתְקַטֵּל
fs	קֹטֶלֶת	מִתְקַטֶּלֶת
mp	קֹטְלִים	מִתְקַטְּלִים
fp	קֹטְלוֹת	מִתְקַטְּלוֹת

---

[3] The Hithpael Infinitive Absolute appears only three times in the Hebrew Bible.

34.11 Hithpael Participle Diagnostics.

1. מִתְ prefix in every form. This unique prefix makes identification of the Hithpael Participle an easy matter.

2. Pathach under the first consonant of the verbal root.

3. Daghesh Forte in the second consonant of the verbal root.

*Hithpael Participle
Strong Verb*

מִתְקַטֵּל

34.12 Metathesis. It has been emphasized that the Hithpael stem is easy to recognize with few exceptions. For the most part, these exceptions are occasioned by a phenomenon known as metathesis. *Metathesis* is a term used to describe *the transposition of two contiguous (side-by-side) consonants* in order to smooth out a word's pronunciation. In Hebrew, whenever the ת of the Hithpael prefix or preformative precedes verbal roots beginning with ס, שׁ, שׂ or צ (sibilant or "s" sound consonants), the two consonants will switch places. For example, we would expect the Hithpael Perfect 3ms form of שָׁמַר to be הִתְשַׁמֵּר. Because of metathesis, however, the Hithpael Perfect 3ms form of שָׁמַר is הִשְׁתַּמֵּר. Notice how the ת of the Hithpael prefix has switched places with the שׁ of the verbal root. Once again, this switching of the two consonants is called metathesis. You will need to be familiar with this phenomenon in order to correctly reconstruct the verbal root in those verbs in which metathesis occurs. Note the following additional examples.

סָתַר	he hid	הִסְתַּתֵּר	he hid himself
שָׂכַר	he hired	הִשְׂתַּכֵּר	he hired himself (earned wages)
צָדֵק	he is just	הִצְטַדֵּק[4]	he justified himself

---

[4] When the first consonant of the verbal root is צ (3 times), the ת of the Hithpael prefix will switch places with the first consonant of the verbal root. Additionally, the ת of the Hithpael prefix will change to ט (הִצְטַדֵּק ≻ הִתְצַדֵּק).

34.13 Assimilation of ת. When the first consonant of a verbal root is ז, ד, ט or ת, the ת of the Hithpael preformative or prefix will assimilate into the first consonant of the verbal root and remain as a Daghesh Forte.

דָּבַר he spoke   הִדַּבֵּר he spoke with

טָמֵא he was unclean   הִטַּמֵּא he became unclean

34.14 Summary.

1. In every form of every Hithpael strong verb conjugation, there is a Pathach under the first consonant of the verbal root and a Daghesh Forte in the second consonant of the verbal root. In the Perfect, Imperative, Infinitive Construct and Infinitive Absolute, the prefix is הִת. The preformatives for the Imperfect are יִת, תִּת, אֶת or נִת and the prefix for the Participle is מִת. These distinctive preformatives and prefixes make the Hithpael stem easy to identify with most verbs.

2. *Metathesis* is a term used to describe the transposition of two contiguous (side-by-side) consonants in order to smooth out a word's pronunciation. Whenever the ת of a Hithpael prefix or preformative precedes verbal roots beginning with ס, שׁ, שׂ or צ (sibilant or "s" sound consonants), the two consonants will switch places. Additionally, with ז, ד, ט or ת, the ת of the Hithpael preformative or prefix will assimilate into the first consonant of the verbal root and remain as a Daghesh Forte.

Hithpael Stem - Strong Verb

Perfect	Imperfect	Imperative	Infinitive Construct	Infinitive Absolute	Participle
הִתְקַטֵּל	יִתְקַטֵּל	הִתְקַטֵּל	הִתְקַטֵּל	הִתְקַטֵּל	מִתְקַטֵּל
הִתְקַטֵּל	יִתְקַטֵּל	הִתְקַטֵּל	הִתְקַטֵּל	הִתְקַטֵּל	מִתְקַטֵּל
הִתְקַטְּלָה	תִּתְקַטֵּל	הִתְקַטְּלִי			מִתְקַטֶּלֶת
הִתְקַטַּ֫לְתָּ	תִּתְקַטֵּל	הִתְקַטְּלוּ			מִתְקַטְּלִים
הִתְקַטַּלְתְּ	תִּתְקַטְּלִי	הִתְקַטֵּ֫לְנָה			מִתְקַטְּלוֹת
הִתְקַטַּ֫לְתִּי	אֶתְקַטֵּל				
הִתְקַטְּלוּ	יִתְקַטְּלוּ				
הִתְקַטַּלְתֶּם	תִּתְקַטֵּ֫לְנָה				
הִתְקַטַּלְתֶּן	תִּתְקַטְּלוּ				
הִתְקַטַּ֫לְנוּ	תִּתְקַטֵּ֫לְנָה				
	נִתְקַטֵּל				

34.15 Vocabulary.

פָּלַל	(Hithpael) to pray (84)
מִקְדָּשׁ	sanctuary (75)
עֵז	goat (74)
קִיר	wall (73)
שׁוֹפָר	ram's horn, trumpet (72)
עוֹף	flying creatures, fowl, insects (71)

34.16 In The Lord His God. Prepositional phrases can sometimes provide important information. In the Amalekite raid against David's town of Ziklag in 1 Sam 30, the prepositional phrase in verse 6, בַּיהוָה אֱלֹהָיו (in the Lord his God), may serve as an illustration.

The attack against Ziklag has left David and his band of men in complete despair. The settlement is destroyed and their possessions are gone but, more devastatingly, wives and children have been taken captive.

Matters get worse as David's band of discontented wanderers (1 Sam 22:2) turn against him and are ready to stone him. David has been in tight spots before, but now the end seems imminent. However, this climactic catalogue of misfortune is abruptly interrupted by the declaration, "but David strengthened himself *in the Lord his God*" (30:6). We are not told specifically how David regained control of his troops but this sentence may be regarded as the turning point of the narrative. Hereafter, David gradually gains the initiative and eventually recovers completely from his loss (30:18).

The verb חָזַק (Hithpael, "to strengthen oneself") has for a general range of meaning "political strength," "military strength" or "courage." In 1 Sam 30:6, the definition "courage" seems to fit the context best. The phrase יְהוָה plus אֱלֹהִים plus pronominal suffix is quite common in the Hebrew Bible and occurs frequently in the covenantal context of Deuteronomy. The frequency drops significantly, however, when the phrase is found in association with a preposition. With the preposition בְּ, it is attested either in a positive context: "Believe in the Lord your God" (בַּיהוָה אֱלֹהֵיכֶם [2 Chr 20:20]) or negative: "Against the Lord your God you have transgressed" (בַּיהוָה אֱלֹהָיִךְ [Jer 3:13]).

1 Sam 30:6 is noteworthy because it is the only instance where the verb, "to strengthen oneself" is modified by the phrase "in the Lord his God." By way of contrast, even close parallels fail to convey the same relationship between the verb and the prepositional phrase. Solomon "strengthened himself [חָזַק in the Hithpael] with regard to his kingdom, and the Lord his God was with him" (2 Chr 2:1). And, Jonathan "strengthened [חָזַק in the Piel] his hand in God" (1 Sam 23:16). Thus it seems "in the Lord his God" takes on an important function. It determines precisely the nature of the strength that David found: it was not a martial courage found deep within himself; it was not a regaining of emotional composure; instead, it was a personal courage grounded in covenantal trust and loyalty to his God.

Tom Petter
Ph.D. candidate
University of Toronto
Toronto, Canada

Chapter 35

The Hithpael Stem - Weak Verbs

35.1 **Introduction.** In this chapter, we will study selected weak verb classes (Geminate, III-ה and II-Guttural) in the Hithpael stem. It is important to observe that most of the strong verb diagnostics are retained in Geminate and III-ה verbs. It is only the II-Guttural class of weak verbs that exhibit significant variation from the strong verb diagnostics. This variation is due to the fact that the guttural in second root position cannot take the Daghesh Forte of the Hithpael stem. Your study of II-Guttural verbs in the Piel (27.7-11) and Pual (29.5-9) will have prepared you for this study of Hithpael II-Guttural verbs.

35.2 **Geminate Paradigms and Diagnostics.**

Perfect	Imperfect	Imperative	Infinitive Construct	Infinitive Absolute	Participle
הִתְפַּלֵּל	יִתְפַּלֵּל	הִתְפַּלֵּל	הִתְפַּלֵּל	הִתְפַּלֵּל	מִתְפַּלֵּל
הִתְפַּלֵּל	יִתְפַּלֵּל	הִתְפַּלֵּל	הִתְפַּלֵּל	הִתְפַּלֵּל	מִתְפַּלֵּל
הִתְפַּלְלָה	תִּתְפַּלֵּל	הִתְפַּלְלִי			מִתְפַּלֶּלֶת
הִתְפַּלַּלְתָּ	תִּתְפַּלֵּל	הִתְפַּלְלוּ			מִתְפַּלְלִים
הִתְפַּלַּלְתְּ	תִּתְפַּלְלִי	הִתְפַּלֵּלְנָה			מִתְפַּלְלוֹת
הִתְפַּלַּלְתִּי	אֶתְפַּלֵּל				
הִתְפַּלְלוּ	יִתְפַּלְלוּ				
הִתְפַּלַּלְתֶּם	תִּתְפַּלֵּלְנָה				
הִתְפַּלַּלְתֶּן	תִּתְפַּלְלוּ				
הִתְפַּלַּלְנוּ	תִּתְפַּלֵּלְנָה				
	נִתְפַּלֵּל				

35.3   Geminate Notes.

1. Most Geminate verbs retain all of the Hithpael strong verb diagnostics.

2. With the Geminate verb פָּלַל (to pray), however, there is one minor exception. Note that the Daghesh Forte in the second consonant of the verbal root may be given up when this consonant is followed by Shewa as in the Perfect 3cp (הִתְפַּלְלוּ). In light of the fact that all other strong verb diagnostics are retained, this minor variation should not present any significant difficulty.

35.4   III-ה Paradigms and Diagnostics.

Perfect	Imperfect	Imperative	Infinitive Construct	Infinitive Absolute	Participle
הִתְגַּלָּה	יִתְגַּלֶּה	הִתְגַּלֵּה	הִתְגַּלּוֹת		מִתְגַּלֶּה
הִתְגַּלָּה	יִתְגַּלֶּה	הִתְגַּלֵּה	הִתְגַּלּוֹת		מִתְגַּלֶּה
הִתְגַּלְּתָה	תִּתְגַּלֶּה	הִתְגַּלִּי			מִתְגַּלָּה
הִתְגַּלִּיתָ	תִּתְגַּלֶּה	הִתְגַּלּוּ			מִתְגַּלִּים
הִתְגַּלִּית	תִּתְגַּלִּי	הִתְגַּלֶּינָה			מִתְגַּלּוֹת
הִתְגַּלִּיתִי	אֶתְגַּלֶּה				
הִתְגַּלּוּ	יִתְגַּלּוּ				
הִתְגַּלִּיתֶם	תִּתְגַּלֶּינָה				
הִתְגַּלִּיתֶן	תִּתְגַּלּוּ				
הִתְגַּלִּינוּ	תִּתְגַּלֶּינָה				
	נִתְגַּלֶּה				

35.5   III-ה Notes.

1. All of the strong verb diagnostics are retained in the Hithpael forms of this weak verb class.

2. The endings that are present on these III-ה Hithpael conjugations are precisely the same ones that were seen on the Qal and all of the other derived stems previously studied. See the summary of endings on III-ה verbs, located in the appendix of the grammar

(page 445) and, in color, on the CD-ROM.

35.6 **II-Guttural Paradigms and Diagnostics: Virtual Doubling.** You know that a Daghesh Forte in the second consonant of the verbal root is a diagnostic feature of the Piel, Pual and Hithpael. A guttural in second root position, however, will reject this Daghesh Forte. In your study of Piel and Pual II-Guttural verbs, you learned that the guttural's rejection of the Daghesh Forte results in either virtual doubling or compensatory lengthening. Hithpael II-Guttural verbs respond in the same way. The following II-Guttural verb exhibits virtual doubling.

Perfect	Imperfect	Imperative	Infinitive Construct	Infinitive Absolute	Participle
הִתְנַחֵם	יִתְנַחֵם	הִתְנַחֵם	הִתְנַחֵם	הִתְנַחֵם	מִתְנַחֵם
הִתְנַחֵם	יִתְנַחֵם	הִתְנַחֵם	הִתְנַחֵם	הִתְנַחֵם	מִתְנַחֵם
הִתְנַחֲמָה	תִּתְנַחֵם	הִתְנַחֲמִי			מִתְנַחֶמֶת
הִתְנַחַמְתָּ	תִּתְנַחֵם	הִתְנַחֲמוּ			מִתְנַחֲמִים
הִתְנַחַמְתְּ	תִּתְנַחֲמִי	הִתְנַחֵמְנָה			מִתְנַחֲמוֹת
הִתְנַחַמְתִּי	אֶתְנַחֵם				
הִתְנַחֲמוּ	יִתְנַחֲמוּ				
הִתְנַחַמְתֶּם	תִּתְנַחֵמְנָה				
הִתְנַחַמְתֶּן	תִּתְנַחֲמוּ				
הִתְנַחַמְנוּ	תִּתְנַחֵמְנָה				
	נִתְנַחֵם				

35.7 **II-Guttural Notes: Virtual Doubling.**

1. With the exception of the Daghesh Forte in the second consonant of the verbal root, all of the other strong verb diagnostics are retained.

2. The guttural consonant in second root position rejects the Daghesh Forte of the Hithpael stem. II-Guttural verbs with virtual doubling retain the diagnostic Pathach under the first root consonant.

35.8   II-Guttural Paradigms and Diagnostics: Compensatory Lengthening.

Perfect	Imperfect	Imperative	Infinitive Construct	Infinitive Absolute	Participle
הִתְבָּרֵךְ	יִתְבָּרֵךְ	הִתְבָּרֵךְ	הִתְבָּרֵךְ	הִתְבָּרֵךְ	מִתְבָּרֵךְ
הִתְבָּרֵךְ	יִתְבָּרֵךְ	הִתְבָּרֵךְ	הִתְבָּרֵךְ	הִתְבָּרֵךְ	מִתְבָּרֵךְ
הִתְבָּרְכָה	תִּתְבָּרֵךְ	הִתְבָּרְכִי			מִתְבָּרֶכֶת
הִתְבָּרַכְתָּ	תִּתְבָּרֵךְ	הִתְבָּרְכוּ			מִתְבָּרְכִים
הִתְבָּרַכְתְּ	תִּתְבָּרְכִי	הִתְבָּרֵכְנָה			מִתְבָּרְכוֹת
הִתְבָּרַכְתִּי	אֶתְבָּרֵךְ				
הִתְבָּרְכוּ	יִתְבָּרְכוּ				
הִתְבָּרַכְתֶּם	תִּתְבָּרֵכְנָה				
הִתְבָּרַכְתֶּן	תִּתְבָּרְכוּ				
הִתְבָּרַכְנוּ	תִּתְבָּרֵכְנָה				
	נִתְבָּרֵךְ				

35.9   II-Guttural Notes: Compensatory Lengthening.

1. In this II-Guttural (ר) paradigm with compensatory lengthening, only the distinctive prefixes and preformatives of the strong verb diagnostics remain.

2. The ר in second root position rejects the Daghesh Forte of the Hithpael stem and causes the preceding Pathach to undergo compensatory lengthening. Compared to the Hithpael strong verb diagnostics, there is neither the Daghesh Forte in the second consonant of the verbal root nor is there the Pathach beneath the first root consonant. Despite these significant changes, the distinctive preformatives and prefixes in the various conjugations should make stem identification easy.

35.10 Summary: Hithpael Diagnostics.

	Perfect	Imperfect	Imperative	Infinitive Construct	Infinitive Absolute	Participle
Strong	הִתְקַטֵּל	יִתְקַטֵּל	הִתְקַטֵּל	הִתְקַטֵּל	הִתְקַטֵּל	מִתְקַטֵּל
Geminate	הִתְפַּלֵּל	יִתְפַּלֵּל	הִתְפַּלֵּל	הִתְפַּלֵּל	הִתְפַּלֵּל	מִתְפַּלֵּל
III-ה	הִתְגַּלָּה	יִתְגַּלֶּה	הִתְגַּלּוֹת			מִתְגַּלֶּה
II-Gutt[1]	הִתְנַחֵם	יִתְנַחֵם	הִתְנַחֵם	הִתְנַחֵם	הִתְנַחֵם	מִתְנַחֵם
II-Gutt[2]	הִתְבָּרֵךְ	יִתְבָּרֵךְ	הִתְבָּרֵךְ	הִתְבָּרֵךְ	הִתְבָּרֵךְ	מִתְבָּרֵךְ

35.11 Vocabulary.

Nouns

עֵד	witness (69)
צָרָה	distress (70)
שֻׁלְחָן	table (71)
שׁוֹר	bull, steer, ox (79)
תְּפִלָּה	prayer (77)
בַּרְזֶל	iron (76)

35.12 In the Cool of the Day? Our knowledge of Hebrew is not complete, and may never be. But study of other, sister languages in the ancient Near East (cognate studies) can sometimes increase our understanding of biblical Hebrew. A case in point is Gen 3:8, a verse that has long

---

[1] II-Guttural with virtual doubling

[2] II-Guttural with compensatory lengthening

been mistranslated and misunderstood. Cognate studies can sweep away the guesswork that has long characterized translations of this verse and give us an accurate translation that also makes more sense theologically.

The *crux interpretum* has been the Hebrew phrase, לְרוּחַ הַיּוֹם. The traditional English translation has been "in the cool of the day" or something of that sort. This translation is based on a guess made by the Septuagint translators who thought that רוּחַ meant "wind" and יוֹם meant "day." Hence, the sense would be something like "in the windy or breezy part of the day." St. Jerome followed suit in his Latin (Vulgate) translation, and so the standard interpretation was established.

Now רוּחַ can certainly mean "wind," and יוֹם can certainly mean "day." But anyone who knows Hebrew and reads the phrase in question finds the whole expression rather odd. It is odd enough to raise the question, Can't there be some other way to translate this phrase? And there is.

Cognate studies, specifically in Akkadian, have revealed a cognate word for the Hebrew יוֹם (day). It is the Akkadian word, *umu*, which also means "day." We call this *umu*[1] because studies have revealed a homonym, or an *umu*[2] in Akkadian that means "storm." The question naturally arises, What if there is a cognate word in Hebrew, a יוֹם[2] that means not "day" but "storm"? There is such a Hebrew cognate, rarely used in the Hebrew Bible, but attested nevertheless. Holladay notes it in his lexicon, although not in Gen 3:8.[3]

On this understanding, the translation of Gen 3:8 changes significantly. It now reads: "Then the man and his wife heard the thunderous voice of Yahweh God as he was going back and forth in the garden in the *wind of the storm* and they hid from Yahweh God among the trees of the garden."

Yahweh has come to judge his disobedient servants. So he comes in the first storm theophany, a manner of coming later associated in the Old Testament with the "Day of Yahweh." Since he comes in stormy glory, other terms in the verse merit an altered translation. "Voice"

---

[3] W. L. Holladay, *A Concise Hebrew and Aramaic Lexicon of the Old Testament* (Grand Rapids: Eerdmans, 1971) 131.

(קוֹל) now becomes "thunderous voice" as at Sinai (Ex 19:16). "Walking" (מִתְהַלֵּךְ) now becomes "going back and forth" like the lightning flashes of Ps 77:17-19.

We can now translate accurately and sensibly a verse that has long seemed puzzling. More than one sermon has portrayed God and Adam walking together in the garden "in the cool of the day," as though they were taking a pleasant after-dinner stroll. The linguistic clarification brings with it greater theological clarity. Yahweh God is coming in storm theophany to judge his disobedient servants as he will come again on the day of Yahweh - as Jesus puts it, on the clouds with great power and glory - to judge a disobedient world.[4]

Jeffrey J. Niehaus
Professor of Old Testament
Gordon-Conwell Theological Seminary
South Hamilton, Massachusetts

---

[4] For a fuller discussion of the verse and its theological significance, see J. J. Niehaus, *God at Sinai* (Grand Rapids: Zondervan, 1995) 155-159.

35.13 Advanced Information: The Hithpolel Stem. The Hithpolel is the equivalent of the Hithpael stem for certain Biconsonantal (and Geminate) verbs. Like the Polel (27.15) and Polal (29.13), the Hithpolel of Biconsonantal verbs is characterized by a Holem Waw after the first consonant and the duplication of the second root consonant. Finally, note that the Hithpolel is distinguished from the Polel only by its distinctive prefixes (for example, הִתְ).

Perfect	Imperfect	Imperative	Infinitive Construct	Infinitive Absolute	Participle
הִתְרוֹמֵם	יִתְרוֹמֵם	הִתְרוֹמֵם	הִתְרוֹמֵם		מִתְרוֹמֵם
הִתְרוֹמְמָה	תִּתְרוֹמֵם	הִתְרוֹמְמִי			מִתְרוֹמֶמֶת
הִתְרוֹמַ֫מְתָּ	תִּתְרוֹמֵם	הִתְרוֹמְמוּ			מִתְרוֹמְמִים
הִתְרוֹמַ֫מְתְּ	תִּתְרוֹמְמִי	הִתְרוֹמֵ֫מְנָה			מִתְרוֹמְמוֹת
הִתְרוֹמַ֫מְתִּי	אֶתְרוֹמֵם				
הִתְרוֹמְמוּ	יִתְרוֹמְמוּ				
הִתְרוֹמַמְתֶּם	תִּתְרוֹמֵ֫מְנָה				
הִתְרוֹמַמְתֶּן	תִּתְרוֹמְמוּ				
הִתְרוֹמַ֫מְנוּ	תִּתְרוֹמֵ֫מְנָה				
	נִתְרוֹמֵם				

35.14 Advanced Information: The Verb חָוָה. The verb חָוָה (to bow down, worship) appears 173 times in the Hebrew Bible and requires special attention because it occurs only in a stem called the Hishtaphel.[5] These verbal forms are easy to identify because of the distinctive prefixes of the Hishtaphel stem (for example, הִשְׁתַּ in the Perfect). Note also that חָוָה is a III-ה verb and will exhibit the distinctive endings of this weak verb class, inflecting quite regularly. The following chart lists the prefixes of the Hishtaphel stem along with some of the more common forms of this verb. This chart is followed by a number of biblical examples.

---

[5] Some older lexical sources identify the verbal root as שָׁחָה and the stem as Hithpalel.

Perfect (הִשְׁתּ)

הִשְׁתַּחֲוָה 3ms he worshipped

הִשְׁתַּחֲווּ 3cp they worshipped

הִשְׁתַּחֲוִיתֶם 2mp you worshipped

Imperfect (יִשְׁתּ)

יִשְׁתַּחֲוֶה 3ms he will worship

וַיִּשְׁתַּחוּ 3ms he worshipped (Waw Conversive)

תִּשְׁתַּחֲוֶה 2ms you will worship

אֶשְׁתַּחֲוֶה 1cs I will worship

יִשְׁתַּחֲווּ 3mp they will worship

Imperative (הִשְׁתּ)

הִשְׁתַּחֲווּ 2mp (you) worship!

Inf Construct (הִשְׁתּ)

הִשְׁתַּחֲוֹת to worship, bow down

Participle (מִשְׁתּ)

מִשְׁתַּחֲוֶה ms worshipping, bowing down

מִשְׁתַּחֲוִים mp worshipping, bowing down

וְהִשְׁתַּחֲווּ לַיהוָה בְּהַר הַקֹּדֶשׁ
(And) they will worship the Lord on the holy mountain.
(Isa 27:13)

וַיִּשְׁתַּחוּ אַבְרָהָם לִפְנֵי עַם הָאָרֶץ
(And) Abraham bowed down before the people of the land.
(Gen 23:12)

וְנִשְׁתַּחֲוֶה וְנָשׁוּבָה אֲלֵיכֶם
(And) we will worship and we will return to you.
(Gen 22:5)

נָפְלוּ לִפְנֵי יְהוָה לְהִשְׁתַּחֲוֹת לַיהוָה
(They) fell down before the Lord to worship the Lord.
(2 Chr 20:18)

Chapter 36

Introduction to the Hebrew Bible

36.1   **The Masoretic Text and *BHS*.** At this point in your study of Hebrew, you have translated (both in the grammar and in the workbook) a few hundred biblical phrases and verses from various sections of the Hebrew Bible. The text that you have been translating is called the Masoretic Text (abbreviated MT). The term "Masoretic" is derived from the Hebrew word מָסוֹרָה (tradition) and refers to the textual tradition of Jewish scholars known as Masoretes. These scholars labored in the preservation of the biblical text between the sixth and tenth centuries A.D.

The Masoretes perfected a system of vowel pointing that was added to the consonantal text, thereby graphically representing the vowel tradition that had been transmitted orally until that time. You will recall that Hebrew, in its earliest stages, did not have a written vowel system (2.1). Additionally, the Masoretes developed a system of symbols to mark word accent in order to assist in the reading and recitation of the text. They also collected and prepared an elaborate set of notes that accompanied the text in the top, bottom and side margins. These laborious efforts (vowel pointing, a system of accents and notes) helped to ensure the accurate transmission of the biblical text. This Tiberian[1] Masoretic text was regarded by early scholars as authoritative and is similarly accepted by modern scholarship. It is the textual tradition that is used for what is now the standard edition of the Hebrew Bible, entitled *Biblia Hebraica Stuttgartensia*.[2] The text of *BHS*, as it is commonly abbreviated, is a copy of the Leningrad Codex, an eleventh century A.D. manuscript located in the Leningrad Public Library. Your first exposure to the pages of *BHS* can be a bit intimidating with its myriad of marks, symbols and enigmatic entries that surround the Hebrew

---

[1] The term "Tiberian" refers to the city of Tiberias, on the western shore of the Sea of Galilee, where the Masoretes lived and worked. The standard Masoretic text is also know as the Ben Asher text, named after the family of Tiberian scholars who completed the final editing.

[2] K. Elliger and W. Rudolph, eds., *Biblia Hebraica Stuttgartensia*. Stuttgart: Deutsche Bibelgesellschaft, 1983.

text. In the following discussion, we will identify and briefly explain some of the major features located on the pages of your Hebrew Bible. For your reference, the first page of the book of Genesis is printed below. Additionally, in the left margin, we have identified some of the basic *BHS* page components.

Book Title

GENESIS בראשית

בְּרֵאשִׁ֖ית בָּרָ֣א אֱלֹהִ֑ים אֵ֥ת הַשָּׁמַ֖יִם וְאֵ֥ת הָאָֽרֶץ׃ 2 וְהָאָ֗רֶץ 1 1 [ס]

הָיְתָ֥ה תֹ֙הוּ֙ וָבֹ֔הוּ וְחֹ֖שֶׁךְ עַל־פְּנֵ֣י תְה֑וֹם וְר֣וּחַ אֱלֹהִ֔ים מְרַחֶ֖פֶת עַל־פְּנֵ֥י

הַמָּֽיִם׃ 3 וַיֹּ֥אמֶר אֱלֹהִ֖ים יְהִ֣י א֑וֹר וַֽיְהִי־אֽוֹר׃ 4 וַיַּ֧רְא אֱלֹהִ֛ים אֶת־

הָא֖וֹר כִּי־ט֑וֹב וַיַּבְדֵּ֣ל אֱלֹהִ֔ים בֵּ֥ין הָא֖וֹר וּבֵ֥ין הַחֹֽשֶׁךְ׃ 5 וַיִּקְרָ֨א

אֱלֹהִ֤ים ׀ לָאוֹר֙ י֔וֹם וְלַחֹ֖שֶׁךְ קָ֣רָא לָ֑יְלָה וַֽיְהִי־עֶ֥רֶב וַֽיְהִי־בֹ֖קֶר י֥וֹם

אֶחָֽד׃ פ 6 וַיֹּ֣אמֶר אֱלֹהִ֔ים יְהִ֥י רָקִ֖יעַ בְּת֣וֹךְ הַמָּ֑יִם וִיהִ֣י מַבְדִּ֔יל

בֵּ֥ין מַ֖יִם לָמָֽיִם׃ 7 וַיַּ֣עַשׂ אֱלֹהִים֮ אֶת־הָרָקִיעַ֒ וַיַּבְדֵּ֗ל בֵּ֤ין הַמַּ֙יִם֙ אֲשֶׁר֙

מִתַּ֣חַת לָרָקִ֔יעַ וּבֵ֣ין הַמַּ֔יִם אֲשֶׁ֖ר מֵעַ֣ל לָרָקִ֑יעַ וַֽיְהִי־כֵֽן׃ 8 וַיִּקְרָ֧א

אֱלֹהִ֛ים לָֽרָקִ֖יעַ שָׁמָ֑יִם וַֽיְהִי־עֶ֥רֶב וַֽיְהִי־בֹ֖קֶר י֥וֹם שֵׁנִֽי׃ פ

9 וַיֹּ֣אמֶר אֱלֹהִ֗ים יִקָּו֨וּ הַמַּ֜יִם מִתַּ֤חַת הַשָּׁמַ֙יִם֙ אֶל־מָק֣וֹם אֶחָ֔ד וְתֵרָאֶ֖ה

הַיַּבָּשָׁ֑ה וַֽיְהִי־כֵֽן׃ 10 וַיִּקְרָ֨א אֱלֹהִ֤ים ׀ לַיַּבָּשָׁה֙ אֶ֔רֶץ וּלְמִקְוֵ֥ה הַמַּ֖יִם

קָרָ֣א יַמִּ֑ים וַיַּ֥רְא אֱלֹהִ֖ים כִּי־טֽוֹב׃ 11 וַיֹּ֣אמֶר אֱלֹהִ֗ים תַּֽדְשֵׁ֤א הָאָ֙רֶץ֙

דֶּ֔שֶׁא עֵ֚שֶׂב מַזְרִ֣יעַ זֶ֔רַע עֵ֣ץ פְּרִ֞י עֹ֤שֶׂה פְּרִי֙ לְמִינ֔וֹ אֲשֶׁ֥ר זַרְעוֹ־ב֖וֹ

עַל־הָאָ֑רֶץ וַֽיְהִי־כֵֽן׃ 12 וַתּוֹצֵ֨א הָאָ֜רֶץ דֶּ֠שֶׁא עֵ֣שֶׂב מַזְרִ֤יעַ זֶ֙רַע֙ לְמִינֵ֔הוּ

וְעֵ֧ץ עֹֽשֶׂה־פְּרִ֛י אֲשֶׁ֥ר זַרְעוֹ־ב֖וֹ לְמִינֵ֑הוּ וַיַּ֥רְא אֱלֹהִ֖ים כִּי־טֽוֹב׃ 13 וַֽיְהִי־

עֶ֥רֶב וַֽיְהִי־בֹ֖קֶר י֥וֹם שְׁלִישִֽׁי׃ פ 14 וַיֹּ֣אמֶר אֱלֹהִ֗ים יְהִ֤י מְאֹרֹת֙

בִּרְקִ֣יעַ הַשָּׁמַ֔יִם לְהַבְדִּ֕יל בֵּ֥ין הַיּ֖וֹם וּבֵ֣ין הַלָּ֑יְלָה וְהָי֤וּ לְאֹתֹת֙ וּלְמ֣וֹעֲדִ֔ים

וּלְיָמִ֖ים וְשָׁנִֽים׃ 15 וְהָי֤וּ לִמְאוֹרֹת֙ בִּרְקִ֣יעַ הַשָּׁמַ֔יִם לְהָאִ֖יר עַל־הָאָ֑רֶץ

וַֽיְהִי־כֵֽן׃ 16 וַיַּ֣עַשׂ אֱלֹהִ֔ים אֶת־שְׁנֵ֥י הַמְּאֹרֹ֖ת הַגְּדֹלִ֑ים אֶת־הַמָּא֤וֹר

Cp 1 ¹Mm 1. ²Mm 2. ³Mm 3. ⁴Mm 3139. ⁵Mp sub loco. ⁶Mm 4. ⁷Jer 4,23, cf Mp sub loco. ⁸Hi 38,19. ⁹Ch 24,20. ¹⁰Mm 5. ¹¹Mm 6. ¹²Mm 3105. ¹³וחד לחשך Hi 28,3. ¹⁴Mm 200. ¹⁵Mm 7. ¹⁶Mm 1431. ¹⁷Mm 2773. ¹⁸Mm 3700. ¹⁹Mm 736. ²⁰לַיַּ֫צָּה חד Ps 66,6. ²¹Mm 722. ²²Mm 2645. ²³Qoh 6,3.

Cp 1,1 ᵃ Orig Βρησιθ vel Βαρησηθ (-σεθ), Samar båråšit ‖ 6 ᵃ huc tr 7ᵃ⁻ᵃ cf 𝔊 et 9.11.15.20. 24.30 ‖ 7 ᵃ⁻ᵃ cf 6ᵃ; ins וירא אלהים כי־טוב cf 4.10.12.18.21.31 et 8 (𝔊) ‖ 9 ᵃ 𝔊 συναγω-γήν = מקוה cf מקוה המים 10 ‖ ᵇ 𝔊 + καὶ συνήχθη τὸ ὕδωρ τὸ ὑποκάτω τοῦ οὐρανοῦ εἰς τὰς συναγωγὰς αὐτῶν καὶ ὤφθη ἡ ξηρά = וַיִּקָּו֨וּ הַמַּיִם מִתַּ֤חַת הַשָּׁמַיִם אֶל־מִקְוֵיהֶם וַתֵּרָא הַיַּבָּשָׁה ‖ 11 ᵃ⁻ᵃ 𝔊𝔙 cj עשב c דשא ‖ ᵇ l c pc Mss ⲙ𝔊𝔖𝔙ᵐ𝔙 וְעֵץ cf 12 ‖ ᶜ prb dl cf 12.

36.2   Looking at *BHS*. Open your Hebrew Bible to Gen 1:1. Remember to
open it from the right. After several pages of introduction, you will
locate the first page of the Hebrew Scriptures at the beginning of
Genesis (page 1 of *BHS*).

1. *Book Title.* The main body of the page is given to the biblical text
    in Hebrew. At the top of the page, the book is identified as
    Genesis with the Hebrew word בראשית in bold characters to
    the right. This is the Hebrew name of the book. You will notice
    that Gen 1:1 begins with this same word but it is vocalized
    בְּרֵאשִׁית (in the beginning). Ancient literary works were
    frequently titled by the first word or phrase of the composition.
    Similarly, the book of Exodus is titled ואלה שמות at the top of
    page 86, and the first verse begins וְאֵלֶּה שְׁמוֹת (these are the
    names of). Within the Pentateuch (Torah), the books of Leviticus
    (page 158) and Deuteronomy (page 283) are also named in this
    way. The book of Numbers (page 209), however, does not take
    its Hebrew name from the first word or phrase of the book. It is
    called במדבר (בְּמִדְבַּר, in the wilderness), the fifth Hebrew word
    in the first verse. Many books, especially the prophetical works
    (and others), are named after the main character. You should be
    able to identify the Hebrew titles for most Old Testament books.

2. *Chapter and Verse.* Like most English Bibles, the text of the Hebrew
    Bible is divided into chapters and verses. There was no such
    numbering system in the original Hebrew texts. This was the
    work of Christian scholars in the thirteenth century and later.
    You should also note that the chapter and verse divisions of the
    Hebrew Bible do not always correspond with the divisions of
    our English Bibles. This phenomenon is especially common in
    the book of Psalms. The elements of English punctuation (such
    as a comma, period, semicolon, question mark, exclamation point,
    etc.) do not appear in the Hebrew Bible. The end of each verse is
    marked, however, with what looks like a large colon (:). This
    symbol is called Sof Pasuq and means "end of verse" in Hebrew.
    The Sof Pasuq is the equivalent of a period in English punctuation.[3]

---

[3] Though the Sof Pasuq designates the end of a verse, its presence does not
always mark the end of a sentence. See, for example, the use of Sof Pasuq at the
end of Gen 22:16.

In Gen 1:1, this symbol occurs after the **ץ** of the last word (הָאָֽרֶץ׃).

3. *Accent Marks.* On any page of *BHS*, you will see a number of symbols (placed either above or beneath words) that you do not recognize. Most of these symbols are accent marks.[4] Imposed upon the text is a complex system of conjunctive and disjunctive accents that serves to mark the stress in individual words and, more importantly, to facilitate the reading, recitation and understanding of the text by marking logical units of thought.[5]

The disjunctive accents are the most important of the two types because they usually divide a verse into two or more units of thought. The use of the major disjunctive accents is comparable to using a comma, semicolon or period in an English sentence. It is important to be able to identify the major disjunctive accents in order to more easily recognize a verse's primary units of thought. The two major disjunctive accents are Athnak and Silluq. The Athnak marks the end of the first major division in a verse. In Gen 1:1, this accent mark occurs under the ה in אֱלֹהִים (God). The Silluq marks the end of the second major division in a verse and usually appears under the accented syllable of the last word in a verse. In Gen 1:1, this accent mark occurs under the א in הָאָֽרֶץ (the earth). Note that the Silluq is similar in appearance to the Metheg (3.7). In the recitation of the text, these are the major points of pause. The conjunctive accents do not divide semantic units. They appear on words between the disjunctive accents and serve to mark some kind of close syntactical connection to the next word. For now, become familiar with the major disjunctive accents noted above.[6]

---

[4] There are two systems of accent used in the Hebrew Bible, though there is some overlap between the two. The books of Psalms, Proverbs and Job employ an accent system that differs from the other books. Some accents are placed after the stressed syllable (postpositive) and others are placed before the stressed syllable (prepositive) but most accent marks appear on the stressed syllable.

[5] Accents are also closely related to the musical rendition of the Hebrew text called "cantillation."

[6] For a full discussion of Hebrew accents, consult W. R. Scott, *A Simplified Guide to BHS* (Berkeley: BIBAL, 1987) 23-34 or P. Joüon, *A Grammar of Biblical Hebrew* (Rome: Pontifical Biblical Institute, 1996) 61-74.

36.3 **Pausal Forms.** It was noted above that the accents Athnak and Silluq mark the two major points of pause in the recitation of the text. Words that occur at these major points of verse division are said to be "in pause" because of the reader's inclination to pause or break the stride of recitation at these points. Words that are "in pause" will often show slight changes in their spelling. The following are some of the most common changes:

1. Pathach will change to Qamets. For example, קָטַל (he killed) will become קָטָל and עַם (people) will become עָם.

2. Seghol will change to Qamets in some Segholate nouns. For example, אֶרֶץ (earth, land) will become אָרֶץ.

3. The Shewa connecting vowel of the 2ms pronominal suffix will change to Seghol. For example, סוּסְךָ (your horse) will become סוּסֶךָ.

4. Words that are accented on the ultima may undergo an accent shift to the penultima with resulting vowel change. For example, the Shewa of the Qal Perfect 3fs (כָּתְבָה) may become Qamets (כָּתָבָה) when in pause because of the retraction of the accent. In this example, a Vocal Shewa is changed to a full vowel. Similarly, אֲנִי (with accent on the ultima) becomes אָנִי when in pause. Here, a Hateph vowel is changed to a full vowel.

36.4 **The Masorah of *BHS*.** As noted above, one of the important and interesting contributions of the Masoretes was their system of marginal notes. These notes are called the Masorah and are traditionally categorized into two main groups: the marginal Masorah and the final Masorah. The category of marginal Masorah is further divided into the Masorah parva (small Masorah) in the outer side margins and the Masorah magna (large Masorah), traditionally located in the top and bottom margins of the text. The Masorah parva consists of word-use statistics, similar documentation for expressions or certain phraseology, observations on full or defective writing, references to the Kethiv-Qere readings (see 36.5) and more. Though some of this information seems trivial and inconsequential to the modern reader, these observations are the result of a passionate zeal to safeguard the accurate transmission of the sacred text. The Masorah magna, in measure, is an expanded Masorah parva. Oftentimes, the notations simply provide greater depth or specificity beyond those in the Masorah parva. Traditionally, the Masorah magna was recorded in the top and bottom margins of the text. Though the Masorah magna is not printed in *BHS*, there is a register of notations (located between the last line of Hebrew text and the lowest register of textual variants) that provides access to this information that has been published in separate volumes. Given that the Masorah magna is abbreviated Mm, this is sometimes called the "Mm register."

The final Masorah is located at the end of biblical books or after certain sections of the text, such as at the end of the Torah. The final Masorah contains information and statistics regarding the number of words in a book or section, the middle word of a book or even the middle consonant of a book. For example, after the conclusion of Deuteronomy, we learn that the book has 955 verses and that the precise midpoint falls on עַל־פִּי in Deut 17:10. Additionally, we learn that the Torah has 5,845 verses, 79,856 words and 400,945 letters. The purpose for this statistical information was to ensure accuracy in the transmission of the text with the production of subsequent copies that were done by hand.

36.5 **The Kethiv-Qere.** The most important of the Masoretic notes are those that detail the Kethiv-Qere that are located in the Masorah parva in the outside margins of *BHS*. Given that the Masoretes would not alter the sacred consonantal text, the Kethiv-Qere notes were a way of "correcting" or commenting on the text for any number of reasons (grammatical, theological, aesthetic, etc.) deemed important by the copyist. The consonantal (uncorrected) wording of the text is the Kethiv, a term that is a transliteration of the Aramaic כְּתִיב ("what is written"). The Kethiv is the reading that comes literally from the consonantal text. The reading that is suggested for "correction" by the Masorete is the Qere, a term that is a transliteration of the Aramaic קְרִי ("what is to be read"). The Qere is signaled by a small circle that is written above the word in the text. This circle refers the reader to a marginal note where the consonants to be read are given. The vowel points of the Qere were placed under the consonants in the text. In the Masorah parva, in the outside margin, the Qere is noted with the consonant ק, over which is located a dot (קֹ), an abbreviation for Qere. The word(s) to be read in the margin are printed above this symbol (for example, see הִיצָא in the outside margin at Gen 8:17). There are hundreds of Kethiv-Qere notations in the Hebrew Bible of varying significance.

A few common words are always read differently than the reading suggested by the consonantal text. This phenomenon is known as a "perpetual Kethiv-Qere." Perhaps the most important example is the divine name יהוה which was never pronounced out of reverence. The consonantal spelling (Kethiv) is יהוה but the perpetual Qere is אֲדֹנָי. The vowels of אֲדֹנָי were superimposed on the four consonants of the divine name, producing יְהֹוָה or יְהוָה.[7] Because of its frequency, this Qere reading was not written in the margin with every occurrence. In this case, the vowels of אֲדֹנָי with the consonants of the divine name served as a reminder to ensure reverence.[8]

36.6   **The Textual Apparatus of *BHS* and Textual Criticism**. At the bottom of each page of *BHS*, below the Mm register, there is a collection of editorial notes in what is called the *textual apparatus*. In these notes, the editors of *BHS* have assembled a selection of important readings, textual variants and (conjectural) emendations that do not appear in the Leningrad Codex (the text of your Hebrew Bible). The textual apparatus of *BHS* provides students with a point of entry into the exegetical discipline of textual criticism.

In the study of biblical (textual) criticism, the term "autograph" refers to the original copy of an author's writing, such as that produced by the prophet Isaiah. The original copy of every book of the Bible has been lost, that is, no autograph of any biblical book has survived or is known at the present time. All known biblical manuscripts are only later copies of the original autographs. From ancient times and until the invention of the printing press, biblical manuscripts were copied by hand with the inevitable result that textual corruptions or errors were introduced into the text, despite the painstaking efforts of scribes to preserve the accuracy of the text. Some books and sections of the Old Testament are relatively free of textual problems (the Pentateuch, Judges, Jonah). Other sections present the reader with an array of textual difficulties (Samuel-Kings, Psalms, Job, Ezekiel, Zechariah).

---

[7] In some instances, the Qere reading tells the reader to pronounce אֱלֹהִים.

[8] Other examples of perpetual Qere include הוּא (Kethiv) for הִיא (Qere) and יְרוּשָׁלַם (Kethiv) for יְרוּשָׁלַיִם (Qere).

Textual problems are generally categorized as either unintentional or intentional. Unintentional errors in the copying of a manuscript include the confusion of letters that look alike, the confusion of letters that sound alike, the accidental omission of a letter(s) or a word(s), the accidental repeating of a letter(s) or a word(s), incorrect word division and a number of other similar errors. Intentional errors in the copying of a manuscript include the altering of a text because the scribe deemed the wording to be disrespectful to God, the substitution of a euphemism for a word or expression that the scribe deemed to be indelicate or offensive and, lastly, the introduction of glosses into the text for the purpose of clarification or explanation.[9] Because of these kinds of errors, most scholars acknowledge the need to do textual criticism in order to restore what is considered to be a more original reading of the text. To this end, the discipline of textual criticism has two primary purposes: (1) to reconstruct the biblical text as close to its original wording as can be established in light of existing manuscript evidence and (2) to document and better understand the transmission of the text through time.

In its fullest dimension, textual criticism involves the task of assembling and translating the full range of ancient manuscript evidence, discerning all the known variant readings, evaluating the quality of each ancient witness, evaluating the quality of each reading, determining the most original reading and sometimes even the conjectural emendation of the text. The *BHS* textual apparatus has done a good deal of this work already, though neither exhaustively nor perfectly. There are a number of works currently available that explain the layout, symbols and use of this apparatus.[10]

---

[9] For an excellent discussion of scribal errors with illustrative examples, see E. R. Brotzman, *Old Testament Textual Criticism* (Grand Rapids: Baker, 1994) 107-121.

[10] The most important and helpful resources are E. R. Brotzman, *Old Testament Textual Criticism*. Grand Rapids: Baker, 1994; W. R. Scott, *A Simplified Guide to BHS*. Berkeley: BIBAL, 1987; R. Wonnenberger, *Understanding BHS: A Manual for the Uses of Biblia Hebraica Stuttgartensia*. Rome: Pontifical Biblical Institute, 1984; P. Rüger, *An English Key to the Latin Words and Abbreviations and Symbols of Biblia Hebraica Stuttgartensia*. Stuttgart: German Bible Society, 1985; E. Würthwein, *The Text of the Old Testament*. Grand Rapids: Eerdmans, 1979.

As a postscript to this brief introduction to textual criticism, it is important to emphasize that the text of the Old Testament has been transmitted with remarkable care and accuracy. The need for textual criticism should not undermine, in any measure, our belief in the inspiration and authority of the Old Testament or our confidence in its providential preservation through the centuries.

36.7   **The Ordering of the Books of the Hebrew Bible**. The Hebrew Bible is composed of twenty-four books arranged in three major divisions: the Law (תּוֹרָה), the Prophets (נְבִיאִים), and the Writings (כְּתוּבִים). The Hebrew Scriptures are sometimes referred to as the Tanak (also Tanach), an acronym derived from the initial letters of the names of the three divisions. The Law is composed of the books of Genesis, Exodus, Leviticus, Numbers and Deuteronomy. The remaining two divisions of the Hebrew Bible have a different ordering and numbering of books compared to the various Christian Bibles. The Prophets comprise eight books: the former Prophets, consisting of Joshua, Judges, 1 and 2 Samuel (counted as one book), 1 and 2 Kings (also counted as one book); and the four Latter Prophets, containing Isaiah, Jeremiah, Ezekiel and the Twelve (the Minor Prophets counted as one). The Writings number eleven books that are ordered in various ways.[11] The sequential ordering in *BHS* is Psalms, Job, Proverbs, Ruth, Song of Songs (Canticles), Ecclesiastes (Qoheleth), Lamentations, Esther, Daniel, Ezra-Nehemiah (counted as one book) and 1 and 2 Chronicles (also counted as one book). You should become familiar with the arrangement and sequential ordering of the biblical books in *BHS*.

36.8   **Selected Resources for Further Study**.

    1.   **Reference Grammars**.

        Gesenius' Hebrew Grammar. Edited and enlarged by E. Kautzsch. Revised by A. E. Cowley. Oxford: Oxford University Press, 1910.

---

[11] The study of the development and ordering of the Hebrew canon is an interesting and complex topic, especially for the Writings. For a helpful introduction, see R. K. Harrison, *Introduction to the Old Testament* (Grand Rapids: Eerdmans, 1969) 260-288.

Joüon, P. *A Grammar of Biblical Hebrew*. 2 vols. Translated and revised by T. Muraoka. Rome: Pontifical Biblical Institute, 1996.

Waltke, B. K., and M. O'Connor. *An Introduction to Biblical Hebrew Syntax*. Winona Lake: Eisenbrauns, 1990.

2. **Hebrew Lexicons**.

Brown, F., S. R. Driver, and C. A. Briggs. *The New Brown-Driver-Briggs-Gesenius Hebrew and English Lexicon*. Peabody: Hendrickson, 1979.

Holladay, W. L. *A Concise Hebrew and Aramaic Lexicon of the Old Testament*. Grand Rapids: Eerdmans, 1988.

Köhler, L., W. Baumgartner, and J. Stamm. *The Hebrew and Aramaic Lexicon of the Old Testament*. 5 vols. New York: E. J. Brill, 1994-2000.

3. **Understanding and Using *BHS* for Old Testament Exegesis**.

Brotzman, E. R. *Old Testament Textual Criticism: A Practical Introduction*. Grand Rapids: Baker, 1994.

Kelly, P. H., D. S. Mynatt, and T. G. Crawford. *The Masorah of Biblia Hebraica Stuttgartensia*. Grand Rapids: Eerdmans, 1998.

Scott, W. R. *A Simplified Guide to BHS*. Berkley: BIBAL, 1987.

Soulen, R. N. *Handbook of Biblical Criticism*. Altanta: John Knox, 1981.

Stuart, D. *Old Testament Exegesis: A Primer for Students and Pastors*. Philadelphia: Westminster, 2001.

Wonneberger, R. *Understanding BHS: A Manual for the Users of Biblia Hebraica Stuttgartensia*. Rome: Pontifical Biblical Institute, 1984.

Würthwein, E. *The Text of the Old Testament*. Grand Rapids: Eerdmans, 1979.

4. **Vocabulary Guides**.

Landes, G. M. *A Student's Vocabulary of Biblical Hebrew*. New York: Charles Scribner's Sons, 1961.

Mitchel, L. A. *A Student's Vocabulary for Biblical Hebrew and Aramaic*. Grand Rapids: Zondervan, 1984.

5. **Electronic Resources**.

Mac platform: *Accordance Bible Software*. Developed by OakSoft Software, Inc. (www.oaksoft.com)

PC platform: *BibleWorks*. Developed by Hermeneutika (www.bibleworks.com)

36.9   **A Still Small Voice?** The prophet Elijah has a famous triumph over the prophets of Baal on Mt. Carmel (1 Kgs 18:17-40). The Lord shows who is truly God by answering the prophet's prayer with fire. For a time, God's people seem to repent. But in the next chapter, in a move of questionable courage, Elijah flees Queen Jezebel when she threatens to have him killed in retaliation. With angelic aid, he makes it to Mt. Horeb, where he encounters Yahweh in storm theophany, much as Moses had long before. When Moses and Israel encountered Yahweh, he came in a dark cloud with "thunderous sounds" (קֹלֹת, Ex 19:16), such that the mountain trembled - as did the people! Now, however, Elijah meets God and hears, according to the traditional translations, "a still small voice" (קוֹל, KJV) or a "gentle whisper" (קוֹל, NIV). What is wrong with this picture?

Whenever Yahweh appears in storm theophany in the Old Testament, the Hebrew word קוֹל is properly and logically translated "thunder," "thunderous voice," or the like. The translation in 1 Kgs 19:12 should be the same. The storm theophany genre leads us to expect it, and a study by J. Lust vindicates this expectation. Lust has shown that the key terms of the phrase, קוֹל דְּמָמָה דַקָּה (traditionally translated "still small voice" or the like) carry a very different meaning from that to which we are accustomed.[12] The Hebrew קוֹל, of course, can mean "voice," "sound," "thunder," "thunderous voice," etc., depending on context. The theophanic context here would lead us to choose "thunderous voice." But what about the other terms? Lust has argued that דְּמָמָה comes from the root דמם² (to roar). Likewise, דַקָּה comes from דקק (to crush, grind small). Traditionally, the adjective דַקָּה was

---

[12] J. Lust, "A Gentle Breeze or a Roaring, Thunderous Sound?" *Vetus Testamentum* 25 (1975) 110-115.

interpreted figuratively, i.e., "made small, gentle." Lust, however, suggests the sense, "crushing." So, instead of a "still, small voice," Elijah hears a "roaring, crushing sound." Or, I would suggest, a "roaring, crushing, thunderous voice."[13]

Here is a case in which either translation is possible. But genre considerations make the new translation preferable. If it is to be adopted, the quality of Yahweh's voice makes perfect sense. His voice always sounds thunderous in storm theophany. But his voice is not merely thunder. God speaks words. And this one fact distinguishes him from Baal in a passage that is partly anti-Baal polemic. We read that Elijah encountered wind, earthquake and fire, but that Yahweh was not in any of these. We would translate, "not yet." The Lord is not yet in any of these cosmic phenomena because they only precede and announce his coming, just as they did at Mt. Sinai (Ex 19:16-19). On the other hand, such phenomena are all that a Baal worshipper might ever expect of Baal, because Baal was himself the storm! What a difference: between worshipping the storm and the Maker of the storm - between worshipping the creature and the Creator!

Jeffrey J. Niehaus
Professor of Old Testament
Gordon-Conwell Theological Seminary
South Hamilton, Massachusetts

---

[13] Cf. discussion in J. J. Niehaus, *God at Sinai* (Grand Rapids: Zondervan, 1995) 247-248.

Appendix

Strong Verbs

Perfect

	Qal	Niphal	Piel	Pual	Hiphil	Hophal (1)	Hophal (2)	Hithpael
3ms	קָטַל	נִקְטַל	קִטֵּל	קֻטַּל	הִקְטִיל	הָקְטַל	הֻקְטַל	הִתְקַטֵּל
3fs	קָטְלָה	נִקְטְלָה	קִטְּלָה	קֻטְּלָה	הִקְטִילָה	הָקְטְלָה	הֻקְטְלָה	הִתְקַטְּלָה
2ms	קָטַלְתָּ	נִקְטַלְתָּ	קִטַּלְתָּ	קֻטַּלְתָּ	הִקְטַלְתָּ	הָקְטַלְתָּ	הֻקְטַלְתָּ	הִתְקַטַּלְתָּ
2fs	קָטַלְתְּ	נִקְטַלְתְּ	קִטַּלְתְּ	קֻטַּלְתְּ	הִקְטַלְתְּ	הָקְטַלְתְּ	הֻקְטַלְתְּ	הִתְקַטַּלְתְּ
1cs	קָטַלְתִּי	נִקְטַלְתִּי	קִטַּלְתִּי	קֻטַּלְתִּי	הִקְטַלְתִּי	הָקְטַלְתִּי	הֻקְטַלְתִּי	הִתְקַטַּלְתִּי
3cp	קָטְלוּ	נִקְטְלוּ	קִטְּלוּ	קֻטְּלוּ	הִקְטִילוּ	הָקְטְלוּ	הֻקְטְלוּ	הִתְקַטְּלוּ
2mp	קְטַלְתֶּם	נִקְטַלְתֶּם	קִטַּלְתֶּם	קֻטַּלְתֶּם	הִקְטַלְתֶּם	הָקְטַלְתֶּם	הֻקְטַלְתֶּם	הִתְקַטַּלְתֶּם
2fp	קְטַלְתֶּן	נִקְטַלְתֶּן	קִטַּלְתֶּן	קֻטַּלְתֶּן	הִקְטַלְתֶּן	הָקְטַלְתֶּן	הֻקְטַלְתֶּן	הִתְקַטַּלְתֶּן
1cp	קָטַלְנוּ	נִקְטַלְנוּ	קִטַּלְנוּ	קֻטַּלְנוּ	הִקְטַלְנוּ	הָקְטַלְנוּ	הֻקְטַלְנוּ	הִתְקַטַּלְנוּ

Imperfect

	Qal	Niphal	Piel	Pual	Hiphil	Hophal (1)	Hophal (2)	Hithpael
3ms	יִקְטֹל	יִקָּטֵל	יְקַטֵּל	יְקֻטַּל	יַקְטִיל	יָקְטַל	יֻקְטַל	יִתְקַטֵּל
3fs	תִּקְטֹל	תִּקָּטֵל	תְּקַטֵּל	תְּקֻטַּל	תַּקְטִיל	תָּקְטַל	תֻּקְטַל	תִּתְקַטֵּל
2ms	תִּקְטֹל	תִּקָּטֵל	תְּקַטֵּל	תְּקֻטַּל	תַּקְטִיל	תָּקְטַל	תֻּקְטַל	תִּתְקַטֵּל
2fs	תִּקְטְלִי	תִּקָּטְלִי	תְּקַטְּלִי	תְּקֻטְּלִי	תַּקְטִילִי	תָּקְטְלִי	תֻּקְטְלִי	תִּתְקַטְּלִי
1cs	אֶקְטֹל	אֶקָּטֵל	אֲקַטֵּל	אֲקֻטַּל	אַקְטִיל	אָקְטַל	אֻקְטַל	אֶתְקַטֵּל
3mp	יִקְטְלוּ	יִקָּטְלוּ	יְקַטְּלוּ	יְקֻטְּלוּ	יַקְטִילוּ	יָקְטְלוּ	יֻקְטְלוּ	יִתְקַטְּלוּ
3fp	תִּקְטֹלְנָה	תִּקָּטַלְנָה	תְּקַטֵּלְנָה	תְּקֻטַּלְנָה	תַּקְטֵלְנָה	תָּקְטַלְנָה	תֻּקְטַלְנָה	תִּתְקַטֵּלְנָה
2mp	תִּקְטְלוּ	תִּקָּטְלוּ	תְּקַטְּלוּ	תְּקֻטְּלוּ	תַּקְטִילוּ	תָּקְטְלוּ	תֻּקְטְלוּ	תִּתְקַטְּלוּ
2fp	תִּקְטֹלְנָה	תִּקָּטַלְנָה	תְּקַטֵּלְנָה	תְּקֻטַּלְנָה	תַּקְטֵלְנָה	תָּקְטַלְנָה	תֻּקְטַלְנָה	תִּתְקַטֵּלְנָה
1cp	נִקְטֹל	נִקָּטֵל	נְקַטֵּל	נְקֻטַּל	נַקְטִיל	נָקְטַל	נֻקְטַל	נִתְקַטֵּל

		Qal	Niphal	Piel	Hiphil	Hithpael
Imperative	2ms	קְטֹל	הִקָּטֵל	קַטֵּל	הַקְטֵל	הִתְקַטֵּל
	2fs	קִטְלִי	הִקָּטְלִי	קַטְּלִי	הַקְטִילִי	הִתְקַטְּלִי
	2mp	קִטְלוּ	הִקָּטְלוּ	קַטְּלוּ	הַקְטִילוּ	הִתְקַטְּלוּ
	2fp	קְטֹלְנָה	הִקָּטַלְנָה	קַטֵּלְנָה	הַקְטֵלְנָה	הִתְקַטֵּלְנָה
Infinitive Construct		קְטֹל	הִקָּטֵל	קַטֵּל	הַקְטִיל	הִתְקַטֵּל
Infinitive Absolute		קָטוֹל	הִקָּטֹל נִקְטֹל	קַטֹּל	הַקְטֵל	הִתְקַטֵּל
Active Participle	ms	קֹטֵל		מְקַטֵּל	מַקְטִיל	מִתְקַטֵּל
	fs	קֹטֶלֶת		מְקַטֶּלֶת	מַקְטֶלֶת	מִתְקַטֶּלֶת
	mp	קֹטְלִים		מְקַטְּלִים	מַקְטִילִים	מִתְקַטְּלִים
	fp	קֹטְלוֹת		מְקַטְּלוֹת	מַקְטִילוֹת	מִתְקַטְּלוֹת
Passive Participle	ms	קָטוּל	נִקְטָל	מְקֻטָּל	מָקְטָל	
	fs	קְטוּלָה	נִקְטָלָה	מְקֻטָּלָה	מָקְטָלָה	
	mp	קְטוּלִים	נִקְטָלִים	מְקֻטָּלִים	מָקְטָלִים	
	fp	קְטוּלוֹת	נִקְטָלוֹת	מְקֻטָּלוֹת	מָקְטָלוֹת	

I-Guttural Verbs

	Qal (1)	Qal (2)	Niphal	Hiphil	Hophal
Perfect					
3ms	עָמַד	חָזַק	נֶעֱמַד	הֶעֱמִיד	הָעֳמַד
3fs	עָמְדָה	חָזְקָה	נֶעֶמְדָה	הֶעֱמִידָה	הָעֳמְדָה
2ms	עָמַדְתָּ	חָזַקְתָּ	נֶעֱמַדְתָּ	הֶעֱמַדְתָּ	הָעֳמַדְתָּ
2fs	עָמַדְתְּ	חָזַקְתְּ	נֶעֱמַדְתְּ	הֶעֱמַדְתְּ	הָעֳמַדְתְּ
1cs	עָמַדְתִּי	חָזַקְתִּי	נֶעֱמַדְתִּי	הֶעֱמַדְתִּי	הָעֳמַדְתִּי
3cp	עָמְדוּ	חָזְקוּ	נֶעֶמְדוּ	הֶעֱמִידוּ	הָעֳמְדוּ
2mp	עֲמַדְתֶּם	חֲזַקְתֶּם	נֶעֱמַדְתֶּם	הֶעֱמַדְתֶּם	הָעֳמַדְתֶּם
2fp	עֲמַדְתֶּן	חֲזַקְתֶּן	נֶעֱמַדְתֶּן	הֶעֱמַדְתֶּן	הָעֳמַדְתֶּן
1cp	עָמַדְנוּ	חָזַקְנוּ	נֶעֱמַדְנוּ	הֶעֱמַדְנוּ	הָעֳמַדְנוּ
Imperfect					
3ms	יַעֲמֹד	יֶחֱזַק	יֵעָמֵד	יַעֲמִיד	יָעֳמַד
3fs	תַּעֲמֹד	תֶּחֱזַק	תֵּעָמֵד	תַּעֲמִיד	תָּעֳמַד
2ms	תַּעֲמֹד	תֶּחֱזַק	תֵּעָמֵד	תַּעֲמִיד	תָּעֳמַד
2fs	תַּעַמְדִי	תֶּחֶזְקִי	תֵּעָמְדִי	תַּעֲמִידִי	תָּעֳמְדִי
1cs	אֶעֱמֹד	אֶחֱזַק	אֵעָמֵד	אַעֲמִיד	אָעֳמַד
3mp	יַעַמְדוּ	יֶחֶזְקוּ	יֵעָמְדוּ	יַעֲמִידוּ	יָעֳמְדוּ
3fp	תַּעֲמֹדְנָה	תֶּחֱזַקְנָה	תֵּעָמַדְנָה	תַּעֲמֵדְנָה	תָּעֳמַדְנָה
2mp	תַּעַמְדוּ	תֶּחֶזְקוּ	תֵּעָמְדוּ	תַּעֲמִידוּ	תָּעֳמְדוּ
2fp	תַּעֲמֹדְנָה	תֶּחֱזַקְנָה	תֵּעָמַדְנָה	תַּעֲמֵדְנָה	תָּעֳמַדְנָה
1cp	נַעֲמֹד	נֶחֱזַק	נֵעָמֵד	נַעֲמִיד	נָעֳמַד

Imperative	2ms	קְטֹל	הִקָּטֵל	חֲזַק	הַקְטֵל	
	2fs	קִטְלִי	הִקָּטְלִי	חִזְקִי	הַקְטִילִי	
	2mp	קִטְלוּ	הִקָּטְלוּ	חִזְקוּ	הַקְטִילוּ	
	2fp	קְטֹלְנָה	הִקָּטַלְנָה	חֲזַקְנָה	הַקְטֵלְנָה	
Infinitive Construct		קְטֹל	הִקָּטֵל	חֲזֹק	הַקְטִיל	
Infinitive Absolute		קָטוֹל	הִקָּטֹל	חָזוֹק	הַקְטֵל	
			נִקְטֹל			
Active Participle	ms	קֹטֵל		חָזֵק	מַקְטִיל	
	fs	קֹטֶלֶת		חֲזָקָה	מַקְטִילָה	
	mp	קֹטְלִים		חֲזָקִים	מַקְטִילִים	
	fp	קֹטְלוֹת		חֲזָקוֹת	מַקְטִילוֹת	
Passive Participle	ms	קָטוּל	נִקְטָל			מֻקְטָל
	fs	קְטוּלָה	נִקְטָלָה			מֻקְטָלָה
	mp	קְטוּלִים	נִקְטָלִים			מֻקְטָלִים
	fp	קְטוּלוֹת	נִקְטָלוֹת			מֻקְטָלוֹת

I-א Verbs

	Qal (1)	Qal (2)	Qal (2)
Perfect			
3ms	אָמַר	אָכַל	טָמֵא
3fs	אָמְרָה	אָכְלָה	טָמְאָה
2ms	אָמַרְתָּ	אָכַלְתָּ	טָמֵאתָ
2fs	אָמַרְתְּ	אָכַלְתְּ	טָמֵאת
1cs	אָמַרְתִּי	אָכַלְתִּי	טָמֵאתִי
3cp	אָמְרוּ	אָכְלוּ	טָמְאוּ
2mp	אֲמַרְתֶּם	אֲכַלְתֶּם	טְמֵאתֶם
2fp	אֲמַרְתֶּן	אֲכַלְתֶּן	טְמֵאתֶן
1cp	אָמַרְנוּ	אָכַלְנוּ	טָמֵאנוּ
Imperfect			
3ms	יֹאמַר	יֹאכַל	יִטְמָא
3fs	תֹּאמַר	תֹּאכַל	תִּטְמָא
2ms	תֹּאמַר	תֹּאכַל	תִּטְמָא
2fs	תֹּאמְרִי	תֹּאכְלִי	תִּטְמְאִי
1cs	אֹמַר	אֹכַל	אֶטְמָא
3mp	יֹאמְרוּ	יֹאכְלוּ	יִטְמְאוּ
3fp	תֹּאמַרְנָה	תֹּאכַלְנָה	תִּטְמֶאנָה
2mp	תֹּאמְרוּ	תֹּאכְלוּ	תִּטְמְאוּ
2fp	תֹּאמַרְנָה	תֹּאכַלְנָה	תִּטְמֶאנָה
1cp	נֹאמַר	נֹאכַל	נִטְמָא

Imperative	2ms	אֱמֹר	אֱכֹל	אֱמֹר
	2fs	אִמְרִי	אִכְלִי	אִמְרִי
	2mp	אִמְרוּ	אִכְלוּ	אִמְרוּ
	2fp	אֱמֹרְנָה	אֱכֹלְנָה	אֱמֹרְנָה
Infinitive Construct		אֱמֹר	אֱכֹל	אֱמֹר
Infinitive Absolute		אָמוֹר	אָכוֹל	אָמוֹר
Active Participle	ms	אֹמֵר	אֹכֵל	אֹמֵר
	fs	אֹמֶרֶת	אֹכֶלֶת	אֹמֶרֶת
	mp	אֹמְרִים	אֹכְלִים	אֹמְרִים
	fp	אֹמְרוֹת	אֹכְלוֹת	אֹמְרוֹת
Passive Participle	ms	אָמוּר	אָכוּל	אָמוּר
	fs	אֲמוּרָה	אֲכוּלָה	אֲמוּרָה
	mp	אֲמוּרִים	אֲכוּלִים	אֲמוּרִים
	fp	אֲמוּרוֹת	אֲכוּלוֹת	אֲמוּרוֹת

II-Guttural Verbs

	Qal	Niphal	Piel (vd)	Piel (cl)	Pual (vd)	Pual (cl)	Hithpael (vd)	Hithpael (cl)
Perfect								
3ms	בָּחַר	נִבְחַר	בֵּחַם	בֵּרַךְ	בֹּחַם	בֹּרַךְ	הִתְבָּחֵם	הִתְבָּרֵךְ
3fs	בָּחֲרָה	נִבְחֲרָה	בֵּחֲמָה	בֵּרְכָה	בֹּחֲמָה	בֹּרְכָה	הִתְבָּחֲמָה	הִתְבָּרְכָה
2ms	בָּחַרְתָּ	נִבְחַרְתָּ	בֵּחַמְתָּ	בֵּרַכְתָּ	בֹּחַמְתָּ	בֹּרַכְתָּ	הִתְבָּחַמְתָּ	הִתְבָּרַכְתָּ
2fs	בָּחַרְתְּ	נִבְחַרְתְּ	בֵּחַמְתְּ	בֵּרַכְתְּ	בֹּחַמְתְּ	בֹּרַכְתְּ	הִתְבָּחַמְתְּ	הִתְבָּרַכְתְּ
1cs	בָּחַרְתִּי	נִבְחַרְתִּי	בֵּחַמְתִּי	בֵּרַכְתִּי	בֹּחַמְתִּי	בֹּרַכְתִּי	הִתְבָּחַמְתִּי	הִתְבָּרַכְתִּי
3cp	בָּחֲרוּ	נִבְחֲרוּ	בֵּחֲמוּ	בֵּרְכוּ	בֹּחֲמוּ	בֹּרְכוּ	הִתְבָּחֲמוּ	הִתְבָּרְכוּ
2mp	בְּחַרְתֶּם	נִבְחַרְתֶּם	בֵּחַמְתֶּם	בֵּרַכְתֶּם	בֹּחַמְתֶּם	בֹּרַכְתֶּם	הִתְבָּחַמְתֶּם	הִתְבָּרַכְתֶּם
2fp	בְּחַרְתֶּן	נִבְחַרְתֶּן	בֵּחַמְתֶּן	בֵּרַכְתֶּן	בֹּחַמְתֶּן	בֹּרַכְתֶּן	הִתְבָּחַמְתֶּן	הִתְבָּרַכְתֶּן
1cp	בָּחַרְנוּ	נִבְחַרְנוּ	בֵּחַמְנוּ	בֵּרַכְנוּ	בֹּחַמְנוּ	בֹּרַכְנוּ	הִתְבָּחַמְנוּ	הִתְבָּרַכְנוּ
Imperfect								
3ms	יִבְחַר	יִבָּחֵר	יְבַחֵם	יְבָרֵךְ	יְבֹחַם	יְבֹרַךְ	יִתְבָּחֵם	יִתְבָּרֵךְ
3fs	תִּבְחַר	תִּבָּחֵר	תְּבַחֵם	תְּבָרֵךְ	תְּבֹחַם	תְּבֹרַךְ	תִּתְבָּחֵם	תִּתְבָּרֵךְ
2ms	תִּבְחַר	תִּבָּחֵר	תְּבַחֵם	תְּבָרֵךְ	תְּבֹחַם	תְּבֹרַךְ	תִּתְבָּחֵם	תִּתְבָּרֵךְ
2fs	תִּבְחֲרִי	תִּבָּחֲרִי	תְּבַחֲמִי	תְּבָרְכִי	תְּבֹחֲמִי	תְּבֹרְכִי	תִּתְבָּחֲמִי	תִּתְבָּרְכִי
1cs	אֶבְחַר	אֶבָּחֵר	אֲבַחֵם	אֲבָרֵךְ	אֲבֹחַם	אֲבֹרַךְ	אֶתְבָּחֵם	אֶתְבָּרֵךְ
3mp	יִבְחֲרוּ	יִבָּחֲרוּ	יְבַחֲמוּ	יְבָרְכוּ	יְבֹחֲמוּ	יְבֹרְכוּ	יִתְבָּחֲמוּ	יִתְבָּרְכוּ
3fp	תִּבְחַרְנָה	תִּבָּחַרְנָה	תְּבַחֵמְנָה	תְּבָרֵכְנָה	תְּבֹחַמְנָה	תְּבֹרַכְנָה	תִּתְבָּחֵמְנָה	תִּתְבָּרֵכְנָה
2mp	תִּבְחֲרוּ	תִּבָּחֲרוּ	תְּבַחֲמוּ	תְּבָרְכוּ	תְּבֹחֲמוּ	תְּבֹרְכוּ	תִּתְבָּחֲמוּ	תִּתְבָּרְכוּ
2fp	תִּבְחַרְנָה	תִּבָּחַרְנָה	תְּבַחֵמְנָה	תְּבָרֵכְנָה	תְּבֹחַמְנָה	תְּבֹרַכְנָה	תִּתְבָּחֵמְנָה	תִּתְבָּרֵכְנָה
1cp	נִבְחַר	נִבָּחֵר	נְבַחֵם	נְבָרֵךְ	נְבֹחַם	נְבֹרַךְ	נִתְבָּחֵם	נִתְבָּרֵךְ

Imperative	2ms						
	2fs						
	2mp						
	2fp						
Infinitive Construct							
Infinitive Absolute							
Active Participle	ms						
	fs						
	mp						
	fp						
Passive Participle	ms						
	fs						
	mp						
	fp						

III-ח/ע Verbs

		Qal	Niphal	Piel	Pual	Hiphil	Hophal
Perfect	3ms	שָׁלַח	נִשְׁלַח	שִׁלַּח	שֻׁלַּח	הִשְׁלִיחַ	הָשְׁלַח
	3fs	שָׁלְחָה	נִשְׁלְחָה	שִׁלְּחָה	שֻׁלְּחָה	הִשְׁלִיחָה	הָשְׁלְחָה
	2ms	שָׁלַחְתָּ	נִשְׁלַחְתָּ	שִׁלַּחְתָּ	שֻׁלַּחְתָּ	הִשְׁלַחְתָּ	הָשְׁלַחְתָּ
	2fs	שָׁלַחַתְּ	נִשְׁלַחַתְּ	שִׁלַּחַתְּ	שֻׁלַּחַתְּ	הִשְׁלַחַתְּ	הָשְׁלַחַתְּ
	1cs	שָׁלַחְתִּי	נִשְׁלַחְתִּי	שִׁלַּחְתִּי	שֻׁלַּחְתִּי	הִשְׁלַחְתִּי	הָשְׁלַחְתִּי
	3cp	שָׁלְחוּ	נִשְׁלְחוּ	שִׁלְּחוּ	שֻׁלְּחוּ	הִשְׁלִיחוּ	הָשְׁלְחוּ
	2mp	שְׁלַחְתֶּם	נִשְׁלַחְתֶּם	שִׁלַּחְתֶּם	שֻׁלַּחְתֶּם	הִשְׁלַחְתֶּם	הָשְׁלַחְתֶּם
	2fp	שְׁלַחְתֶּן	נִשְׁלַחְתֶּן	שִׁלַּחְתֶּן	שֻׁלַּחְתֶּן	הִשְׁלַחְתֶּן	הָשְׁלַחְתֶּן
	1cp	שָׁלַחְנוּ	נִשְׁלַחְנוּ	שִׁלַּחְנוּ	שֻׁלַּחְנוּ	הִשְׁלַחְנוּ	הָשְׁלַחְנוּ
Imperfect	3ms	יִשְׁלַח	יִשָּׁלַח	יְשַׁלַּח	יְשֻׁלַּח	יַשְׁלִיחַ	יָשְׁלַח
	3fs	תִּשְׁלַח	תִּשָּׁלַח	תְּשַׁלַּח	תְּשֻׁלַּח	תַּשְׁלִיחַ	תָּשְׁלַח
	2ms	תִּשְׁלַח	תִּשָּׁלַח	תְּשַׁלַּח	תְּשֻׁלַּח	תַּשְׁלִיחַ	תָּשְׁלַח
	2fs	תִּשְׁלְחִי	תִּשָּׁלְחִי	תְּשַׁלְּחִי	תְּשֻׁלְּחִי	תַּשְׁלִיחִי	תָּשְׁלְחִי
	1cs	אֶשְׁלַח	אֶשָּׁלַח	אֲשַׁלַּח	אֲשֻׁלַּח	אַשְׁלִיחַ	אָשְׁלַח
	3mp	יִשְׁלְחוּ	יִשָּׁלְחוּ	יְשַׁלְּחוּ	יְשֻׁלְּחוּ	יַשְׁלִיחוּ	יָשְׁלְחוּ
	3fp	תִּשְׁלַחְנָה	תִּשָּׁלַחְנָה	תְּשַׁלַּחְנָה	תְּשֻׁלַּחְנָה	תַּשְׁלַחְנָה	תָּשְׁלַחְנָה
	2mp	תִּשְׁלְחוּ	תִּשָּׁלְחוּ	תְּשַׁלְּחוּ	תְּשֻׁלְּחוּ	תַּשְׁלִיחוּ	תָּשְׁלְחוּ
	2fp	תִּשְׁלַחְנָה	תִּשָּׁלַחְנָה	תְּשַׁלַּחְנָה	תְּשֻׁלַּחְנָה	תַּשְׁלַחְנָה	תָּשְׁלַחְנָה
	1cp	נִשְׁלַח	נִשָּׁלַח	נְשַׁלַּח	נְשֻׁלַּח	נַשְׁלִיחַ	נָשְׁלַח

	Col 1	Col 2	Col 3	Col 4	Col 5
Imperative 2ms	הִשָּׁלַח	הִשְׁתַּלַּח	שַׁלַּח	הַשְׁלַח	
2fs	הִשָּׁלְחִי	הִשְׁתַּלְּחִי	שַׁלְּחִי	הַשְׁלִיחִי	
2mp	הִשָּׁלְחוּ	הִשְׁתַּלְּחוּ	שַׁלְּחוּ	הַשְׁלִיחוּ	
2fp	הִשָּׁלַחְנָה	הִשְׁתַּלַּחְנָה	שַׁלַּחְנָה	הַשְׁלַחְנָה	
Infinitive Construct	הִשָּׁלַח	הִשְׁתַּלַּח	שַׁלַּח	הַשְׁלִיחַ	
Infinitive Absolute	הִשָּׁלוֹחַ / הִשָּׁלֵחַ	שַׁלֵּחַ	שַׁלֵּחַ	הַשְׁלֵחַ	
Active Participle ms		מִשְׁתַּלֵּחַ	מְשַׁלֵּחַ	מַשְׁלִיחַ	
fs		מִשְׁתַּלַּחַת	מְשַׁלַּחַת	מַשְׁלִיחָה	
mp		מִשְׁתַּלְּחִים	מְשַׁלְּחִים	מַשְׁלִיחִים	
fp		מִשְׁתַּלְּחוֹת	מְשַׁלְּחוֹת	מַשְׁלִיחוֹת	
Passive Participle ms	נִשְׁלָח		מְשֻׁלָּח	מֻשְׁלָח	
fs	נִשְׁלָחָה		מְשֻׁלָּחָה	מֻשְׁלָחָה	
mp	נִשְׁלָחִים		מְשֻׁלָּחִים	מֻשְׁלָחִים	
fp	נִשְׁלָחוֹת		מְשֻׁלָּחוֹת	מֻשְׁלָחוֹת	

III-א Verbs

		Qal	Niphal	Piel	Pual	Hiphil	Hophal	Hithpael
Perfect	3ms	מָצָא	נִמְצָא	מִצֵּא	מֻצָּא	הִמְצִיא	הֻמְצָא	הִתְמַצֵּא
	3fs	מָצְאָה	נִמְצְאָה	מִצְּאָה	מֻצְּאָה	הִמְצִיאָה	הֻמְצְאָה	הִתְמַצְּאָה
	2ms	מָצָאתָ	נִמְצֵאתָ	מִצֵּאתָ	מֻצֵּאתָ	הִמְצֵאתָ	הֻמְצֵאתָ	הִתְמַצֵּאתָ
	2fs	מָצָאת	נִמְצֵאת	מִצֵּאת	מֻצֵּאת	הִמְצֵאת	הֻמְצֵאת	הִתְמַצֵּאת
	1cs	מָצָאתִי	נִמְצֵאתִי	מִצֵּאתִי	מֻצֵּאתִי	הִמְצֵאתִי	הֻמְצֵאתִי	הִתְמַצֵּאתִי
	3cp	מָצְאוּ	נִמְצְאוּ	מִצְּאוּ	מֻצְּאוּ	הִמְצִיאוּ	הֻמְצְאוּ	הִתְמַצְּאוּ
	2mp	מְצָאתֶם	נִמְצֵאתֶם	מִצֵּאתֶם	מֻצֵּאתֶם	הִמְצֵאתֶם	הֻמְצֵאתֶם	הִתְמַצֵּאתֶם
	2fp	מְצָאתֶן	נִמְצֵאתֶן	מִצֵּאתֶן	מֻצֵּאתֶן	הִמְצֵאתֶן	הֻמְצֵאתֶן	הִתְמַצֵּאתֶן
	1cp	מָצָאנוּ	נִמְצֵאנוּ	מִצֵּאנוּ	מֻצֵּאנוּ	הִמְצֵאנוּ	הֻמְצֵאנוּ	הִתְמַצֵּאנוּ
Imperfect	3ms	יִמְצָא	יִמָּצֵא	יְמַצֵּא	יְמֻצָּא	יַמְצִיא	יֻמְצָא	יִתְמַצֵּא
	3fs	תִּמְצָא	תִּמָּצֵא	תְּמַצֵּא	תְּמֻצָּא	תַּמְצִיא	תֻּמְצָא	תִּתְמַצֵּא
	2ms	תִּמְצָא	תִּמָּצֵא	תְּמַצֵּא	תְּמֻצָּא	תַּמְצִיא	תֻּמְצָא	תִּתְמַצֵּא
	2fs	תִּמְצְאִי	תִּמָּצְאִי	תְּמַצְּאִי	תְּמֻצְּאִי	תַּמְצִיאִי	תֻּמְצְאִי	תִּתְמַצְּאִי
	1cs	אֶמְצָא	אֶמָּצֵא	אֲמַצֵּא	אֲמֻצָּא	אַמְצִיא	אֻמְצָא	אֶתְמַצֵּא
	3mp	יִמְצְאוּ	יִמָּצְאוּ	יְמַצְּאוּ	יְמֻצְּאוּ	יַמְצִיאוּ	יֻמְצְאוּ	יִתְמַצְּאוּ
	3fp	תִּמְצֶאנָה	תִּמָּצֶאנָה	תְּמַצֶּאנָה	תְּמֻצֶּאנָה	תַּמְצֶאנָה	תֻּמְצֶאנָה	תִּתְמַצֶּאנָה
	2mp	תִּמְצְאוּ	תִּמָּצְאוּ	תְּמַצְּאוּ	תְּמֻצְּאוּ	תַּמְצִיאוּ	תֻּמְצְאוּ	תִּתְמַצְּאוּ
	2fp	תִּמְצֶאנָה	תִּמָּצֶאנָה	תְּמַצֶּאנָה	תְּמֻצֶּאנָה	תַּמְצֶאנָה	תֻּמְצֶאנָה	תִּתְמַצֶּאנָה
	1cp	נִמְצָא	נִמָּצֵא	נְמַצֵּא	נְמֻצָּא	נַמְצִיא	נֻמְצָא	נִתְמַצֵּא

Imperative	2ms	מְצָא	הִמָּצֵא	מַצֵּא		הַמְצֵא
	2fs	מִצְאִי	הִמָּצְאִי	מַצְּאִי		הַמְצִיאִי
	2mp	מִצְאוּ	הִמָּצְאוּ	מַצְּאוּ		הַמְצִיאוּ
	2fp	מְצֶאנָה	הִמָּצֶאנָה	מַצֶּאנָה		הַמְצֶאנָה
Infinitive Construct		מְצֹא	הִמָּצֵא	מַצֵּא		הַמְצִיא
Infinitive Absolute		מָצוֹא	הִמָּצֹא	מַצֵּא		הַמְצֵא
Active Participle	ms	מֹצֵא		מְמַצֵּא		מַמְצִיא
	fs	מֹצֵאת		מְמַצֵּאת		מַמְצֵאת
	mp	מֹצְאִים		מְמַצְּאִים		מַמְצִיאִים
	fp	מֹצְאוֹת		מְמַצְּאוֹת		מַמְצִיאוֹת
Passive Participle	ms	מָצוּא		מְמֻצָּא	מֻמְצָא	
	fs	מְצוּאָה		מְמֻצָּאָה	מֻמְצָאת	
	mp	מְצוּאִים		מְמֻצָּאִים	מֻמְצָאִים	
	fp	מְצוּאוֹת		מְמֻצָּאוֹת	מֻמְצָאוֹת	

III-ה Verbs

		Qal	Niphal	Piel	Pual	Hiphil	Hophal	Hithpael
Perfect	3ms	גָּלָה	נִגְלָה	גִּלָּה	גֻּלָּה	הִגְלָה	הָגְלָה	הִתְגַּלָּה
	3fs	גָּלְתָה	נִגְלְתָה	גִּלְּתָה	גֻּלְּתָה	הִגְלְתָה	הָגְלְתָה	הִתְגַּלְּתָה
	2ms	גָּלִיתָ	נִגְלֵיתָ	גִּלִּיתָ	גֻּלֵּיתָ	הִגְלֵיתָ	הָגְלֵיתָ	הִתְגַּלִּיתָ
	2fs	גָּלִית	נִגְלֵית	גִּלִּית	גֻּלֵּית	הִגְלֵית	הָגְלֵית	הִתְגַּלִּית
	1cs	גָּלִיתִי	נִגְלֵיתִי	גִּלִּיתִי	גֻּלֵּיתִי	הִגְלֵיתִי	הָגְלֵיתִי	הִתְגַּלִּיתִי
	3cp	גָּלוּ	נִגְלוּ	גִּלּוּ	גֻּלּוּ	הִגְלוּ	הָגְלוּ	הִתְגַּלּוּ
	2mp	גְּלִיתֶם	נִגְלֵיתֶם	גִּלִּיתֶם	גֻּלֵּיתֶם	הִגְלֵיתֶם	הָגְלֵיתֶם	הִתְגַּלִּיתֶם
	2fp	גְּלִיתֶן	נִגְלֵיתֶן	גִּלִּיתֶן	גֻּלֵּיתֶן	הִגְלֵיתֶן	הָגְלֵיתֶן	הִתְגַּלִּיתֶן
	1cp	גָּלִינוּ	נִגְלֵינוּ	גִּלִּינוּ	גֻּלֵּינוּ	הִגְלֵינוּ	הָגְלֵינוּ	הִתְגַּלִּינוּ
Imperfect	3ms	יִגְלֶה	יִגָּלֶה	יְגַלֶּה	יְגֻלֶּה	יַגְלֶה	יָגְלֶה	יִתְגַּלֶּה
	3fs	תִּגְלֶה	תִּגָּלֶה	תְּגַלֶּה	תְּגֻלֶּה	תַּגְלֶה	תָּגְלֶה	תִּתְגַּלֶּה
	2ms	תִּגְלֶה	תִּגָּלֶה	תְּגַלֶּה	תְּגֻלֶּה	תַּגְלֶה	תָּגְלֶה	תִּתְגַּלֶּה
	2fs	תִּגְלִי	תִּגָּלִי	תְּגַלִּי	תְּגֻלִּי	תַּגְלִי	תָּגְלִי	תִּתְגַּלִּי
	1cs	אֶגְלֶה	אֶגָּלֶה	אֲגַלֶּה	אֲגֻלֶּה	אַגְלֶה	אָגְלֶה	אֶתְגַּלֶּה
	3mp	יִגְלוּ	יִגָּלוּ	יְגַלּוּ	יְגֻלּוּ	יַגְלוּ	יָגְלוּ	יִתְגַּלּוּ
	3fp	תִּגְלֶינָה	תִּגָּלֶינָה	תְּגַלֶּינָה		תַּגְלֶינָה	תָּגְלֶינָה	תִּתְגַּלֶּינָה
	2mp	תִּגְלוּ	תִּגָּלוּ	תְּגַלּוּ	תְּגֻלּוּ	תַּגְלוּ	תָּגְלוּ	תִּתְגַּלּוּ
	2fp	תִּגְלֶינָה	תִּגָּלֶינָה	תְּגַלֶּינָה	תְּגֻלֶּינָה	תַּגְלֶינָה	תָּגְלֶינָה	תִּתְגַּלֶּינָה
	1cp	נִגְלֶה	נִגָּלֶה	נְגַלֶּה	נְגֻלֶּה	נַגְלֶה	נָגְלֶה	נִתְגַּלֶּה

		Qal	Niphal	Piel	Pual
Imperative	2ms	גְּלֵה	הִגָּלֵה	גַּלֵּה	
	2fs	גְּלִי	הִגָּלִי	גַּלִּי	
	2mp	גְּלוּ	הִגָּלוּ	גַּלּוּ	
	2fp	גְּלֶינָה	הִגָּלֶינָה	גַּלֶּינָה	
Infinitive Construct		גְּלוֹת	הִגָּלוֹת	גַּלּוֹת	
Infinitive Absolute		גָּלֹה	הִגָּלֹה	גַּלֵּה	
			נִגְלֹה		
Active Participle	ms	גֹּלֶה	נִגְלֶה	מְגַלֶּה	
	fs	גֹּלָה	נִגְלָה	מְגַלָּה	
	mp	גֹּלִים	נִגְלִים	מְגַלִּים	
	fp	גֹּלוֹת	נִגְלוֹת	מְגַלּוֹת	
Passive Participle	ms	גָּלוּי			מְגֻלֶּה
	fs	גְּלוּיָה			מְגֻלָּה
	mp	גְּלוּיִם			מְגֻלִּים
	fp	גְּלוּיוֹת			מְגֻלּוֹת

I-נ Verbs

		Qal (1)	Qal (2)	Qal (Irreg.)	Niphal	Hiphil	Hophal
Perfect	3ms	נָפַל	נָגַשׁ	נָתַן	נִגַּד	הִגִּיד	הֻגַּד
	3fs	נָפְלָה	נָגְשָׁה	נָתְנָה	נִגְּדָה	הִגִּידָה	הֻגְּדָה
	2ms	נָפַלְתָּ	נָגַשְׁתָּ	נָתַתָּ	נִגַּדְתָּ	הִגַּדְתָּ	הֻגַּדְתָּ
	2fs	נָפַלְתְּ	נָגַשְׁתְּ	נָתַתְּ	נִגַּדְתְּ	הִגַּדְתְּ	הֻגַּדְתְּ
	1cs	נָפַלְתִּי	נָגַשְׁתִּי	נָתַתִּי	נִגַּדְתִּי	הִגַּדְתִּי	הֻגַּדְתִּי
	3cp	נָפְלוּ	נָגְשׁוּ	נָתְנוּ	נִגְּדוּ	הִגִּידוּ	הֻגְּדוּ
	2mp	נְפַלְתֶּם	נְגַשְׁתֶּם	נְתַתֶּם	נִגַּדְתֶּם	הִגַּדְתֶּם	הֻגַּדְתֶּם
	2fp	נְפַלְתֶּן	נְגַשְׁתֶּן	נְתַתֶּן	נִגַּדְתֶּן	הִגַּדְתֶּן	הֻגַּדְתֶּן
	1cp	נָפַלְנוּ	נָגַשְׁנוּ	נָתַנּוּ	נִגַּדְנוּ	הִגַּדְנוּ	הֻגַּדְנוּ
Imperfect	3ms	יִפֹּל	יִגַּשׁ	יִתֵּן	יִנָּגֵד	יַגִּיד	יֻגַּד
	3fs	תִּפֹּל	תִּגַּשׁ	תִּתֵּן	תִּנָּגֵד	תַּגִּיד	תֻּגַּד
	2ms	תִּפֹּל	תִּגַּשׁ	תִּתֵּן	תִּנָּגֵד	תַּגִּיד	תֻּגַּד
	2fs	תִּפְּלִי	תִּגְּשִׁי	תִּתְּנִי	תִּנָּגְדִי	תַּגִּידִי	תֻּגְּדִי
	1cs	אֶפֹּל	אֶגַּשׁ	אֶתֵּן	אֶנָּגֵד	אַגִּיד	אֻגַּד
	3mp	יִפְּלוּ	יִגְּשׁוּ	יִתְּנוּ	יִנָּגְדוּ	יַגִּידוּ	יֻגְּדוּ
	3fp	תִּפֹּלְנָה	תִּגַּשְׁנָה	תִּתֵּנָּה	תִּנָּגַדְנָה	תַּגֵּדְנָה	תֻּגַּדְנָה
	2mp	תִּפְּלוּ	תִּגְּשׁוּ	תִּתְּנוּ	תִּנָּגְדוּ	תַּגִּידוּ	תֻּגְּדוּ
	2fp	תִּפֹּלְנָה	תִּגַּשְׁנָה	תִּתֵּנָּה	תִּנָּגַדְנָה	תַּגֵּדְנָה	תֻּגַּדְנָה
	1cp	נִפֹּל	נִגַּשׁ	נִתֵּן	נִנָּגֵד	נַגִּיד	נֻגַּד

		Qal	Niphal	Piel	Pual	Hiphil	Hophal
Imperative	2ms	פְּעַל	הִפָּעֵל	פַּעֵל		הַפְעֵל	
	2fs	פִּעֲלִי	הִפָּעֲלִי	פַּעֲלִי		הַפְעִילִי	
	2mp	פִּעֲלוּ	הִפָּעֲלוּ	פַּעֲלוּ		הַפְעִילוּ	
	2fp	פְּעַלְנָה	הִפָּעַלְנָה	פַּעֵלְנָה		הַפְעֵלְנָה	
Infinitive Construct		פְּעֹל	הִפָּעֵל	פַּעֵל		הַפְעִיל	
Infinitive Absolute		פָּעוֹל	הִפָּעֹל	פַּעֵל		הַפְעֵל	
Active Participle	ms	פֹּעֵל	נִפְעָל	מְפַעֵל		מַפְעִיל	
	fs	פֹּעֶלֶת	נִפְעֶלֶת	מְפַעֶלֶת		מַפְעֶלֶת	
	mp	פֹּעֲלִים	נִפְעָלִים	מְפַעֲלִים		מַפְעִילִים	
	fp	פֹּעֲלוֹת	נִפְעָלוֹת	מְפַעֲלוֹת		מַפְעִילוֹת	
Passive Participle	ms	פָּעוּל			מְפֻעָל		מֻפְעָל
	fs	פְּעוּלָה			מְפֻעֶלֶת		מֻפְעֶלֶת
	mp	פְּעוּלִים			מְפֻעָלִים		מֻפְעָלִים
	fp	פְּעוּלוֹת			מְפֻעָלוֹת		מֻפְעָלוֹת

I-ʾ Verbs

		Qal (1)	Qal (2)	Niphal	Hiphil	Hophal
Perfect	3ms	יָשַׁב	יָרַשׁ	נוֹשַׁב	הוֹשִׁיב	הוּשַׁב
	3fs	יָשְׁבָה	יָרְשָׁה	נוֹשְׁבָה	הוֹשִׁיבָה	הוּשְׁבָה
	2ms	יָשַׁבְתָּ	יָרַשְׁתָּ	נוֹשַׁבְתָּ	הוֹשַׁבְתָּ	הוּשַׁבְתָּ
	2fs	יָשַׁבְתְּ	יָרַשְׁתְּ	נוֹשַׁבְתְּ	הוֹשַׁבְתְּ	הוּשַׁבְתְּ
	1cs	יָשַׁבְתִּי	יָרַשְׁתִּי	נוֹשַׁבְתִּי	הוֹשַׁבְתִּי	הוּשַׁבְתִּי
	3cp	יָשְׁבוּ	יָרְשׁוּ	נוֹשְׁבוּ	הוֹשִׁיבוּ	הוּשְׁבוּ
	2mp	יְשַׁבְתֶּם	יְרַשְׁתֶּם	נוֹשַׁבְתֶּם	הוֹשַׁבְתֶּם	הוּשַׁבְתֶּם
	2fp	יְשַׁבְתֶּן	יְרַשְׁתֶּן	נוֹשַׁבְתֶּן	הוֹשַׁבְתֶּן	הוּשַׁבְתֶּן
	1cp	יָשַׁבְנוּ	יָרַשְׁנוּ	נוֹשַׁבְנוּ	הוֹשַׁבְנוּ	הוּשַׁבְנוּ
Imperfect	3ms	יֵשֵׁב	יִירַשׁ	יִוָּשֵׁב	יוֹשִׁיב	יוּשַׁב
	3fs	תֵּשֵׁב	תִּירַשׁ	תִּוָּשֵׁב	תּוֹשִׁיב	תּוּשַׁב
	2ms	תֵּשֵׁב	תִּירַשׁ	תִּוָּשֵׁב	תּוֹשִׁיב	תּוּשַׁב
	2fs	תֵּשְׁבִי	תִּירְשִׁי	תִּוָּשְׁבִי	תּוֹשִׁיבִי	תּוּשְׁבִי
	1cs	אֵשֵׁב	אִירַשׁ	אִוָּשֵׁב	אוֹשִׁיב	אוּשַׁב
	3mp	יֵשְׁבוּ	יִירְשׁוּ	יִוָּשְׁבוּ	יוֹשִׁיבוּ	יוּשְׁבוּ
	3fp	תֵּשַׁבְנָה	תִּירַשְׁנָה	תִּוָּשַׁבְנָה	תּוֹשֵׁבְנָה	תּוּשַׁבְנָה
	2mp	תֵּשְׁבוּ	תִּירְשׁוּ	תִּוָּשְׁבוּ	תּוֹשִׁיבוּ	תּוּשְׁבוּ
	2fp	תֵּשַׁבְנָה	תִּירַשְׁנָה	תִּוָּשַׁבְנָה	תּוֹשֵׁבְנָה	תּוּשַׁבְנָה
	1cp	נֵשֵׁב	נִירַשׁ	נִוָּשֵׁב	נוֹשִׁיב	נוּשַׁב

		Qal	Niphal	Piel	Pual
Imperative	2ms	קְטֹל	הִקָּטֵל	קַטֵּל	
	2fs	קִטְלִי	הִקָּטְלִי	קַטְּלִי	
	2mp	קִטְלוּ	הִקָּטְלוּ	קַטְּלוּ	
	2fp	קְטֹלְנָה	הִקָּטַלְנָה	קַטֵּלְנָה	
Infinitive Construct		קְטֹל	הִקָּטֵל	קַטֵּל	קֻטַּל
Infinitive Absolute		קָטוֹל	הִקָּטֹל	קַטֵּל	קֻטֹּל
Active Participle	ms	קֹטֵל	נִקְטָל	מְקַטֵּל	
	fs	קֹטֶלֶת	נִקְטָלָה	מְקַטֶּלֶת	
	mp	קֹטְלִים	נִקְטָלִים	מְקַטְּלִים	
	fp	קֹטְלוֹת	נִקְטָלוֹת	מְקַטְּלוֹת	
Passive Participle	ms	קָטוּל			מְקֻטָּל
	fs	קְטוּלָה			מְקֻטֶּלֶת
	mp	קְטוּלִים			מְקֻטָּלִים
	fp	קְטוּלוֹת			מְקֻטָּלוֹת

Biconsonantal Verbs

		Qal (ו-class)	Qal (ˑ-class)	Qal (וֹ-class)	Hiphil	Hophal
Perfect	3ms	קָם	שָׂם	בָּא	הֵקִים	הוּקַם
	3fs	קָ֫מָה	שָׂ֫מָה	בָּ֫אָה	הֵקִ֫ימָה	הוּקְמָה
	2ms	קַ֫מְתָּ	שַׂ֫מְתָּ	בָּ֫אתָ	הֲקִימ֫וֹתָ	הוּקַ֫מְתָּ
	2fs	קַמְתְּ	שַׂמְתְּ	בָּאת	הֲקִימ֫וֹת	הוּקַמְתְּ
	1cs	קַ֫מְתִּי	שַׂ֫מְתִּי	בָּ֫אתִי	הֲקִימ֫וֹתִי	הוּקַ֫מְתִּי
	3cp	קָ֫מוּ	שָׂ֫מוּ	בָּ֫אוּ	הֵקִ֫ימוּ	הוּקְמוּ
	2mp	קַמְתֶּם	שַׂמְתֶּם	בָּאתֶם	הֲקִימוֹתֶם	הוּקַמְתֶּם
	2fp	קַמְתֶּן	שַׂמְתֶּן	בָּאתֶן	הֲקִימוֹתֶן	הוּקַמְתֶּן
	1cp	קַ֫מְנוּ	שַׂ֫מְנוּ	בָּ֫אנוּ	הֲקִימ֫וֹנוּ	הוּקַ֫מְנוּ
Imperfect	3ms	יָקוּם	יָשִׂים	יָבוֹא	יָקִים	יוּקַם
	3fs	תָּקוּם	תָּשִׂים	תָּבוֹא	תָּקִים	תּוּקַם
	2ms	תָּקוּם	תָּשִׂים	תָּבוֹא	תָּקִים	תּוּקַם
	2fs	תָּק֫וּמִי	תָּשִׂ֫ימִי	תָּב֫וֹאִי	תָּקִ֫ימִי	תּוּקְמִי
	1cs	אָקוּם	אָשִׂים	אָבוֹא	אָקִים	אוּקַם
	3mp	יָק֫וּמוּ	יָשִׂ֫ימוּ	יָב֫וֹאוּ	יָקִ֫ימוּ	יוּקְמוּ
	3fp	תְּקוּמֶ֫ינָה	תְּשִׂימֶ֫ינָה	תְּב֫וֹאנָה	תְּקִימֶ֫ינָה	תּוּקַ֫מְנָה
	2mp	תָּק֫וּמוּ	תָּשִׂ֫ימוּ	תָּב֫וֹאוּ	תָּקִ֫ימוּ	תּוּקְמוּ
	2fp	תְּקוּמֶ֫ינָה	תְּשִׂימֶ֫ינָה	תְּב֫וֹאנָה	תְּקִימֶ֫ינָה	תּוּקַ֫מְנָה
	1cp	נָקוּם	נָשִׂים	נָבוֹא	נָקִים	נוּקַם

Imperative				
2ms	קוּם	שִׂים	בּוֹא	
2fs	קוּמִי	שִׂימִי	בֹּאִי	
2mp	קוּמוּ	שִׂימוּ	בֹּאוּ	
2fp	קֹמְנָה	שֵׂמְנָה	בֹּאנָה	
Infinitive Construct	קוּם	שִׂים	בּוֹא	
Infinitive Absolute	קוֹם	שׂוֹם	בּוֹא	
Active Participle				
ms	קָם	שָׂם	בָּא	
fs	קָמָה	שָׂמָה	בָּאָה	
mp	קָמִים	שָׂמִים	בָּאִים	
fp	קָמוֹת	שָׂמוֹת	בָּאוֹת	
Passive Participle				
ms	קוּם	שׂוּם	בּוֹא	מוּקָם
fs				מוּקֶמֶת
mp				מוּקָמִים
fp				מוּקָמוֹת

Geminate Verbs

		Qal (1)	Qal (2)	Niphal	Piel	Hiphil	Hophal	Hithpael
Perfect	3ms	סָבַב	תַּם	נָסַב	הִלֵּל	הֵסֵב	הוּסַב	הִתְהַלֵּל
	3fs	סָבְבָה	תַּמָּה	נָסַבָּה	הִלְלָה	הֵסֵבָּה	הוּסַבָּה	הִתְהַלְלָה
	2ms	סַבּוֹתָ	תַּמּוֹתָ	נְסַבּוֹתָ	הִלַּלְתָּ	הֲסִבּוֹתָ	הוּסַבּוֹתָ	הִתְהַלַּלְתָּ
	2fs	סַבּוֹת	תַּמּוֹת	נְסַבּוֹת	הִלַּלְתְּ	הֲסִבּוֹת	הוּסַבּוֹת	הִתְהַלַּלְתְּ
	1cs	סַבּוֹתִי	תַּמּוֹתִי	נְסַבּוֹתִי	הִלַּלְתִּי	הֲסִבּוֹתִי	הוּסַבּוֹתִי	הִתְהַלַּלְתִּי
	3cp	סָבְבוּ	תַּמּוּ	נָסַבּוּ	הִלְלוּ	הֵסֵבּוּ	הוּסַבּוּ	הִתְהַלְלוּ
	2mp	סַבּוֹתֶם	תַּמּוֹתֶם	נְסַבּוֹתֶם	הִלַּלְתֶּם	הֲסִבּוֹתֶם	הוּסַבּוֹתֶם	הִתְהַלַּלְתֶּם
	2fp	סַבּוֹתֶן	תַּמּוֹתֶן	נְסַבּוֹתֶן	הִלַּלְתֶּן	הֲסִבּוֹתֶן	הוּסַבּוֹתֶן	הִתְהַלַּלְתֶּן
	1cp	סַבּוֹנוּ	תַּמּוֹנוּ	נְסַבּוֹנוּ	הִלַּלְנוּ	הֲסִבּוֹנוּ	הוּסַבּוֹנוּ	הִתְהַלַּלְנוּ
Imperfect	3ms	יָסֹב	יִתַּם	יִסַּב	יְהַלֵּל	יָסֵב	יוּסַב	יִתְהַלֵּל
	3fs	תָּסֹב	תִּתַּם	תִּסַּב	תְּהַלֵּל	תָּסֵב	תּוּסַב	תִּתְהַלֵּל
	2ms	תָּסֹב	תִּתַּם	תִּסַּב	תְּהַלֵּל	תָּסֵב	תּוּסַב	תִּתְהַלֵּל
	2fs	תָּסֹבִּי	תִּתַּמִּי	תִּסַּבִּי	תְּהַלְלִי	תָּסֵבִּי	תּוּסַבִּי	תִּתְהַלְלִי
	1cs	אָסֹב	אִתַּם	אֶסַּב	אֲהַלֵּל	אָסֵב	אוּסַב	אֶתְהַלֵּל
	3mp	יָסֹבּוּ	יִתַּמּוּ	יִסַּבּוּ	יְהַלְלוּ	יָסֵבּוּ	יוּסַבּוּ	יִתְהַלְלוּ
	3fp	תְּסֻבֶּינָה	תִּתַּמְנָה	תִּסַּבֶּינָה	תְּהַלֵּלְנָה	תְּסִבֶּינָה	תּוּסַבֶּינָה	תִּתְהַלֵּלְנָה
	2mp	תָּסֹבּוּ	תִּתַּמּוּ	תִּסַּבּוּ	תְּהַלְלוּ	תָּסֵבּוּ	תּוּסַבּוּ	תִּתְהַלְלוּ
	2fp	תְּסֻבֶּינָה	תִּתַּמְנָה	תִּסַּבֶּינָה	תְּהַלֵּלְנָה	תְּסִבֶּינָה	תּוּסַבֶּינָה	תִּתְהַלֵּלְנָה
	1cp	נָסֹב	נִתַּם	נִסַּב	נְהַלֵּל	נָסֵב	נוּסַב	נִתְהַלֵּל

	Qal	Niphal	Piel	Pual	Hiphil	Hophal	Hithpael
Imperative							
2ms	קְטֹל	הִקָּטֵל	קַטֵּל		הַקְטֵל		הִתְקַטֵּל
2fs	קִטְלִי	הִקָּטְלִי	קַטְּלִי		הַקְטִילִי		הִתְקַטְּלִי
2mp	קִטְלוּ	הִקָּטְלוּ	קַטְּלוּ		הַקְטִילוּ		הִתְקַטְּלוּ
2fp	קְטֹלְנָה	הִקָּטַלְנָה	קַטֵּלְנָה		הַקְטֵלְנָה		הִתְקַטֵּלְנָה
Infinitive Construct	קְטֹל	הִקָּטֵל	קַטֵּל		הַקְטִיל		הִתְקַטֵּל
Infinitive Absolute	קָטוֹל	הִקָּטֹל	קַטֹּל		הַקְטֵל		הִתְקַטֵּל
Active Participle							
ms	קֹטֵל		מְקַטֵּל		מַקְטִיל		מִתְקַטֵּל
fs	קֹטֶלֶת		מְקַטֶּלֶת		מַקְטֶלֶת		מִתְקַטֶּלֶת
mp	קֹטְלִים		מְקַטְּלִים		מַקְטִילִים		מִתְקַטְּלִים
fp	קֹטְלוֹת		מְקַטְּלוֹת		מַקְטִילוֹת		מִתְקַטְּלוֹת
Passive Participle							
ms	קָטוּל						
fs	קְטוּלָה						
mp	קְטוּלִים						
fp	קְטוּלוֹת						

Strong Verb Diagnostics
At-A-Glance

	Perfect	Imperfect	Imperative	Infinitive Construct	Infinitive Absolute	Participle
Qal	קָטַל	יִקְטֹל	קְטֹל	קְטֹל	קָטוֹל	קֹטֵל
Niphal	נִקְטַל	יִקָּטֵל	הִקָּטֵל	הִקָּטֵל	נִקְטוֹל הִקָּטוֹל	נִקְטָל
Piel	קִטֵּל	יְקַטֵּל	קַטֵּל	קַטֵּל	קַטֵּל	מְקַטֵּל
Pual	קֻטַּל	יְקֻטַּל				מְקֻטָּל
Hiphil	הִקְטִיל הִקְטַלְתְּ	יַקְטִיל	הַקְטֵל הַקְטִילִי	הַקְטִיל	הַקְטֵל	מַקְטִיל
Hophal	הֻקְטַל הָקְטַל	יֻקְטַל יָקְטַל				מֻקְטָל מָקְטָל
Hithpael	הִתְקַטֵּל	יִתְקַטֵּל	הִתְקַטֵּל	הִתְקַטֵּל	הִתְקַטֵּל	מִתְקַטֵּל

Niphal Diagnostics
At-A-Glance

	Perfect	Imperfect	Imperative	Infinitive Construct	Infinitive Absolute	Participle
Strong	נִקְטַל	יִקָּטֵל	הִקָּטֵל	הִקָּטֵל	נִקְטוֹל הִקָּטוֹל	נִקְטָל
III-א	נִמְצָא	יִמָּצֵא	הִמָּצֵא	הִמָּצֵא	נִמְצוֹא	נִמְצָא
III-ה	נִבְנָה נִבְנֵיתָ	יִבָּנֶה	הִבָּנֶה	הִבָּנוֹת	נִבְנֹה הִבָּנֵה	נִבְנֶה
I-Gutt	נֶעֱזַב נֶעֱזָב	יֵעָזֵב	הֵעָזֵב	הֵעָזֵב	נַעֲזוֹב הֵעָזוֹב	נֶעֱזָב
I-נ	נִצַּל	יִנָּצֵל	הִנָּצֵל	הִנָּצֵל	הִנָּצֵל נִצּוֹל	נִצָּל
I-י	נוֹשַׁב	יִוָּשֵׁב	הִוָּשֵׁב	הִוָּשֵׁב		נוֹשָׁב

Piel Diagnostics
At-A-Glance

	Perfect	Imperfect	Imperative	Infinitive Construct	Infinitive Absolute	Participle
Strong	קַטֵּל קִטֵּל	יְקַטֵּל	קַטֵּל	קַטֵּל	קַטֵּל	מְקַטֵּל
III-ח/ע	שַׁלַּח שִׁלַּח	יְשַׁלַּח	שַׁלַּח	שַׁלַּח	שַׁלֵּחַ	מְשַׁלֵּחַ
III-א	מִצֵּא מִצֵּא	יְמַצֵּא	מַצֵּא	מַצֵּא	מַצֵּא	מְמַצֵּא
III-ה	גִּלָּה	יְגַלֶּה	גַּלֵּה	גַּלּוֹת	גַּלֵּה	מְגַלֶּה
Geminate	הִלֵּל	יְהַלֵּל	הַלֵּל	הַלֵּל	הַלֵּל	מְהַלֵּל
II-Gutt¹	נִחַם נִחַם	יְנַחֵם	נַחֵם	נַחֵם	נַחֵם	מְנַחֵם
II-Gutt²	בֵּרֵךְ בֵּרַךְ	יְבָרֵךְ	בָּרֵךְ	בָּרֵךְ	בָּרֵךְ	מְבָרֵךְ

---

[1] II-Guttural verbs with virtual doubling

[2] II-Guttural verbs with compensatory lengthening

Pual Diagnostics
At-A-Glance

	Perfect	*Imperfect*	*Participle*
Strong	קֻטַּל	יְקֻטַּל	מְקֻטָּל
III-א	מֻצָּא	יְמֻצָּא	מְמֻצָּא
III-ה	גֻּלָּה	יְגֻלֶּה	מְגֻלֶּה
II-Gutt[1]	נֻחַם	יְנֻחַם	מְנֻחָם
II-Gutt[2]	בֹּרַךְ	יְבֹרַךְ	מְבֹרָךְ

---

[1] II-Guttural with virtual doubling
[2] II-Guttural with compensatory lengthening

Hiphil Diagnostics
At-A-Glance

	Perfect	Imperfect	Imperative	Infinitive Construct	Infinitive Absolute	Participle
Strong	הִקְטִיל הִקְטַ֫לְתָּ	יַקְטִיל	הַקְטֵל הַקְטִ֫ילִי	הַקְטִיל	הַקְטֵל	מַקְטִיל
I-Gutt	הֶעֱמִיד הֶעֱמַ֫דְתָּ	יַעֲמִיד	הַעֲמֵד הַעֲמִ֫ידִי	הַעֲמִיד	הַעֲמֵד	מַעֲמִיד
III-ע/ח	הִשְׁלִיחַ הִשְׁלַחְתְּ	יַשְׁלִיחַ	הַשְׁלַח הַשְׁלִיחִי	הַשְׁלִיחַ	הַשְׁלֵחַ	מַשְׁלִיחַ
III-א	הִמְצִיא הִמְצֵ֫אתָ	יַמְצִיא	הַמְצֵא הַמְצִ֫יאִי	הַמְצִיא	הַמְצֵא	מַמְצִיא
III-ה	הִגְלָה הִגְלִ֫יתָ	יַגְלֶה	הַגְלֵה	הַגְלוֹת	הַגְלֵה	מַגְלֶה
I-נ	הִצִּיל הִצַּ֫לְתָּ	יַצִּיל	הַצֵּל הַצִּ֫ילִי	הַצִּיל	הַצֵּל	מַצִּיל
I-י	הוֹשִׁיב הוֹשַׁ֫בְתָּ	יוֹשִׁיב	הוֹשֵׁב הוֹשִׁ֫יבִי	הוֹשִׁיב	הוֹשֵׁב	מוֹשִׁיב
Bicon	הֵקִים הֲקִימֹ֫ות	יָקִים	הָקֵם הָקִ֫ימִי	הָקִים	הָקֵם	מֵקִים

Hophal Diagnostics
At-A-Glance

	Perfect	*Imperfect*	*Participle*
Strong (u)	הָקְטַל	יָקְטַל	מָקְטָל
Strong (o)	הָקְטַל	יָקְטַל	מָקְטָל
I-Guttural	הָעֳמַד	יָעֳמַד	מָעֳמָד
III-ה	הָגְלָה	יָגְלֶה	מָגְלֶה
I-נ	הֻצַּל	יֻצַּל	מֻצָּל
I-י	הוּשַׁב	יוּשַׁב	מוּשָׁב
Bicon	הוּקַם	יוּקַם	מוּקָם
Geminate	הוּסַב	יוּסַב	מוּסָב

443

Hithpael Diagnostics
At-A-Glance

	Perfect	Imperfect	Imperative	Infinitive Construct	Infinitive Absolute	Participle
Strong	הִתְקַטֵּל	יִתְקַטֵּל	הִתְקַטֵּל	הִתְקַטֵּל	הִתְקַטֵּל	מִתְקַטֵּל
Geminate	הִתְפַּלֵּל	יִתְפַּלֵּל	הִתְפַּלֵּל	הִתְפַּלֵּל	הִתְפַּלֵּל	מִתְפַּלֵּל
III-ה	הִתְגַּלָּה	יִתְגַּלֶּה	הִתְגַּלֵּה	הִתְגַּלּוֹת		מִתְגַּלֶּה
II-Gutt¹	הִתְנַחֵם	יִתְנַחֵם	הִתְנַחֵם	הִתְנַחֵם	הִתְנַחֵם	מִתְנַחֵם
II-Gutt²	הִתְבָּרֵךְ	יִתְבָּרֵךְ	הִתְבָּרֵךְ	הִתְבָּרֵךְ	הִתְבָּרֵךְ	מִתְבָּרֵךְ

---

[1] II-Guttural with virtual doubling
[2] II-Guttural with compensatory lengthening

Summary of Endings on III-ה Verbs
Qal and Derived Stems

Ending	Qal	Niphal	Piel	Pual	Hiphil	Hophal	Hithpael
Perfect — הָ	גָּלָה	נִגְלָה	גִּלָּה	גֻּלָּה	הִגְלָה	הָגְלָה	הִתְגַּלָּה
Imperfect — הֶ	יִגְלֶה	יִגָּלֶה	יְגַלֶּה	יְגֻלֶּה	יַגְלֶה	יָגְלֶה	יִתְגַּלֶּה
Imperative — הֵ	גְּלֵה	הִגָּלֵה	גַּלֵּה		הַגְלֵה		הִתְגַּלֵּה
Inf Construct — ֹת	גְּלוֹת	הִגָּלוֹת	גַּלּוֹת		הַגְלוֹת		הִתְגַּלּוֹת
Participle — הֶ	גֹּלֶה	נִגְלֶה	מְגַלֶּה	מְגֻלֶּה	מַגְלֶה	מָגְלֶה	מִתְגַּלֶּה

Hebrew-English Lexicon

Hebrew words occurring fifty times or more,
including less frequently occurring words that appear
in the grammar and workbook

א

אָב — father; אָבוֹת (plural); אֲבִי (ms construct)

אָבַד — to perish; (Piel) destroy; (Hiphil) exterminate

אָבָה — to be willing, consent, agree

אֶבְיוֹן — poor, oppressed

אֲבִימֶלֶךְ — Abimelech

אֵבֶל — mourning

אֲבָל — truly, indeed, however

אֶבֶן — stone (fs)

אַבְנֵר — Abner

אַבְרָהָם — Abraham

אַבְרָם — Abram

אַבְשָׁלוֹם — Absalom

אֵד — fresh water, surface water (mist?)

אֱדוֹם — Edom; אֲדוֹמִי Edomite(s)

אָדוֹן — lord, master, Lord (see אֲדֹנָי)

אָדָם — man, Adam

אֲדָמָה — ground, land

אֶדֶן — pedestal, socket

אֲדֹנָי — Lord

אָהַב — to love, like

אַהֲבָה — love

אֹהֶל — tent; אֹהֶל מוֹעֵד tent of meeting

אַהֲרוֹן — Aaron

אוֹ — or

אוּלַי — perhaps

אָוֶן — wickedness, iniquity

אוֹצָר — supply, storehouse, treasure

אוֹר — light

אוֹר — (Hiphil) to give light, shine

אוֹת — sign; אֹתוֹת (plural)

אָז — then, formerly, since; (מִן + אָז) מֵאָז from then, from that time

אָזַן — (Hiphil) to listen

אֹזֶן — ear (fs); אָזְנֵי (dual construct)

אָח — brother; אַחִים (plural); אֲחִי (ms construct)

אַחְאָב — Ahab

אֶחָד — one (ms)

446

אָחוֹר	back, behind
אָחוֹת	sister (fs)
אָחַז	to seize, hold fast
אֲחֻזָּה	property, possession
אַחַר	after, behind (more frequently as אַחֲרֵי)
אַחֵר	another; אַחֶרֶת (fs)
אַחֲרוֹן	behind, last
אַחֲרִית	end, outcome (fs)
אַחַת	one (fs)
אֵי־מִזֶּה	from what place
אֵיב	enemy; אוֹיֵב (full spelling)
אַיֵּה	where?
אִיּוֹב	Job
אֵיךְ	how?
אֵיכָה	how? where?
אַיִל	ram
אֵילָם	porch, vestibule (spelling varies as אוּלָם or אֵלָם)
אֵימָה	fear, terror, dread
אַיִן	there is not, there are not; אֵין (construct)
אֵיפֹה	where?
אִישׁ	man, husband; אֲנָשִׁים (plural); אַנְשֵׁי (mp construct)
אַךְ	only, surely
אָכַל	to eat, devour
אֹכֶל	food

אָכְלָה	food
אֵל	God, mighty one, god
אֶל	to, toward, unto
אַל	no, not
אֵלֶּה	these
אֱלֹהִים	God, gods; אֱלֹהֵי (mp construct)
אַלּוּף	tribal chief
אֵלִיָּה	Elijah; also as אֵלִיָּהוּ
אֱלִישָׁע	Elisha
אָלַם	(Piel) to bind sheaves
אֲלֻמָּה	sheaf
אַלְמָנָה	widow
אֶלְעָזָר	Eleazar
אֶלֶף	thousand, tribe, clan
אֵם	mother (fs)
אִם	if, then, or
אָמָה	female slave
אַמָּה	forearm, cubit
אֱמוּנָה	steadiness, firmness
אָמַן	(Niphal) to be steady, firm, trustworthy, faithful; (Hiphil) believe
אָמֵץ	to be strong, brave
אָמַר	to say
אֱמֹרִי	Amorite(s)
אֱמֶת	trustworthiness, stability, truth (fs)
אַמְתַּחַת	sack; אַמְתְּחֹת (plural)
אֱנוֹשׁ	man, men (collective)

אֲנַ֫חְנוּ — we

אֲנִי — I

אָנֹכִי — I (alternate form of אֲנִי)

אֲנָשִׁים — men, husbands (plural of אִישׁ); אַנְשֵׁי (mp construct)

אָסָא — Asa

אָסִיר — prisoner

אָסַף — to gather, assemble

אָסַר — to bind; (Niphal, Pual) be fettered, imprisoned

אֶסְתֵּר — Esther

אַף — nose, nostril, anger

אַף — also, even

אֶפְרַ֫יִם — Ephraim; אֶפְרָתִי Ephraimite

אֵ֫צֶל — beside, near, next to

אַרְבַּע — four; אַרְבָּעָה (fs)

אֲרוֹן — ark, chest (with definite article הָאָרוֹן)

אָרוּר — accursed

אֶ֫רֶז — cedar

אֹ֫רַח — way, path

אֲרִי — lion

אַרְיֵה — lion (alternate of אֲרִי)

אֹ֫רֶךְ — length

אֲרָם — Aram, Syria; אֲרַמִּי Aramean(s), Syrian(s)

אֶ֫רֶץ — earth, land (fs); אֲרָצוֹת (plural); אַרְצוֹת (construct)

אַ֫רְצָה — toward the earth, to the ground (אֶ֫רֶץ with directional ending ה ָ)

אָרַר — to curse

אֵשׁ — fire (fs)

אִשָּׁה — woman, wife; אֵ֫שֶׁת (fs construct); נָשִׁים (plural); נְשֵׁי (construct)

אִשֶּׁה — offering by fire

אַשּׁוּר — Assyria

אָשֵׁם — to be guilty; also אָשַׁם

אֲשֶׁר — who, which, that

אֵת/אֶת־ — with, beside; אִתִּי (with 1cs suffix)

אֵת/אֶת־ — definite direct object marker (not translated); אֹתִי (with 1cs suffix)

אַתְּ — you (2fs)

אַתָּה — you (2ms)

אָתוֹן — female donkey (fs)

אַתֶּם — you (2mp)

אֶתְמוֹל — yesterday

אַתֵּן — you (2fp)

אַתֵּ֫נָה — you (2fp)

בּ

בְּ	in, against
בְּאֵר	well, pit (fs)
בָּבֶל	Babylon (Babel)
בֶּגֶד	garment
בִּגְלַל	(בְּ + גְּלָל) on account of
בְּהֵמָה	cattle, animal(s)
בּוֹא	to go in, enter, come; (Hiphil) to bring, carry
בּוֹר	pit, cistern
בּוֹשׁ	to be ashamed
בָּחוּר	young man; בַּחוּרִים (plural)
בָּחַר	to choose
בָּטַח	to trust
בֶּטֶן	belly, womb (fs)
בִּין	to understand, perceive
בֵּין	between
בִּינָה	understanding, intelligence
בַּיִת	house; בָּתִּים (plural); בֵּית (ms construct); בָּתֵּי (mp construct)
בֵּית־אֵל	Bethel
בָּכָה	to weep, mourn
בְּכֹר	firstborn; בְּכוֹר (full spelling)
בַּל	not (mostly in poetry)
בִּלְתִּי	not, except (negates Infinitive Construct); frequently as לְבִלְתִּי
בָּמָה	high place, funerary installation; בָּמוֹת (plural)
בֵּן	son; בָּנִים (plural); בֶּן־ (ms construct); בְּנֵי (mp construct)
בָּנָה	to build
בִּנְיָמִין	Benjamin
בַּעֲבוּר	because of, for the sake of
בַּעַד	distance, behind, through; בְּעַד (construct)
בְּעֵינֵי	in the eyes of, in the opinion of
בַּעַל	owner, husband, Baal
בָּעַר	to consume, burn
בָּקַע	to split, break open
בָּקָר	cows, herd, cattle
בֹּקֶר	morning
בָּקַשׁ	(Piel) to seek
בָּרָא	to create
בָּרָד	hail
בַּרְזֶל	iron
בָּרַח	to run away, flee
בְּרִית	covenant (fs)
בָּרַךְ	(Piel) to bless, kneel
בְּרָכָה	blessing; בִּרְכַּת (construct)

בָּשָׂר   flesh

בָּשָׁן   Bashan

בַּת   daughter (fs); בָּנוֹת (plural)

בְּתוֹךְ   in the midst of

בְּתוּלָה   virgin

ג

גָּאַל   to redeem

גָּבַה   to be high, exalted

גָּבֹהַ   high; גְּבֹהִים (plural)

גְּבוּל   boundary, territory, border

גִּבּוֹר   warrior, mighty man (גִּבּוֹר חַיִל mighty warrior)

גְּבוּרָה   strength

גִּבְעָה   hill, (cultic) high place; גְּבָעוֹת (plural)

גָּבַר   to excel, swell, rise

גֶּבֶר   young man, strong man

גָּד   Gad; גָּדִי Gadite(s)

גָּדַל   to be(come) strong, great; (Piel) bring up, let grow, nourish; (Hiphil) to make great, magnify

גָּדוֹל   great

גּוֹי   people, nation

גּוּר   to sojourn, stay as a foreigner

גּוֹרָל   lot, allotment

גָּלָה   to reveal, uncover, depart, go into captivity

גָּלַל   to roll, roll away

גָּלָל   on account of (frequently with inseparable preposition, בִּגְלַל)

גִּלְעָד   Gilead; גִּלְעָדִי Gileadite(s)

גַּם   also, indeed

גָּמַל   to wean

גָּמָל   camel; גְּמַלִּים (plural)

גַּן   garden; גָּן (alternate spelling)

גָּנַב   to steal

גַּנָּה   vineyard, garden

גָּעַר   to rebuke

גֶּפֶן   vine (fs)

גֵּר   stranger, sojourner, alien

גֹּרֶן   threshing-floor

גָּרַשׁ   (Piel) to drive away

גַּת   winepress (fs)

ד

דָּבַק   to stick, cling to, cleave

דָּבַר   (Piel) to speak

דָּבָר   word, matter, thing; דִּבְרֵי (mp construct)

דְּבַשׁ   honey

דָּג   fish

דָּוִד   David; דָּוִיד (full spelling)

דּוֹד   beloved, lover

דּוֹר generation, lifetime, lifespan; דּוֹרוֹת (plural)

דִּין to judge

דַּל poor

דֶּלֶת door (fs)

דָּם blood; דָּמִים (plural); דַּם (ms construct); דְּמֵי (mp construct)

דָּמַם to be astonished, silent

דָּן Dan; דָּנִי Danite(s)

דָּנִיֵּאל Daniel

דַּעַת knowledge (fs)

דֶּרֶךְ way, road (ms, fs)

דָּרַשׁ to seek

ה

הַ the (with Daghesh Forte in the following consonant)

הֲ interrogative particle (not translated)

הֶבֶל breath, vanity, idol

הֶבֶל Abel

הוּא he, that

הוּא she (alternate form of the 3fs independent personal pronoun הִיא)

הִיא she, that

הָיָה to be, happen, become

הֵיכָל palace, temple

הָלַךְ to go, walk

הָלַל (Piel) to praise; (Hithpael) boast

הֵם they (3mp)

הֵמָּה they (3mp)

הָמוֹן tumult, turmoil, multitude

הֵן they (3fp)

הֵנָּה they (3fp); those (fp)

הֵנָּה here, to this place

הִנֵּה behold! lo!; הִנְנִי or הִנֶּנִּי (with 1cs suffix)

הָפַךְ to turn, overturn, destroy

הֲפֵכָה destruction

הַר mountain, mountain range; הָרִים (plural)

הָרַג to kill

הָרָה to conceive, become pregnant

ו

וְ and, or, also, even

ז

זֹאת this (fs)

זָבַח to slaughter, sacrifice

זֶבַח sacrifice

זֶה this (ms)

זָהָב gold

זַיִת   olive, olive tree

זָכָר   man, male

זָכַר   to remember; (Hiphil) to summon, recall, make known

זֵכֶר   remembrance, memorial

זָנָב   tail (as of a snake)

זָנָה   to commit fornication, be a harlot

זֵעָה   sweat; זֵעַת (fs construct)

זָעַק   to cry out; (Niphal) called to arms; (Hiphil) send out a call to arms

זְקוּנִים   old age

זָקֵן   (adjective) old; (noun) old man, elder; זְקַן (construct)

זָר   strange, different, illicit

זְרוֹעַ   arm, forearm, power, strength (fs)

זָרַע   to sow, scatter seed

זֶרַע   seed, descendant

זָרַק   to sprinkle, scatter

ח

חֶבְרוֹן   Hebron

חָג   procession, feast, festival; חַג (alternate spelling)

חָדַל   to cease, desist, stop

חָדָשׁ   new, fresh

חֹדֶשׁ   new moon, month; חֳדָשִׁים (plural)

חָוָה   (Hishtaphel) to bow down, worship

חַוָּה   Eve

חוֹמָה   wall

חוּץ   outside; חוּצָה (חוּץ with directional ending) to the outside

חָזָה   to see, perceive

חִזָּיוֹן   vision; חֶזְיֹנוֹת (plural)

חָזַק   to be(come) strong; (Hiphil) seize, grasp

חָזָק   hard, strong

חִזְקִיָּה   Hezekiah; הִזְקִיָּהוּ (alternate spelling)

חָטָא   to sin, miss the goal

חַטָּאת   sin, sin-offering, expiation (fs); חַטָּאוֹת (plural); חַטַּאת (fs construct)

חַי   life, lifetime; (adjective) living, alive

חָיָה   to live, be (stay) alive

חַיָּה   animal(s), living thing

חַיִּים   life, lifetime (see חַי above)

חִיל   to be in labor, pain

חַיִל   strength, wealth, army; חֵיל (ms construct)

חֵיק   bosom

חָכַם	to be(come) wise	חָסִיד	one who is faithful, devout
חָכָם	wise	חָפֵץ	to please, delight, take pleasure
חָכְמָה	experience, shrewdness, wisdom	חָפַשׂ	to search out; (Piel) look; (Hithpael) disguise oneself
חֵלֶב	fat		
חָלָב	milk	חֵץ	arrow
חָלָה	to be(come) weak, tired, sick	חֲצִי	half
חֲלוֹם	dream; חֲלוֹמוֹת (plural)	חָצֵר	permanent settlement, court, enclosure
חָלָל	(adjective) slain	חֹק	statute, prescription, rule, ordinance; חֻקִּים (plural)
חָלַל	(Niphal) to be defiled; (Piel) pollute, profane; (Hiphil) begin		
		חֻקָּה	statute, prescription; חֻקּוֹת (plural)
חָלַם	to dream	חֶרֶב	sword (fs)
חָלַק	to divide, apportion; (Piel) scatter	חֹרֵב	Horeb
חֵלֶק	part, portion	חָרָה	become hot, burning, angry
חֵמָה	heat, rage, wrath, poison	חָרַם	to devote to the ban, consecrate
חֲמוֹר	(male) ass, donkey		
חָמָס	violence, wrong	חֶרְפָּה	reproach, disgrace
חָמֵשׁ	five; חֲמִשָּׁה (fs)	חָרַשׁ	to be deaf
חֲמִשִּׁים	fifty	חָשַׂךְ	to withhold
חֵן	favor, grace	חָשַׁב	to account, regard, value, think; (Piel) calculate, plan, think about
חָנָה	to encamp		
חָנַן	to be gracious to, favor; (Hithpael) implore favor or compassion	חָשַׁךְ	to be(come) dim, dark
		חֹשֶׁךְ	darkness
חֶסֶד	loyalty, kindness, devotion, steadfast love	חֵת	Heth; חִתִּי Hittite(s)
חָסָה	to seek refuge		

חֹתֵן	father-in-law
חָתַת	to be shattered, filled with terror

ט

טָבַח	to slaughter
טָהוֹר	clean, pure
טָהֵר	to be clean, pure
טוֹב	to be good, pleasant (cf. יָטַב)
טוֹב	good
טָמֵא	to be unclean; (adjective) unclean
טַף	children
טֶרֶם	not yet, before, frequently as בְּטֶרֶם with the same meaning

י

יְאֹר	Nile river, river
יָבֵשׁ	to be dry, dry up
יָד	hand (fs); יָדוֹת (plural); יַד (fs construct); יָדַיִם (dual); יְדֵי (dual construct)
יָדָה	(Piel) to throw, cast; (Hiphil, Hithpael) thank, praise, confess
יָדַע	to know, notice; (Hiphil) to teach, declare, make known
יְהוּדָה	Judah; יְהוּדִי Judahite, Judean
יְהוָה	Yahweh, the Lord; יָהּ or יָהּ (shortened, often poetic forms)
יְהוֹיָדָע	Jehoiada
יְהוֹנָתָן	Jonathan
יְהוֹשֻׁעַ	Joshua
יְהוֹשָׁפָט	Jehoshaphat
יוֹאָב	Joab
יוֹאָשׁ	Joash
יוֹם	day; יָמִים (plural); יְמֵי (mp construct)
יוֹמָם	in the daytime, by day
יוֹסֵף	Joseph
יַחַד	(noun) community; (adverb) together, at the same time (frequently spelled יַחְדָּו with the same meaning)
יַחְדָּו	see יַחַד above
יָטַב	to be good; (Hiphil) treat kindly, graciously
יַיִן	wine
יָכַח	(Niphal) to dispute; (Hiphil) reprove, give judgement, settle quarrels
יָכֹל	to be able
יָלַד	to bring forth, bear; (Piel) help at birth, serve as midwife

יֶלֶד	male child, boy	יָרָה	(Hiphil) to instruct, teach
יַלְדָּה	girl	יְרוּשָׁלַם	Jerusalem; also spelled יְרוּשָׁלַיִם
יָם	sea, west; יַמִּים (plural); יְמֵי (mp construct)	יָרֵחַ	moon
יָמָּה	westward (יָם with directional ending ה ָ)	יְרִיעָה	curtain, tent (fabric)
		יָרֵךְ	thigh; יֶרֶךְ (construct)
יָמִין	right hand (side), south (fs)	יִרְמְיָה	Jeremiah; יִרְמְיָהוּ (alternate spelling)
יָסַף	to add, continue to do more or again; (Hiphil) enhance, increase	יָרַשׁ	to inherit, subdue, possess, dispossess, tread; (Hiphil) drive out, take possession of
יַעַן	on account of, because		
יַעַן אֲשֶׁר	because	יִשְׂרָאֵל	Israel
יָעַץ	to give counsel, advice	יֵשׁ	there is (are)
יַעֲקֹב	Jacob	יָשַׁב	to sit, dwell
יַעַר	thicket	יְשׁוּעָה	deliverance, salvation
יָפֶה	beautiful, handsome	יִשְׁמָעֵאל	Ishmael; יִשְׁמְעֵאלִי Ishmaelite
יָצָא	to go (come) out, go (come) forth; (Hiphil) make come out, lead out	יָשַׁע	(Niphal) to be saved, receive help; (Hiphil) save, help, rescue
יִצְחָק	Isaac	יֵשַׁע	salvation, help (יִשְׁעִי with 1cs suffix)
יָצַק	to dish up (food), pour out (liquid)		
יָצַר	form, shape, fashion	יָשָׁר	straight, right, upright, just
יָקַץ	to wake up	יָתוֹם	orphan
יָקָר	precious	יָתַר	(Niphal, Hiphil) be left, remain
יָרֵא	to fear, be afraid		
יָרַד	to go down; (Hiphil) bring down, throw down	יֶתֶר	remainder, remnant
יַרְדֵּן	Jordan		

כ

כְּ	as, like, according to כָּמֹונִי (with 1cs suffix)
כַּאֲשֶׁר	as, when
כָּבֵד	to be heavy, honored; (adjective) heavy
כָּבֹוד	glory, honor, possessions
כָּבַס	(Piel) to wash (clothes)
כֶּבֶשׂ	young ram
כִּבְשָׂה	ewe-lamb
כֹּה	thus, so
כָּהַן	(Piel) to perform the duties of a priest
כֹּהֵן	priest
כֹּוכָב	star; כֹּוכָבִים (plural)
כּוּן	(Niphal) to be firm, established; (Polel) establish; (Hiphil) establish, set up
כֹּחַ	strength, power
כִּי	because, for, that, when, but, indeed, truly
כַּיֹּום	today, this day (כְּ + הַיֹּום)
כָּכָה	so, thus
כִּכָּר	that which is round, i.e., loaf of bread, talent, region, proper name for the southern portion of the Ghor

כֹּל	all, each, every, whole; כָּל־ (construct)
כָּלָה	to cease, come to an end, finish, complete
כְּלִי	vessel, utensil; כֵּלִים (plural); כְּלֵי (construct)
כְּמֹו	as, like (cf. כְּ above)
כֵּן	thus, so
כָּנַע	(Niphal) to be subdued, humbled
כְּנַ֫עַן	Canaan; כְּנַעֲנִי Canaanite
כָּנָף	wing, corner, edge
כִּסֵּא	seat, throne; כִּסְאֹות (plural)
כָּסָה	(Piel) to cover, conceal
כְּסִיל	foolish, stupid, insolent
כֶּסֶף	silver, money
כָּעַס	to be irritated, angry; (Hiphil) provoke, insult, offend
כַּף	hand, palm (fs)
כָּפַר	to cover; (Piel) expiate
כְּרוּב	cherub
כֶּרֶם	vineyard
כָּרַת	to cut (off), make a covenant
כַּשְׂדִּים	Chaldea, Chaldeans
כָּשַׁל	to stumble, totter
כָּתַב	to write
כֻּתֹּנֶת	tunic (also as כְּתֹנֶת)

כָּתֵף shoulder (fs)

ל

לְ to, toward, for

לֹא no, not

לֵאמֹר saying (used to introduce a direct quote)

לֵב heart, mind, will

לֵבָב heart, mind, will (alternate spelling of לֵב)

לְבַד alone, besides (בַד with לְ prefix)

לַבָּה flame; לַבַּת (construct)

לְבִלְתִּי not, except (negates Infinitive Construct); see בִּלְתִּי

לָבָן Laban

לָבַשׁ to put on, clothe

לֶהָבָה flame

לוּחַ tablet; לוּחוֹת (plural)

לֵוִי Levi, Levite(s)

לָחַם (Niphal) to fight

לֶחֶם bread, food

לָחַץ to crowd, press, oppress, torment

לַחַץ oppression, affliction

לַיְלָה night

לִין to spend the night, lodge

לָכַד to seize, capture

לָכֵן therefore

לָמַד to learn; (Piel) teach

לָמָה why; לָמָּה (alternate spelling)

לְמַעַן for the sake of, on account of, in order that

לִפְנֵי before, in the presence of

לָקַח to take, lay hold of, seize

לִקְרָאת toward, over against, opposite

לָשׁוֹן tongue

מ

מְאֹד very, exceedingly

מֵאָה one hundred

מְאוּמָה anything

מֵאָז from then, from that time (מִן + אָז)

מֵאַיִן from where? (מִן + אַיִן)

מָאַן (Piel) to refuse

מָאַס to reject, refuse

מָאתַיִם two hundred

מַבּוּל flood, deluge

מִבְטָח trust, confidence

מִגְדָּל tower

מָגֵן shield

מַגֵּפָה stroke, plague

מִגְרָשׁ pasture, untilled ground

מִדְבָּר pasturage, wilderness, steppe

מִדְבָּ֫רָה	toward the wilderness (מִדְבָּר with directional ending הָ)	מַטֶּה	rod, staff, tribe
מָדַד	to measure	מַטְמוֹן	treasure
מִדָּה	measure	מָטָר	rain
מַדּ֫וּעַ	why?	מִי	who?
מִדְיָן	Midian; מִדְיָנִי Midianite	מַ֫יִם	water; מֵי (construct)
מָה	what? how?	מָכַר	to sell
מָהַר	(Piel) to hasten, hurry, do something quickly or in a hurry	מָלֵא	(verb) to be full; (Piel) fill, fulfill
מוֹאָב	Moab; מוֹאָבִי Moabite(s)	מָלֵא	(adjective) full
מוֹלֶ֫דֶת	descendants, offspring, (with 3ms suffix מוֹלַדְתּוֹ)	מַלְאָךְ	messenger
		מְלָאכָה	work
מוּסָר	chastening, correction	מָלוֹן	lodging place
מוֹעֵד	appointed place, appointed time, season	מִלְחָמָה	war, battle; מִלְחֶ֫מֶת (construct)
מוּת	to die; (Hiphil) kill, have executed	מָלַט	(Niphal) to escape; (Piel) save, deliver
מָ֫וֶת	death; מוֹת (construct)	מָלַךְ	to reign, be king; (Hiphil) make someone king
מִזְבֵּ֫חַ	altar; מִזְבְּחוֹת (plural)	מֶ֫לֶךְ	king; מַלְכֵי (mp construct)
מִזְמוֹר	psalm		
מִזְרָח	sunrise, east	מַלְכָּה	queen; מְלָכוֹת (plural)
מַחֲזֶה	vision	מַלְכוּת	dominion, kingdom, reign (fs)
מַחֲלָה	sickness	מִלִּפְנֵי	from before, from the presence of, on account of
מַחֲנֶה	camp, army; מַחֲנִים and מַחֲנוֹת (plural); מַחֲנֵה (construct)		
		מַמְלָכָה	kingdom; מַמְלֶ֫כֶת (construct)
מָחָר	tomorrow	מִמַּ֫עַל	above, on top of (מֵעַל with מִן)
מַחֲשָׁבָה	thought, idea		
		מָן	manna

מִן	from	מֶרְכָּבָה	chariot; מִרְכֶּבֶת (construct)
מִנְחָה	gift, offering	מִרְעֶה	pasture
מָנַע	to retain, hold back, withhold	מָרַר	to be bitter
מִסְפָּר	number	מַשָּׂא	burden, message
מְעַט	a few, a little	מֹשֶׁה	Moses
מֵעַל	upwards, above	מָשַׁח	to anoint
מַעֲשֶׂה	work, deed, act	מָשִׁיחַ	anointed one; מְשִׁיחַ (construct)
מִפְּנֵי	from before, from the presence of, on account of	מִשְׁכָּן	dwelling, tabernacle
מָצָא	to find	מָשַׁל	to govern, rule
מַצֵּבָה	standing-stone	מִשְׁמָר	jail, place of confinement
מַצָּה	unleavened bread; מַצּוֹת (plural)	מִשְׁמֶרֶת	guard, obligation, service (fs)
מִצְוָה	commandment; מִצְוֹת (plural)	מִשְׁפָּחָה	family, clan; מִשְׁפַּחַת (construct)
מִצְרִי	Egyptian (gentilic of מִצְרַיִם)	מִשְׁפָּט	judgement, custom, justice
מִצְרַיִם	Egypt; מִצְרִי Egyptian; מִצְרִים Egyptians	מִשְׁתֶּה	banquet
מִקְדָּשׁ	sanctuary	מֵת	dead
מָקוֹם	place; מְקוֹמוֹת (plural)	מִתּוֹךְ	from the midst of
מִקְנֶה	possession (of land or cattle); מִקְנֵה (construct)		

נ

מַר	bitter
מַרְאֶה	sight, appearance; מַרְאֵה (construct)
מְרַגֵּל	spy
מָרוֹם	height

נָא	please, now (used after volitional conjugations and often untranslated)
נְאֻם	utterance, declaration (נְאֻם יְהֹוָה declares the Lord)
נָבָא	(Niphil, Hithpael) to prophesy

נָבוֹן intelligent, discerning

נָבַט (Piel, Hiphil) to look at, regard

נָבִיא prophet

נָגַד (Hiphil) to make known, report, tell

נֶגֶב dry country, south, Negev

נֶגֶד opposite, before, in front of

נָגִיד chief, leader, prince

נָגַע to touch, reach

נֶגַע blow, assault, plague

נָגַף to strike, smite

נָגַשׂ to beat, drive, force; taskmaster (Participle)

נָגַשׁ to draw near, approach

נָדַח (Niphal) to be scattered, go astray

נָדַר to vow

נֶדֶר vow; נֵדֶר (alternate spelling)

נָהָר river, stream; נְהָרוֹת and rarely נְהָרִים (plural)

נָוֶה pasturage, abode, residence

נוּחַ to rest, settle down, make quiet; (Hiphil) lay, deposit

נוּס to flee, escape

נָחַל to obtain, receive property

נַחַל stream, small river, wadi

נַחֲלָה inheritance, property, possession

נָחַם (Niphal) to be sorry, repent; (Piel) comfort, console

נָחָשׁ snake

נְחֹשֶׁת copper, bronze

נָטָה to turn, stretch out, spread out

נָטַע to plant

נָכָה (Niphal) to be hit; (Hiphil) to smite

נָכַר (Niphal) to pretend; (Hiphil) investigate, recognize

נָסָה (Niphal) to put someone to the test

נֶסֶךְ libation, drink-offering; נֵסֶךְ (alternate spelling)

נָסַע to depart

נַעַל shoe, sandal

נַעַר youth, young man

נַעֲרָה young girl

נְפִילִים giants; נְפִלִים (alternate spelling)

נָפַל to fall

נֶפֶשׁ life, soul (fs)

נָצַב	(Niphal) to take one's stand, be stationed; (Hiphil) establish
נָצַח	(Piel) to lead, supervise
נָצַל	(Niphal) to be delivered; (Hiphil) snatch away
נָצַר	to watch, guard
נְקֵבָה	female
נָקַם	to take revenge, vengeance
נָשָׂא	to lift up, bear, carry
נָשַׂג	(Hiphil) to overtake
נָשִׂיא	prince
נָשִׁים	women, wives (plural of נְשֵׁי ;(אִשָּׁה) (construct)
נָשַׁק	to kiss
נָתַן	to give
נָתָן	Nathan
נָתַשׁ	to uproot, tear up, pull up

ס

סָבַב	to turn around, go around, surround
סָבִיב	circuit, all around, round about, surrounding
סְגֻלָּה	personal property
סָגַר	to shut, close; (Hiphil) deliver up
סוּס	horse
סוּסָה	mare

סוּר	to turn aside; (Hiphil) take away, remove, get rid of
סִינַי	Sinai
סֻכָּה	booth, hut
סֶלָה	selah (unexplained technical term of music or recitation)
סֹלֶת	fine wheat, flour
סְנֶה	bush, thorny shrub
סְעָרָה	heavy windstorm, gale
סָפַר	to write, count, number; (Piel) recount, report, enumerate
סֵפֶר	scroll, book
סֹפֵר	scribe, writer
סָרִיס	eunuch, officer
סָתַר	(Niphal) to conceal, hide; (Hiphil) hide

ע

עָבַד	to serve, work, till, cultivate
עֶבֶד	servant
עֲבוֹדָה	work, labor, service; עֲבֹדָה (alternate spelling)
עָבַר	to pass over, transgress
עֵבֶר	side, region, opposite side
עִבְרִי	Hebrew
עֲגָלָה	wagon; עֲגָלוֹת (plural)

עֶגְלָה	heifer	עַיִן	eye, fountain (fs); עֵין (construct)
עֵד	witness	עִיר	city (fs); עָרִים (plural)
עַד	to, unto, as far as (spatial); until, while (temporal)	עַל	on, upon, against, over
		עַל־דְּבַר	on account of, because of
עֵדָה	congregation, assembly, testimony, witness	עַל־כֵּן	therefore
עֵדוּת	warning sign, reminder, precept, commandment (fs); עֵדֹת (plural)	עַל־פְּנֵי	on the surface of, in front of, before
		עֹל	yoke
עֵדֶן	Eden	עָלָה	to go up
עֵדֶר	flock, herd	עֹלָה	burnt offering; עֹלוֹת (plural)
עוּד	(Hiphil) to warn, admonish	עֶלְיוֹן	Most High, upper
עוֹד	yet, still, again	עָלַץ	to rejoice
עוֹלָם	remote time, forever, eternity, everlasting; (לְעֹלָם וָעֶד) forever and ever)	עַם	people; עַמִּים (plural)
		עִם	with
		עָמַד	to stand
עָוֹן	transgression, iniquity, guilt	עֹמֶד	place where one stands or is stationed
עוֹף	flying creatures, birds, insects	עַמּוּד	pillar, column
		עַמּוֹן	Ammon; עַמּוֹנִי Ammonite
עוּר	to arouse, awake	עָמָל	distress, trouble, effort
עוֹר	skin, leather	עֵמֶק	valley
עֵז	goat (fs)	עָנָה	to answer
עֹז	strength, power, might	עָנָה	to bend down, be afflicted, humble; (Piel) oppress, humiliate
עָזַב	to leave, forsake, abandon		
עָזַר	to help, assist	עָנִי	afflicted, poor
עֵזֶר	help, assistance	עֳנִי	misery, affliction

עָנָן — cloud(s)

עָפָר — dirt, dust

עֵץ — tree; עֵצִים (plural)

עֵצָה — advice, counsel

עָצוּם — mighty, vast

עָצַם — to be mighty, vast, numerous

עֶצֶם — bone (fs)

עֶרֶב — evening

עֲרָבָה — desert, plain

עֶרְוָה — nakedness, shame

עָרוּם — clever, subtle, shrewd

עָרַךְ — to arrange, set in order

עֹרֶף — neck, back of neck

עֵשֶׂב — grass, green plants, vegetation

עָשָׂה — to do, make; (Piel) press, squeeze

עֵשָׂו — Esau

עֶשֶׂר — ten, decade

עֶשְׂרִים — twenty (plural of עֶשֶׂר)

עָשִׁיר — rich, wealthy

עֵת — time (fs)

עַתָּה — now

פ

פֵּאָה — side, rim, corner

פָּגַע — to meet, encounter

פֶּגֶר — corpse, carcass

פָּדָה — to buy (off), ransom, redeem

פֶּה — mouth; פִּי (construct)

פֹּה — here; פּוֹ or פֹּא (alternate spellings)

פּוּץ — to scatter, disperse

פָּחַד — to tremble

פַּחַד — trembling, terror

פָּלָא — (Niphal) to be extraordinary, wonderful

פָּלַל — (Hithpael) to pray

פְּלִשְׁתִּי — Philistine; פְּלֶשֶׁת Philistia; פְּלִשְׁתִּים Philistines

פֶּן־ — lest

פָּנָה — to turn about, turn aside

פָּנִים — face; פְּנֵי (construct)

פֶּסֶל — idol, image

פָּעַל — to do, make

פַּעַם — foot, step, time (fs)

פַּעֲמַיִם — twice

פָּקַד — to visit, number, appoint, miss, take care of, muster

פַּר — young bull

פָּרַד — (Niphal) to divide, branch off; (Hiphil) separate

פָּרָה — heifer, cow

פְּרִי — fruit

פַּרְעֹה — Pharaoh

פָּרַץ	to make a breach, burst out
פָּרַר	(Hiphil) to break out, burst forth, shake
פָּרַשׂ	to spread out, flaunt
פָּרָשׁ	horseman, rider, horse
פָּשַׁט	to take off, strip off
פֶּשַׁע	rebellion, revolt, transgression
פָּתַח	to open; (Piel) loosen, free
פֶּתַח	gate, opening, entrance

צ

צֹאן	flock, small herd of sheep and / or goats
צָבָא	(verb) to serve in war
צָבָא	(noun) host, army; צְבָאוֹת (plural)
צַדִּיק	righteous, just
צָדֵק	to be right, just, righteous; (Hiphil) give justice
צֶדֶק	righteousness, what is right, just
צְדָקָה	righteousness
צָוָה	(Piel) to command, order, direct
צוּר	rock, boulder, cliff
צִיּוֹן	Zion

צֵל	shadow, shade, protection
צָלַח	to be strong, effective, succeed
צֶלֶם	image, likeness
צֵלָע	rib, side (fs)
צָמַד	(Niphal) to commit oneself to, attach oneself to
צֶמַח	growth, sprout, bud
צָעַק	to cry out
צְעָקָה	outcry, wailing, call for help
צָעַר	to be trifling, insignificant
צָפוֹן	north (fs)
צָפוֹנָה	northward (צָפוֹן with directional ending הָ)
צַר	adversary, foe
צָרָה	distress
צָרַף	to smelt gold, refine
צָרַר	to wrap up, be hostile toward

ק

קָבַץ	to gather
קָבַר	to bury
קֶבֶר	grave
קָדַד	to bow down, kneel down
קָדוֹשׁ	holy

קָדִים — east side, east

קָדַם — to be in front, walk at the head

קֶדֶם — east, in front, east(ward); קֵדֶם (alternate spelling)

קֵדְמָה — eastward (קֶדֶם with directional ending ה ָ)

קָדַשׁ — to be holy; (Piel) make holy, consecrate, sanctify; (Hiphil) consecrate, designate as holy

קֹדֶשׁ — (adjective) holy; (noun) holy thing

קָהָל — assembly, congregation

קוֹל — voice, sound

קוּם — to rise, arise, stand

קָטַל — to kill

קָטֹן — small, insignificant

קָטַר — (Piel) to send an offering up in smoke; (Hiphil) make smoke, make a sacrifice go up in smoke

קְטֹרֶת — smoke (of sacrifice), incense

קִיא — to vomit

קַיִן — Cain

קִיר — wall

קָלַל — to be small, of little account; (Piel) declare cursed; (Hiphil) make light

קְלָלָה — curse; קִלְלַת (construct)

קָנָא — (Piel) to be jealous of, be zealous for

קָנָה — to acquire, buy

קָנֶה — (measuring) reed, tube

קֵץ — end, limit, boundary

קָצֶה — end, border, extremity; קְצֵה (construct)

קָרָא — to call, read (aloud), summon, proclaim

קָרָא — to happen, encounter, meet, befall

קָרַב — to draw near, approach; (Hiphil) bring, bring near

קֶרֶב — inward part, midst, in the midst of (also spelled בְּקֶרֶב with the same meaning)

קָרְבָּן — offering, gift

קָרָה — to meet, encounter, befall

קָרוֹב — near, imminent

קֶרֶן — horn

קָרַע — to tear up, away

קֶרֶשׁ — plank, board

קָשָׁה — difficult

קֶשֶׁת — bow (weapon), rainbow (fs)

ר

רָאָה	to see; (Niphal) appear
רֹאשׁ	head, chief, top
רִאשׁוֹן	first; רִישׁוֹן (alternate spelling); רִאשֹׁנִים or רִאשֹׁנוֹת (plural)
רֵאשִׁית	beginning, first
רֹב	multitude, abundance
רַב	much, many, great, numerous
רָבָה	to be(come) numerous, be great; (Hiphil) multiply, make many
רְבִיעִי	fourth, one-fourth
רָגַל	(Piel) to spy out
רֶגֶל	foot (fs)
רָדַף	to pursue, persecute
רוּחַ	wind, spirit (fs)
רוּם	to be(come) high, exalted; (Hiphil) raise, lift up, exalt
רוּץ	to run
רֹחַב	breadth, width
רַחוּם	compassionate
רָחוֹק	far, distant, distance
רָחַץ	to wash (off), bathe
רָחַק	be(come) far (away), distant

רִיב	(verb) to contend, quarrel, dispute, conduct a lawsuit
רִיב	(noun) contention, lawsuit, legal speech
רִיבָה	contention, lawsuit, legal speech (see רִיב above)
רֵיחַ	odor, scent
רָכַב	to ride, mount
רֶכֶב	chariot, chariotry
רְכוּשׁ	property; רְכֻשׁ (alternate spelling)
רָנַן	to shout (for joy)
רֵעַ	friend, fellow, companion
רָע	evil, bad; רַע (alternate spelling)
רָעָב	hunger, famine
רָעֵב	to be(come) hungry; (adjective) hungry
רָעָה	to feed, graze, tend (flocks)
רֹעֶה	shepherd
רָעַע	to be wicked, evil
רָפָא	to heal (someone)
רָפָה	to relax, become slack, desist; (Hiphil) abandon, forsake
רָצָה	to be pleased with, like
רָצוֹן	pleasure, favor
רָצַח	to kill

רַק	only
רֵשִׁית	beginning (see רֵאשִׁית above)
רָשַׁע	to be(come) guilty
רָשָׁע	guilty, wicked

שׂ

שָׂבַע	to satisfy, be satiated
שָׂדֶה	open field; שָׂדוֹת (plural)
שֵׂיבָה	old age, gray-headedness
שִׂים	to set, place, put
שָׂכַל	to have success; (Hiphil) understand
שְׂמֹאל	left (side), left hand
שָׂמַח	to rejoice; (Piel) gladden
שִׂמְחָה	joy, rejoicing
שָׂנֵא	to hate
שָׂעִיר	male goat, demon
שָׂפָה	lip, shore, bank
שַׂק	sackcloth; שַׂקִּים (plural)
שַׂר	official, leader, prince; שָׂרִים (plural)
שָׂרָה	Sarah
שָׂרַי	Sarai
שָׂרַף	to burn
שָׂרָף	seraph, fiery serpent; שְׂרָפִים (plural)

שׁ

שָׁאוּל	Saul
שְׁאוֹל	Sheol, underworld (fs)
שָׁאַל	to ask (for), demand
שְׁאֹלָה	to Sheol (שְׁאוֹל with directional ending הָ)
שְׁאֵלָה	request
שָׁאַר	to remain; (Niphal, Hiphil) be left over
שְׁאֵרִית	remainder, remnant, what is left
שָׁבָה	to take captive
שְׁבוּעָה	oath
שֵׁבֶט	rod, staff, tribe
שְׁבִיעִי	seventh
שָׁבַע	(Niphil, Hiphil) to swear
שֶׁבַע	seven; שִׁבְעָה (fs)
שָׁבַר	(I) to break; (II) buy grain; (Hiphil) to sell grain
שֶׁבֶר	grain
שָׁבַת	to cease, rest
שַׁבָּת	Sabbath, rest
שָׁדַד	to devastate, lay waste, overpower
שָׁוְא	worthless(ness), in vain, vainly
שׁוּב	to turn, return; (Hiphil) bring back, lead back
שׁוֹפָר	ram's horn, trumpet

שׁוֹר	bull(ock), steer
שָׁחַט	to slaughter, kill
שָׁחַת	(Niphal) to be corrupt, spoiled; (Piel) spoil, wipe out, ruin; (Hiphil) destroy
שִׁיר	(verb) to sing
שִׁיר	(noun) song
שִׁירָה	song (see שִׁיר above)
שִׁית	to put, set, place
שָׁכַב	to lie down, have sexual intercourse
שָׁכַח	to forget
שָׁכַם	(Hiphil) to rise early
שָׁכֵן	to dwell, settle
שָׁכֵן	neighbor; שְׁכֵנוֹת (plural)
שָׁכַר	to be(come) drunk
שֵׁכָר	intoxicating drink (perhaps a kind of beer)
שָׁלוֹם	peace, health
שָׁלַח	to stretch out, let go, send
שֻׁלְחָן	table
שְׁלִישִׁי	third, one-third
שָׁלַךְ	(Hiphil) to throw, throw down, cast
שָׁלַל	to plunder
שָׁלָל	plunder, booty
שָׁלֵם	to be whole, complete; (Piel) repay; (Hiphil) make peace with

שֶׁלֶם	peace offering; שְׁלָמִים (plural); שַׁלְמֵי (mp construct)
שְׁלֹמֹה	Solomon
שָׁלֹשׁ	three; שְׁלֹשָׁה (fs)
שֵׁם	name; שֵׁמוֹת (plural)
שָׁם	there
שָׁמַד	(Niphal) to be destroyed, exterminated; (Hiphil) exterminate
שָׁמָּה	there, to that place
שְׁמוּאֵל	Samuel
שָׁמַיִם	heaven(s), sky
שָׁמֵם	to be astonished, be desolate, be appalled
שֶׁמֶן	oil
שְׁמֹנֶה	eight; שְׁמֹנָה (fs)
שָׁמַע	to hear, heed (with אֶל or לְ), to obey (with בְּקוֹל or לְקוֹל)
שָׁמַר	to keep, guard, watch, observe; (Niphal) be careful, be on one's guard
שֹׁמְרוֹן	Samaria
שֶׁמֶשׁ	sun
שֵׁן	tooth, crag (fs)
שָׁנָה	year; שָׁנִים (plural)
שֵׁנִי	second
שְׁנַיִם	two (masculine)
שְׁנָתַיִם	two years

שַׁעַר	gate
שִׁפְחָה	female slave
שָׁפַט	to judge, enter into controversy; (Niphal) plead, go to court
שֹׁפֵט	judge
שָׁפַךְ	to pour out, spill, shed
שָׁקָה	(Hiphil) to give drink to
שֶׁקֶל	shekel (unit of weight)
שֶׁקֶר	lie, falsehood, deception
שָׁרַת	(Piel) to minister, serve
שֵׁשׁ	six; שִׁשָּׁה (fs)
שָׁתָה	to drink
שְׁתַּיִם	two (also as שְׁנַיִם)

תּ

תֹּאַר	form, appearance
תְּהִלָּה	glory, praise
תָּוֶךְ	midst, middle, within, through; בְּתוֹךְ in the midst, in the middle
תּוֹלְדוֹת	line of descendants, generation; תּוֹלְדוֹת (construct)
תּוֹעֵבָה	abomination
תּוֹרָה	teaching, law, Torah
תַּחַת	beneath, below, under, instead of
תֵּימָן	south

תֵּימָנָה	southward (תֵּימָן with directional ending הָ)
תְּלֻנּוֹת	complaining, grumbling; תְּלוּנֹת (alternate spelling)
תְּמוּנָה	image, form, shape
תָּמִיד	continually, regularly
תָּמִים	whole, entire, blameless
תָּמַם	to be complete, finished
תָּעָה	to wander off, stagger, be confused
תִּפְאֶרֶת	ornament, decoration (fs)
תְּפִלָּה	prayer
תָּפַשׂ	to seize, take hold of, capture
תִּקְוָה	hope, expectation
תָּקַע	to drive, thrust, strike
תְּרוּמָה	tribute, contribution
תֵּשַׁע	nine; תִּשְׁעָה (fs)

Subject Index

*The items listed in this index refer to section numbers,
not page numbers.*

Dig Deeper in Hebrew with the Zondervan
Hebrew Reference Series

A Reader's Hebrew-English Lexicon
of the Old Testament

Terry A. Armstrong, Douglas L. Busby, Cyril F. Carr

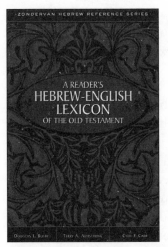

Few pastors continue to read their Hebrew Old Testament after seminary. One reason is that it is too time-consuming, since many words have to be looked up in the dictionary.

A Reader's Hebrew-English Lexicon of the Old Testament, now for the first time complete in one volume, enables the pastor and the student to read the Hebrew Old Testament with relative ease. Listed in sequence by chapter and verse are all words that occur fewer than fifty times in the Old Testament, complete with translation (based on the *Brown-Driver-Briggs Hebrew and English Lexicon*) and numbers indicating how often the word occurs in the particular book and in the Old Testament as a whole. At the end of each entry is the page number in *Brown-Driver-Briggs Hebrew and English Lexicon* where a discussion of the word can be found. Appendixes list all Hebrew words occurring more than fifty times in the Old Testament and all Aramaic words occurring more than ten times.

Hardcover   ISBN: 0-310-36980-0

GRAND RAPIDS, MICHIGAN 49530

w w w . z o n d e r v a n . c o m

The Interlinear NIV Hebrew-English Old Testament

John R. Kohlenberger III

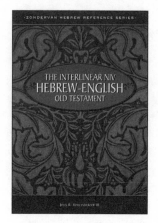

These four volumes in one binding include the standard Hebrew text Biblia Hebraica Stuttgartensia, the NIV (North American version) as the English parallel text, a word-for-word translation for renderings of specific Hebrew words, and an introduction on how to use the interlinear text.

Main Features:

- The standard Hebrew text, Biblia Hebraica Stuttgartensia, with all necessary variant readings and major textual conjectures in footnotes
- The New International Version (North American Edition) as the English parallel text, complete with special indentation and paragraphing, section headings, and footnotes
- A grammatically literal, word-for-word translation with English phrases reading in normal left-to-right order for renderings of specific Hebrew words
- A complete introduction explaining translation techniques and characteristics of the Hebrew and English texts
- A special introduction for the general reader on how to use an interlinear for word studies and learning Hebrew

ISBN: 0-310-40200-X

GRAND RAPIDS, MICHIGAN 49530

www.zondervan.com

The Hebrew-English Concordance to the Old Testament

John R. Kohlenberger III and James A. Swanson

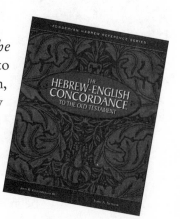

The Hebrew-English Concordance to the Old Testament is the exhaustive index to the Biblia Hebraica Stuttgartensia, 4th edition, and the Hebrew text underlying the New International Version of the Bible. It replaces the venerable *Englishman's Hebrew and Chaldee Concordance of the Old Testament* by George Wigram, published over 150 years ago.

Main Features:

- Lists all occurrences of a given Hebrew word (even when there is no direct English equivalent) in Hebrew alphabetical order
- Shows the interrelationship between the English and Hebrew texts, including redundant cognates and repeated Hebrew words, as well as multiple-word translations
- Uses the Goodrick-Kohlenberger numbering system (with cross-reference to Strong's numbers), allowing for accurate identification of Hebrew words and use with *The NIV Exhaustive Concordance*
- Keyed to *Brown-Driver-Briggs Hebrew and English Lexicon*, *Koehler and Baumgartner's Hebrew and Aramaic Lexicon*, and *Holladay's Concise Hebrew and Aramaic Lexicon*
- Complete NIV-to-Hebrew index

ISBN: 0-310-20839-4

GRAND RAPIDS, MICHIGAN 49530

w w w . z o n d e r v a n . c o m

The Analytical Hebrew and Chaldee Lexicon

Benjamin Davidson

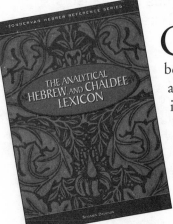

Originally published in 1848, *The Analytical Hebrew and Chaldee Lexicon* has become a standard reference tool for scholars and students who wish to continue developing their foundational knowledge of Hebrew.

In the words of the author, "Multitudes of Hebrew students, after having overcome the first difficulties under the instruction of a living teacher, abandon further study for lack of a guide through the yet untrodden intricacies of the language. Our aim has been to provide a permanent instructor."

The success of this lexicon in fulfilling its role, guiding countless students of Hebrew to greater levels of expertise, is attested to by its enduring popularity over 150 years after its first printing.

Features:

- The various forms of all the Hebrew and Aramaic (formerly referred to as Chaldee) words in the Old Testament are listed in alphabetical order.
- For every word, a full grammatical analysis of each form is supplied, plus an indication of its root.
- The book also contains a lexical part where the meanings of these roots are supplied.
- Under each main lexical entry, both the root and its derivatives are listed.
- A complete set of noun and verb charts with explanatory comments provides a concise but complete summary of both Hebrew and Aramaic grammatical systems.
- Irregular forms are cross-referenced to the grammatical introduction.
- The Scripture passage for every grammatical form that occurs only once in the Bible, and for peculiar forms, is referenced at the bottom of the page.

ISBN: 0-310-24085-9

GRAND RAPIDS, MICHIGAN 49530

www.zondervan.com

Discover the Basics of Greek with the aid of a CD-ROM!

Basics of Biblical Greek

Includes an Interactive Study Aid CD-ROM

William D. Mounce

The first textbook to take an integrated approach to teaching and learning New Testament Greek is now the first to include a CD-ROM.

Basics of Biblical Greek enables students to immediately start working with verses from the New Testament, tying the lessons directly to the biblical text. It makes learning Greek a natural process and shows from the very beginning how an

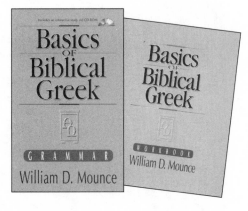

understanding of Greek helps in understanding the New Testament. Written from the student's perspective, this approach combines the best of the deductive and inductive methods. The workbook features a parsing section and is usefully perforated with hole-punched pages for loose-leaf binders.

Features:

- Combines the best of the deductive and the inductive approaches.
- Explains the basics of English grammar before teaching Greek grammar.
- Uses from the very beginning parts of verses from the New Testament instead of "made up" exercises.
- Includes at the beginning of every lesson a brief devotional, written by a well-known New Testament scholar, that demonstrates how the principles taught in the lesson apply directly to an understanding of the biblical text.
- Has been field-tested at a number of colleges and seminaries.

Grammar
Hardcover   ISBN: 0-310-23211-2

Workbook
Softcover   ISBN: 0-310-40091-0

We want to hear from you. Please send your comments about this book to us in care of the address below. Thank you.

GRAND RAPIDS, MICHIGAN 49530

www.zondervan.com